FEDERAL CENSORSHIP:

OBSCENITY IN THE MAIL

Federal Censorship

OBSCENITY IN THE MAIL

by James C. N. Paul
UNIVERSITY OF PENNSYLVANIA

and Murray L. Schwartz
UNIVERSITY OF CALIFORNIA, LOS ANGELES

The Free Press of Glencoe, Inc.
A DIVISION OF THE CROWELL-COLLIER PUBLISHING COMPANY

CONTENTS

PREFACE

WE HOPE THAT this work will have value as a study of sex censorship in operation. We hope that it will be useful in promoting further discussion and analysis of the balance to be struck between curbing sex expression considered to be noxious and protecting the freedom of men to create, publish, read, think, and talk about the conditions of life and the phenomena of sex.

Using federal controls over the mails as the focal problem, we have attempted to trace the development and to discuss the future evolution of laws designed to suppress circulation of obscene publications. We have made both general proposals for the future development of the law and particular recommendations with respect to Postal and Customs operations—federal censorship. Our study attempts to show how these federal programs have evolved, how they have worked in the recent past, how they work today, the justifications for them, and the dangers which are their price.

The mails are a vital channel for publishing and for access to materials which citizens may want to see or read. Thus, the programs carried on by the federal government to police the mails are of great significance for several reasons: because of the importance of the mails as an avenue for distribution; because these are national censorship programs having nationwide ramifications in other fields of anti-obscenity law enforcement; because the legal standards and constitutional principles which have developed in this federal field are illustrative of the law governing the operations of other units of government, state and local, as they attempt to suppress things deemed obscene.

The Post Office Department and the Bureau of Customs have been empowered to close the mails, as an avenue of circulation, to any publication which officials in these agencies consider obscene. In common terms, this is a "censorship" operation because it forceably prevents circulation of publications which government officials decide to suppress. While "censorship" may be regarded as an epithetical, color word, while use of color words is regrettable, and while Postal and Customs officials eschew (and some resent) use of the word "censorship" to describe their operations, we have used that term to characterize what the government is doing—with apologies to the many fine persons in government who have so graciously helped us. We do this on the premise that one should call a spade a spade.

Part I of this book traces the rise, development, and operation of controls of obscenity, criminal and censorial. It starts with John Milton's time and proceeds to the early legislation, the English Obscene Publications Act of 1857, and the famous *Hicklin* decision of 1868. Attention is then turned to parallel developments in this country, to Anthony Comstock and the adoption of the federal statute he fathered and which still bears his name, and to the actual operation and impact of federal censorship to 1930.

The next step in this history (Part II) begins with the year 1930, when the United States Congress—in fact, the Senate—for the only time in its history debated seriously and at length the problems involved in a system of federal censorship. The proponents of censorship carried the day. But the warnings voiced by their opponents found echoes in the ensuing years as the courts became more concerned about the catch-all application of the statutes.

In Part III we treat the experience of the recent (post World War II) past—the *modus operandi* of censorship and the substantive results, the persisting problems. It might be noted that much of this experience is now ancient history, in the sense that it no longer reflects precisely what Postal and Customs officials are doing, thanks to their own recent reforms and the pressure of new court decisions. But even that which is ancient history should still be instructive, because it shows how rapidly legal standards and social norms can change in this field.

Part IV discusses court decisions of the last few years, particularly those Supreme Court rulings which have, parodoxically, both clarified and obfuscated the law. We have attempted to explain the background of the cases and to interpret their ramifications—concluding that the law is indeed in a state of flux. Part V discusses recent censorship experience following these decisions.

Part VI analyzes various objectives of anti-obscenity laws, those that have been articulated and those that have been more "felt" than articulated. Recognizing the urgency of the pressure for some legislation in favor of suppression, we propose new criteria for the determination of when and how government may prevent the dissemination of works deemed obscene; we then proceed to examine the role of the U.S. government, which, after all, has never been considered the primary, sovereign guardian of sexual morality under our federal scheme of government. Finally we make some specific recommendations for Post Office and Customs censorship, assuming that there will be retention of some sort of a system of federal censorship.

This work deals strictly with the problem of obscene publications; other closely related aspects of federal censorship of the mails have largely been ignored. Thus, the federal laws say that "filthy" matter shall be barred, and likewise with abortifacient matter, information on birth control, and "libelous" matter which appears on the envelope or wrapper of a piece of mail. All these proscriptions pose problems having to do with distinguishing permissible expression from contraband expression, and to a greater or lesser extent they all touch on the area of "sex censorship." But, except for a limited discussion of these restrictions, we have bypassed them in order to avoid spreading our discussion and analysis too thin and in the interest of concentrating on what has been, along with control of foreign, subversive political expression (until that censorship was abandoned as it recently was) the biggest and most challenging phase of federal mail censorship.[1]

1. For the same reason—to advance the discussion without clogging it with detail—we have largely ignored the fact that the basic Postal statute proscribes not only "obscene" matter but also "lewd," "lascivious," "inde-

In the interests of readability we have dispensed with footnotes, other than an occasional explanatory or illustrative, but purely textual, note at the bottom of a page. Appendix I presents a series of notes to each chapter and section, setting forth major source materials and references upon which we have specifically relied for our text; these notes are arranged chapter by chaper, in a way which we hope will be sufficiently convenient to those readers who will want to make use of this information. Appendix II presents an alphabetical listing of major secondary works which we have consulted. Cases discussed in the text or cited in Appendix I are set forth in a table labeled Appendix III. Appendix IV sets forth the text of the principal statutes with which we deal.

* * * * *

This book is the product of a study of a number of aspects of federal censorship control of the mails. The study was conducted through the Institute of Legal Research of the Law School of the University of Pennsylvania, pursuant to a grant from The Fund For The Republic, Inc., a non-profit corporation created by the Ford Foundation. The authors were co-directors of the project.

In planning our total project we were fortunate in persuading Professor Stephen Bailey, formerly Woodrow Wilson Professor of History at Princeton University, now at Syracuse University, Dean Henry Brandis, Jr., of the Law School of the University of North Carolina, Erwin Canham, editor of the *Christian Science Monitor* and past president of the U.S. Chamber of Commerce, Charles Horsky, eminent Washington attorney, and Mrs. Katherine Macy, past president of the Young Women's Christian Association, to act in an advisory capacity. Their suggestions at the outset regarding the problems to be posed and the courses of investigation to be pursued were extremely helpful. But we must add, too, the customary dis-

---

cent," and "immoral" matter, and the fact that the tariff statute has, in the past, spoken of published material which is "obscene and immoral." We have treated these statutory proscriptions—"immoral," "indecent," "lewd," "lascivious," etc.—as if they were question-begging synonyms of the term "obscene," i.e., as if they were words of no independent significance. That is what the courts have done, with only a few exceptions, and the older decisions which do suggest distinctions and shadings for these words—which treat them in any fashion other than as surplusage—are, it seems clear, obsolete sports. In short, these words are vestigial, meaningless appendages to the Comstock Act.

claimer: responsibility for errors in the text and values and opinions expressed rests entirely with us.

Our study of anti-obscenity law has also profited from the work done by our friend and colleague, Professor Louis B. Schwartz of the University of Pennsylvania Law School, who served as draftsman for the American Law Institute's Model Penal Code provisions on obscenity. Professor Schwartz's essay on the law—in the form of comments to and an explanation of the Model Penal Code—was of inestimable value, and we have enjoyed the added advantage of discussing it with him. The significance of his work in this field can best be attested by the rapidity with which courts, and some legislatures, have assimilated the Model Penal Code proposals into law.

As far as our own research operations were concerned, we attempted first to tackle the available traditional legal resources: statutes, judicial decisions, legislative reports and debates. It is interesting that the period during which our study took place has probably been the most active, judicially as well as politically, of any comparable period in the century of American experience with obscenity controls.

We also attempted to contact, by personal interview and correspondence, those organizations, publishers, libraries, and individuals who seemed most likely to have had experience with the operation of the federal laws.

We found practically everyone who was contacted completely co-operative. Thus, the American Civil Liberties Union made available to us its extensive historical files in New York and in the Princeton Library. Trade, library, and publishers' associations not only published notices of our study and solicited comments from their members but also called attention to the letter questionnaires which we had circulated among individuals. A great many private attorneys were consulted; nearly all gave freely of their time, making file material available within the limits imposed by professional confidences. To list all these various groups and individuals would be, frankly, an exhaustive task. However, we should like to thank, by name, Mr. James Fitzpatrick, General Counsel to New York's Joint Legislative Committee to Study Offensive and Obscene Publications, for his interest and help. We owe a considerable debt to Morris L. Ernst, Esq.; even if he may not agree with all our thinking he was the source of much stimulation.

Finally, and most important, we made an intensive examination of the "government in operation." This aspect of our effort would have been impossible without the co-operation of the appropriate officials, and if there are deficiencies or errors in our explanations of the mechanics of government enforcement, this should not be attributed to lack of co-operation. We were given access to many Postal and Customs files, as well as permission to interview officials involved in the administration of the programs. Thus, our "field study" of the government agencies was limited only by our own predilections and financial resources. We express, here, our sincere appreciation to the Post Office Department, the Treasury Department and its Bureau of Customs, the Department of Justice, and the Library of Congress for this wholehearted co-operation.

Specifically, we should like to acknowledge the interest and help extended to our study by Mr. Abe M. Goff, General Counsel of the Post Office until 1958; Mr. William C. O'Brien, former Assistant General Counsel; Mr. James C. Haynes, Chief Hearing Examiner of the Post Office; Mr. David H. Stephens, Chief of Postal Inspection Service; Mr. Huntington Cairns, of the National Gallery of Art; and Mr. Irving Fishman, Deputy Collector of Customs of the Port of New York, all of whom extended more hospitality and assistance than we had any right to expect. The continuing friendship of Irving Fishman is a by-product asset which we prize. We should also like to thank Herbert B. Warburton, General Counsel of the Post Office Department until 1961, and Charles Ablard, former Judicial Officer of the Department, for their co-operation and warm hospitality during the latter stages of our work.

Our field study of government operations included examination of files in Washington, interviews, and study of the operations of the General Counsel and his staff, the Hearing Examiners, and the Postal Inspection Service. In addition, we examined files and interviewed Postal personnel in New York, Chicago, Los Angeles, San Francisco, Philadelphia, Minneapolis, and St. Paul. In Washington, we interviewed Customs personnel, including the Assistant to the Commissioner of Customs, the attorneys in the Penalty Section, and Mr. Cairns, the Bureau's special legal advisor. The Customs' field study included interviews of and examination of the files maintained by the Collectors and members of their staffs in New York, Philadelphia, Baltimore, Minneapolis, St. Paul, Chicago,

Los Angeles, and San Francisco. Finally, we conducted extensive interviews with U.S. Attorneys in New York, Chicago, Philadelphia, Los Angeles, and San Francisco. To all of the many government officials who helped us in this field research we owe a warm expression of gratitude.

Throughout this Preface the word "we" has been used. Much of the basic field research is the product of the investigations of many lawyers throughout the country: William J. Brown, George Brunn, Frederick Davis, John B. Henderson, Charles D. Kelso, William P. Kennedy, Paula Markowitz, Stanford Shmukler, Michael I. Sovern and our project's associate director, Alan N. Spector, who gave unstintingly of his energies for an extended period of time. Their research, particularly the contribution of Alan Spector, has supplied much of the basic information for this study. But we, the authors, take full responsibility for its contents and conclusions.

Among the secretaries who have helped us, Mrs. Andrew Fritz, Executive Secretary of the Institute of Legal Research deserves our greatest thanks—for her patience, endurance and wholehearted help with the long task of preparing a jointly authored manuscript for the press.

One final acknowledgement. When this project was undertaken, it was agreed that The Fund For The Republic, Inc., would furnish the financial support, but that we would assume full responsibility for formulating the objectives of the study and for selecting personnel and methods of research and execution of the project, following the traditions of scholarly research to the best of our ability. Not only was the Fund true to this policy, but its officers gave help and encouragement in countless other ways.

In a field charged with emotion, we have attempted to be rational, recognizing that many would probably maintain that where "obscenity" is concerned this may be impossible. We do not pretend that any of the recommendations we have set forth are either "dramatic" or "final." We do hope, however, that this study of this frustrating subject—censorship, freedom, and the control of obscene publications—will help those who will continue to try to comprehend the persisting problems.

J.C.N.P.
M.L.S.

PART I

The Evolution of the Law and Censorship to 1930

Since 1842, there have been federal statutes in this country authorizing federal officials to censor obscene publications by suppressing their circulation. The first censorship statute dealt solely with the importation of pictorial matter. Until it was enacted there had been, in Anglo-American jurisprudence, very little anti-obscenity law at all, nor was there any American precedent for censorship laws which put government officials in the business of policing sex expression and banning distribution of things proscribed under some broad legal standard.

Within the latter half of the nineteenth century there was developed in this country, and in others, a network of anti-obscenity prohibitions. Sweeping criminal statutes were enacted. A distinguished English court pronounced what was said to be the "common law" on the subject, though there had been virtually none before: the judges set forth both a concept of obscene expression and a most inclusive standard defining it, a standard to which the creations of men in the forms of books or pictures must conform if people were to circulate them at all without incurring the risk of punishment. Courts in America borrowed this ground-breaking English precedent, reading the new standard into our statutes and justifying it on the assumption that the restrictions were needed to protect the young and the susceptible from the impact of improper art or writing. Federal legislation dealing first with foreign commerce, then the mails, then interstate commerce as channels of distribution, became integral parts of the national network of anti-obscenity laws. The power of censorship—a power long thought to be odious to our constitutional heritage—evolved, unchallenged and uncriticized, to become an entrenched operation of the U.S. government.

Detailed examination of these background developments is the point of departure for this study. The history is both intrinsically interesting and a valuable perspective to the study of contemporary enforcement of our national sex censorship laws.

I.   CENSORSHIP AND THE ANGLO-AMERICAN CONSTITUTIONAL TRADITION

"I DENY NOT," wrote poet-pamphleteer John Milton, in his *Areopagitica,* in the seventeenth century, "but that it is of the greatest concernment in the church and commonwealth, to have a vigilant eye how books demean themselves as well as men."

Milton wrote when the printing press was still a new, mistrusted development. The "concernment" of the state at that time was with authors who might use it to agitate questions about the validity of religious dogma, the divine right of kings, or, conversely, the infallibility of a Roundhead parliament. Licensing—which meant one must have government permission to own a press or to publish anything—was, in theory anyway, a most efficient way to police the content of mass-produced communication on these matters or anything else which might become the "concernment" of those in power.

Milton condemned licensing with both broad, philosophical arguments for free speech generally, as well as with specific objections aimed particularly at censorship as a device to repress expression of men's thoughts. *Areopagitica* may ramble and rave in places; and perhaps its contemporary impact was slight; but it bristles with quotes, concepts, and dogmas which have become the argument armament of the advocates of press freedom.

[3]

Said Milton, in passages long familiar to students of censorship: I share the "concernment" of church and state about the dangers present in reading some of what is written; but the way to repudiate what is bad is through open debate and open scorn, not suppression. "So truth be in the field," who knows her to lose in the struggle with falsehood for men's minds? Truth "is strong next to the almighty," and "she needs no licensing" to aid her cause; "her confuting" is the "surest suppressing," for if men rely on censors to protect them from seeing the sin or subversion in books, then they become weak—incapable of discernment, more prone to be influenced by bad ideas, and mere puppets under the manipulation of the censorial powers that be. Moreover, censors have a way of making mistakes themselves; and if the Commonwealth sets up guards over what can be published and read, then we, its citizens, must worry all the more about who will guard these guards and whether the guards are good enough to guard us. If the censors become too zealous, as is their tendency because they are paid to find fault, then a whole "flowery crop of knowledge" may be suppressed before we can know it; "an oligarchy of twenty ingrossers" may yet "bring famine upon our minds." And finally:

> If we think to regulate printing, thereby to rectify manners, we must regulate all recreations and past-times, all that is delightful to man. No music must be heard, no song be set or sung, but what is grave and *Doric*. There must be licensing dancers, that no [wrong] gesture, motion, or deportment be taught . . .; it will ask more than the work of twenty licensers to examine all the lutes, the violins, and the guitars in every house; they must not be suffered to prattle as they do, but must be licensed what they may say. And who shall silence all the airs and madrigals, that whisper softness in chambers?

Licensing was eventually abandoned; but only later, in England and America, did freedom of the press become an operating political principle, and one to which the government itself was committed. Of course, "how much freedom"—how much policing of the marketplace of human expression—has remained a controversial question.

The First Amendment, passed by our First Congress in response to a national demand for assurance against meddling with publishing, put it bluntly: "Congress shall make *no* law . . . abridging

freedom of the press." Precisely what this was originally intended to
mean—whether no law was to mean no laws at all—has long been
debated. Certainly condemned were laws which were fresh in the
framers' minds, laws which had been used by the Crown to harass
political and social dissidents who were heroes to eighteenth-century
Americans. Thus, the First Amendment must have been intended
to say at least: there should be no government licensing system
such as had existed in Milton's time; no stamp taxes such as had
been used to suppress the circulation of colonial newspapers, books,
and magazines; no similar techniques of suppressing at the source all
circulation of unpopular writings;[1] no prosecutions for "seditious
libel"—a fancy label for the crime of simply criticizing the government—such as had been used against John Peter Zenger, John
Wilkes, and many other agitators for liberty revered here.

Doubtless, the First Amendment was intended to mean more.
Madison (its principal author) and Jefferson argued, in hindsight,
the extreme position. As part of their states' rights campaign against
the anti-Republican sedition law, they seemed to maintain that "no
law" meant no federal law at all: just as Congress was surely barred
from policing religious thought, or dogma, so with the content of
things published in the press; the states alone possessed the power,
if any power existed, to deal with gross intemperance, defamation
or any similar "licentiousness" put out by the press. Some modern
scholars and advocates have today revived this claim that "no law"
means, simply, no law, though perhaps the statements of people
like Madison, on which much reliance is placed, must be read in
the context of their essentially partisan fight against the Federalists
and the follies of their anti-sedition law. And other, recent histori-

1. According to Blackstone, writing as the oracle of eighteenth-century,
English Common Law, but not necessarily the oracle of the framers of the
First Amendment, the gist of "freedom of the press" was simply freedom
from all "previous restraint," which, in today's terms, probably could be
translated to mean freedom from any kind of bureaucratic government activity which interfered with the free circulation of publications. "Every free
man," he wrote, "has an undoubted right to lay what sentiment he pleases
before the public." The way to suppress publishers of noxious matter, said
Blackstone, was to prosecute them criminally—not censor their circulations
civilly. As to grounds for criminal liability, the law might prescribe punishment for whatever was "mischievous," but as to techniques for control, the
traditional processes of the criminal courts supplied the only remedy; there
should be no censorship—no governmental action which prevented publication.

cal investigations of the contemporary understanding suggest that
the scope of protection bestowed by the First Amendment was far
from clear, possibly far from radical. Perhaps it was perceived more
as a general exhortation aimed at congress than a specific law, en-
forceable in the courts, forbidding enforcement of other laws. Indeed, our first freedom has been given content only recently—
largely since 1920—as concrete cases were finally brought before
the Supreme Court, as the court began to spell out some theories
and rules which do protect unpopular speech, disfavored publications.

Be all that as it may, a system of national licensing or any overt
censorship would surely have been condemned in the eighteenth
century. As Milton put it, the strategems and methods of this kind
of operation were odious.

Moreover, eighteenth-century American lawmakers combined op-
timistic idealism with hardheaded realism; they surely knew how
abusive a free press could be, for many were victimized by as much
abuse as any generation of politicos in history. Yet their views on
the value of freedom were positive. Freedom to publish was not just
a natural right. Government was not just obliged to tolerate the
free flow of ideas. The condition of freedom—open access to the
minds of men—was a positive good despite all its evils, a necessary
adjunct to a political system which reposed such a large measure of
responsibility in the citizen elector. Thus, the First Amendment was
a statement of affirmative faith. Men needed this freedom, including the freedom to publish or to read what was thought heretical
or socially noxious by most of the community. For this kind of
freedom supplied the surest way of finding insights to truth, the
most effective way to expose false assumptions, errors, and hypocrisy. To secure this freedom it was necessary to eschew all sem-
blance of governmental obstruction or censoring of the press. Milton's arguments were eloquently restated by Thomas Jefferson when
he pronounced an epitaph to the discredited Sedition Act of the
Adams administration.

> If there be any among us who would wish to dissolve this Union
> or to change its republican form, let them stand undisturbed as
> monuments of the safety with which error of opinion may be
> tolerated where reason is left free to combat it. I know, indeed,
> that some honest men fear that a republican government cannot

be strong; that this government is not strong enough. . . . I believe this, on the contrary, the strongest government on earth. I
believe it is the only one where every man, at the call of the laws,
would fly to the standard of the law, and would meet invasions of
the public order as his own personal concern. Sometimes it is said
that man cannot be trusted with the government of himself. Can
he, then, be trusted with the government of others? Or have we
found angels in the forms of kings to govern him? Let history
answer this question.

The same affirmation of the positive value of freedom of the press
is reflected in Congress' first efforts to establish a national postal
system. If anything stands out in the debates, it is the desire to
promote circulation of newspapers and periodicals. Congress talked
less of the boon to commerce and far more of the boon to demo-
cratic values than Congress would probably talk today were it to
do the job all over again. Not a word was said about keeping bad
publications out of the mails, though it is clear that many spokesmen were targets for abuse by the very papers they proposed to have
carried, and at rates low enough to provide the widest possible
dissemination.

In 1836, an issue of national censorship—the question whether
the U.S. government could engage in any regulation of the content
of publications in the mail—was presented in clear form and for
the first time to Congress. The Abolitionist movement had emerged,
a fighting faith dedicated to the overthrow of slavery, expounded by
zealous advocates—radical iconoclasts, old-fashioned moralists,
pious preachers, and masters of invective. In numbers the movement may have been small, but because it was vocal and dangerous
to a *status quo* which few other Americans dared or wanted to
disturb, and perhaps, too, because anti-slavery touched a sensitive
nerve of the national conscience, the feeling against the Abolitionist
propagandists ran strong.

To President Andrew Jackson it was an outrage that "incendiary"
tracts, put out by these radicals, should be disseminated in such vast
volume—especially in the South—by the government itself, cour-
tesy of the U.S. mails. Surely the government should not be a party
to stirring up bitterness and worse. Jackson's Postmaster General
had already sanctioned some extra-legal suppression by postal employees. "Old Hickory" now invited Congress to join him in stop-

ping the "incendiaries": a law was needed instructing postmasters to destroy their writings whenever they found them.

Congress refused to pass the law. Partisan politics was an influence; in the Senate a curious coalition of Whigs and Calhoun Democrats was bent on embarrassing the President, no doubt. But some of the senatorial giants made common cause on First Amendment grounds. "Congress has no right in any form or in any manner, to interfere with the freedom of the press," Calhoun wrote—as chairman of an *ad hoc* committee which brought an adverse report (archly adding that the states, of course, should be free to make and enforce any law they chose to stop postal delivery of whatever they, the states, wanted to proscribe). Henry Clay, though no philosophical ally to Calhoun, was "alarmed": the bill would establish a "precedent" for censoring which could lead to "incalculable mischief." Daniel Webster was "shocked": "Congress had not the power, drawn from the character of [any publication] or paper to decide whether it should be carried in the mail or not." These declarations rallied others. The Senate and the House repudiated Andrew Jackson's bill, avowing that they had no power to pass it. They went on to pass a statute prohibiting tampering with anyone's mail.

It was the first time, and the only time for a long period, that Congress explored the question, Can the government censor, on any ground, what it carries in the mail? Political conditions and conceptions changed. The First Amendment came, in a sense, to lie fallow.

Within a decade after the debates of 1836, an ostensibly different form of censorship appeared in the federal law. This resulted as legislatures, courts, and the public began to seek ways to stop the circulation of a quite different kind of objectionable publication.

2. THE NINETEENTH-CENTURY EMERGENCE OF ANTI-OBSCENITY LAW: THE TARIFF ACT OF 1842, LORD CAMPBELL'S ACT, HICKLIN'S CASE, COMSTOCK'S LAW

IN MILTON'S TIME, even when censorship had been total, there was little written law, at least in the secular sources, on the question of how "Books [should] demean themselves" with respect to their treatment of the fact of sex and the fascinating, omnipresent matter of relationships between the sexes. Contemporary tracts like Prynne's *Histriomastix* and Jeremy Collier's *Short View of Profaneness* bear testimony to the fact that there was much that was shocking to some, and also to the fact that little was done by way of law enforcement to suppress it. Government had reckoned with the proposition that books could stimulate heresies and sedition, and on those fronts it bore down hard. But in the nineteenth century there was a fresh awareness of the possibility that the arts could stimulate glands—or perhaps just undesirable thoughts and feelings about sex; and it became commonly assumed that this sort of communication could promote a promiscuity subversive of the norms by which men sought to live. So it became the law, but only long after Milton's death, that people who by word, deed, or picture portray sex through "obscene" forms could be punished; and the obscene portrayal itself became, like the deodands of ancient English law, evil *per se,* to be exorcised so that no man should see it.

There were few attempts, at the time, to square the belief favoring suppression of all things obscene with the belief that the press should be free. The writings of some of freedom's great nineteenth century advocates—John Stuart Mill, for example, were silent or ambiguous on the problem. Typical, no doubt, was the thinking of Robert G. Ingersoll, a great orator (it was he who nominated James G. Blaine before an enraptured convention and dubbed him the "plumed knight") and a well-known nineteenth century American defender of freedom of the press. Ingersoll vigorously championed the cause of agnosticism, fought in the courts, in Congress and in many public forums for the rights of virulent, atheist publishers who had outraged the community. Ingersoll even crusaded for repeal of the First Postal anti-obscenity law, because, as will be seen, it was used to persecute "free thinkers" as well as pornographers; but he glibly assumed that obscenity was a recognizable species of speech apart, that there simply was no freedom to publish it and no reason to grant such freedom: nothing should ever be tolerated in print which would "cover the cheek of modesty with the blush of shame."

Perhaps it was assumed then, as it sometimes is now, that obscene communication performs no useful service in the development of ideas or art, that it has no intellectual value to men; consequently its suppression can not be thought to be inconsistent with the objectives of the First Amendment. In any event, freedom of speech came to mean, de facto and de jure, freedom of clean speech only.

Historians have stressed, perhaps overstressed, the "prudery" which "the Victorians" superimposed over the conditions of life in their time. It is trite, now, to dwell on this and to berate the "Comstockery" of the age. The fact remains that there were strong pressures for legislating more morality with respect to all men's vices as they were then perceived. Gambling, drinking, and similar habits were the targets of new, vigorous laws just as much as was immodest or erotic expression in the arts.

The nineteenth century was a period of popularization of the printed word. Books, notably fiction, circulated among an ever-widening audience; larger newspapers and magazines (and pictures to illustrate them) could be assembled more cheaply, and more and more people could read them. There is evidence that, not withstanding all the pressure for morality, pornography—that age-old by-product of our culture—also enjoyed the boom in mass communication produced by literacy, mass production, and urbanization. It is not surprising that this increase in pornography should cause concern, as it did, especially in the much publicized reports of the many, aggressive anti-vice societies which were, in turn, a development and a reflection of this vice-conscious era. But the demands for counteraction seldom drew the line anywhere near crude pornography. The concept of obsceneness was far broader. As a Massachusetts minister, with Hawthorne's *Scarlet Letter* in mind, put it: There should be no "toleration" whatsoever of any "popular and gifted writer when he perpetrates bad morals—let all brokerage of lust be put down at the very beginning."

Yet until the middle of the nineteenth century there was very little legislation or legal precedent to implement such counsel through the force of law. True, an old English vagrancy statute of the eighteenth century (copied in some places here) punished "obscene exhibitions," and three New England states had legislated against public dissemination of "prints" and "books" which were "obscene" as well as "blasphemous." There was also common law authority—a few cases and some very general pronouncements in the leading texts—to the effect that public exhibition or sale of obscene things, including books, was criminal even in the absence of a statute. But in the actual cases which had arisen, the courts seemed more concerned with the scandalous behavior of the particular individuals who had been indicted than with the general repression of a particular publication. The cases at common law involved prosecutions akin to cases of blasphemy, cursing, lewd behavior, and indecent exposure, and were analogized in this way in the search for precedents; these were prosecutions, so it was said, for "breaches of the peace" or for reckless affronts to the rudimentary norms of individual deportment in public places.

Beginning about the mid-nineteenth century, the concept of this crime was subtly but significantly changed; the focus shifted from the defendant's personal conduct to the ideas or the content of the expression he was disseminating. Whereas the defendant's public use of obscene creations was once the basis of prosecution, that now became unimportant; obscenity was bad in itself, without regard to conduct or to the actual effect of its previous dissemination, and virtually all distribution was proscribed, regardless of motive, audience reached, or actual harm done. Thus, the law moved, almost unconsciously, into the business of banning books.

In 1842, Congress, without any debate whatsoever, indeed without any explanation appearing in any of the official annals reflecting the evolution of this law, inserted a provision in the Tariff Act, authorizing Customs officers to confiscate "prints" and "pictures" which were "obscene or immoral" and to bring court proceedings authorizing their destruction. In hindsight it was a novel measure, a type of censorship statute and the first of its kind in this country. Yet it slipped into the law unnoticed, and for a while it occasioned little controversy. Its significance as a technique to control reading and press freedom was not appreciated, and perhaps could not have been appreciated. For, perhaps those who framed this new law foresaw only that it would permit seizure of disgusting pictures. And what was wrong with that?

In England, events shortly occurred which were to influence the future interpretation of this tariff ban on obscenity and to spur the growth of anti-obscenity law generally. These developments were, in one sense only a reflection of the times, but they mark the first clear instance of a new legal departure.

In 1857, Lord Chief Justice John Campbell, a jurist-author and untiring reformer on many fronts, brought forward in the House of Lords a bill to facilitate criminal prosecutions of purveyors of obscenity. Sitting as a trial judge, he had presided over a number of trials of some notorious denizens of "Holywell Street" in London. These men, so he learned, were entrepreneurs of pictures and pamphlets apparently of a tawdry, lurid, or erotic character, perhaps of outright pornography, too. Thanks to the aggressive methods of these hucksters, there existed, according to the Chief Justice's report to Parliament, "an alarming trade . . . of the most infamous" commodities. Bales of material "printed in Paris"—"poison more deadly than arsenic"—were secreted in London "warehouses," from whence the stuff was taken and hawked in back alleys and dingy shops or peddled via the mails and via traveling salesmen who were touring the realm (and even visiting cloistered halls in Oxford and Cambridge and young ladies' boarding schools, according to an earlier report of one of the anti-vice societies).

Due very largely to the efforts of private groups, something had been done to thwart this business. But the investigations and prosecutions initiated by anti-vice groups were not enough, for the private citizen lacked, under common law, sufficient legal privileges to enable him to search for and to seize the offensive matter and arrest the offenders. Besides, said Campbell, the "spies and informers" who were hired by the anti-vice societies to do the actual dirty work were men of "doubtful character." They bungled their cases. They made appalling witnesses. In Lord Campbell's opinion, the situation called for more government action than had yet been forthcoming. The police should be both spurred and given clear-cut authority to do what needed to be done. With this explanation he introduced a statute resolving all doubts about the criminality of sales of obscene books or the possession of them for purposes of sale, providing stiff penalties as well as procedures for the issuance of warrants authorizing searches and confiscation.

In a strict sense, the principal thrust of the "Obscene Publications Act" was in its adjective rather than its substantive parts. Lord Campbell experienced little doubt—though it would now appear that the contours of the crime were most vague—that the Holywell purveyors were guilty of an offense at common law whenever they negotiated sales of their wares or attempted to do so; to him the real issue was simply whether it was necessary to create or to codify police powers to make searches and seizures. But the bill was not debated in this context in Parliament. The controversy centered, not around law enforcement search and seizure powers, but over the question of standards: should Parliament pass any anti-obscenity law at all.

Lord Campbell's opposition felt, despite all the clamor about Holywell Street, that the statute contemplated a wider orbit of action, that the bill could be a spearhead for a new crusade. It was, they pointed out, a proposal to prevent all circulation of all "obscene" books, though the term "obscene" was nowhere defined and never had been in the law; and Campbell's critics demanded to know just how far this grant of authority could be stretched if zealous police and puritanical judges, spurred on by anti-vice groups, undertook to enforce the law against the arts.

Perhaps the sharpness of this opposition was occasioned by the presence in the opposite aisle of Lord Lyndhurst, a former Chief Justice himself and, as such, a subject of a chapter that was a lot less than a eulogy in Campbell's very recently published, multivolume work, *The Lives of the Chief Justices*. Lyndhurst, it was said, believed that his juristic talents surpassed those of his unsolicited, critical biographer. Perhaps this supplied motivation for his lawyer-like dissection of pitfalls present in Campbell's proposal, and Lyndhurst (with stinging asides on Campbell's talents as a writer) raised a hue and cry against the bill. Campbell's opponents reviewed a list of salacious "classics," e.g., works by Rochester, Wycherly, Congreve, and other Restoration dramatists—why, there was hardly a play published in the reign of Charles II which might not offend contemporary standards. Lyndhurst called attention to the tableaux of nymphs and satyrs and gods and goddesses in the Louvre and elsewhere, to licentious Latin poets like Ovid, to passages in Shakespeare and, indeed, in the works of contemporary authors. Pictures were conjured up of staid, upright booksellers and art dealers being marched off to jail for selling great masterpieces —a parade of potential, horrible results to supply rhetoric to his question: where will the government draw the line in defining what shall be "obscene?"[2]

In the Commons, Lyndhurst spurred like opposition: "A more preposterous bill has never been set down from the House of Lords —and that is saying a great deal." One M.P. called attention to the existence of the United States Tariff Law and its ban on imported obscenity; he reported the fact that the Collector of the Port of New York had recently confiscated a "well-known work, describing with figures, the principal statues, paintings, etc. of the Royal Museum at Naples," a book worth at least thirty pounds, "and we have it in the Library attached to this House." Admitting the noxious nature of Holywell pornography, opponents asserted that the common virtues were common enough to spare the populace

2. "No one could be more decorous than Lord Lyndhurst as he rolled up his stately periods around some point of international or constitutional law. But he had his weaknesses and his prejudices. He liked sailing near the wind, and he could not abide John Campbell. On the second reading of his 'noble and learned friend's Bill,' he delivered one of the most amusing speeches to be found in the innumerable volumes of Hansard. He entertained the Lords spiritual and temporal by describing all the most improper pictures by celebrated painters, and all the most improper poems by celebrated poets. . . . Whether this strange harangue be regarded as a scandalous exhibition of senile depravity, or the vivacious outburst of a temperament which years could not impair, it was certainly a remarkable performance for a man of eighty-five" H. Paul, *History of Modern England* (1888), II, 83–84.

from the corruption which Campbell feared would envelop London and then England, without help from Parliament; it was forlorn foolishness and risky presumptuousness to suppose that Parliament could "make people virtuous" or quell salacity and indecency in print by passing laws to jail publishers and booksellers.

Lord Campbell and his defenders insisted that the classics were somehow privileged by dint of antiquity and that they would not be disturbed by future enforcement of the law. But Campbell insisted, too, that there was far too much modern fiction afoot which was capable of corrupting the populace, that was shocking to modern modesty. Holywell Street was a glaring example of what might happen without a vigorous government cleanup, and why (as the Archbishop put it) should there be so much "misplaced sympathy" with those hucksters of filth?

The onus of "misplaced sympathy" defeated the opposition. The bill passed, and shortly thereafter the Chief Justice reported to the House of Lords that the new law had provided a basis for "repeated assaults" and, finally, "victory" over the peddlers. Dared by Lyndhurst to produce, for purposes of inspection, samples of the "abominations" which had been confiscated, the Chief Justice assured his colleagues that he would do nothing of the sort, lest he "alarm" the "modesty" of England's peers.

But Holywell Street was not the last "assault." A decade later the law was interpreted by Campbell's successor, Lord Chief Justice Cockburn, in a fashion which undoubtedly would have confirmed Lyndhurst's fears, had he been alive to express them.

The case was *Queen v. Hicklin.* The offense: selling a virulent, anti-Catholic tract called *The Confessional Unmasked,* both authored and published by the defendant Hicklin as part of the campaign of the Protestant Electoral Union to keep Catholics out of Parliament. Offensive in parts, perhaps, this was no Holywell Street item. Indeed, the prosecution assumed and the Court admitted that Hicklin had a purpose which transcended a pornographer's one-track intention to put out something simply calculated to induce sexual reflexes. The defense was based on the argument that Hicklin was certainly within his rights if he chose to pamphleteer against the vices he thought he saw in the confession; even if his argument proceeded by alleging that the confessional was an indecent practice, and even if he sought to prove these allegations by purported graphic documentation of conversations and conduct between priest and penitent, still, it was Hicklin's right to publish these things when he did so to present an otherwise legitimate argument, and when the alleged obscene passages in his narration comprised only a small part of the total work.

Here Hicklin's defense collapsed. The Court laid it down as law that every passage in a book must be judged independently and apart from every other passage; and if any excerpt, read in isolation, was obscene then the book was contraband, though the balance of its text be unexceptionable and its message and motivation even laudable. Thus, a jury—judging Hicklin's or any other book—was to ignore the work as a whole; they need know nothing of the book's substance or quality, not even what it was about; their job, and the court's, was to examine only the passage or passages brought to their attention and conveniently marked by the prosecution, and to decide whether any of these were obscene. And the meaning of "obscene"?

Lord Cockburn declared: "I think the test is this, whether the tendency of the matter charged as obscenity [i.e., the isolated passages to be examined] is to deprave and corrupt those whose minds are open to immoral influences, and into whose hands a publication of this sort may fall."

Studied in context, that oft-quoted sentence carried broader implications than an initial reading might impart. For Cockburn's ruling meant that:

(1) The law was concerned with the "tendency" of the printed word to "corrupt" or to "deprave," and a broad innuendo was attached to those vague epithets; they were used in the inflated sense of their time and referred to bad thoughts or desires, not bad conduct; a book need induce no actual sexual misbehavior before its capacity to corrupt could be found, nor need it even tend to do that; enough that excerpts in it could simply stimulate sexual thoughts in impressionable minds.

(2) The law would automatically presume that a work offered for distribution to the public at large might fall into the hands of the young or those susceptible to libidinous imaginings—a class assumed to be large; and it was this kind of audience which the law, as now formulated, was to protect by making criminal all circulation

of any expression which could corrupt the corruptible, regardless of whether that harm actually had occurred.

These English developments—Campbell's statute and Cockburn's test—seemed to translate a social urge into legal doctrine.

The same pattern unfolded in America. Legislatures enacted statutes (often using Campbell's act as a model) and courts (often with unthinking acquiescence) read the *Hicklin* standard into them. What was done by our national government is a reflection of what was done by state and local governments. There was increased lawmaking, given impetus by increased agitation against the evil; there was little analysis of the consequences of creating vague laws giving vast power to men whose only qualification to regulate reading was derived from their official positions.

Even as Parliament was debating Lord Campbell's bill to suppress "obscene publications," Congress (again with no reported discussion) enlarged the tariff barrier first erected in 1842. The prohibition against importing "prints" and "pictures" was amended to include "daguerreotypes" and "photographs," "images" and "figures," and all other "obscene articles," but not yet, apparently, the printed word alone.

Then, in 1865, Congress dealt for the first time with obscenity in the mails, but in a casual way, considering the novelty of the problem. The Postmaster General had reported that "great numbers" of "obscene books and pictures" were being "sent to the Army." Indeed, even without a statute, postal employees had occasionally assumed the authority to confiscate materials which they thought were morally objectionable. Now the situation was getting worse; there was said to be an increasing flow of bad things; there ought to be a law. The Post Office asked for one which would (1) authorize seizure by any postmaster of any "obscene" material which he might find; (2) authorize criminal prosecutions (with imprisonment up to a year) against those who used the mails to disseminate such material.

The proposal came up for enactment in the Senate. Discussion was brief and rather perfunctory. There was vague mention of "censorship": perhaps we shouldn't simply authorize postmasters to seize whatever they think is bad, said a senator from Vermont. It would, indeed, be "a very bad precedent to give authority to postmasters to take anything out of the mails," declared Maryland's

Reverdy Johnson, whose reputation as a lawyer commanded respect. Why so? Did he, too, fear the possibility of excessive censorship? Apparently not so much that, but he did fear the possibility that postal officials would go around "breaking seals" and snooping into private business in their quest for this noxious contraband; the authorization to snoop ought to be excised. Agreed, said Senator Sherman; we should change our bill, but we should enact the "prohibition against carrying [obscenity] when it is known to the postmaster" (i.e., when it can be detected without breaking seals). The upshot of all this ambiguous debate was that some deletions were made; but if the senators were really concerned about preventing censorship of the mails, then they surely bungled. For if one reads what was left of the bill as passed—without benefit of this legislative history—one might infer that Congress had indeed authorized the Post Office to censor.[3] In any event, this new law was passed with no further debate, without concern about the meaning of obscenity, the difference between legitimate and illegitimate sex expression, or the proper way to combat whatever evil existed.

No sooner had the U.S. government taken up the business of policing the post than there was more pressure for more lawmaking to enlarge the operation.

In 1873, just in the wake of the Crédit Mobilier scandal, when American political morality seemed at its lowest ebb, when corruption in high places (notably Congress) was the consuming topic in Washington, Anthony Comstock arrived on Capitol Hill as the young (he was only 28) lobbyist for the New York YMCA's "Committee for the Suppression of Vice," soon to become the famous New York Society For the Suppression of Vice. Plumpish,

3. The deleted portion of the bill stated that "all . . . obscene publications . . . discovered in the mails shall be seized and destroyed . . . as the Postmaster General shall direct." The statute, as enacted after this deletion, stated, "No obscene book, pamphlet [etc.] . . . shall be admitted into the mails," and went on to impose criminal penalties on those who put such materials into the mails. This first clause, enjoining admission into the mails, may have been meant to give postmasters the authority to refuse to accept mail where, without breaking seals, the postmaster could examine the item and conclude that it was obscene. In essence, then, the act of 1865 may well have contemplated the possibility of some sort of an administrative censorship operation, though precisely how much no one could say. The debates were very summary, and passage was really perfunctory. There were no debates at all in the House. For a detailed account of the legislative history of the Act of 1865 see the chapter notes in Appendix I.

bewhiskered—appearing benign and far older than his age—Comstock was a dynamo of activity with a compulsive hatred for all things sexually immodest.

He had already achieved some fame and plenty of experience in the business of battling vice. As an angered private citizen, working in a purely unofficial capacity by taking time off from his Brooklyn dry goods store, he had spent the past year personally tracking down offenders—American counterparts of the Holywell vendors—in the back streets of New York and reporting his successes to the YMCA, the police, the courts. "I have," he boasted to one Congressman, "seized and destroyed . . . more than 5 tons [of] obscene books and pamphlets." At least fifty "dealers" had been arrested, and six "publishers" had died shortly after public exposure of their sins—one a suicide. (It seemed that the vengeance of the Lord had revealed itself through this crusader's work—at least so he suggested.)

Comstock had also investigated the business of mail-order dissemination. At regular intervals he would purchase lowbrow newspapers and magazines (like *New Varieties* and *Illustrated Police Gazette*) and scan the ads. Some were suspicious, for example, an offer to send a mail-order catalogue listing pictures of magnificent "views of Rome." Now who would expect to find lovers of ancient architecture reading *New Varieties?* Comstock wrote for the catalogue. Sure enough, it solicited orders for "fancy books." Not "fancy," but "vile," he concluded when he received his copy. Upon this and several other occasions he had turned such evidence over to the United States Marshal. Sometimes he did more, traveling to distant cities to instigate arrests; indeed, he probably knew more about enforcement of the law of 1865 than anyone in the government, and he soon concluded that its coverage was insufficient to promote the kind of vigorous suppression which the times demanded.

Acting in the same capacity—as a citizen-guardian of the mails—Anthony Comstock was also mixed up in something of a *cause célèbre* at the very time of his descent on Congress, in the winter of 1873. He had recently instigated the arrest of those famous sisters, Victoria Woodhull and Tennessee Claffin, two fabulous females who, in defiance of the double standard and the assumed natural law of the times, had combined careers as Wall Street speculators, political advocates, and journalists with great success. These two ladies were also permanent champions of women's rights and, sometimes, advocates of free love. For the advancement of all these various interests they published *Woodhull and Claflin's Weekly*. Included in the *Weekly*'s pages were reports on financial matters (dull) and political comment (avowedly "radical") and an occasional story dealing with some choice scandal in the upper echelons of society.

In the fall of 1872 there was detailed, but apparently in prose quite prim, an allegation that Henry Ward Beecher had been intimate with another man's wife. Worse yet, the *Weekly* seemed to forgive the adultery, but not the hypocrisy of covering it up.

Despite the hesitancy of U.S. prosecutors, Comstock swore out a federal warrant to force the government to do its duty. The sisters had mailed obscenity, he charged, and he personally journeyed to Wall Street with two marshals in tow to see their arrest effectuated. There followed a protracted hearing before a U.S. Commissioner—who simply couldn't make up his mind. The sisters retained "Counselor Howe" (of Howe and Hummel fame), and he took some pains to elicit Mr. Comstock's opinion on such painful questions as: Were certain Old Testament accounts of adultery obscene? Was biblical usage of the word "virginity" immoral? (Comstock had previously objected to the word in the *Weekly*.) And if the Old Testament was mailable, why pick on the similar but less graphic prose of the defendants?

Another wealthy, Wall Street erratic, George Francis Train—"Citizen Train," self-styled—picked up Mr. Howe's line of argument. To vent his disgust at the persecution of Victoria and Tennessee, Train published a tract called *The Train Lique*. And in Train's own words (from his autobiography): "Every verse I used was worse than anything published by these women. I was immediately arrested on a charge of obscenity, and taken to the Tombs. I was never tried on this charge, but was kept in jail as a lunatic, and then dismissed, under the ban of declared lunacy, and have so remained for thirty years. Although the public pretended to be against me, it was very eager to buy the edition of my paper that gave these extracts from the Bible. The price of the paper rose from five cents a copy to twenty, forty, sixty cents, and even to one dollar. In a few days it was selling surreptitiously for two dollars a copy."

Indeed, the whole affair—Train's and the sisters'—became a

pruriently publicized circus which terminated in a legal stalemate, and the prosecutions were dropped. But this experience only fired the wrath and zeal of Anthony Comstock. He reported to the YMCA Committee his belief that the federal mail statute needed more teeth. That group quickly commissioned him to go to Washington. Some outstanding gentlemen were on the YMCA Committee, and it appears that through the good offices of Justice Strong of the Supreme Court an interview was arranged with Congressman Merriam of New York and Senator Windom of Minnesota. Indeed, Strong did more (according to Comstock's authorized biographer); he not only wrote a letter of introduction, but he scratched out a draft bill for the New York lobbyist to present to the gentlemen,

Comstock's goal was an expanded law which would suppress circulation, not only of obscene books, but also obscene things (articles and gadgets), advertisements of obscenity or purported obscenity, and all information on contraception, abortion, and physical implements designed for such purposes. This broad coverage was imperative, he urged, for "vice" in the mails was a "hydraheaded monster," and he who combated it needed a sword which could cut through all legal technicalities to smite down every evil scheme disclosed, every businessman who dealt in things immoral or offensive.

The old law was inadequate, and "I know whereof I speak," Anthony Comstock told Mr. Merriam, demonstrating his case by extracting horrendous exhibits from a great cloth bag which he carried about. These apparently included the lowbrow publications and their advertisements, gadgets purportedly designed to stimulate sexual potency, the "fancy books," the bogus sex literature, contraceptive and abortifacient matter, and other "abominations" which were sold via the ads. Comstock had, indeed, learned all about the mail-order commerce in these things, and he explained it, tirelessly, to any congressman who would listen: the use of advertisements to attract the prurient, the suspected volume of these various mailing operations, and the evil impact which (he was certain) this stuff was having on the country's virtue. A sort of chamber of horrors exhibit of all this "dirty trash" was set up in the Vice-president's office and shown to all who manifested an interest. Alarming reports from anti-vice societies were also spread about, and some congressmen were referred to Lord Campbell's experience and his great reform of English law.

Comstock soon become a familiar figure on the floors of Congress, at receptions, and in Washington churches, and even at presidential receptions where, so he confided to his diary, the "ladies" wore shamelessly "low dresses" and "painted faces." No doubt his exhibits and his puritanical fervor were the subject of off-color satire in the cloakrooms, and plainly there did develop some informal opposition to his bill and some aversion for the man. But on the floors of both houses, no word was spoken against him or his proposal.

A group in Congress was enlisted to steamroller the measure into the statute books. They couldn't act fast enough to suit Anthony Comstock, who prayed and hovered over every stage of the proceedings, and fulminated and agonized in the pages of his diary over the fate of "my bill," as he called it. Indeed, the principal reason for the delay was that too many cooks now wanted to stir the broth, and Comstock's original bill, while in committee, became a veritable potpourri of anti-obscenity legislation. A crusading fervor prompted new proposals. A spokesman from a Washington anti-vice society wanted inclusion of a statute for the District of Columbia. Then ex-General Ben Butler, the mercurial politico from Massachusetts (and certainly known far and wide among ladies of the South as the "Beast of New Orleans" for his alleged Civil War atrocities against female virtue), sequestered all drafts of the bills with the avowed purpose of expanding and rewriting them, himself, so that Congress could exercise its constitutional power to the hilt to cope with the menace, not only in the mails and foreign commerce but also in all federal territory. Butler was later to become an open critic of Comstock, but now he was his advocate, and the new draft bill which emerged from the Judiciary Committee was truly an omnibus measure.

It was also long and verbose. The postal code said in effect: No "obscene," "lewd," or "lascivious" publication "shall be carried in the mail"; further, "any person" who "knowingly" mailed or "received" these things was guilty of a crime; he should be sent to jail for up to ten years. Similarly with the mailing of abortifacient "things" or information about them, or with any "thing designed

or intended . . . for indecent or immoral use." Similarly with advertisements for any of this offensive matter.

Another part of the bill dealt with importation; it was essentially
a redraft of the old 1842 tariff law—but with the notable addition
of "books" and "pamphlets"; Congress was now asked to ban access
to all foreign literature which might be deemed "obscene." Other
parts of the bill, modeled after Lord Campbell's act, prohibited
selling obscene publications in the District of Columbia and the
territories and sending them through the channels of interstate
commerce.

It took many words for Congress to spell all this out; even so,
close reading of this text might have suggested many questions of
detail, for the drafting was sloppy. But, disregarding technicalities, there were two issues which were fundamental and yet treated
ambiguously: (1) Was the mail statute purely a criminal statute?
Or did it also mean to authorize Postal officials to engage in an
independent, censorship operation to purge the mails of obscenity?
(2) What was the definition of the term "obscene"? On both counts
the legislation was silent. Nor was there much time to debate details. The session was wearing on; it was now into February, and
Congress had to clear the decks for adjournment in the first week
in March, when President Grant would start his second term and a
new session would begin. Comstock and his friends on the floor
were desperately anxious to be done with it all by then. Alas, the
Credit Mobilier scandals and other matters kept interfering with
attempts to get the bill up for a vote.

In the middle of February Senator Buckingham asked unanimous
consent to take it up. But Casserly of California objected: we've
barely had time to read this bill, he said; there may be a "great
many important questions"; for example, "I do not know whether
it can be left to employees of a custom house to determine with
safety what kind of literature or what sort of matter is to be admitted."

Casserly had certainly put his finger on something important, but
no one bothered to answer him. The bill was passed over, the
further discussion was delayed for a few days. Then Buckingham
called it up again and, at the same time, started offering amendments to tinker with some minor language details. Casserly made a
confused speech which apparently signified his endorsement; he

now had no qualms about Customs censorship because, as he now read the bill, material seized by the Customs clerks would be referred to the courts for forfeiture proceedings, and the courts would be passing on the legality of every seizure. (This assumption was wrong, as will be seen.) Buckingham ignored these comments and went on proposing minor amendments. Finally, Senator Roscoe Conkling of New York said he was too confused to go on; none of us even have copies of the bill before us; "If I were to be questioned now as to what [it] contains, I could aver nothing certain in regard to it." No doubt others shared his ignorance.

So passage was delayed again, and Comstock's diary records the deep despair of a crusader frustrated by politicians. But it is questionable whether Conkling was really interested in allaying his own ignorance or debating the bill, and certainly Comstock despaired too soon. A short while later the bill was printed, called up, and rammed through without a further murmur or quibble. And a few days after that, sandwiched between spates of passsionate oratory on Credit Mobilier and morality in government, the House—also without any debate at all (but with some thirty votes against it)— enacted this comprehensive, verbose piece of legislation, which was characterized thereafter, and rightly so, as the "Comstock Act."

"O how can I express the joy of my Soul or speak the mercy of God," was the diary recording of that protagonist, who stayed on to be sworn in as a "special agent" for the Post Office Department and to watch the festivities of Grant's second inaugural, noting with apparent satisfaction that the inclement weather forced the painted ladies to keep their shawls on throughout the dancing at the grand ball that evening.

3. THE MENTAL SANITATION TEST IS
IMPORTED, AND THE POST OFFICE
ASSUMES CENSORSHIP POWERS

COMSTOCK DID NOT treat his special agent's commission as a mere memento of those hectic Washington days. He used the power which the Postmaster General had bestowed; indeed, as contemporary newspaper accounts show, he soon piled up an astounding record of confiscations, investigations, and convictions. And yet like law enforcement officers of modern times he constantly accused the courts of failing to appreciate the menace of obscenity. Nevertheless the courts did give him much leeway. One of Comstock's cases, the prosecution against D. M. Bennett, developed a court decision which became a definitive landmark, the *Hicklin* precedent of federal law.

The cantankerous Bennett was a freewheeling publisher of free thought and free love tracts. In 1877 he wrote and circulated "An Open Letter to Jesus Christ," an event which touched off a vice-society raid of his premises and an abortive prosecution for mailing obscenity. In 1878 he published a tract called *Cupid's Yokes,* a "dull little sociological treatise" so we are told by a modern critic, "filled with antiquated phrases about 'legalized prostitution' and 'relics of barbarism.' " Bennett was now "everything vile in Blasphemy and Infidelism," according to Comstock, who had already sworn a mortal vengeance. That day came when Bennett responded to the letter of one "G. Brackett" ordering "a copy of that Heywood book you advertise, Cupid's something or other, you know what I mean." For G. Brackett was in truth A. Comstock; and after Bennett mailed the book, Postal inspectors descended upon him, and he was jailed and indicted in New York. The incident was widely publicized and controversial. Bennett was a "crank," no doubt, but he had some support in respectable newspapers. His trial was widely publicized—with the *Herald* taking Bennett's side and the *Times* for the prosecution.

The case was quickly tried, for the act of mailing was conceded, and the disputed issue was the alleged obscenity of the book. A marked edition was put in evidence. Defense witnesses (including some clergymen) who sought to testify about the work—to summarize its total content, to explain its theme and motive, to defend its merit—were silenced when the trial judge declared all this irrelevant.

Let me read the whole work to the jury, urged the defense attorney. No, was the court's response, the marked excerpts alone are to be judged. Let me read the marked passages and then read similar passages from other, well-known and respected books (such as an essay of Montaigne) to show that other authors have used similar illustrations and language to make a point, urged the defense counsel.

Again the objection was sustained. The jurors were told: read *only* the passages marked by the prosecutor; if any are obscene, then the book is obscene. And you may find them obscene if they "tend" to "deprave the minds of those open to such influences," if they would "suggest impure and libidinous thoughts in the minds of the young and inexperienced."

The jury responded with a verdict of guilty. (One juror was said to have told a newsman that no other verdict was possible in obedience to the judge's instructions.)

Bennett's lawyers appealed. The trial judge had followed the already well-known *Hicklin* precedent, and the big question, of course, was whether that formula for determining the legality of a book should be read into the federal statutes. Bennett's lawyers argued, in essence: The *Hicklin* method of enforcing these laws, at least as applied against *Cupid's Yokes,* was too arbitrary, too harsh. Alternative criteria to determine obscenity, more liberal to freedom of expression, were proposed. They were rejected. We think, declared Judge Blatchford for the Court of Appeals, that the *Hicklin* decision—which he erroneously assumed was a reflection of very ancient common law—is "very sound".

Bennett went to the penitentiary for thirteen months.

President Hayes, deluged with demands from clergymen and a special report from agent Comstock exposing Bennett's past indiscretions, refused a pardon. Meanwhile, Judge Blatchford's opinion, prolix but carefully drafted, became an influential precedent in the multitude of Comstock Act prosecutions which soon followed. Some years later, when the Supreme Court was finally confronted with one of these cases, the *Hicklin* formula for testing the obscene content—and thus the legality—of a publication was apparently regarded as so settled that the defense attorneys did not even suggest review of the question. Indeed, the high Court, in its first dictum on the subject, and without analysis, made the same assumption— quoting verbatim from the *Bennett* case. That precedent of uncritical acceptance was, in turn, followed in a series of later, *obiter* observations by Supreme Court Justices on the meaning of the term "obscene."

In 1876 Congress was forced to tinker again with the Comstock Act to iron out an ambiguity in its penalty clause, and once again a verbose bill was rushed to the floor. It is only a restatement of all we intended to say three years ago, plus a strengthening of the lottery laws, declared the bill's managers; aside from that, the new statute will in "no wise change the law. . . ." A few ambiguous questions were asked. We ought to act "carefully," James Garfield told his colleagues in the House—recalling several of the more controversial prosecutions of recent years. And a New York congressman promised to divulge some startling information about "postal oppression of an honorable and innocent man." He never did (at least on the floor), and Garfield's caveats were forgotten. The bill passed, and no one seemed particularly concerned that the Comstock Act, in its revised form, now ordained that "obscene" publications were "declared [to be] non-mailable matter and shall not be conveyed in or delivered by mail," and then went on to provide for criminal liability.

This new language (about obscenity being "non-mailable matter") certainly seemed to authorize the Post Office to engage in censorship. But there also appeared to be another, quite different reason for rewriting the statute in this form: The Act of 1873 listed a great many items—ranging from obscene publications to advertisements to gadgets and devices which might be used for various purposes; anyone who mailed these was to be guilty of a crime. But in his haste, the draftsman of the Act of 1873 had written the law so that, after listing all the proscribed items, the statute said, in effect: anyone who mails the "hereinbefore mentioned *articles* or *things*" shall be guilty of a crime. A sharp-eyed lawyer had apparently noted that nothing was specifically said about publications in this penalty clause: did the terms "articles and "things" comprehend "writings" and "pictures"? Apparently it was that ambiguity which was to be clarified in 1876. The method chosen by the new draftsman was to list all the proscribed items and then declare that they were "non-mailable matter," and anyone who mailed "non-mailable matter" was guilty of a crime. Thus, it may well have been that the draftsman had no idea of using the term "non-mailable" in the sense that it would authorize official censoring powers for the Post Office. Certainly not a word was said in the debates about bestowing any independent, administrative power to confiscate mail in transit. On the contrary, Chairman Cannon of the House Post Office Committee (and manager for the bill) declared: "Nor, sir, does this bill give any right to any postmaster to open or interfere with anybody's mail. It is like anything else, before you can convict you must offer and make proof," referring, presumably, to the fact that the law was to be enforced exclusively through criminal proceedings in the courts, with the burden put upon the government; there should be no stoppage of mail by Postal officials unless the criminal remedy was to be invoked.

It is probable that in 1876, as in 1873, Congress simply did not appreciate the problem of censorship, just as few foresaw any other significant dangers to freedom in anti-obscenity legislation. The pressures of the times, it would appear, inhibited such critical analysis. True, the activities of Comstock had become notorious, and, as is evident from remarks made in the brief debates in 1876 (over the revision of the Comstock Act) there were some in Congress who thought the New Yorker was abusing the power bestowed in 1873. But they hardly pressed their objections.

Again, the prosecution of D. M. Bennett must have disturbed

some. For it had enraged many atheistic and "free thinking" groups, an element of the population which was vociferous even if small in number. The protest of these groups against Comstock and his law came to a head when a petition, prepared under the auspices of the "National Liberal League" and purporting to bear the names of 50,000 men and women (including spokesmen of the standing of Robert Ingersoll and James Parton, the noted biographer) was presented to Congress. Repeal the Comstock Act, was the petition's message: This law is a usurpation of power which should be exclusively vested in the states; this law is being used to persecute Americans for expressing radical religious beliefs by mailing "free thinking" tracts. The erratic Ben Butler, formerly a conservative and an author of parts of the Comstock Act but now the Greenback Party's candidate for President and a preacher of a new political gospel, mustered courage to introduce the petition; but he disclaimed support of it. Nor was a word ever said thereafter about the grievances of the petitioners; the Senate and House Committees to which the petition was referred promptly brought out summary recommendations to table it, and these were accepted without debate.

The protest of the 50,000 deserved a more extended treatment than it received. Experience had surely shown that zealous men like Comstock could convert an anti-obscenity law into a broad proscription. Important, too, was the matter of the method and procedures for enforcing the Postal law. As we have seen, it is far from clear that Congress had intended to authorize the Post Office to stop suspect obscene materials in transit except as an incident to the arrest or indictment of the man who mailed them. But the Department did gradually develop a system of administrative censorship, and this censorship became an operation distinct and apart from criminal enforcement of the anti-obscenity law. Suspect books or magazines or newspapers would be stopped; it might well be that neither the Department of Justice nor the local U.S. Attorney had any disposition to indict the publisher; it might well be that those officials would conclude that the publication was not obscene. But if the Postal officials concluded otherwise, they would assert the power to suppress its circulation, by confiscating the material whenever and wherever it appeared.

This censorship power was confirmed, by 1890, in an opinion

of the Attorney General, Charles J. Bonaparte. A responsible daily newspaper had been carrying Tolstoy's *Kreutzer Sonata* in serial form. Postal officials decided that passages in the book were obscene. The paper was told to stop publishing it via the mails. The publisher apparently objected, and the Postmaster General referred the problem to Mr. Bonaparte: Could the Post Office do what it had done? The reply: you may stop the mailing of any issue of any newspaper which reproduces any obscene passage from any book or any article. Thus the Attorney General upheld, but without any careful analysis, the legality of a censorship practice which had long since been developed.

The publisher's only remedy in the *Kreutzer Sonata* case, and in any similar case, was to expurgate Tolstoy or to hire an attorney and sue in court for an injunction—a court order telling the Postal officials to cease their interference. But the courts, it appears, were reluctant to override the "discretion" of postal officials. The Postmaster General and his subordinates, it was assumed, were well equipped to decide what was "obscene"; that was their job, and their judgment was only to be set aside in cases of clear "abuse." Thus, the plain fact was that by the simple act of seizing a publication, postal officials were able to throw a heavy burden of exculpation entirely upon the citizen who wanted to distribute it. Censorship thrives in such a regime precisely because the censor is so little accountable except to his own notions of what should be censored.

4. THE EXPANSION OF FEDERAL CENSORSHIP BY CONGRESS, THE COURTS, AND THE EXECUTIVE

WAS ALL THIS constitutional? In particular, one might ask, what of the First Amendment? "Congress shall make no law . . . abridging freedom of speech or of the press." The Comstock law—now being enforced by both criminal prosecutions and administrative censorship—obviously affected the citizen's right to publish and to circulate books, magazines, and other forms of expression. Likewise, it affected the right of adult citizens to decide for themselves what books, magazines, and other expression they should read. And these rights are the essence of our First Freedom.

Curiously, the Supreme Court had attempted an *obiter* answer to the question of the validity of the Postal anti-obscenity law even before the *Bennett* case, even before the statute had been authoritatively interpreted by any reported decision, even before the Post Office Department began to exercise the very broad censorial powers which it was exercising by the end of the nineteenth century. The Court's pronouncement came forth in *Ex parte Jackson,* a case which actually had nothing to do with obscenity. Mr. Jackson had mailed a lottery advertisement, thus running afoul of another Postal statute adopted in 1876, which made this kind of mailing criminal. In an unusual proceeding, Jackson attempted to obtain a writ of *habeas corpus* directly from the Supreme Court of the United States,

[31]

using as his sole argument the contention that Congress had no power to suppress lottery or, indeed, any other matter placed in the mails.

It would appear that there was no elaborate argument of this proposition, no intensive exploration of its many facets. Counsel for petitioner Jackson called the Court's attention to the events which had transpired in Congress during the tenure of President Jackson and suggested that these had set a precedent and had settled the constitutional issues. He cited the clear-cut rebuff to President Jackson as a worthy precedent—a legislative decision disavowing all power to police the mails, which the Court should now embrace. But the Court declined.

Justice Field wrote the opinion; it bears the earmarks of haste, and it might be criticized for its summary treatment of difficult problems, for the rambling disorganization of the discourse, and for addressing itself to questions never raised in the litigation before the court. But for all that, the opinion covered the ground on the Postal censorship power in the grand manner of a court confident that it could settle all these issues for the future. The essence of the opinion: The government owns the mails; it establishes the rates and other physical qualifications for carriage; and in like fashion, Congress may impose such conditions as it chooses concerning the content of communication acceptable for carriage. The Comstock Act was cited as an example of precisely the kind of power which the Court had in mind, with the plain implication that its validity was beyond doubt.

Were there *any* constitutional limitations on the scope of this power to regulate the content of mail? The First Amendment might be a limitation, wrote Justice Field, except for the fact that other channels of communication were left open, unregulated; so no one could complain if the mails were closed to those forms of expression which Congress deemed noxious. In short: the First Amendment did not seem to apply to the post—the expressions of the Senate in 1836 and all the traditional arguments against censorship to the contrary notwithstanding.

On the other hand, said the Court, the Fourth Amendment did apply. Though the question was not at all involved, Justice Field went on at length to declare that sealed packages and letters could never be opened, even to enforce lottery laws or obscenity laws or the like, unless the enforcement official first obtained a search warrant.

The Court's dictum declaring the immunity of sealed mail from official search has never really been disputed; the Post Office, while sometimes regretting the handicap which this disability imposes on law enforcement, has never denied its wisdom, and Congress has subsequently legislated it into the Postal code. The Court's dictum denying mail communication the dignity and status of First Amendment protection failed to sit so well.[4] It was shortly challenged by some Louisiana newspapermen. Lotteries were perfectly legal in that state, and newspapers depended on lottery ads for much of their revenue. The newsmen wanted the Court to rule that Congress had no power to interfere with Louisiana's power to regulate gambling according to its own desires, no general power to use postal laws as a springboard to regulate morality. And again the claim was pressed that the power to ban the newspapers because of their textual content was a threat to freedom of the press.

This time the Court spoke through Chief Justice Fuller, who explained that the opinion would have to be short because it had originally been assigned to Justice Bradley for preparation; due to his untimely death the work had devolved on the Chief Justice, who lacked time and was "constrained . . . to waive any elaboration of our views. . . ." It seems unfortunate that Bradley's legal craftsmanship was never devoted to the issue. Fuller's summary opinion simply reiterated and reaffirmed all that was said in the *Jackson* opinion and, indeed, embroidered on the nature of Congress' plenary power to regulate the character of all mail communications.

Subsequent dicta in subsequent decisions did likewise. In 1903 the Court upheld the constitutionality of a statute permitting the Post Office to seize, summarily, *all incoming mail* addressed to a person believed to be using the post to perpetrate frauds. Again the opinion swept over the ground in the grand manner: Congress owns

4. The narrow "First Amendment" question in the Jackson case was simply whether Congress could prohibit lottery communication—not any or all communication, commercial or otherwise, deemed injurious by any majority at any time in Congress. Lottery communication, like false or fraudulent advertising, would hardly seem to be a form of "idea" communication which must be given protection under constitutional guarantees of free speech; if the Court wanted to make short shrift of Jackson's First Amendment claim, it might have just said this, and stopped there.

the Post Office; it may "annex such conditions" to use of the mails as it "chooses," including conditions stating what shall be mailable and conditions imposing sanctions which close mail service to those who violate the laws on mailability. Thus were the constitutional obstacles to the assumption of broad censorship powers swept aside.

In turn, these Supreme Court cases made it all the easier for Congress to pass more laws and for the Post Office to aggrandize its power in the period 1873–1930.

Envelopes or postcards bearing defamatory statements were declared "non-mailable." Purely private communications—even a letter from a husband to his wife—were brought under the purview of the Comstock Act. So was any vulgar expression which was thought to be simply "filthy" rather than "obscene": some court decisions had suggested a hiatus here, whereupon Congress, prompted by the Post Office, filled the gap. Pictures of prize fights were also declared non-mailable. The Espionage Act in 1917 added treasonable and seditious matter to the index. The theory seemed to be that any text which Congress disapproved might be kept out of the mails. Thus, a bill was proposed, indeed seriously urged, in 1915, which would have permitted Postal officials to cut off *all* mail service to *any* publisher who put out books which were "immoral" *or* "libelous." Aimed at radical religious propagandists, this law was so obviously broad and vague that it failed.

As far as the business of suppressing obscene matter was concerned, the Post Office gradually built up an increasingly strong censorship operation. The practice of banning a publication deemed obscene by declaring it "non-mailable" became well established. But that was only one technique of suppression. Invoking a law which was originally designed to curb mail frauds, the Department asserted and exercised the power to cut off all incoming mail addressed *to* any person, publisher, or bookseller who used a "fictitious" business name to sell material considered by Postal officials to be obscene. This "mail block" sanction became a potent weapon; today, as a censorship technique, its constitutionality, at least in some aspects, may be debatable; but only a few decades ago it was used freely with little policing from the courts.

Perhaps the most potent sanction of all was the threat to revoke the mailing permits of magazine publishers who printed obscenity.

This sanction, too, was developed at the turn of the century. It was potent precisely because it gave the Department so much leverage. The fact is that, to the extent that any mass produced magazine or newspaper uses the mails to reach its readers, the so-called "privilege" to go at special low rates is vital to its ability to circulate. Since the very beginnings of governmental postal service in America, even prior to the Revolution, special low rates for papers and periodicals were promulgated precisely to promote a press which could reach an audience.

In contemporary jargon, this cheap-rate "privilege" has been characterized as a "subsidy," but historically it has been called a "necessity," and in the eighteenth century this necessity was assumed as a matter of course. George Washington once believed, apparently, that any postal charge on papers and periodicals was probably too much. Congress never went that far, but it consistently adhered to the policy that magazines and papers published for the world at large should never be obliged to pay their own carriage, but rather only a token rate. Of course, conditions for the special rate were laid down from the beginning and modified from time to time by Congress. In essence these statutory qualifications for enjoyment of cheap rates, as worked out over the years, concerned the question: is this publication a newspaper or a magazine which is disseminated to an audience of subscribers—as opposed, say, to a vehicle for advertising or an unsolicited pamphlet?

During Woodrow Wilson's administration, if not before, the Post Office interpreted the law to add another qualification for enjoyment of low rates. It related to internal content rather than external nature. Said the Postmaster General: we have the power to revoke the permits of any publisher who has been putting out any non-mailable matter. It was not an obscenity case, but a sedition case, which brought this bold assertion of power to a head. For, during World War I, the Postmaster General bore down with a heavy hand on alleged subversive propagandists.

The *Milwaukee Leader* was one of those—a small, left-wing, pacifist journal. While the nation was fighting enemies abroad, it printed and circulated vigorous anti-war articles at home. In the opinion of Postal officials these articles were "non-mailable" under the Espionage Act. So the Post Office cut off the *Leader's* second-class privilege—its vital "subsidy." No statute expressly authorized revocation on any such grounds; this was conceded. But Postal lawyers thought the power was implied, automatically, from the very existence of the non-mailability statutes. Surely, they said, if a periodical violated the laws by introducing into the post that which Congress forbade, it must forfeit further privilege to enjoy a low rate at the expense of the taxpayer. The *Milwaukee Leader* disputed this claim, went to court to win back its "privilege," and carried the fight all the way to the Supreme Court.

It lost. The Court agreed with the government. Once a publisher puts out non-mailable matter—be it sedition or obscenity—he "abuses" his "privilege" to enjoy the postal subsidy which Congress has authorized. The Post Office, in its discretion, may revoke the privilege and refuse to reinstate it unless and until, in the Department's discretion, the publication will "mend its ways" and abide by the laws. "Government," said the Court, is a "practical business"; the power to revoke was a "practical," efficient way to secure enforcement of the prohibitions against non-mailable matter, including obscene matter. Again the Court alluded to the government's plenary, proprietary power over the postal system.

Justice Holmes and Justice Brandeis dissented. "The question of the rate has nothing to do with the question of whether the matter is mailable," Holmes wrote, "and I am satisfied that the Postmaster cannot determine in advance that a certain newspaper is going to be non-mailable and on that ground deny to it not the use of the mails but the rate of postage that the statute says shall be charged." He agreed with Brandeis that this revocation power, neither expressly bestowed nor even expressly suggested in the long history of congressional legislation on postal rates, was "illegal" and probably unconstitutional. The power simply carried the censorial discretion and the censorial sanctions of the Department too far. The Postmaster General could first decide—even in retrospect—that past issues of a paper were non-mailable; then he could decide that no future issues could go at rates which made mass circulation economically possible. All this power lay in the hands of one man or a few appointed subordinates, and in many cases it might amount to the power to close down a publishing business for good, to a forefeiture of use of the mails on the basis of an administrator's decision that the law had been violated in the past. Too much discretion, too much power, Brandeis feared. "I say again—because it cannot be stressed too strongly" that the Postmaster General cannot be allowed the power to become a "universal censor of publications."

Of course, the Postmaster General never has become the "universal censor." But in a relatively short period, as the result of the combined action of courts, legislators, and administrators, the federal government had certainly made it its business to suppress circulation of much sex expression. The *Hicklin* standard, which emphasized "mental sanitation" as a *sine qua non* of legality, was established. The courts had flashed the green light for censorship by characterizing the government's power over the mails as proprietary and plenary, while the citizen's right to use the post was a revocable "privilege." Zealous administrators, however well motivated, were in a position to interfere, substantially, with freedom: freedom to write, freedom to publish and circulate, freedom to read.

5.   HOW THE CENSORS WENT ABOUT

THEIR WORK AND WHAT THEY

CENSORED

FROM ITS INCEPTION until the 1930's, federal enforcement of the anti-obscenity laws was affected by adherence to the *Hicklin* formula and to informal administrative procedures. Books, magazines, and other works were judged by broad criteria which used possible impact on the minds of children as the basis for banning works written for adults, criteria which called for no evaluation of the total work but, rather, only isolated passages read out of context. Administrative decision-making was virtually unpoliced by the courts and unregulated by rules which forced officials to discriminate.

As far as Postal enforcement was concerned, no procedures were established authorizing any formal administrative review. Decisions to ban a book, would be made, in theory, by the Postmaster General, but in fact by men on his legal staff, headed by the Department's Solicitor. The lawyers assigned this work would simply inspect the challenged item and make up their minds. There was no particular obligation—even in the revocation of second-class mailing permits—to hear arguments bringing out both sides of the case, nor to hear opinions of any other persons who might be qualified to discuss the value of the challenged work. There were no formal rules requiring a separation of the function of attacking a publication as obscene from the function of judging that claim impartially. Once a decision was rendered by the Solicitor in the name of the Department, there was no procedure for further departmental review. The citizen denied access to the mails could always go to court—if he was prepared to pay the cost and bear the possible stigma of defending a book which the government denounced as obscene. But the courts continued to defer to the Postal "experts." Their decisions should stand, it was said, in the absence of a clear "abuse of discretion." Thus, great power devolved upon the few men who actually made the Department's decisions in the name of the Postmaster General.

In legal theory, Customs administration of the tariff law's anti-obscenity bar differed from Postal censorship because a decision by the Bureau to ban a book was, *supposedly,* subject to automatic review in the courts. Since the very beginning, in 1842, the statute had required a court proceeding—a "libel" (i.e., forfeiture) action —before there could be confiscation of a suspect work. In practice, however, these court forfeiture proceedings became simply *pro forma* ratifications of seizures made by Customs officials. Very seldom, if ever, did the courts (or even the U.S. Attorneys who filed the petitions for forfeiture) adopt the practice of reviewing, on their own initiative, the merits of the materials seized by the officials. Thus, a Customs decision to ban would stand unless and until it was challenged in the courts by an importer willing to expend the time, energy, and money necessary to litigate it.

Presumably because of the expense or because of ignorance of their rights or for fear of future difficulty or embarrassment with the government, few importers ever went to court. Nor, apparently, was any procedure developed in the handling of these cases whereby an importer was advised, through receipt of an informative notice, that he had a right to ask the government to prove its case in the courts before there could be any final authorization to destroy what the Bureau's employees had seized. On the contrary, there developed practices allowing these officials to bypass the court proceedings after they had seized a book: without being expressly advised of his rights to a day in court, the importer was notified that an obscene item addressed to him had been seized, and he was asked—perhaps urged—to assent to immediate destruction of this "prohibited importation." Though there was often no specific explanation to the importer, the assent was treated as a waiver of the necessity for a court decree. Similarly, practices developed whereby matter was often turned over to Postal officials for confiscation under the Postal laws, thus avoiding the need for court condemnation proceedings required by the Tariff Act for Customs seizures.

The initial decision regarding whether a work should be seized rested with the collector (or his deputies) of the port where it arrived. During the nineteenth century, it would appear that these officials were quite autonomous. The Bureau circulated only the most generally phrased regulations, with no special instructions about the meaning of the word "obscene," no lists of prohibited titles, and no records of what its employees in various ports across the country were doing. Indeed, on some occasions, advice seems to have been refused when it was sought by local officials who were uncertain about seizing a particular work. Later, there developed a more centralized system of enforcement which called for referrals, supervisory decisions, and informal appeals in Washington.

Still later, following establishment of the Customs Court, a new form of administrative review was introduced. Created in 1926, the Customs Court was, in fact, simply an agency formerly known as the Board of Appraisers and given a new name and new status. The Board of Appraisers had never been told by Congress to review decisions of collectors in obscenity cases, nor, apparently, did it ever exercise such authority. By statute, in 1926, the Board was given its new name, but no new powers. The function and jurisdiction of the Customs Court was expressly declared to be the same as the Board; its job was to review claims about the evaluation of merchandise for tax purposes. Yet, the practice developed of referring contested obscenity seizure cases—censorship issues—to this newly created "court," though there would appear to be nothing indicating any legislative design to make it operative in that field. On the contrary, the expertise of the court, as contemplated by the statutes, lay in another field—the valuation of merchandise; nor is there any reason to believe that its judges, formerly called Appraisers and, generally, appointees from the ranks of patronage applicants, were now thought to be qualified to decide whether a book was "obscene" or to exercise the influence which they did, for a brief period, upon federal control over access to books published abroad.

In a rather cavalier fashion, the Customs Court promulgated rulings, broad in their implications, to the effect that such and such a book was unfit for any importation, any circulation, or any reading here.

Consider its decision in a case involving Marie Stopes' *Enduring Passion,* certainly a well-known book and one designed to provide sex education to the inexperienced and special help to frigid spouses. The importer's plea that the book should be admitted for distribution in the United States because it was the work of a doctor, known and respected, because its discussion was scientific, useful and needed, was rejected. Were the importer a doctor we might make an exception, said the Customs judges. Apart from that, we must treat each case on the assumption that the book may circulate freely. Is this one obscene? Look at the contents: "Excessive Virility," "Undersexed Husbands," and "The Frigid Wife." Here was material "alluring the reader and exciting in him a morbid curiosity" to read on about the sex act. Obviously it was obscene; the subject matter itself was obscene; the law was designed to prevent circulation of precisely this kind of discussion. The court went on to intimate that Dr. Stopes should have known better than to write what she did.

In a like fashion, the court dismissed expert testimony that Pierre Louys was a gifted author, "an extraordinary poet" whose *Aphrodite* and *The Songs of Bilitis* and other pieces were "genuine works of art" with a "wide literary reputation." The trouble was that Louys wrote—indeed, rhapsodized—about sexual behavior and attitudes of the ancients, and much of what the ancients did was now immoral. Again, the very subject was obscene even when presented in the "well chosen" words of the poet, indeed, perhaps more so: "Impure suggestion clothed in pleasing attire allures and corrupts, when bold filth would disgust and repel."

Seldom did the Customs Court overrule a collector's seizure. On the whole, its rulings were cryptic and unedifying, albeit stated in virile prose. Thus, Balzac's *Droll Stories* was "obscene in every sense of that term." J. M. March's *The Wild Party* was "thoroughly rotten and putrid. We can conceive of no moral calamity so appallingly disastrous to the Nation as to make available to its youth such vile obscenity." *The Decameron* was obscene in its text. *The Golden Ass* of Apuleius was obscene. An expensive folio of nude model studies for distribution to artists was obscene. Flaubert's *Temptation of St. Anthony* was obscene. George Moore's *Story Teller's Holiday* was "obscene within any fair meaning of the word." It mattered not that one expert witness characterized Moore as the "Supreme Master of English [writing]" whose gifts of expression were well worth the study of Americans. The law's standard must be applied, and here the court referred to one of its favorite formulations of the *Hicklin* test: "What is [the] probable, reasonable effect [of this book] on the sense of decency, purity and chastity of society extending to the family made up of men and women, young boys and girls—the family, which is the common nursery of mankind?" Judged by that standard of criticism, Moore's writing, however masterful, was unfit for consumption, and his books were contraband. Finally, consider the fate of another set of books stoutly defended by an importer who begged the court to refrain from ordering their destruction: the opinion was only abstracted, and the titles remain unrecorded, but the result was emphatic: ". . . a mere cursory glance . . . is sufficient to convince anyone that [these books] abound in obscenity of the vilest character. The court . . . could not view with patience the claim that the work is a literary classic, if anything it was a master-piece in utter degeneracy." This kind of exposition of the law could hardly be offset by the few equally cryptic and positive rulings which cleared such books as Longus' *Daphnis and Chloe* and Rad-clyffe Hall's *The Well of Loneliness.*

Apart from the cases which went into the Customs Court and the even fewer cases which went into other federal courts, most decisions closing the mails and the channels of commerce were actually made by a handful of men in Washington, the Customs and Postal lawyers who exercised supervision over anti-obscenity en-forcement in the field. All doubtful cases were referred to them. Though each agency operated independently, there was then, as there is now, informal exchange. But, during the twenties, it would appear that the two agencies saw eye to eye much more than they have in the recent past.

In 1929, after a conference over policy and after taking inventory of their accumulated index, these officials published a "Joint Mem-orandum" explaining the yardstick by which the U.S. government had been measuring suspect matter. "In passing upon such literature," ran the text of this explanation of policy, we have "considered, primarily, its evil influence upon the impressionable minds of those persons the statutes, according to the courts, aim to protect, i.e., the young and inexperienced. In examining the text it is sought to determine if the psychological effect of the language would be to create in the mind of the individual libidinous thoughts and unduly excite the sexual functions or arouse the animal passions." Here was the *Hicklin* test put in Freudian terms and government syntax. Appended to this brief statement was a list of works found unfit for the public. Regrettably, the list was treated as confidential and never published; both agencies have regularly refused to disclose to the public, even on request, the titles of the books they have banned. Today the list is lost, and we are left with only fragmentary evidence of the scope of censorship as it then was practiced.

Undoubtedly then, as now, the two agencies, but particularly Customs, were confronted with both private and commercial distributions of patent pornography. Undoubtedly then, as now, there flowed through the mails and the channels of foreign commerce an abundance of material, trash, judged by any reasonable, contemporary standard, which was deliberately designed to cater to prurient tastes. In underscoring the more controversial aspects of federal censorship of the recent past, it must be remembered and emphasized that there have always been Holywell peddlers. If anti-obscenity enforcement has never eliminated their traffic, surely it has curbed it. Certainly, however, censorship of the kind which went on for the first thirty years of the twentieth century was a high price to pay for such protection.

The case of Marie Ware Dennett is an example of the cost. In 1915, Mrs. Dennett, perhaps a progressive mother for her era, concluded that her two sons, aged ten and fourteen, were far too ignorant of the facts of life. Nor was there, to her way of thinking, any simple, readable book which would serve as a source of enlightment. So she wrote for her children a short text setting forth the lesson to be taught. It was effective for its purposes. Friends borrowed it. Other parents asked for copies, and thanks to this demand a medical journal published it as an article in 1918. It was also published in a journal called *The Modern School*.

In fact, the work, which was entitled *The Sex Side of Life: An Explanation for Young People,* seemed so successful for its purposes that Mrs. Dennett had it published as a pamphlet. Modest advertisements were inserted in newspapers and journals and it sold well, on a mail-order basis, going through reprint after reprint. Mrs. Dennett became director of the Planned Parenthood League. Her sudden fame was destined to be her undoing. There were some who objected to her pamphlets on the ground that they would exert an evil influence, and among those suspicious were some New York postal clerks. They stopped a shipment of the booklets offered for mailing, held up all further deliveries, and sent a copy of the work to Washington, to the Solicitor of the Post Office Department, with a query: Can this booklet lawfully be distributed through the mails? The Solicitor responded that it was obscene; the New York Post Office officials were instructed that no copies, henceforth, should be carried.[5]

The incident illustrates not only enforcement procedures but also the Department's interpretation and application of the Comstock law against books explaining sex. In this one area alone, the law had a severe impact, for the simple reason that so many publishers and authors (like Mrs. Dennett) depended on the mails. Many mail-order operations, involving dissemination of works by admittedly reputable doctors, were scotched. Of course, the Comstock Act expressly forbade circulation of information on contraception, which effectively blocked Margaret Sanger from the mails without even raising a question about the obsceneness of her birth-control preachments. The statute was also interpreted to forbid information on how best to practice conception. Similarly, works by Havelock Ellis and Freud were banned. Here again the law's mental sanitation mandate posed a barrier. Only one exception was recognized: doctors could mail to other doctors any work which was

5. Mrs. Dennett did try, again and again, to persuade the Solicitor to reverse the ban. Finally, she went back into business and began mailing the pamphlet first class, under the protection of the seal, deliberately daring the government to bring criminal proceedings to "test" the legality of the ban. Although she was prosecuted and convicted, on appeal her work was cleared of the taint of obscenity. This happened in 1930, and the decision of the appellate court in the *Dennett* case was the first in a long series which "reformed" the legal standards during the period 1930–50. This is discussed in the next chapter.

deemed medically reputable by the Postal lawyers. But the public remained insulated.

The principle under which sex education materials could be censored out of the mails was also applied to other non-fiction. Thus, in 1911, the official report of a commission appointed by the mayor of Chicago to report on vice conditions in the city was found to be obscene; Americans could not use the mails to describe or to learn what a very distinguished group of Chicagoans had found out about organized prostitution in the nation's second largest city; too much "corruption" of another sort might ensue.

In 1907, an issue of the *American Journal of Eugenics* was stopped. It advertised a book called The *History of Prostitution.* That was enough. Wrote the Solicitor: "From its very name [this book] is clearly indecent and unfit for circulation through the mails"; consequently, any magazine advertising it was also non-mailable.

A small-town newspaper editor wrote an editorial which deplored "society's" treatment of an unwed mother: "Love had its way, and God blessed the union with the most stupendous fruit of the Universe, a human child; and 'society' steps in and cries 'shame' and causes the mother to kill both herself and the child. . . . Society is as guilty of the murder of this girl as though she had been put to death by the public hangman." This, said the Department, was obscene, and the editor was put in jail for it, although later released on appeal. Likewise with an individual who advertised a home to care for unwed mothers. The minds of youth should not be turned by this kind of communication was the theory of those charged with enforcing the statute.

In like fashion, René Fulop-Miller's biography, *Rasputin, the Holy Devil* was declared non-mailable, though the work itself had been reviewed favorably and had been published openly in this country. This depiction of the debauchery of the final Czarist years —a tragedy with important historical consequences—was, in the Department's view, a violation of the obscenity law's limitations on what Americans could read.

Just as frank, non-fictional depiction of sex as a dynamic affecting human behavior and productive of social problems ran the risk of censorship, so with fictional depiction. Thus, Kuprin's *Yama,* a representation of the degradation of prostitution, was obscene.[6] Any author whose work was to pass to readers via the United States mails must conform to *Hicklin*'s mental sanitation test. *"Ulysses* [by James Joyce] as you are doubtless aware, is a very obscene book," wrote the Solicitor to the Chief Postal Inspector in 1923; the Bureau of Customs agreed, and ruled that no American should be allowed to acquire Joyce's new work from any of the foreign sources, which were the only sources selling it over the counter. Indeed, condemnation of the work was so strong that both the Post Office and the Bureau pressed hard for the prosecution of anyone who used the mails to introduce Americans to the "stream of consciousness" of Joyce's people in Dublin. The artistic merit of the work was irrelevant to U.S. censorship, nor were there even nagging doubts about the book's probable, total lack of appeal to any but the most stolid intellectual readers. It had dirty passages in it; no one should see it.

To describe in detailed, non-euphemistic terms what a modern man might think, say, and do when it came to sex was to create something automatically evil and contraband. Not only was D. H. Lawrence's *Lady Chatterley's Lover* banned (it is a "gross exposition of obscenity, filth and lewdness," wrote a Customs official), but so was his *Women in Love.* An issue of a magazine entitled *The Little Review* was stopped by the Post Office when it ran a story about the dismal doings of a disillusioned British soldier who seduced a girl and left her as an unwed mother in order to protest the follies and injustices of war. Even more debatable were rulings like the ban on Anatole France's *The Gods are Athirst* and Radclyffe Hall's *The Well of Loneliness.* Senator Millard Tydings was appalled and disgusted to learn that he had been cheated in his

6. The Modern Library published an English translation in 1929, and Arthur Garfield Hays wrote, in the Foreword: "The book deals with life in a Russian house of ill-fame. It is realistic and tragic. It is well dedicated by Kuprin 'To Mothers and Youths.' No evil is ever met by shutting it out of sight. In time the world will learn that facing facts is the beginning of progress. Ignorance is the greatest evil. Bigotry is never justified. It is high time that the reading public be credited with some intelligence and that the test of a book should be its real value, its sincerity and its honesty, rather than its appeal to the ignorant, vicious and sensually inclined. Books are today banned because of their effect on this class, who rarely read books anyhow."

reading of *All's Quiet on the Western Front* because the work could be imported only in expurgated editions; the government would not, apparently, trust him with the original version. A good many ancient books, generally characterized as "classics," which had been regaling readers round the world for centuries, were also banned by both Postal attorneys and Customs officials during the period 1900–1930: *The Golden Ass* of Apuleius, Aristophanes' *Lysistrata,* and many editions of Ovid's *Ars Amoris* (in both Latin and English) were on the index. "All editions of Boccaccio's *Decameron* coming before this office have been declared nonmailable," reported the Solicitor in 1928. *The Heptameron of Margaret of Navarre* apparently suffered a like fate. Burton's seventeen-volume edition of the *Arabian Nights*—very expensive and very limited in circulation—was obscene. The president of Oklahoma University reported that "several editions of classics" consigned to him were "destroyed by Customs officials." A rare edition of Rabelais, destined for A. Edward Newton, the Philadelphia bibliophile, was confiscated by Customs (the Post Office also condemned this work). Mr. Newton's reaction was instantaneous:

> In order that you may not be the laughing-stock of the world, I beg that the volume be sent to me immediately; but for no other reason, for one can secure a copy at any well-ordered bookshop or library in the United States.
>
> I am not a youth seeking to gloat, surreptitiously, over a smutty book, but a student of mature years, the possessor of an important library, and the author of . . . [various books on book collecting]. Moreover, I have a copy of the first edition of Rabelais, which is worth several thousand dollars.
>
> If you keep or destroy my Rabelais, it will be in my power to make you and your department ridiculous the world over.

A professor of French at Harvard ordered a shipment of Voltaire's *Candide* for his students. A Customs official in Boston, relying on a previous ruling, seized them because they were "unexpurgated"; the professor and angry Harvard colleagues demanded an explanation from Washington and were told that Voltaire was on the list—though these particular books were later released to the recipients. French classics destined for a Baltimore attorney were seized, and that gentleman, too, stormed the Collector's office and berated officials with questions about their competence to judge books and writers, eliciting an admission that the ruling was made by a man who "did not make a practice of reading much" and could not answer with certainty whether Geoffrey Chaucer was a living or a dead, let alone an obscene, poet.

There was, in short, little discrimination. Suspect materials were judged abstractly, not in the setting of the concrete cases which arose or with regard to the merit of the work regardless of its failure to pass muster under the current "tests" for obsceneness. All pornographic expression was automatically bad, whether revealed in a cheap French postcard or in the illustrations of a rare Rabelais; apparently, all of those deliberately bawdy classics which are part of our culture were automatically banned. Thus, *The Memoirs of Fanny Hill,* that enduring eighteenth-century work depicting, flagrantly, from cover to cover, one sex act after another, and Brantone's *Lives of the Gallant Ladies,* were both obscene and equally prohibited. Nudity was bad: thus, cheap pictorial matter and fifteen-dollar art students' books were both banned; indeed, the Bureau of Customs confiscated a reproduction of Michelangelo's Sistine Chapel art, as well as some rare Chinese paintings destined for the Field Museum in Chicago. Cheap anthologies of smoker jokes were banned, as was a higher-brow edition of Harvard's *Lampoon* which, on one page, burlesqued the famous painting of "Washington Crossing the Delaware" and, on another, presented a nude young lady. Likewise with a too-Rabelaisian edition of Virginia's *Virginia Reel.* Two other cases based on flippancy may be revealing. In the famous "Hatrack case," H. L. Mencken's *American Mercury* was barred from the mails after it had satirized the Watch and Ward Society. Mencken and Arthur Garfield Hays stormed to Washington and berated the Solicitor. Would he ban the Bible for its sexual episodes, they asked? The reply was the perennial: we will *not* discuss other cases, hypothetical or real, with people who protest our decisions. The ban stood until Judge Mack of the District Court enjoined it, observing that "no one but a moron would be affected by [this article]." While the Bible itself was never banned, an Oklahoma wit of a somewhat lower brow than Mencken found that his flippant little booklet of verse purporting to annotate various Old Testament episodes could not be sold via the mails. The Solicitor checked this verse:

Once Rachel got disgusted,
No children could she bear,
She rowed and fussed at Jacob,
A most unhappy pair;
Then Jacob got disgusted,
Refused to go to bed,
'Til Rachel coaxed Miss Bilhal
To take her place instead.

PART II

Developments from 1930 to 1945: How Law and Censorship Responded to Social Changes

By 1930, after federal enforcement had stirred controversy for several decades, there were a few powerful legal critics whose contributions to the problem of sex censorship were beginning to receive more recognition. Theodore Schroeder, a lawyer and prodigious author, had broken new ground in many ways when he challenged the historical and scientific assumptions underlying the law of obscenity. Were basic nineteenth-century norms about sexual modesty universal to all civilized cultures, past and present? Were nineteenth-century assumptions about the psychological impact of immodesty or indecency valid? How meaningful were the legal tests and doctrines? What had been their impact on freedom of the arts and on the advancement of scientific knowledge?

On its merit and because it reflected a new stress upon a scientific and functional analysis of the law, Schroeder's work, especially his book *"Obscene" Literature and Constitutional Law,* has a special interest to today's scholar. But it was radical for its time. In 1913 Judge Learned Hand, in a single short opinion, had exposed the follies of censorship which set up possible harm to children as the overriding standard.[1] Morris Ernst and William Seagle published *To The Pure* in 1929. The book marshaled the arguments for free-

---

1. The case was *United States v. Kennerly.* As a trial judge, Hand felt obliged to follow the law as laid down by the higher courts. But he wrote: ". . . I hope it is not improper for me to say that the [Hicklin] rule as laid down, however consonant it may be with mid-Victorian morals, does not seem to me to answer to the understanding and morality of the present time . . . I question whether in the end men will regard that as obscene which is honestly relevant to the adequate expression of innocent ideas, and whether they will not believe that truth and beauty are too precious to society at large to be mutilated in the interests of those most likely to pervert them to base uses. Indeed, it seems hardly likely that we are even today so lukewarm in our interest in letters or serious discussion as to be content to reduce our treatment of sex to the standard of a child's library in the supposed interest of a salacious few, or that shame will for long prevent us from adequate portrayal of some of the most serious and beautiful sides of human nature. . . . Yet, if the time is not yet when men think innocent all that which is honestly germane to a pure subject, however little it may mince its words, still I scarcely think that they would forbid all which might corrupt the most corruptible, or that society is prepared to accept for its own limitations those which may perhaps be necessary to the weakest of its members. If there be no abstract definition, such as I have suggested, should not the word 'obscene' be allowed to indicate the present critical point in the compromise between candor and shame at which the community may have arrived here and now? . . . To put thought in leash to the average conscience of the time is perhaps tolerable, but to fetter it by the necessities of the lowest and least capable seems a fatal policy."

dom—the vagueness of the standard, the subjectiveness of its test, the capricious excesses reflected in the experience of enforcement, the absence of scientific data showing a cause-and-effect relationship between sex expression and sexual misbehavior—and advanced the inquiry, perhaps, as far as any single work on the subject ever has. Other protagonists added to an ever growing volume of protest during the twenties and early thirties. The courts of New York State, in a series of decisions in the same period, began clearing works which other courts and the Post Office and the Bureau of Customs were declaring obscene. The time was ripe for frank reappraisal of the federal censorship laws.

I. THE SENATE REVIEWS CUSTOMS CENSORSHIP: THE TARIFF ACT OF 1930

THE FIRST SIGNIFICANT challenge came in the Senate; the attack was spearheaded by Bronson Cutting of New Mexico. A well-read, Boston-raised Brahmin, Cutting had become interested in the plight of a constituent who, wanting to read D. H. Lawrence's *Lady Chatterley's Lover,* had run afoul of Customs censorship. Cutting asked the Bureau: why can't you release this book—this powerful work by a gifted writer—to an adult American who wants to read it? The reply came from no less an authority than Secretary of the Treasury Andrew Mellon: the Bureau makes "no exceptions," not even exceptions "in favor of so called classics or the work of leading writers of the day." Senator Cutting, a Lawrence fancier himself, was appalled that the censorial barrier which sealed *Lady Chatterley* from Americans should be total. Further investigation of how this censorship had been working produced further shock.

In the meantime, in October, 1929, the tariff laws came up for revision. Senator Smoot and Congressman Hawley were managing an omnibus measure. The House had acted; the Senate was wading through the bill, considering it, item by item, as a Committee of the Whole, and the debate droned through lambs wool, coconut oil, soap, the status of the Philippines, and finally came upon Section 305.

This part of the bill recodified the old prohibition against importing obscene matter, and it also proposed to add a new one of a totally different nature: literature "advocating treason, insurrection or forcible resistance to any law" or containing any "threat" to "inflict bodily harm upon any person" in the United States was to be prohibited. Senator Cutting made it known that he would offer an amendment to remove all of these censorship items from the law. He apologized for diverting his colleagues from the mainstream of tariff matters. But, "in the opinion of some of us the question of free speech and free thought [involved in section 305] is of such great importance that it even outweighs" all the rest of the tariff issues put together. For the moment Cutting turned his fire on Customs censorship of obscene matter, and it is that phase of the debate which is of primary concern here.

A *New York Times* correspondent who was watching the proceedings reported that, "As Mr. Cutting began his address, nearly every member turned his chair to face the New Mexico Senator, an action unusual in the chamber." On both sides of the aisle men "listened attentively." In 1842, Cutting declared, the law had permitted seizure of pictorial matter alone. Later, books had been added. With that step "censorship" had come in, and now it was being practiced at the ports on a wholesale basis. He described and ridiculed many recent rulings regarding works by Aristophanes, Voltaire, Rabelais, and others. This was a "kindergarten" operation! And to protect the American people from what? No one could be sure. The law seemed incapable of articulating either objectives or a sensible formula to implement them; and untrained officials, incapable of making sensible judgments, had simply been delegated the job of protecting the entire populace from books considered dangerous to moral standards. There had been much abuse, and what good had been won? Were morals better? Youth purer? He proposed that all this censorial power to ban obscene publications be scrapped. Let the states, alone, worry about this problem—if, in fact, there was need for worry by government.

It was late at night when Cutting and his supporters (notably Millard Tydings) finished with their first attack. The next day's debate was largely concerned with attacks on the new proposals to ban the "treasonable," "forcible resistance," and "incitement to bodily harm" matter. But the obscenity question was debated too:

Alabama's Tom Heflin feared for the future of Southern woman-hood if the ban were dropped just as much as he feared for the Union if books espousing any sort of subversion could come in. But Hugo Black, his junior colleague, supported Cutting and suggested that criminal prosecutions, with jury trials and procedural safe-guards, constituted the only safe basis for suppression; otherwise the risk of censorship abuse would remain too great.

Because the Senate still sat as a Committee of the Whole, it was possible to tinker piecemeal with the language of the bill. Though Cutting wanted total abolition of all "censorship," the Senate would not go that far. The eventual outcome was that, by a close vote, two items were stricken from the class of non-importable works: (1) treasonable matter, (2) obscene *books* (the ban on pictures was retained). Cutting had momentarily won a victory. But Senator Smoot, who was as wedded to this protective feature of his tariff bill as he was to any other, vowed that there would be reconsidera-tion of the obscenity issue at a later date when the Senate dissolved itself as a Committee of the Whole and proceeded to a final vote on the legislation.

So what had transpired was only a preliminary skirmish. Further debates, however, were put off for several months. In the meantime, in many parts of the country, many people awaited them with interest. By raising the whole issue of federal censorship, Cutting had evoked widespread controversy. Congress was urged by many groups to stick by the Cutting Amendment. At the very least, urged one petition, set up a commission to "supervise entry of literature with the view that . . . accredited libraries may import . . . works otherwise deemed objectionable." This suggestion was signed by a formidable roster of learned men, including 28 "university presi-dents," 30 "judges, lawyers and law professors," 38 "editors," 100 "professors of liberal arts," and 20 "novelists and poets."

"Mr. President, it is doubtful if any measure of public legislation has ever evoked such a general consensus among enlightened American opinion in its support as the Cutting Amendment," said Senator Wheeler, as he read similar statements into the record. "It was most refreshing to read Senator Cutting's words of common sense, of broad-minded liberalism," wrote Nicholas Murray Butler; "How even a single Senator would dare to vote to put some un-known official or group of officials in a Washington department in supervision of what we shall read is beyond my belief." There were similar sentiments from John Dewey, William Allen White, a large group of Yale professors, another group of Harvard professors led by Zechariah Chafee, and many others. Surprisingly, perhaps, there were relatively few recorded petitions urging Congress to retain the law as it was.

On March 17, 1930, the Senate came back to Section 305 of the tariff bill. Senator Smoot was ready and certain that he could persuade his colleagues to reverse the earlier vote. "This question is one that strikes at the morals of every young boy and girl in the United States," were his opening words. He had in his hand some books which would "so disgust Senators" that "they would never dream of agreeing to the [Cutting] amendment . . . I did not believe there were such books in the world—books that the Senator from New Mexico referred to and said ought to be in the libraries of the people of the United States. They are lower than beasts!"

The books included *Lady Chatterley's Lover* and Harris' *My Life and Loves,* and the Senator later admitted that he had ready only a few pages of each—that was enough for him. But his polemic against this "filth" was powerful; he raised the specter of obscenities "by the thousands" flowing through our ports, of the impotence of state law enforcement to stop it, of the consequent dangers to our own standards of acceptability, to youth, to the family. As "a father" I protest, cried Smoot; "Lady Chatterley" will come in "over my dead body." D. H. Lawrence must have "a soul so black that it would obscure the darkness of hell." If this is what the literati like Cutting wanted to admit with all their talk about protecting "classics," then censorship was the safer risk. He read the "test" of obscenity from the *Hicklin* opinion. The protection of the family; this was the heart of the law; it should stay as law; and on this issue you must stand and be counted, he warned his colleagues. "I thus conclude . . . I appeal to the Senate to throw the arm of protection around the army of boys and girls who must constitute the citizenship of our country."[2]

2.   Senator Smoot (Republican, Ut.)
           Is planning a ban on smut.
           Oh root-ti-toot for Smoot of Ut.
           And his reverent occiput.
is the way Ogden Nash began his well-known satire which appeared in a contemporary issue of the *New Yorker.*

The curious thing is that Smoot's proposal to reinsert the obscene book ban (which the Cutting amendment had removed from Section 305) also contained an entirely new, and very striking, proviso which would, perhaps, permit some *Lady Chatterleys* to creep into the stream of American culture: "*Provided further,* that the Secretary of the Treasury may, in his discretion, admit the so-called classics or books of recognized and established literary or scientific merit, but may, in his discretion, admit such classics or books only when imported for non-commercial purposes." Smoot did call attention to this clause; but he offered no explanation of its origin or purpose. The proviso had been drafted in response to the pleas and pressures of some of the professors and lawyers who had previously concerned themselves with Customs censorship. Yet there was only fleeting discussion, on the Senate floor, of this unusual proposal to open a loophole based on the unstated assumption that an "obscene" book could still be a work of "literary merit." Does the proviso mean, asked Senator Johnson (a Cutting supporter), that Andrew Mellon the Secretary of Treasury was to have special authority to determine whether a book was meritorious and hence let some people read it despite its obscenity? Yes, said Smoot. "That," snorted Johnson, "strikes me as ludicrous and humorous." And there the matter of discretionary dispensations was dropped and apparently forgotten as Smoot launched into his oration.

When he finished, it appeared that Smoot had rallied much support for re-enactment of some sort of ban on obscene books. Senator Hugo Black, who had voted for the Cutting amendment, now favored retention of a law ordaining seizure of "bad books," provided, and on this he was emphatic, that the law was clear that the courts should make the decision; Customs "censors" should be stripped of power to impose the prohibition.[3] This line of argument

3. Said Senator Black: "Oh I have seen some [books] . . . that would shock the morals of a man who has not been in church for 40 years. There is no question about there being bad books in this country. . . . but there are some that might offend some minds and not offend others. There is a twilight zone; and the question is: Who shall determine whether books within that twilight zone shall be circulated or shall not be circulated? . . . If the Senator [Smoot] will propose a method whereby these books can be seized and brought into court in the first instance, and have the [importer's] right tried, I will support him." By 1957, as we shall see, Hugo Black, now Mr. Justice Black, had revised his opinion both about the validity of banning "bad books"—even those which would "shock the morals" of the

proved persuasive; there was much talk to the effect that the problems could be solved if only the Bureau's discretion could be curtailed. So the language of the Smoot amendment was revised on the floor, then and there, by a group of compromisers—revised to say that all seized books be forthwith turned over to the U.S. Attorney for court proceedings to test their admissibility; claimants to the book were entitled to a jury determination of its obscenity if they wanted one; the jurisdiction of the Customs Court was eliminated. Smoot accepted the changes, and then the discussion of what had been done droned on into the evening hours, becoming at times almost incomprehensible.

The next day Cutting spoke. He twitted Smoot for his hyperbole on *Lady Chatterley:* "his [Smoot's] favorite work . . . He has [probably] been reading it since the Christmas holidays." Indeed said Cutting, the Senator from Utah had probably now stimulated a nationwide curiosity among literate Americans to taste the forbidden fruit. The Senator should now go on to read Lawrence's little essay on *Pornography and Obscenity;* this work would "fill some of the hours which have previously been filled by 'Lady Chatterley's Lover.' " It might also shed some light on the "soul" of D. H. Lawrence and the folly of damning great authors indiscriminately.[4]

Again, the gist of the Cutting argument was simply an appeal that Americans be trusted, as they were before 1870, to regulate their own reading habits with respect to access to foreign literature. It was neither necessary nor safe—nor virtuous in a civic sense—to permit the federal government to do that job for them. This time

---

non churchgoer—and about the competency of courts or juries to make any meaningful distinctions, especially when judging books of the "twilight" zone category.

4. Lawrence wrote:

"But even I would censor genuine pornography, rigorously. It would not be very difficult. In the first place, genuine pornography is almost always underworld, it doesn't come into the open. In the second, you can recognize it by the insult it offers invariably, to sex, and to the human spirit.

"Pornography is the attempt to insult sex, to do dirt on it. This is unpardonable. Take the very lowest instance, the picture post-card sold underhand, by the underworld, in most cities. What I have seen of them have been of an ugliness to make you cry. The insult to the human body, the insult to a vital human relationship! Ugly and cheap they make human nudity, ugly and degraded they make the sexual act, trivial and cheap and nasty."

Cutting failed to hold the line. The Senate voted 54 to 24 for the Smoot amendment as revised. There were many who shared the view of the Senator from Utah that the protection of the family and the prevention of "corruption" (that never-defined condition which obscenity circulation would produce) were simply overriding considerations, that a federal law, rigidly enforced, was an essential strand in a network of statutes designed to prevent this subversion of American mores and morals. There were others—like Senator Black—who agreed with Cutting that there had been serious "abuses" in enforcement of the law, who wanted to stop them, and who believed that they could be stopped in the future by thrusting greater responsibility for law enforcement on the courts. For the courts would know enough to discriminate between "good" and "bad" books.

I "congratulate the senator from New Mexico," said Black; you have "lost a vote" but won a "victory." Perhaps congratulations were in order. An implied caveat against indiscriminate confiscation of meritorious works which circulated freely in the country had been spread across the pages of the *Congressional Record*. A special exemption for at least some admission of obscene works of recognized "literary merit" had crept, unceremoniously, into the law. And, with the elimination of the Customs Court and the spelling-out of the forfeiture proceedings in the district courts, the procedure for seizure and condemnation had been clarified.

But other difficulties had been left unsolved because of superficial consideration. For example, Senator Black and others seemed to think that the revised statute would throw the full burden of making decisions in all cases upon the courts; but he overlooked the fact that under traditional Customs practice the courts only reviewed a seizure on its merits when and if the importer expended the effort and money to fight the case; the burden of invoking court review had always rested with the importer, who had seldom been informed that such review was his for the asking. Would the new law force abandonment of old practices? Did it require automatic referral to the courts and, automatically, a court decision on the merits in *every* instance of seizure, without expense, effort, or embarrassment to the importer? The answer proved to be no.

Again, Senator Black and others assumed that federal judges and jurors could enforce the law intelligibly by using existing legal doctrine to make a Solomon-like judgment between the "good" and the "bad."

This overlooked the fact that existing federal law, employing the *Hicklin* formula, still judged books by prognosticating the psychic response that they would generate in childish or susceptible minds. The compromisers who had cut the ground from under Cutting made assumptions about the "corrupting" impact of pictorial or written communication depicting nudity or sexual activity. No one challenged Bronson Cutting when he disputed these assumptions; instead it was tacitly assumed that he was simply wrong. Finally, with all the talk about *Lady Chatterley,* no one faced up to the possibility that this book and others might have both qualities of obsceneness and also qualities of great literary art. Was it right that no American adult should be allowed to import the book unless he could prevail on Andrew Mellon to give him special permission?

Yet, considering the time and the circumstances, it is surprising that the Senate debated as soberly as it did. Popular assemblies have always been unlikely places for the rewriting of obscenity laws to make them *less* stringent. Relaxation of restrictive laws has come, so far, through efforts of the courts to rewrite the law under the guise of interpreting statutes, of spelling out tighter standards and broader constitutional limitations.

2. # THE COURTS REWRITE THE OB-
    SCENITY STANDARD: ULYSSES AND
    OTHER CELEBRATED CASES

BY 1930, AS NOTED, the New York state courts were
already breaking new ground in the quest for standards better suited
to the tastes, concepts, and outlook of the new generation of the
twentieth century—an era of rising skirts, burgeoning trends in the
entertainment media, retreat from prohibition, contempt for Comstock, a vogue for Freud, Havelock Ellis, and others. Of course, the
influence of such cultural changes on law is a nebulous thing, but
during a period spanning the "New Deal" and running through
World War II, a series of notable federal decisions proceeded to
purge the *Hicklin* formula from the federal law and to guarantee
a far greater freedom of expression.

Perhaps the first significant case was a United States Court of
Appeals decision in 1930 which set aside the conviction of Mary
Ware Dennett for selling her pamphlet on sex education. This
book, said the judges, was a "sincere," "truthful," and "scientific"
statement; unless the subject matter was automatically uncommuni-
cable, no matter how presented, the obscenity laws should never be
used as a basis to ban such a work, let alone put the author in jail.
To make all sex instruction obscene would be intolerable. Nor,
added the court, was there anything bad about the method used by
Mrs. Dennett to disseminate her book; she had not pandered it to a
prurient audience by suggestive and sensational advertising.

Then, in 1933, came the famous *Ulysses* litigation. An actress had imported the volume, and New York Customs officers, familiar with the Bureau's blanket ban, confiscated it, refusing to tell the lady precisely where it was obscene for fear of embarrassing her by reading "the dirtiest language" imaginable. Of course there were "dirty passages" in the narration of the stream of consciousness and the doings of Joyce's characters—"dirt" which perhaps was more emetic than aphrodisiac; the book spoke in terms which are familiar language in many walks of life but which were still not then repeated in print. But, "dirty" passages or not, Random House, Inc. was at that very time printing this work with the design of selling it to the American public at large. So Random House intervened in the case, demanding the court hearing which the tariff law required and demanding exculpation of the work. The publishers' plea, in essence, was: Just read this book; just read the *whole* book, and judge the alleged obsceneness of some of its passages in the context of the mosaic of which they are but a part.

The plea was sympathetically received by a very literate judge, John Woolsey of the District Court in New York. He did read the whole book, carefully. He was satisfied that is was a good book and that its "unusual frankness" was "sincerely motivated" as an attempt at "honest" depiction of a "slice of life" in Dublin. "When such a real artist in words, as Joyce undoubtedly is, seeks to draw a true picture of the lower class in a European city, ought it to be impossible for the American public legally to see that picture?," asked Judge Woolsey.[5] To pose the issue in those terms was to suggest the answer: *Ulysses* was not obscene.

Judge Woolsey's opinion clearing the book, and, on appeal, Judge Augustus Hand's opinion, affirming clearance, formulated new law designed to explain why such books were not now to be confiscated. The opinions implied that the function of obscenity laws was to prevent the "promotion of lust" engendered by "lewd thoughts" and "sex impulses" but immature or susceptible people

5. Or as the Court of Appeals put it: "The question is whether such a book of artistic merit and scientific insight should be regarded as obscene within . . . the Tariff Act?" The literature about the meaning and merit of *Ulysses* is of course voluminous. Of particular interest, when considering the question of the author's "sincerity"— indeed his agony—in composing *Ulysses,* are the recently published letters which Joyce wrote while he was writing the book.

were ruled out as the measuring stick. The "promotion of lust" must occur in normal adults; "l'homme moyen sensuel" was Woolsey's characterization. Moreover, this harm must result, not from reading selected "dirty" passages, but as a result of reading the whole book; thus, the "dominant effect" of the entire book must be stimulation of libidinous impulses and thoughts. Furthermore, it was to be assumed that if a book had literary, scientific, or educational merit and if the author's apparent reason in writing its allegedly obscene parts was germane to the book's purpose, then the courts should be wary about concluding that the "dominant effect" would be harmful. So the "merit" of the work was relevant, and to find out if the book had merit, that is, to determine the author's purpose and success, the courts should, in appropriate cases, receive the benefit of testimony from students of the author's art—critics, teachers, and whoever else might be qualified to explain the meaning of the work and the relevancy of its objectionable parts to the author's objectives.

These rather sophisticated propositions made up the new *Ulysses* formula; and with its projection came repudiation of the *Hicklin* law.[6] Instantly there was national acclaim both for the clearance of *Ulysses* and for these new legal standards. True, the new formula had not been promulgated by the Supreme Court; a lawyer might warn that the decision was binding only on federal courts in the Second Circuit and that the *Hicklin* case might still be followed by courts in other areas. But the *Ulysses* opinions had been written by distinguished judges, and it was commonly assumed that their

6. Judge Augustus Hand summed up the new interpretation this way: "While any construction of the statute that will fit all cases is difficult, we believe that the proper test of whether a given book is obscene is its dominant effect. [I.e., is promotion of lust the dominant effect of reading the whole book?] In applying this test, relevancy of the objectionable parts to the theme, the established reputation of the work in the estimation of approved critics, if the book is modern, and the verdict of the past, if it is ancient, are persuasive pieces of evidence; for works of art are not likely to sustain a high position with no better warrant for their existence than their obscene content."

Judge Manton wrote a vigorous dissent, asserting that the court had no right to overrule the *Hicklin* standard, which had been so long accepted and was so well established by precedent as "the law." He asserted that as recently as 1930 Congress had impliedly re-enacted the *Hicklin* test; that test was necessary for "the protection of the great mass of our people . . . The people need and deserve a [high] moral standard; it should be a point of honor with men of letters to maintain it."

decision would be binding on federal censors, as well as a persuasive authority in other jurisdictions. Random House was apparently prepared to accept the risk of further harassment (by state enforcement); its first American edition soon emerged triumphant with an introduction which set forth the history of *Ulysses'* liberation from the grasp of Customs. Morris Ernst, the book's successful advocate, ventured this prediction in its Foreword: Henceforth no book which sold openly and was openly discussed would be subject to federal confiscation.

Then, in 1940, the United States Court of Appeals for the District of Columbia postulated another test, the "community standard," as a second, alternative formula to be used in cases involving pictorial matter alleged to be obscene. A Washington bookseller named Parmelee sought to import six copies of a work called *Nudism in Modern Life.* The title reflected the content. The book contained a good many pages of admittedly unobjectionable text plus twenty-three photo illustrations of nudists at work and at play. Concluded the Customs Bureau: this massing of unretouched photographs of unsegregated nudes between the covers of one book made the work unfit for circulation. Mr. Parmelee retained a lawyer, insisted that the Bureau justify the seizure in court, and finally won his case on appeal.

These pictures are not obscene, said the court; their display in a "serious" work on nudism was not too much of an affront to the sensibilities of reasonable, contemporary Americans. The pictures might well be stimulating, but so are many pictures of nudes—for example, those massed in works on art; and as regards pictorial matter, at least, libidinous reactions should no longer be the only frame of reference. Particularly for pictorial matter, "perhaps the most useful" test, the court declared, was one suggested many years before by Judge Learned Hand: "Should not the word obscene be allowed to indicate the present critical point in the compromise between candor and shame at which the community may have arrived here and now?" The *Parmelee* decision postulated this "community standard" test, apparently as an adjunct to the *Ulysses* formula. So long as pictures, viewed in the context of their setting, did not go beyond that optimal point where current tastes in candor and shame would cry, "Hold, enough," their circulation was permissible.

Thus, the *Parmelee* and the *Ulysses* cases, and others of the same period, rejected the *Hicklin* standard with its inflexible insistence on "mental sanitation" to protect the susceptible and introduced a groping quest for law that would be more rational, more consistent with the needs of the twentieth century.

3.

FEDERAL CENSORSHIP FROM 1930 TO 1945: THE DIVERGENT RESPONSES TO NEW COURT STANDARDS, THE POSTAL FIGHT TO CLEAN UP THE MAGAZINE INDUSTRY

HOW DID FEDERAL CENSORSHIP respond to these court decisions?

The Bureau of Customs recognized that the *Ulysses* case called for a more discriminating appraisal of suspect books than had been given in the past, and so it hired an expert consultant: Huntington Cairns, a Baltimore lawyer, author, and social scientist in his own right. Cairns' job was to advise the Bureau so it could avoid, if possible, another calamity like the *Ulysses* case; to help the Bureau exercise Secretary Morgenthau's discretionary power to admit, in special cases, obscene "classics" and obscene books of "literary merit."[7] As a sort of unofficially anointed "high priest" of tariff obscenity enforcement, Cairns was able, for a long time, to keep the Bureau out of controversy. Shortly after his retention, he visited several of the large ports to learn firsthand the problems of Customs censorship. By 1937 the Bureau had adopted new procedures which stripped collectors and their deputies of all decision-making power,

7. Compare John Milton's statement in his *Areopagitica:* "It cannot be denied but that he who is made to sit upon the birth or death of books whether they be wafted into this world, or not, had need to be a man above the common measure, both studious, learned and judicious; there may be else no mean mistakes in what is passable or not; which is also no mean injury."

[68]

giving Washington (and thus the Bureau's new expert) plenary control. There was no more confiscation of accepted literature like *Candide* or the *Decameron* or the works of Rabelais—unless the illustrations in such books (which were usually judged separately) were considered too erotic or vulgar. Apart from the *Parmelee* (*Nudism in Modern Life*) case, the Bureau seems to have lost no reported litigation. Of course, there were some banned books (e.g., D. H. Lawrence's *Lady Chatterley,* works by Ovid, De Sade, and Frank Harris and, later, works by the celebrated—or, to others, notorious—Henry Miller) which were important (if the volume of words written about these volumes is any index) and enjoyed some reputable acclaim and a "black market" circulation among literati as well as prurient collectors. But it is doubtful if the courts during this period would have reversed many of these decisions, if any; indeed, the ban on Miller's two *Tropics* was sustained by two federal courts as late as 1953.

Thus, Customs censorship during this period, 1930–45, did diminish considerably. To a great extent, the problems which remained were simply inherent in the existing legal concept of obscenity and in Congress' command—backed up, of course, by strong national pressures that the circulation of obscenity be regulated. The services rendered by Mr. Cairns during this period seem unique and valuable.

The Post Office hired no expert, rejected various proposals that it do so, and adhered to the earlier procedures whereby rulings were made, *ex parte,* by the Solicitor on the basis of recommendations of one or more members of his staff. In terms of the substance of its decisions, the Department was indeed loathe to revise its ideas about obsceneness notwithstanding the "new law" laid down in *Ulysses,* for the new standards might lead to results too extreme, results surely unintended by the courts.

Consider the ruling in the case of Lillian Smith's *Strange Fruit.* This "book is a plea for social equality," wrote the Post Office lawyer who judged it. "The book aspires to fill the role of 'Uncle Tom's Cabin' in the life of the modern negro problem . . . The book is obscene in that it deals with the sexual relations of a ne'er-do-well son of a respected white southern family with a mestee. Some incidents are too much detailed (p. 198, 238–239, etc.) but the worst part is the filthy language at pp. 225–226. It is obscene in that it is disgusting, repulsive, nauseating. Under the standards laid down . . . in the 'Ulysses' case . . . this book would *not* [emphasis added] be held to be obscene in that the sexual scenes are merely incidental to the principal theme of the book—the social degradation of the negro in the South." But *Strange Fruit* was simply too strong a draught for this lawyer, who went on to recommend exclusion, though the book had already sold freely and widely. The Solicitor accepted his advice.

Tobacco Road suffered a similar fate in 1941. "I have not found a passage that one would care to remember or quote," declared a subordinate who advised a ban. The advice was accepted, although the Solicitor noted (1) that the book would probably be cleared under *Ulysses,* and (2) that, unfortunately, "such harm as they [the books] were calculated to do had already been done in view of their wide distribution . . . " *God's Little Acre* suffered a like fate during the thirties and forties and later, even after a U.S. Attorney adamantly refused a request to prosecute a New Yorker who had persisted in mailing it.

Other works which sold openly in bookstores were still suppressed when found in the mails. For example, John O'Hara's *Appointment in Samarra,* Norman Lindsay's *The Cautious Amorist,* and Tiffany Thayer's *Thirteen Women* were declared non-mailable in 1941. So were Hemingway's *For Whom the Bell Tolls* and Diana Fredericks' *Diana.* And on the non-fiction side, Julian Strange's *Adventures in Nakedness* and George Ryley Scott's *History of Prostitution,* both published by reputable New York firms, were banned. Various writings by Havelock Ellis on sex were allowed to go only to doctors.

Still, some ancient precedents were overruled. Zola's *Nana* and Balzac's *Droll Stories* were finally cleared. So was the *Arabian Nights.* "While there are numerous passages in *The Grapes of Wrath* which, taken by themselves, must be regarded as obscene," observed a Department lawyer in 1941, still the book itself "has much literary merit" and was, therefore, not obscene "under the [court] decisions" (presumably *Ulysses* in particular). A book entitled *The Five Arrows,* written by Allan Chase and published by Random House, was "a Communist propaganda novel," in the opinion of the Post Office lawyer who read it, and it contained a "lewd scene" where the hero "slept with the U.S. Ambassador's daughter." But "in view of the decision of the courts" the book "cannot be declared non-mailable"; there was a note of reluctance in this report. Likewise, the Department resisted both a suggestion from a Southern Postmaster that *Gone with the Wind* might be obscene and pressure from a Southern Congressman in favor of banning Richard Wright's *Native Son.*

Even while older, stricter rulings were being rejected—although reluctantly and slowly—harm was sometimes done before the Postal lawyers changed their minds. In 1940 a bookdealer was stopped when he sought to mail 35,000 copies of a catalogue which listed *Candide, Droll Stories,* and *Let's Make Mary.* In 1939 an entire issue of the magazine *Studio,* a 45-year-old monthly, was stopped in the New York Post Office when nudes by contemporary artists—including Matisse—were found inside the covers. A few months later, an issue of a non-profit, graphic arts magazine, *PM,* was stopped by the New York Postmaster on the grounds that its nudes —including figures by Abner Dean and Peter Arno—were "obscene." Another art magazine, *View,* was stopped in New York, and when the Postmaster was finally pinned down, the objectionable matter, it was found, consisted of nudes by Michelangelo and Picasso. The forensic zeal of the publishers and the American Civil Liberties Union finally persuaded the Solicitor to change his mind in each of these cases.

The uncertainty of it all was epitomized by what was, apparently, coming to be a bane to enforcers of the statute: mass-produced magazines for males, deliberately contrived to titillate: the slick-paper "detectives," the "girlies," the "pulps," and the "adventure" stories which regularly spiced their fare with a sex angle. There is a "treacherous borderline zone," admitted the Postmaster General (probably speaking by his lawyers), when it comes to deciding whether these entertainment materials are "technically obscene." His observation certainly echoed the earlier conclusions of an Attorney General's study of Postal enforcement that obsceneness here was often a matter of "personal judgment," largely "up to one's individual conscience."

In the early forties, despite the fact that both the law and public attitudes were changing in favor of tolerance—indeed, perhaps in a dramatic effort to arrest these trends—the Post Office launched a vigorous campaign against the "borderline" magazines. Not only did the Department bear down with non-mailability rulings; it also began revoking the second-class permits of alleged offenders, relying, of course, on the *Milwaukee Leader* case for authority to do so. Many magazines "for men," put by their own contrivance in that "treacherous zone," now found themselves cited for revocation proceedings. Some publishers pleaded with the Department for precise instructions as to how they might "clean up," and thereafter complained that too often the answer was too hazy—simply an admonition to conform to "good taste." Until 1942 there were no formal, published procedures governing contested revocation cases. Special "boards" were set up to hold "hearings" and to judge whether past performance justified future denial of the second-class rate. And some magazine publishers complained angrily about all this. They found diverse champions: Senator William Langer, Drew Pearson, various newspapers, ranging from the New York *Daily News* to *PM,* and the American Civil Liberties Union.

Pearson and the American Civil Liberties Union suggested that the Department was acting under direct pressure from Catholic groups, especially the National Organization for Decent Literature. Postmaster General Walker indignantly denied this. The charge was never proved; the only evidence produced to support it was a showing that the Post Office had proceeded against many magazines which the church groups had listed as objectionable. On the other hand, Langer, who seemed particularly concerned with the revocation of the *Police Gazette*'s privilege ("one of [our] oldest and best known magazines"), charged that the whole affair was the Postmaster General's political vendetta, a reprisal against a publisher who opposed the Administration. Again, the evidence to support the charge was weak, e.g., a showing that the *Police Gazette's* owners had turned Republican before the revocation axe fell.

Senator Langer did wage, on the Senate floor, a sort of one-man exposé of what was going on, and if some of his claims were extravagant, others reflected the extent to which the Department was purging "cheesecake." A list produced by Langer showed that some seventy publications, according to the Post Office, had either been warned and put on informal probation or lost their permits. The list included titles put out by well-known publishers like Fawcett, Dell, and Frank Munsey Co.; it included titles ranging from *Spark,*

Stocking Parade, and *Peek* to *Real Romance, Front Page Detective, Judge,* and *Argosy.* The *Police Gazette* had lost its permit, even though, according to Langer and others, the issues cited as objectionable had been acceptable to Boston's Watch and Ward Society. In no case had the Department attempted any criminal prosecution, and Langer dared it to do so: these censors are scared, said he, to go before any American jury and try to prove their case.

A number of newspapers across the country joined Langer's protest—as well they might, if for no other reason than self-interest, for surely the "cheesecake" and reporting in many of the detective and romance magazines were similar to the output of the more sensational dailies, similar enough, at any rate, to make it hard to articulate the difference.

Langer introduced a resolution calling for a congressional investigation of Postal censorship. He also introduced legislation, apparently drafted by the American Civil Liberties Union and patterned after the Tariff Act, which would require the Post Office to go to court to effectuate every stoppage of alleged obscene mail matter. These proposals never saw the light of day in the Post Office Committee. Chairman McKellar predicted they would die, and die they did, no doubt because Senator McKellar used self-help to fulfill his lethal prophecy.

The vigorous Postal efforts continued. A "second-class mail privilege" is a publication's "certificate of good moral character," declared Mr. Walker in his *Annual Report* of 1942. Reviewing the statutory qualifications for second-class rates, he suggested (somewhat ambiguously) that he had the power to deny these privileges *even when the magazine had published nothing which was actually non-mailable.* It appeared, then, that many of the magazines which the Post Office wanted to clean up were not even obscene to begin with; but the absence of obscenity was not going to stop the Department from using its revocation power to prod publishers to a higher standard of morality. "Some criticism [of our new policies] is expected," added the Postmaster General.

An accurate prognostication. When the Department took on *Esquire* in 1943, the power now being asserted was fully revealed—as a naked exercise of unprecedented, federal censorship.

The statutory qualifications for a second-class permit required regular issuance of a magazine at least four times a year, from a fixed office of publication, in a printed form with paper covers. The "fourth" qualification stated:

> It [the magazine] must be originated and *published for the dissemination of information of a public character, or devoted to literature, the sciences, arts, or some special industry,* and having a legitimate list of subscribers. Nothing herein contained shall be so construed as to admit to the second-class rate regular publications designed primarily for advertising purposes, or for free circulation, or for circulation at nominal rates. (Emphasis added).

Previously, this ambiguous "fourth" qualification had been interpreted as simply a requirement that a magazine be a magazine and not a vehicle for advertising or a commercial propaganda piece gratuitously circulated. In 1943 a new interpretation was officially endorsed. This "fourth" qualification means, said the Department, that the magazine must be "for the public good." Or again:

> A publication to enjoy these unique mail privileges and special preferences is bound to do more than refrain from disseminating material which is obscene or bordering on the obscene. It is under a positive duty to contribute to the public good and public welfare.

Thus spoke the Postmaster General, concluding that *Esquire* had violated the statute as it had now been interpreted. This magazine, he declared, makes no "contribution" to the "public welfare"; in issue after issue there are too many pictures and too many jokes which, if not obscene, are nearly so. Surely Congress had no intention of subsidizing the mailing of a work which consistently hewed so close to the line. Second-class permits were "privileges" reserved for good magazines. Therefore, let Esquire's permit be revoked until it improved its contents.

When the full implications of this new revocation standard were exposed, outraged protests from publishers, newspapers, and libertarian groups followed. Faced with vastly increased costs of distribution—and perhaps oblivion—*Esquire* went to court, backed by an imposing phalanx of some of the nation's foremost advocates. They deliberately forced further review of the entire question of the alleged indecency of the magazine's pages. Several hundred pounds of *Esquires* were "put in the record." Tell us, demanded the magazine's attorneys, what we have printed which justifies this curtailment of our rates. In reply, the Post Office produced witnesses—educated, sincere citizens to testify why they thought *Esquire* was in bad taste, why, regardless of its obscenity, the material in it was deleterious.

The cross-examination of these government witnesses reflected some of the problems.

Q. Will you look at this Exhibit 133, and tell me if this picture is decent or indecent? A. I think I am being trapped [again], your Honor. . . .

Q. Well, would you mind telling me if that picture is decent or indecent? A. If I had a daughter I shouldn't like to have her photographed in that costume. I have no daughter, I have only sons.

Q. Is that your criterion for decency? A. My criterion for decency is anything that is proper, in order, certainly not harmful to human dignity. This woman is evidently by the ocean. I see the ocean there. She has probably come in and out of the ocean and if she stays there all right for me, but I do not wish to see that picture displayed except where it belongs. I believe in suitability, suitability; I don't like the picture. It is not pleasing to me and to my eye because I don't believe in such poses. . . .

Q. This picture, Exhibit 131, do you think it is decent or indecent?

A. I object to it very much.

Q. Do you think it is decent or indecent? A. Do I have to answer, your honor?

Q. I wish you would, please. A. It is a matter of please?

Q. Yes. A. Then I refuse to answer. You have shown me enough. . . .

Q. I would like to know, Mr. [Counsel for the Post Office], if you don't mind telling me now, just what it is in that article you don't like. I can't find it.

A. I would be glad to read it to counsel.

Q. Thank you.

A. Third column at the bottom of page 144. "He noticed how large the uniform made her behind look."

The government won the first round, in the District Court. But the Court of Appeals reversed—emphatically. It is inconceivable, said the Court, that Congress delegated this kind of revocation power to the Post Office, "the power first to determine what is good for the public to read and then to force compliance" with that judgment through the revocation sanction. And to conclude:

> We intend no criticism of counsel for the Post Office. They were faced with an impossible task. They undertook it with sincerity. But their very sincerity makes the record useful as a memorial to commemorate the utter confusion and lack of intelligible standards which can never be escaped when that task is attempted. We believe that the Post Office officials should experience a feeling of relief if they are limited to the more prosaic function of seeing to it that "neither snow nor rain nor heat nor gloom of night stays these couriers from the swift completion of their appointed rounds."

The government chose to fight again. The case moved on to the Supreme Court, where defeat became a rout. A unanimous court ruled that the fourth qualification "related" only "to the format of the publication and to the nature of its contents, but not to their quality or worth." For this proposition the history of the statute was cited; it was never the intention of Congress to authorize the power now asserted by the Post Office. To cap its construction of the statute, the Court warned that "grave Constitutional questions were immediately raised" should powers of this sort be exercised by the government.

The *Esquire* decision did not overrule the *Milwaukee Leader* case. Nothing conclusive was said about the power to revoke the second-class privileges of magazines which produced, say, two or three consecutive issues clearly non-mailable on the grounds of obscenity. But the courts had emphasized the important legal status of a permit to mail at second-class rate. So long as physical qualifications were met, the "privilege" was more in the nature of a "right"; the power to abridge it was circumscribed by the First Amendment. Certainly it was arguable that the courts would, if pushed to the issue, adopt the Holmes-Brandeis view that the revocation power, as a sanction to supplement obscenity enforcement, was unlawful.

These considerations suggested caution. And the Post Office now became cautious—at least about revoking permits. Interviewed by Roger Baldwin of the American Civil Liberties Union, the Solicitor declared that permits would no longer be revoked whenever a publisher put out a single "non-mailable" issue or widely intermittent, non-mailable issues. Possibly, if a publisher put out a series of non-mailable issues so that the continuity of publication was seriously affected, revocation proceedings might be brought. In fact, since the *Esquire* case the revocation power has been almost totally abandoned, in practice, as an anti-obscenity sanction. Yet, the *Milwaukee Leader* case still stands. Revocation remains a club in the corner—although covered with cobwebs.

PART III

Postwar Developments: Another Period of Evolution, 1946 to 1956

Postwar developments have been complex and frustrating; they reflect a socio-legal schizophrenia. The country has manifestly been torn between the urge to use the force of law to suppress the undesirable with a vengeance and the urge to promote freedom of expression in matters pertaining to sex by extending legal guarantees protecting this freedom.

These postwar developments in federal censorship can best be analyzed by studying first the period of 1946 to 1956, surveying the *modus operandi* of federal censorship, analyzing representative cases, and surveying the social context in which this law enforcement took place.

The decade 1946–56 preceded a period which has produced a new series of important court decisions. These very recent decisions have changed the law, or, more accurately, thrown it into a state of flux that has caused great consternation and, indeed, considerable anger around the country. But evaluation of these very recent decisions and prognostication for the future can best be attempted if one is familiar with the experience which preceded the immediate present. Thus, there follows a survey of what happened between 1946 and 1956.

I.   THE MODERN DILEMMA: MORE JUDICIAL LAWMAKING, MORE FREEDOM, MORE OBSCENITY, AND MORE PRESSURE FOR MORE CENSORSHIP

DURING THIS DECADE, significant appellate court decisions steadily contracted the permissible operation of anti-obscenity and related laws.

A basic motivation behind these decisions was the First Amendment. There were several Supreme Court landmarks. In 1948 a New York statute designed to prohibit publication and sale of at least the more blood-thirsty detective or crime-comic magazines was declared unconstitutional. In 1952 a statute authorizing New York's movie censors to ban "sacrilegious" movies was declared invalid. So, too, was a Texas municipal ordinance permitting the town censors to stop the showing of films which were "prejudicial" to "the best interests" of the community. Two similar state statutes permitting censors to stop exhibition of any "immoral" movies or movies which "tended to debase morals" were struck down in 1954.

In each of these cases the vice of the proscription was the vagueness of the standards; "men of common intelligence" were made to "guess," too much, about their interpretation and application. Thus, the Court spelled out a First Amendment doctrine—particularly applicable where censorship laws were involved—that prohibitions on "speech" (a term which now plainly included entertainment and pictorial media) must be objectively exact, leaving minimal discretion to law enforcement and limited to a demonstrable evil which government was competent to curb.

The validity of the obscenity laws, when tested against this relatively new First Amendment standard condemning broad, vague restraints on speech, was still assumed during the beginning of the decade 1946–56. Obscene expression was "speech" devoid of "social value," "speech" which had long been condemned, not the kind of "speech" which the Constitution protects, suggested the Court in passing comment on two occasions.

Yet in 1948 the Court was confronted with precisely the kind of case which belied the claim that there were no serious First Amendment problems, that nothing which was obscene could have any worth: a New York prosecution of a book publisher for selling Edmund Wilson's *Memoirs of Hecate County*. Conceding that New York could, constitutionally, pass laws prohibiting the sale of obscene books, counsel for the book publisher nevertheless argued that to apply such a law against a work as meritorious as *Hecate County* violated the First Amendment, and he backed up the claim of merit with an array of respectable literary opinion. There was opportunity here for review of fundamental questions now more clearly emerging. But with one Justice not participating, the Supreme Court split four to four, and, having split evenly, followed its tradition of affirming the judgment of the lower court without any expression of opinion or indication of division.

So a question, once ignored, now persisted: Could the obscenity laws, as their scope was defined, stand up under the scrutiny of a searching inquiry into their validity under the First Amendment?

In 1949, a distinguished Pennsylvania judge, Curtis Bok of Philadelphia, and a distinguished federal judge, Jerome Frank of the United States Court of Appeals for the Second Circuit, voiced doubts. They drew an analogy to the "clear and present danger" doctrine which was thought to denote the scope of the protection given political advocacy under the First Amendment. There should be, said Judges Bok and Frank, some definite evidence that an allegedly obscene publication will in fact produce anti-social conduct among the persons who view it before its sale is made criminal. The argument was reinforced by the observations of several experts or purported experts on the science of human behavior. The exhibition of nudity, the depiction of sex in action, and so forth, does not really affect the social behavior of adults exposed to such communication, claimed some of the bolder experts. At least there is no "scientific" evidence that it does, concluded others more guardedly. Therefore, urged Judges Bok and Frank, books and pictures, even if trash, should be left alone unless and until it can be shown by persuasive evidence that their impact produces something more than a mere transitory, psychic response without overt misconduct. This limitation, it was urged, is the price of freedom of expression; otherwise speech is suppressed solely on the basis of prejudice and gestalt reactions—an arbitrary and dangerous business, as experience consistently has demonstrated.

Judicial utterances like these, during the period of 1946–56, encouraged the champions of freedom from censorship to become increasingly articulate—both before the courts and in legal and lay periodicals. Moreover, the strength of this advocacy produced an effect, immeasurable but discernible, on what the courts did and said in cases which fell in this general area.

On the other hand, during this same postwar period, pressures for suppression were strong. The country, it was said many times over, from many varied sources, was being inundated by a flood of harmful trash. Distinguished church and lay leaders identified and deplored what seemed to be a steady erosion of moral values. Beginning in 1948, juvenile crime seemed to increase significantly in volume and became a major subject for news, editorial, TV, movie, and literary coverage. Mr. Hoover of the FBI warned the public frequently and vigorously, that much of the salacious material which was readily available to immature or unstable people was producing sex criminals. Hundreds of other police chiefs, prosecutors, and civic leaders echoed this assertion. And in any event there were trends in mass media which caused great concern among a great many sober-minded people.

The plain fact was that each year more Americans seemed to be spending more money on matter which more openly catered to their prurience. The circulation of "girlie" magazines—including the new, more expensive items like *Playboy* and its imitators—increased steadily. *Playboy* hopped to over a million in a year. The magazine *Confidential* was started on a shoestring, but it soon claimed four million readers, offered a special fare of "exposés" of the "private lives" of "celebrities," concentrating on their sexual misbehavior; it catered to that instinct—whatever it is—that urges men, and women as well, to delve into prurient gossip. The importation and domestic publication and circulation of nudist magazines increased, as did the circulation of pocket books and phenomenally so—a fact that, of course, was not disturbing per se, but was, perhaps, disturbing to the extent that so many paperbounds, regardless of internal content, exploited sex so patently on their covers. It was said that over 29,000,000 Americans read the paperbound works of Mickey Spillane; the obvious popularity of these and other "tough" detective tales so well larded with sex and sadism evoked disturbed comment from many quarters, including commentators who were vigorous opponents of censorship. Not only horror and gore but, again, sadism with a sexual motif pervaded so many "comic" magazines to such an extent that the chastised industry condemned its own iconography and accepted a voluntary censorship code.

Whether this mass media exploitation of sex has produced great social harms, as many law enforcement officers, churchmen, and just plain citizens believe, or whether it was just symptomatic of some deeper problem in our culture, as various social science experts have opined, the phenomenon remained. Demands for sweeping laws which somehow would arrest the development followed— and this occurred even as the courts were restricting the permissible scope of police or censorship action.

In New York State a joint legislative committee was created in 1949 to investigate and report, first, on the problem of comics; then (after comic-book publishers had adopted their own cleanup program) on pocket books, girlie magazines, and mail order materials; and, later, motion pictures. The Committee recruited a full-time staff and worked steadily over a period of years. Its reports contain, by way of exhibits, facts, and figures, a sobering picture of what was happening in New York in the way of mass media exploitation of sex. Say what one may about the Committee's jeremiads or its legal proposals and nostrums, the very fact of this strenuous effort bears testimony to the strength of the drive to suppress. Instances of similar, if less studied and sustained, efforts in many other states and cities are not wanting. Legislature after legislature passed new laws to stop the trend, many patently invalid in light of First Amendment court decisions. But the torrent of bills pouring into the hoppers showed the strength of popular political pressures, even as the rising volume of sales of salacity showed the avarice of American appetites for the forbidden fruits.

Congressional investigators entered the field in 1952 (a House Select Committee under Congressman Gathings) and in 1954 (the so-called Kefauver Senate Judiciary Subcommittee, which investigated juvenile crime). Both committees "exposed" the fact that "obscenity"—a characterization including pocket books with sexually suggestive covers, regardless of content (in the case of the Gathings Committee), "girlie" picture magazines, lurid comics, mail-order nudes, patent pornography—was being distributed in phenomenal quantities at a phenomenal total outlay of the national income.

Inadvertently, perhaps, the Gathings Committee developed some interesting information about the techniques of suppression in its hearings, notably from testimony of Postal officials, who were quite candid about their methods. The committee was lavish with its praise for these and other law enforcement efforts aimed at suppression, and its insensitivity to the perils of censorship, its anti-intellectual utterances, and its general condemnation of the entire publishing industry prompted a torrent of editorial criticism.

More balanced and comprehensive was the work of the Kefauver Committee. It traced the growing volume of crime comics and crime depiction in our culture, noting that much of this material, while perhaps allied as a social problem with obscene matter, was, in a legal sense, a category apart when it came to legislating restraints. The Committee also investigated traffic—particularly mail-order traffic—in obscenity or alleged obscenity. It investigated, perhaps not methodically, but still soberly, the impact which such material may have had on its recipients. Protesting against the launching of any new censorial activities, the Committee made only a few legislative recommendations. Perhaps its major contribution was simply the amount of information which it brought to light. The hearings showed more clearly than other sources had shown before that commercial exploitation of pin-up magazines, "art photo" publications, pictures of "girl wrestlers," "stag movies," "bizarre erotica," "Wolf pacs," "strip sets," paperbound fiction, and things *ejusdem generis,* was big business. The mails were the major avenue for this traffic. Estimates of the total volume of business ran into hundreds of millions of dollars, though no one could really be sure because no one bothered to identify very carefully what it was that was being estimated.

Foreign dealers could, by the same technique, exploit American prurience. Paperback fiction, much of it quite erotic, some of it degenerately pornographic, was now being advertised and sold via the mails in burgeoning commercial operations. These exporters were beyond the reach of our criminal law. And, as a practical matter, criminal prosecution of the importers was usually unwarranted or practically out of the question and thus no deterrent. Customs censorship seemed the only effective curb on the traffic. Doubtless Customs censorship did frustrate much potential exploitation of the United States market, though precisely how effective it was, no one could say.

Thus our obscenity laws posed an increasingly sharp and frustrating dilemma. On the one hand, the freedom of adults to decide for themselves what they were to read was given increased protection by the courts. On the other hand, there was mass commercial exploitation of various species of "speech" that many responsible Americans insisted was causing serious social harms. And Federal censorship played an increasingly important, publicized, controversial role in the total national effort to suppress obsceneness in mass media during the postwar decade 1946–56.

2.   THE MODUS OPERANDI OF CENSORSHIP: CUSTOMS AND POSTAL PROCEDURES, 1946–1956

IN THEORY THE GOALS of the Post Office and of Customs were similar. Customs officials intercepted objectionable publications or movies entering the country by mail or otherwise. The Post Office policed the domestic mails. Both agencies invoked the same theoretical legal standards: the *"Ulysses* test" to screen books (measuring the impact of the work "as a whole" on the "libido" of the average reader); the "community standard test" to judge pictorial matter (does it transgress what the "community" will tolerate by way of depiction of nudity or sexual activity?) The important decisions of each agency were made by a few officials in Washington, who in truth were the nation's chief censors.

Yet both the procedures used to police the mails and the results of that censorship differed between the two agencies. Nor was there any real co-ordination between the Post Office and the Bureau beyond the most casual exchange of information on the rulings each rendered. The Bureau operated under very informal, streamlined procedures; the volume of cases confronting it was smaller and the cases, individually considered, somewhat different in kind. The Bureau was generally more liberal, notably in its rulings on books and in the depiction of nudity in magazines.

The Bureau of Customs

Most of the Customs cases arose at the major ports of entry (New York, Chicago—an important midwestern distribution point for mail from abroad—Los Angeles, and San Francisco). The procedure was as follows: Foreign mail would first be screened by Customs officials, called segregators or inspectors. Although it was impossible to check every package containing a book or magazine, experienced employees had a uncanny ability to root out suspect matter by running regular spot checks or by developing familiarity with the return address, wrapping, or writing appearing on the packages of offending exporters. Suspect items, once detected, were immediately passed to a superior, usually a deputy collector, at the port. He had three choices: (1) to release the material as not obscene; (2) to condemn it without seeking approval from Washington in cases where the particular work in question was clearly covered by a recent ruling; or, when in doubt, (3) to refer it to Washington. In most cases the deputy would forward the material. In Washington the decision would be made by one or two officials in the Bureau's Penalty Section or, if there was doubt, the material would be physically referred to Mr. Huntington Cairns, the Bureau's adviser, whose "advice" was followed as a matter of course. Thus Washington, and to a large extent Mr. Cairns, fixed the minimum standards of fitness for foreign works.

Movies were handled in a special way. With rare exceptions commercial entertainment films came through the New York port, usually by air freight. All were screened for obscene content by a Customs film reviewer who would then prepare a brief memo describing the film and recommending either clearance or detention. If the film was detained by the reviewer, the next and usually key decision would be made by the Deputy Collector. After looking at the whole film or inspecting the alleged objectionable parts or after brief consultation with the reviewer, the Deputy Collector would decide whether the film was objectionable. If his decision was to seize, he would so advise Mr. Cairns's office by memorandum. With rare exceptions Mr. Cairns would sustain the decision without actually seeing the alleged offensive scenes. "We understand each other," was Mr. Cairns's explanation in 1955. The importer would then be notified of the seizure decision. He then would invariably either request permission to cut out (physically and in the presence of Customs officials) the allegedly obscene portions of the film, or, less frequently, where the importer concluded that the deletions would render the film non-commercial, he would request permission to send the item back to its source, thus avoiding considerable expense.

So the Deputy Collector in New York, Irving Fishman, and his adviser, Mr. Cairns, were the *de facto* censors of America's foreign film fare. The standards they applied will be detailed shortly, but here it should be noted that during the period 1946–56, their decisions were seldom disputed seriously and rarely litigated. The need for speed, the realization that if the film couldn't pass Customs it might run afoul of local police or censorship agencies, the fact that the cuts made were usually slight, and the fact that the importer was often in the status of a broker rather than a distributor or exhibitor may account for the surprising amount of acquiescence.

All material seized at the ports was, under the theory of the Tariff statute, supposed to be referred to the courts for their decision. Indeed, it seems to have been the thought of Congress when the statute was passed in 1930 (as manifested by Senator Hugo Black's explanation and emphasis of its virtue) that the courts, not Customs officials, would make the ultimate decisions on what would be banned.

The practice has always been different. The courts have played a passive role. Once Customs officials decided to seize, they would send a form letter to the importer advising him that the named article addressed to him was contraband obscenity and asking him to assent forthwith to its seizure by returning an enclosed form. In most instances the importer returned the form, thereby waiving court proceeding. In most other instances he simply did not respond at all, and the Bureau construed this failure to respond as a demonstration of unwillingness to contest the seizure. The seized article was then stored in a warehouse, and, perhaps once a year, the local U.S. Attorney would file in the federal court a petition to "libel," i.e., condemn the material. The petition would be captioned, for example, "United States v. 1000 Obscene Articles," listing what was to be seized in such general terms as "200 books," "500 magazines," "300 photographs." Notice of this pending action was never sent to the importer who was about to lose his importation for good and all unless he had previously made a specific request indicating that he wanted to contest the seizure. Ordinarily, the only "notice" given of the pending action was the insertion of an advertisement in a legal newspaper that an action entitled, for example, "U.S. v. 1000 Obscene Articles," had been initiated. When the case was called for hearing in court, the U.S. Attorney would explain briefly to the judge that the material had been seized, that there were no claimants, that the articles were obscene and should be condemned, whereupon the judge would sign an order to that effect. In New York, where this practice was studied in 1956, the judge never, and the U.S. Attorney rarely, actually saw the material confiscated by the judicial action.

In rare cases during this period (1946–56) an importer would protest upon notification that his book had been seized. The protest would be in the form of a letter or call to the Deputy Collector. These objections seldom changed any minds, and usually the importer dropped the matter at this point. Occasionally, where the protest was vehement and persuasive, the seizure decision would be reviewed *ex parte* in Washington. But seldom was the work released after this review. Only in a very few instances would the importer go further and carry his fight to the courts by contesting the libel case. The time and expense and the doubtfulness of success all probably discouraged litigation involving, usually, only one or two items of slight monetary value.

Thus the Bureau, not the courts, made the decisions and set the pattern. Despite the importance of the Bureau's role, there was very little of what lawyers call "procedural due process," i.e., a definite opportunity for a formal hearing before a disinterested officer who was not also charged with the task of initiating actions to enforce the law. It has been the theory of the Bureau that this formality, required in analogous adjudicatory situations in other government agencies by the Administrative Procedure Act, is not required in Customs censorship.

Although this theory is probably correct in the case of Customs, it is also probably true that, as a general principle in government, the absence of administrative formality makes it easier for the government official to decide against the contesting citizen in a borderline case. Precisely because there is not the check of a formal adversary hearing nor easy review in the courts, Customs procedure

delegates considerable power to the few who decide what publications shall be suppressed.

Be that as it may, there were few public complaints during the
period 1946–56. Indeed, the Bureau with its informal procedure was
in practice more cautious about impounding publications than the
Post Office, which was forced to follow more formal procedures.
Occasionally controversies arose, as when the San Francisco Collector summarily confiscated a work called *Howl and Other Poems*
by Alan Ginsberg. But this official was reversed by his superiors
in Washington after civil libertarians in the Bay area set up a
vigorous protest and asked the Bureau to review the case.

The restraint which characterized the Customs operation most of
the time seems attributable to the personalities who exercised the
ultimate judgment—men like Huntington Cairns, whose "advice"
was followed as "the law," and the Deputy Collector in New York,
who was regularly confronted with an endless number and variety
of cases, who had little time to spend on censorship work, and yet
whose decisions avoided public controversy and were seldom im-
plausible, given a duty to enforce the law as written.

The Post Office

The Post Office used two methods to police the mails: First, confiscation of obscene publications discovered in transit—the so-called
non-mailability ruling. Second, non-delivery of mail addressed to
persons using the mails to sell objectionable materials—the "unlawful order" or "mail block." Mail blocks were the sanction when
inspectors uncovered the operation of commercial purveyors of
noxious books or pictures. In such a case the local postmaster would
be ordered not to deliver any incoming mail to the alleged offender.
Use of a third possible sanction, criminal prosecution of any disseminator of obscene publications—the "ultimate weapon" reserved, supposedly, for serious offenders—was entirely within the
discretion of the Department of Justice; Postal inspectors could and
did suggest action here, but local U.S. Attorneys and lawyers in the
Criminal Division in Washington would make the choice. While
in theory the statutes seemed to make almost any Postal censorship
case an equally appropriate case for a criminal charge, the fact is
that U.S. prosecutors either could not or would not seek grand jury
indictments in the vast run of cases where Postal lawyers found a

mailing of obscenity. Thus most of the policing of the mails was done by the Post Office, by recourse to the non-mailability or mail block sanction.

The non-mailability sanction operated substantially on a hit-or-miss basis. Frequently an event such as a chance remark by the sender or the breaking of the wrapping on a package rather than any spot checking would arouse the curiosity of some postal employee and lead ultimately to a seizure. At the point of mailing of mass-circulated magazines there was some deliberate scrutiny of content, but primarily for compliance with mail-rate regulations. There was, however, extensive deliberate checking of certain magazines such as the girlies, detectives, men's magazines and the like.

When the Postal employee had concluded on the basis of his own "common sense" that the material was not "fit for the home" (for these were the standards actually used), he passed on the offending publication to the local postmaster, who in turn, would seek a ruling from the Postal Solicitor's office in Washington unless he decided to release the work. The offending publication was then shipped, physically, to Washington to the desk of a lawyer in the Fraud and Mailability Division. During the period of 1950–56, there were about 3,000 referrals to Washington each year. In Washington, a small team of lawyers, usually two or three, spent a part of their time inspecting and evaluating material shipped in from the field. If they concluded that it was obscene, a ruling declaring the work non-mailable would be issued in the name of the Solicitor, their superior. (Only occasionally, however, would the Solicitor in fact review these cases.) When a non-mailability ruling issued, the local postmaster would be told to notify the mailer of the decision. Opportunity was provided for an informal conference in Washington to contest the ruling; the mailer's alternative would be to retain a lawyer and fight the government in court.

Stoppage of suspect obscenity in transit—enforcement of the non-mailability sanction—depended very much on local policing; yet officials in the field were given neither specific instructions to judge "obsceneness" nor any general information reflecting current departmental rulings. They were given only the order to report "obscenity," whatever that might be. Admittedly the standards employed by Postal employees in the field varied. Officials in the New York Post Office, for example, stated that they received for delivery magazines which had been cleared by their counterparts in Chicago (the Post Office of origin) but which they regarded as obscene. Thus, the whole machinery of the non-mailability sanction, the imposition of this censorship, operated sporadically: the best seller, *From Here To Eternity,* happened to be banned only because a carton of paperbacks happened to break open in a big post office and some "dirty words" on the pages happened to catch the eye of a clerk who happened to be less tolerant, probably, than many others.

On the other hand, mail block proceedings originated out of a more deliberate investigation by the Postal Inspection Service. This agency investigates any suspected violations in the vast range of Postal laws, from "con games" to pornography, where additional facts may be needed as legal proof of violation. In the case of obscenity enforcement, a continuous, co-ordinated campaign is aimed at commercial dealers who advertise and distribute under the protection of the seal. Suspect advertisements in girlie magazines are scanned and often answered (under guise of a fictitious name); or the source of mailing of materials sent in by complaining citizens —often outraged parents—is tracked down wherever the complaint seems to have merit.

Out of the thousands of investigations conducted every year during the period 1946–56, between two and three hundred cases were referred by the Service to the Solicitor's office for mail block proceedings. The Service also averaged two hundred arrests each year for criminal violations of the Comstock Act, but at least half of these were for private, home-made pornography frequently produced by persons mentally ill, rather than for commercial exploitation of more borderline matter by large-volume producers.

The ultimate power to wield censorship sanctions rested with the Postmaster General; but by directives he delegated the job to the Solicitor, who in turn delegated it to the chief of the Mailability division, a career employee of a conservative disposition, it seems fair to say, in matters of sex expression. Thus a very few lawyers set the tone of the operation, and the fact that a few men could apparently exercise so much discretion evoked more and more concern from persons familiar with the Post Office *modus operandi.*

As far back as 1940, Postal lawyers had rejected a suggestion that they employ an expert or a committee of experts to advise on anti-obscenity enforcement. The proposal was seriously urged by an Attorney General's Committee on Administrative Procedures, headed by Dean Acheson. The question of obscenity, said the Committee, is "largely a question of one's own conscience." The need is to find one whose conscience is tolerant, whose judgments can proceed on the basis of broad familiarity with the arts and science: a Huntington Cairns, for example. The Committee was quite impressed by Cairns's apparent "success"; but Post Office demurred; its lawyers were not so impressed.

"To the chemist," wrote the Postal lawyers in rejoinder, "there is no such thing as dirt. We must likewise ponder whether to an artist or connoisseur there is any such thing as obscenity." An expert might let anything go through the mail. But the law condemning the obscene was fixed, and the Postal lawyers intended to respect it according to their lights, notwithstanding complaints about censorship.

Indeed, not only did the Post Office refuse to use experts versed in literature, art, or psychology to assist in the investigation or decision-making, but throughout the period 1946–56 it attempted to prevent the use of experts by those who challenged its rulings. Testimony about the merit or probable adverse effect of a work on the viewer was consistently rejected.

Just as they refused to hear the ideas of other witnesses on the obsceneness of a challenged work so also Postal lawyers refused to have their decisions reviewed, independently, by other lawyers in the Department, who, acting outside the aegis of the Mailability Division, might hear both sides of a contested case without having prejudged it.

Where, for example, the Solicitor's office determined *ex parte* that a publication was obscene, it notified the local postmaster not to carry the material in the mails; that official in turn notified the sender, giving him a specified time, usually fifteen days, to contact the Solicitor's office in protest, if he desired to do so. In the meantime, of course, the publication was not delivered.

If the mailer did protest and did take the trouble to journey to Washington to plead his case, he found that he was permitted to argue only to the very lawyers who had decided in the first place that the materials were offensive; and from their disposition there was no appeal to any higher Postal authority. Nor would these lawyers expend much patience listening to witnesses, expert or otherwise; nor would they look at other publications or books as a basis for comparison. The question, they would say, is whether *this* work is obscene; the test is a legal one; the decision is made by inspecting the work and evaluating it; we are the lawyers who have been assigned to make the decision. Rarely would rulings be reversed, even when the protestant was accompanied by vociferous counsel who threatened immediate redress in the courts.

In 1945, this informal, summary method of banning books, which applied both to non-mailability cases and to mail blocks, and which smacked of arbitrariness to many rankled critics of the Department, was branded illegal. The ruling came from the United States Court of Appeals in the District of Columbia, the very site of the department's basic operations and of most Postal litigation at that time. Reversing a ruling that Dr. Paul Popenoe's booklet "Preparing for Marriage," was non-mailable obscenity, Judge Thurman Arnold vigorously condemned the procedures by which the Department could stop, summarily, the distribution of books. Interferences with Popenoe's distribution of his book by summarily seizing it amounted to interferences with both his liberty (the right to publish) and his property (the right to do with the book as he wished). The Fifth Amendment guarantees "due process of law" before liberty and property are taken. There had been no "due process" here. At the very least, said the court, the Department must provide open, formal hearings before an adjudicator who has not already decided the case against the mailer.

The Post Office blatantly ignored that decision and continued to use informal, summary processes to dispose of contested cases. Then, a year later, Congress adopted the Administrative Procedure Act, in response to long-standing agitation for reforms in the administrative processes in many federal agencies. This Act required that any agency determination which affected the individual rights of citizens must be preceded by a hearing following established legal procedures, with ample notice to the parties and opportunity to present evidence and cross-examine adverse witnesses. Perhaps even more fundamental, the Act prohibited agency officials with law enforcing duties from judging the very cases which they had already investigated and prosecuted. There must be a "separation of functions"; and to that end a civil-service force of hearing examiners was created—lawyers who, in a sense, would act as agency judges and whose only function was to hear cases and make their own independent recommendations as to the dispositions.

The hearing before the Examiner was to be a trial in microcosm: both sides could present witnesses and make arguments; a written record of the proceeding would be compiled; the Examiner would then recommend a decision; either side could file "exceptions" and appeal the Examiner's decision. The agency head might still exercise the final responsibility for the decision, but under this Act, the recommendation which was to be his guide was not that of the very person who had previously initiated the proceeding and thus prejudged it.

To the argument that the Act applied to Postal proceedings, the Postal lawyers responded with a firm negative.[1] If the Act applies, they maintained, every disappointed purveyor of obscenity could force us to a time-consuming, expensive administrative hearing. If the Act applies, "we are just hopelessly sunk—that's all—we are just lost," said the Solicitor to a sympathetic Gathings Committee. That Committee promised to make sure, by writing an amendment into the Act, that no court would ever force the Post Office to abandon its "efficient," longstanding method of enforcing the law. But the effort to secure an amendment lapsed. And, alas for the Post Office, the courts held that the Act did apply, first in 1952, with regard to mail block proceedings, and then in 1955 (and thereafter in a string of decisions), with regard to non-mailability cases. In these decisions, as in *Popenoe's* case, the courts emphasized that censorship sanctions affected basic liberties; they emphasized that basic liberties should never be impaired unless due process—a fair hearing—was first accorded.

Formal procedures complying with the Administrative Procedure Act were bad enough from the Department's point of view. But the courts had created an even worse headache. Did the requirement that the Department must hold hearings mean that the Department was required to hold hearings *before* it could impose any censorship sanction? After all, the formal hearing consumed great time and

1. The legal argument was that the determination of whether a work was "obscene" or not was a decision which could be made simply by "inspecting" it. And the Act, by its own terms, did not apply to decisions which could be made solely on the basis of "inspections."

effort. If hearings were now to be required, could the Department at least stop suspect mail pending the time-consuming process of conducting a formal hearing? Unless sanctions could be imposed pending the outcome of formal hearings, the Department's whole censorship operation would not be worth much. For, while the Post Office's hearing examiner was deciding whether a picture or an issue of a magazine was obscene, while lawyers for the suspect disseminator were using dilatory tactics available under the formal hearing procedure, the disseminator could stand smugly by and watch the Post Office deliver vast volumes of offending materials; the Post Office would win no more than an academic victory if it finally prevailed. So, too, with the mail-order disseminator against whom the Department might seek to impose a mail block. Most of the money returns for a dealer's materials were received very shortly after the dealer's solicitation. By the time the Department imposed the mail block, the mail intercepted might mostly be complaints from dissatisfied customers. Justifiably, therefore, the Post Office was reluctant to keep hands off the purveyor's incoming mail until the obscenity question had been finally decided.

A series of cases illustrate the dilemma. In 1955 and 1956, issues of the magazines *Confidential, Playboy,* and *Rogue* were intercepted when deposited for mailing. Counsel for the publishers hurried into court, arguing that the Post Office could not intercept these issues until there had been an administrative hearing under the Administrative Procedure Act and there had been a final decision that the magazines were obscene. The Post Office's rejoinder that such a result would completely vitiate the civil sanctions of the Comstock Act was rejected in each case by the federal district judge, who enjoined any interference with the mailings until the procedures had been followed. The magazines went through.

In like fashion, Postal inspectors would build up a case against a California mail-order distributor of girlie pictures. He would be served with a "complaint" charging a violation of the obscenity laws and proposing a mail block if, after hearings before the examiner, the charge was proven. In the meantime, declared the Postal lawyers, purporting to act for the Postmaster General, all your incoming mail will be held until the hearings are over.

In one of these cases, however, the mail-order operator hired a lawyer and went to court to get an order enjoining the "interim" mail block. The case was carried up on appeal and, pending an appeal, the distributor's lawyer sought a stay from Justice Douglas of the Supreme Court. Justice Douglas denied the request, but he wrote an opinion (speaking, of course, only for himself, not the Court) which clearly implied that "interim" mail blocks of this sort were illegal in the absence of express statutory authorization. The power to cut off mail so summarily, he suggested, might even abridge basic constitutional liberties.

This declaration, even if it lacked the status of an express court ruling declaring "interim" impounding unlawful, was a serious blow. The Post Office, fearing a further court test, abandoned interim mail blocks while it went to Congress for aid. The matter was aired in the Kefauver investigations. Congressmen concerned with the recent revelations about the volume of mail-order materials vowed that the Post Office should have the powers it needed. A number of bills were introduced. Finally, in June of 1956, Congress did enact a law authorizing temporary mail blocks. The new statute, considerably modified to meet objections and secure hasty passage, contained ambiguities and conditions which raised issues to be considered later. Suffice it to say now: The problem of interim mail stoppage, while in one sense technical, has been of basic significance in our present scheme of Postal enforcement.

Another feature of the mail block power was litigated in the courts in 1955, and another sharp blow was dealt Postal censorship. The Post Office imposed a mail block on its perennial adversary, the Sunshine Book Company, a publisher of nudist magazines. Sunshine appealed to the courts, for it was faced with total and indefinite loss of mail service.

The big issue emerging from the litigation that followed was this: assuming the "obscenity" of *some* past issues of Sunshine's magazines, could the Post Office stop *all* of the magazine's incoming mail for the indefinite future? The answer of the Court of Appeals was no. The mail block must be "confined to [incoming mail related to] materials already published, and duly found unlawful. . . . To let the present orders stand would permit the Postmaster General to prevent—in practical effect—the continued publication of a magazine without any advance knowledge that its future issues will be in violation of the law. . . . Grave constitutional issues would then be presented."

This ruling put a severe handicap on the Post Office, or so its lawyers thought. How could a mail block limited by the court's restriction possibly be enforced against an enterprise like the Sunshine Book Company, which continuously published all sorts of material?—especially when almost all incoming mail was sealed matter, making it impossible for Postal officials to open it to determine whether it was deliverable? The United States government asked the Supreme Court to review this case and reverse the ruling. If not, warned the government, the Post Office will be "helpless," the mail block power "nullified," and the mail-order obscenity business will "flourish." The Supreme Court turned a deaf ear to the plea; certiorari was denied.

Still unwilling to take the *Sunshine* decision for an answer, the Postal lawyers defied the ruling and continued to issue total mail blocks against distributors who were putting out both mailable and non-mailable and unlawful material. This immediately produced another case. The Tourlanes Publishing Company printed and distributed a booklet called *Studio Art,* a fancy name for a cheap pamphlet of retouched nudes. The Post Office issued a mail block. Tourlanes went to court, claiming that because they published things aside from *Studio Art*—for example, an "income tax guide"—the mail block had to be limited to incoming mail relating only to non-mailable issues of *Studio Art.*

The lower courts agreed. The government again asked the Supreme Court to hear the matter. It was pointed out that the Tourlanes tax guide was nothing but a "poor condensation" of the instruction booklet "furnished to all tax payers by the Internal Revenue Service." The essential point was, of course, that the Tourlanes case showed how easy it was for a distributor of nudes to avoid mail blocks by purporting to develop some "innocent" line of lawful merchandise. The "statute will soon become a dead letter if the error" of the *Sunshine* case "is not corrected," declared the Solicitor General of the United States in his petition. But there was no correction of the "error." Certiorari was again denied.

The complex, legalistic history recounted above should underscore the fact that the courts were becoming more chary about condoning the broad-gauged censorship sanctions which, in earlier years, had been wielded without question. Again, these so-called procedural issues reflect the struggle which has become the essence of the censorship problem. On the one hand, the Post Office, probably backed up by popular sentiment in the Congress and the nation, will continue to want effective power to deal with those who use the mails to pander. On the other hand, the courts, backed by lawyers and citizens who are hostile to the destructive powers, indeed, the very idea of censorship, will continue to whittle away, wherever opportunity for an effective legal offensive is presented, at laws which permit drastic consequences to be visited upon publishers whose works meet a censor's conception of that amorphous epithet, "obscenity."

3. A DESCRIPTION OF SOME MATE-

RIALS WHICH THE POST OFFICE

CENSORS HAVE CENSORED

WHAT KINDS OF MATERIALS were the subjects of censorship in the period 1946–56? What did this considerable expenditure of the government's time, energy, and money really achieve?

Available statistics are both inadequate and meaningless. In 1955, for example, the Post Office Solicitor's office received 3,052 requests for rulings; how many were actually issued is not known; how many of the materials were cleared can only be estimated; how many publications were actually barred from the mails is not known because a single ruling could have related to many copies of the same issue of a magazine or copies of the same book in a single package. Analysis of what was done must proceed by examining various categories of typical cases.

In the book industry, the great majority of books, for cost reasons, are shipped by freight, not by mail, and thus do not come under Postal censorship. Moreover, of the books which are shipped by mail, only a small percentage is ever screened by any Postal official. It is interesting, however, to compare the titles of books barred from the mails by the Post Office with best-seller lists, remembering that two criteria for obscenity are whether what is written violates a "community standard" and whether it lacks literary value.

The novel *From Here To Eternity* was banned in 1955, long after it had become a best seller. A large commercial package of paperbound editions of another best seller, *The Woman of Rome,* was likewise intercepted and kept out of the mails. *Memoirs of Hecate County,* cleared by Customs, was tabu as of 1956. Simone de Beauvoir's *The Second Sex,* published by Knopf, was declared to be non-mailable "for distribution to the public generally." A pocket edition of *Mademoiselle Fifi* by De Maupassant was banned: the line drawing illustrations depicted female nudity.

Presumably, book rulings issued in the 1940's and mentioned before, for example, bans on *Memoirs of Casanova, For Whom the Bell Tolls, Strange Fruit, Appointment in Samarra, Diana,* and *Thirteen Women,* still stood. *God's Little Acre,* although cleared by several state court decisions, was ruled non-mailable in 1946 and again in 1953. John O'Hara's *Butterfield 8* and *Hope of Heaven* were "obscene and filthy." So was Maxwell Bodenheim's *Replenishing Jessica.* George R. Scott's *History of Prostitution* was obscene, as was *Adventures in Nakedness,* Julian Strange's study of European nudist camps, in rulings issued both before and after the *Parmelee* case, where the Court of Appeals for the District of Columbia had reversed a Customs ban on a similar study of nudism.

Most, if not all, of these hard-cover books had wide acceptance. But there were others in the paperbound category which were not so widely accepted and which could not claim, at least by their external appearance, any vestige of literary merit. *Blonde Temptress, High Priced Party Girls, Immoral Woman, Indiscretions of a French Model, Part Time Wife, The Shame of Vanna Gilbert, Shameless Sue, Sin Island,* and *Vengeful Sinner,* were the titles of paperbounds in one shipment. Books like these may have nothing to recommend them, but their bite is probably weaker than their bark, and the titles listed above did sell over the counter in cigar stores in at least two big eastern cities. Again, the "community standard" seems, in fact, to turn on the question of which community. That was a question the Post Office did not want to consider.

The official files reflect few non-mailability rulings dealing with the world's more renowned erotica or of hard-core pornography. It is doubtful these rulings had much effect on the circulation of such books, although occasionally booksellers were deterred. An individual was told that under no circumstances could he circulate, even to a limited audience, his privately printed copies of Mark Twain's *1601*. Foreign paperbound materials of the type which make up so large a bulk of the Customs exclusionary operation, including Frank Harris' *My Life and Loves,* Henry Miller's *Tropics* and D. H. Lawrence's *Lady Chatterley's Lover* were confiscated whenever detected. These and books by the notorious "Jack Woodford" represent the "worst" items arrested by administrative censorship. This is not to say that straight pornographic works are not disseminated by mail. But it is probable that most circulations of books of this nature go undetected via first class mail and that most cases of large-scale dissemination of such materials, when detected, have been referred straight to the U.S. Attorney for prosecution and not to the General Counsel's office for a ruling.

The rulings on all the books mentioned dealt with small shipments. The large commercial publishers—who seldom resort to the mails for major distributions anyway—report, with few exceptions, no interference by the Post Office, and Postal censorship seems to have had no real impact on their publication policies. The Macmillan Company had to be reminded that the Department had declared *Forever Amber* obscene in 1941, a ban which lasted in theory until 1957 when it was reversed by the Solicitor. Obviously, the ban had no impact on the book's distribution. The publisher of the paperbound *Woman of Rome* saw no point in contesting the Solicitor's adverse ruling in court because the ruling interfered so little with the book's distribution.

Nevertheless, some possibility of more serious regulation of book distribution remains so long as titles put out by established publishers and sold widely over the counters in community bookstores can be declared "obscene" by the federal government.

Suppose, for example, a national book club had decided to publish and distribute by mail a reissue of *From Here to Eternity* or *Woman of Rome,* both previously condemned by the Post Office. Would the Post Office have changed its ruling because of the numbers involved? Theoretically, it should not. But the Post Office obviously was reluctant to tackle a respected book club's mass distribution, even when Postal lawyers thought the book was obscene. It is difficult to escape the feeling, therefore, that, in 1946–56, Postal censorship of books in a real sense picked on the little fellows.

Furthermore, there is something anomalous, even ridiculous, in the Post Office's seizure of a few copies of *From Here to Eternity* while the nation at large reads, discusses, and reviews the same work.

Another fairly recent, celebrated case suggests a different approach towards individual mailings of allegedly obscene books. In 1955 Postal lawyers ruled that an imported, expensive, "unexpurgated" edition of Aristophanes' *Lysistrata* was "plainly obscene . . . well calculated to deprave the morals of persons reading same and almost equally certain to arouse libidinous thoughts." This case involved a single mailing to a single individual, a book collector, who imported without Customs interference. He immediately filed suit, but before the case proceeded any further the Postal lawyers backed down. This edition of *Lysistrata* (the unexpurgated text, the illustrations) may well be obscene, the Solicitor declared in an official press release, but we shall not argue about it. "We decided not to contest the delivery of this single book to an individual collector," he declared, because "our real concern is about the great mass of pornographic material being sent through the mails every day into the homes of American citizens and this is our main target . . ." Permitting individual mailings of books to go through where no demonstrable harm will be done to anyone by delivering the book may be desirable policy, but it surely had not been the general policy of the department until editorial writers over the country began a hue and cry in the *Lysistrata* case. By far the great majority of Post Office bans took absolutely no consideration of the individual circumstances. All that was considered was whether, in the abstract, the work was "obscene."

The result was that postal censorship of literature during the decade 1946–56 was often irrational precisely because it was haphazard and because the weight of censorship so often seemed to fall on transactions involving little if any potential harm to the public and because the Department sometimes went far afield in applying the standards.

While works of current fiction or literature posed only sporadic problems, distribution of other books brought more frequent problems.

Postal lawyers sometimes permitted doctors or social scientists to receive works on psychology, psychiatry, anthropology, or "sexology" which dealt in detail with sex, but mail distribution to members of the public at large was another matter. So far as Postal censorship was concerned, blunt talk by psychiatrists or social scientists could become too blunt for the public.

In 1951, a two-volume work on *Sex Perversion and the Law* was banned. "These volumes are not so much concerned with [describing] the law as with [describing] sex perversions," wrote the lawyer who inspected them, "The author has borrowed mainly from . . . [various psychiatrists]. . . . These two volumes cover the field of aberrations. . . . [they] are obscene and filthy . . ."

Dr. Benjamin Karpman's *The Alcoholic Woman* was an "obscene" creation "when distributed to the public generally"; for the psychodynamics of Dr. Karpman's studies reflected too much "promiscuity" related in "too much detail."

A book called *Bristow Rogers: American Negro,* purporting to be "a psychoanalytical case history" was banned. In the words of the lawyer who reviewed it: "In this book (Rogers) describes his numerous sex activities, which for the most part are with a white young woman. Rogers, in referring to the sex act, uses the— [sic] word for it, and he also from time to time, uses the usually avoided (in books at least) language in other matters, including the bodily functions as well as the parts of the body. Such a book as this probably would be valuable to a student of psychiatry and psychoanalysis and, as to him, would not be obscene. However, when generally distributed, it is my opinion that the book should be regarded as non-mailable."

A ruling grounded on similar considerations proscribed an admittedly reputable work on *Sexual Deviations* written by two admittedly reputable London doctors. Krafft-Ebing's *Psychopathic Sexualis* was banned for the same reasons. On the other hand, the *Kinsey Report* was cleared for general distribution, and it did circulate widely by mail, even though some members of Congress and many members of the public put pressure on the Department to make it non-mailable.

Similar difficulties have been posed by numerous books or pamphlets purporting to offer sex instruction or to explain sex hygiene. With such books the problems are twofold. In the first place, if a sex instruction text contained any amount of detailed information on the practice of contraception, it could be banned simply for teaching contraceptive methods. Such information, thanks to the lobbying of Anthony Comstock, had specifically been declared to be non-mailable as far back as 1873. A book entitled *A Sex Manual* by the dean of the school of medicine of a state university was banned in 1955 solely because it contained chapters on "birth control" and was made available for sale to the public generally, without qualification. This case is typical of many others.

There was, however, a judicially created loophole in the ban on contraceptive instruction. This exception permitted distribution of bona fide instructional books to professional men or their patients or to married persons using prophylactics with the advice of physicians, despite the literal ban of the Comstock Act. Consequently, the Post Office was frequently confronted with publishers, planned-parenthood groups and other agencies which sought to avail themselves of this exemption. After a conference between the publisher and Postal lawyers, the mailings usually were permitted, so long as some creditable assurance was given that the materials were not to be mailed indiscriminately to the public at large. No doubt Postal lawyers had no desire to contest cases where the publisher pressed hard.

There remained, however, the problem of "obsceneness" in connection with these sex-instruction manuals. For, in the view of the Department, frank talk about sex and sexual acts, especially when the emphasis was on its enjoyment, could produce the very stimulation of libidinous feelings and violate the standards of decency of expression which were the very basis of postal censorship.

To put a concrete example: Two doctors printed a manual for married couples, "Vital Facts of Sex." Their attorney brought it to Washington for clearance. The Postal lawyer who read it checked a passage which described the "duties of the wife" in the "fulfillment of successful intercourse ("allow her husband to undress her," "surrender to love," "kiss and caress the husband," "aid him in the movements," work towards a "climax . . . moaning, gasping with delight and frenzied, passionate throbbing.") Here was a word picture which might excite the envy of a pornographer. But the words were penned by sexologists, experts who were not pornographers, whose stated purpose was to write "a little book for the sole purpose of helping that large group of married people who do not understand the greatest part of their married life." Furthermore, cases such as *Walker v. Popenoe* had squarely held that the Government had no business stopping such books when they were "sincere," "truthful," and "educational." Attempting to apply these criteria produced a number of difficult if not arbitrary distinctions.

Another class of books, photography studies featuring nude figures, produced frequent censorship problems. Here the Postal criteria for obsceneness were less flexible. For example, In 1955 a Philadelphia firm imported a small shipment of *Art International*, an expensive ($12) foreign book of photographs by internationally-known photographers, to be offered for sale through professional photo magazines. The book cleared Customs without incident. But Philadelphia postal officials warned the importers not to try to sell it by mail. Faced with real economic loss, which they ultimately suffered, the importers appealed to the General Counsel, who first refused an advisory ruling in advance of an actual case of mailing and then ruled against the book, observing that "This office has consistently held that photographic nudes are non-mailable." The importers asked: why ban our book, containing (as it unquestionably did) the work of the best-known professionals here and abroad, when Customs had cleared it and when so many other model studies were not only advertised for distribution through the mails in photography magazines such as *U.S. Camera,* but were also sold over the counter without incident in bookstores all over the country. The only answer was the General Counsel's cryptic statement, "The photographic nudes in this book are indecent according to the moral standards of the nation and therefore must be regarded as non-mailable."

A volume of recognized standing called *Anthropometry and Anatomy for Artists,* published in London, was cleared for importation by the Bureau of Customs in 1953, but in 1954 the Post Office banned it, even for sale to a limited audience. Peter Gowland's *How to Photograph Women* was banned, and the ruling was upheld even after the publishers journeyed to Washington to argue with the Solicitor. *Skin Divers Manual* was declared obscene because it contained pictures of several female divers "with breasts exposed." Photography magazines which featured anything more than a few pages of nude photography were regularly banned when referred from the field. Exceptions were made only for magazines like *U.S.*

Camera, which sandwiched a few figure studies amongst otherwise unobjectionable matter.

On advice of the magazine's printer, an advance copy of one issue of the magazine *Natural History* was sent to the New York Post Office for clearance because the cover depicted (in the words of the publisher) "a Waiwai Indian girl with the upper part of her body exposed." The New York Postmaster referred the magazine to Washington. Fearful about adverse publicity, the magazine's editors quickly produced a substitute cover to meet their mailing deadline. It was well that they did. Washington ruled that the Waiwai girl, when portrayed as she lived, was non-mailable.

Indeed, the Post Office's rigid policing of nudity in photographs has caused at least one large film developing concern, Eastman Kodak, to set up a sort of private censorship operation of material sent to it for processing. This company has taken the position, perhaps with good legal reasons, that it is just as much bound by the laws prohibiting the mailing of obscene pictures as is any other citizen or concern, even when the pictures belong to someone else. The company's criteria, expressed in 1949, appear to be the same today. ". . . we cannot legally deliver by any method pictures (a) which depict the pubic area of the nude body, either male or female, in such fashion that such area is clearly discernible, or (b) which, even though not completely in the nude, by posture, gesture, or otherwise, in our judgment are such as to incite, especially in the minds of young people, immoral thoughts or deeds." At least until a judicial decision in 1956 to the contrary, the company simply refused to return any developed film it thought obscene under these criteria. This was private censorship foisted on photographers by the government, for the Eastman Company stated that their policy was adopted after consultation with Washington.

From genuine art photographs of nudes to scantily clothed models who disport in the "cheesecake" or "girlie" magazines may be a step in either direction on the scale of indecency or libidinous impact. Surely no discussion is needed to document the extent to which the pages of many of these publications are blatant, banal appeals to prurience; and it is a commonplace that many sober observers of our society have deplored the cultural trends reflected by the steady increase in distribution of these magazines and the increasing audacity of the publishers.

Such magazines made up a large share of the material which came across the Solicitor's desk for an obscenity ruling in the period 1946–56. It is impossible to articulate criteria which have been used to judge them except in terms of the coverage of clothing worn, the pose of the models and over-all impression of the degree of indecency of the publication, including its advertising. Censorship cases include most of the titles which were in common circulation in the cigar stores, though it would appear that few if any of those censored depended on the mails for much of their circulation.

Beginning around 1954 the Post Office was contronted with a type of "girlie" magazine featuring a good deal of nudity and "raciness" in the illustrations and textual matter, which included bawdy stories by such authors as Erskine Caldwell, Balzac, Rabelais, or others whose stories, for one reason or another, can be reprinted at no real cost to the magazine publisher. *Playboy,* now known nationally (and a good deal "cleaner" than it was originally) was the first. Its circulation rose to the million mark quickly. Imitators of the same style were such magazines as *Rogue, Satan, Nugget, Dude, Gent, Escapade* and *Gem,* to name only some. Nearly all were found to be non-mailable. In some instances, notably *Playboy,* the publisher, planning to build up a subscription market, successfully frustrated the ban by attacking the legality of the procedures used to impose it. And, if we follow the traditional theory of the law, the key issue was whether these magazines, which now sell widely and usually with impunity throughout the country, violated the "community standard." But the Post Office, right or wrong, never equivocated: the magazines were continuously banned through the period now under survey.

Humor, more or less prurient or bawdy, also provoked a significant body of administrative decisions on non-mailability during this period. An *Esquire* cartoon depicted a buxom blond in bed being served breakfast by a man and exclaiming, "Louis, you're a Goddam jewel." The magazine was threatened with a non-mailable ruling for printing this tidbit, but was cleared after a conference and acceptance of a warning. *Army Fun,* apparently a common newsstore item, was banned from time to time. Of the marked items in one banned issue, reasonably representative was a cartoon of a girl in a bathtub holding a baseball and warning two boys and a man, also present, "That's the sixth time, wise guy—next time get it yourself." Quite a number of college humor magazines were banned; again the objection was the massing of risque jokes, often complemented by a few "cheesecake" pictures.

Scandal magazines posed an increasing number of problems in this postwar decade. *Confidential* magazine grew so fast that in 1955, a few years after the first issue appeared, it had a circulation of about 4,500,000, with about 50,000 copies going through the mail to subscribers. Purporting to delve into the private lives of public figures, particularly Hollywood people, the magazine aroused storms of protest. "A cat-o'nine-tails" is needed to "penetrate the elephant hide of these lice [the scandal publishers]" wrote a well-known movie columnist in 1955, mixing her metaphors as she gnashed her teeth. "I am going to Washington to persuade the government to 'ban' transportation of these 'sin-and-sex expose magazines,'" declared Hollywood Attorney Jerry Geisler. The extraordinary popularity of *Confidential* was viewed with dismay by many journalists, who feared its impact in other publishing fields, and by citizens, who deplored the phenomenon on general principles.

The Post Office found an issue of *Confidential* obscene in August, 1955, on the basis of the following passages and headings:

Named . . . The Cutie Who Split up the [family of a Hollywood actor].

Nude Body Found in the Apartment of [an actor's] Daughter.

S*H*H; Have you heard the latest about [an entertainer]? What is it [he has] got that the girls go for? Ask that sexy redhead from "Phoenix City" or read it here.

Why [a celebrity] became an Ex-ambassador. [He] has been known as a bottom man for years, but he made his fatal mistake when he switched to bosoms.

The Wild Party That Almost Landed [an actor] in the Coop.

Caught . . . [Actor] in [actress'] Boudoir—[He] knew he shouldn't have been with [Her].

[Actress] wearing only socks when [an actor] walked in.

Juan Peron and his First Teen-age Mistress.

Rave, an imitator of *Confidential,* was found non-mailable in 1954. Marked illustrations included a picture of girl lying down with legs partly drawn up, skirt up to about her thighs, a low-cut blouse, and a picture of woman with transparent covering over her breasts. Marked passages included, "The typical $20 lovely lives in West Hollywood, probably on Havenhurst or North Harper. She'll make anywhere from three to seven calls a night and averages about $500 a week" (back cover) and "In this Issue . . . The Higher the Queerer . . . Pointing out that some of England's noblest family trees bear rotten apples—and asking why these juicy fruits prefer Boy Scouts to gorgeous women?"

Did these magazines, during the period of their great popularity, violate that amorphous aphorism, the "community standard"? Or were the Postal censors attempting to make us more "moral" than we really are? In later years the scandal magazines seemed to fizzle. The public, perhaps, grew bored. And enemies of the magazines found a better legal reprisal—and perhaps one more appropriate for judging their legality—in law suits for defamation and violation of privacy.

There was, and still is, one other important area of Postal anti-obscenity law enforcement: control, via the mail-block power, of mail-order distributors.

As has already been stressed, commercial exploitation of "art photos," pictures of "girl wrestlers," "bizarre pictures," and "stag movies" had become a fact of life in America by 1950. First-class mail became the major vehicle of distribution of advertisements and wares in this multi-million dollar traffic.

The history of one particular trafficker in mail-order pictures, a history unearthed in detail by the Kefauver Committee, supplies a graphic illustration of what has happened a hundred times over in New York, on the west coast and elsewhere.

In 1948 Dorothy Tager and her husband were in the photography business in southern California. He ran the studio; she, the office—under instructions to keep out of the studio. But one day she peeked and learned that her husband was photographing nudes and selling the pictures profitably. Far from expressing outrage, she suggested that the business concentrate on this and use the mails to do so. In fact, she quickly assumed leadership of the enterprise. Post office boxes in various California towns were rented under different names. A mailing list of some 20,000 names was purchased from another dealer; advertisements were sent by sealed first class mail, dumped in different mail boxes to avoid suspicion. Ten pictures for $2.00 was Mrs. Tager's offer. Within less than two weeks, the return orders totaled $4,000. These were quickly filled, and the names of the buyers were carefully filed away; then the rented mail boxes were closed out, and the first mailing operation abandoned before Postal inspectors might become aware of its existence.

But not the business. It was just beginning. New models were hired (including, according to Mrs. Tager, college co-eds), new pictures taken, new lists purchased, new post office boxes rented. This time the gross orders after ten days totaled $7,000. Again, the business was closed down quickly. The effort to reach a potential audience was then expanded in another significant way. Using various trade names, advertisements were put in various "girlie" magazines. They were prepared by a commercial agent. The rate was about $365 for a column; apparently it proved to be a profitable investment, though it surely increased the risk of potential Post Office interference. These magazine advertisements purportedly dealt in the sale of "pinups." But customers who answered were offered "nudes" in a more explicit follow-up, and this proved to be a useful way to build up the file of known customers.

Because both her advertisements and her wares went by first class mail, in plain sealed envelopes sent from different post offices at different times, the inspectors were powerless to intercept them en route. However, once they could get samples of the pictures Mrs. Tager was mailing, they did have recourse to two weapons: (1) they could refer these items to the District Attorney, suggesting criminal prosecution; (2) under the so-called "mail block" statutes, they could ask the department to issue an order impounding all incoming mail sent to the post office box which the Tager business had rented to solicit orders for the item in question.

The trouble with the first course was that federal prosecutions were costly, time consuming, and hard to win. At least, U.S. prosecutors in southern California were reluctant to attempt them in this kind of "borderline" case. A few experiences had seemed to indicate that jurors would not convict. In fact, the Tagers were never indicted.

Neither was the Post Office's "mail block" a very effective weapon. By the time inspectors were able to get a copy of Mrs.

Tager's latest product and refer it to Washington for an official order to stop all incoming mail addressed to "Marian Marsh," Box 100, Santa Barbara (one of Mrs. Tager's many trade names), that particular operation would have paid its huge dividends, and Mrs. Tager was quite ready to abandon it, leaving it to the local post office to impound a piddling remainder of incoming mail to return to the senders. As a Post Office lawyer put it, "She made monkeys out of us."

Indeed, within two years Mrs. Tager had rented over two hundred post office boxes, and her business had branched out to include movies "for men," courses on "art photography," and "wolf pac" card decks (for which the federal amusement tax was duly paid). Supplementary central office spaces were rented. The secretarial force to handle the mailings grew from one to three to fifteen: good pay, no racial discrimination in hiring girls, and good hours (9 to 4:30), boasted Dorothy Tager, who often worked into the wee hours of the night, filing away names for her ever-growing list of "regular customers."

These included, she insisted, men from all sorts of professions: doctors, a "priest," a "politician," a "rich man" who asked that his mail be sent to his gardener's house, and a self-styled "bank president" who sent special lingerie for the models to wear while posing and stopped payment on his checks when he was not satisfied.

Dorothy Tager refused, so she says, the orders of suspected adolescents or "perverts." She constantly criticized her "competitors"—an ever-increasing number—for lowering the standards of the profession by catering to "abnormal" tastes and disseminating "smoking room" stuff. However, she joined with some twenty-six other "operators" to form a trade group, the "Associated Photographers of Strippers and Nudes," dues $25 initially, thereafter $10 per month; objectives: employment of a lawyer, pooling of information on current Postal enforcement techniques and defense stratagems, and maintenance of minimum professional standards. More pornographic materials were, by mutual consent, to be avoided; thus, in a sense, "unfair competitive practices" were regulated.

Originally the attorney was paid from association dues and was more or less simply a clearinghouse of information; but soon he became more active—almost a house counsel, it would seem, fencing away with the Post Office and frequently prevailing or at least delaying the issuance of mail blocks.

What was done by Dorothy Tager was being done, less spectacularly, by others. Mail-order businesses in nudes have mushroomed in southern California. There were, according to Mrs. Tager, about 225 "operators" in 1954, and there may be many more today. New York was another big business area. Sam Roth, the self-styled "American Rabelais," who had long skirmished with the Post Office, ran dozens of enterprises, including the sale of erotic books. He built up a mailing list of 400,000 names and was grossing many thousands each year.

Most of the many operators dealt in pictorial matter—cheesecake items, unimaginative, inartistic pictures of girls unadorned. They skirted the boundaries of the business of producing more outright pornography; apparently most of these operators held that sort of stuff to be contraband, but "mere nudity" was considered "legitimate." The volume of this trash was immense. Whether or not individual pictures were bad, judged abstractly, peddling them involved an open appeal to the customer to enjoy pictorial aphrodisiacs. "Action Movies!" ran the blurb of "Filmfare," a Los Angeles outfit dealing in movies. Take your pick of many: "Boudoir Secrets" (for $8) starring a "ready redhead . . . And when she gets on that couch [in the nude—so the accompanying picture indicates] her imagination runs rampant. So will yours!" In most cases the product probably fell below the promise. But the very fact that the business grew more and more competitive seems to have driven some operators into a line of wares increasingly erotic.

Some operators seem to have aimed at a more specialized audience. Consider the work of Irving Klaw. It sold (until Klaw was finally put out of business by being put into jail by the New York State courts) for a pretty penny—$8 for a booklet of thirty pages or so of pictorial "comic-book" style stories. Indeed, Klaw's efforts were said to have grossed $1,500,000. A Columbia University scholar who studied his booklets describes some of them as follows:

> In these fantasias hapless heroines, I briefly noted, are tied up, strapped down, gagged, masked, thrown to animals, used as ponies, stretched by pulleys, squeezed under weights, rubbed on sandpaper, given electric shocks (the last two in intimate portions of the anatomy), seated on spokes, slid in chutes, fried over fires, slapped

in stocks, choked, currycombed, wrestled with, throttled, sat on, bent double, suspended over boiling cauldrons, tied astride hot steam pipes, whirled centrifugally, hung up by the hair, used as clappers for a giant bell, made to ride wild horses, secured under a low diving-board to be regularly dunked in a pool, and whipped or paddled as a matter of course every few pictures.

However one may feel about legal suppression, via censorship or criminal sanctions, of the wholesale dissemination of the "art" of Mrs. Tager or the "literature" of Mr. Roth, the "fun" of Filmfare or the "fantasy" of Mr. Klaw, there is, to repeat, food for thought in the fact that so many Americans seemed so willing to spend so much for this material. Postal inspectors put the mail business figure at over $100,000,000 in 1955; estimates before the Kefauver Committee put it at even a higher figure, and so it is today. There is room for skepticism over these high figures; but, as a people, we have been remunerating these panderers royally, even while we reviled them openly.

Another difficult problem was posed by the appearance of magazines put out for homosexuals. The General Counsel's files reflect that from time to time magazines featuring pictorial male nudity (e.g., as "art" studies or as illustrations to a "body and health" pamphlet) have been banned on the grounds both of indecency and because they are deemed to be an incitement to homosexuality.

In 1954 the Post Office banned an issue of *One,* a publication which openly proclaimed itself to be "The Homosexual Magazine" and attempted to circulate by mail subscription. According to its editors, *One* was a non-profit corporation formed "to publish a magazine dealing primarily with homosexuality from the scientific, historical and critical point of view . . . to sponsor educational programs, lectures and concerts for the aid and benefit of social variants and to promote among the general public an interest, knowledge and understanding of the problems of variation . . . to sponsor research and promote the integration into society of such persons whose behavior and inclinations vary from the current moral and social standards."

Featured in *One* were articles and fiction, all related to the subject of homosexuality, as well as occasional advertisements for similar foreign publications. The issue condemned by the Post Office was deemed obscene principally because of an admittedly "off color," satirical poem, and a story about two lesbians. The Court of Appeals for the Ninth Circuit, upholding this ban, characterized the story as "cheap pornography" and the poem as "dirty, vulgar and offensive." While certainly the subject matter of these stories—and, indeed, the whole idea of *One*—may arouse an emotionally charged reaction, it does seem, in the light of what followed, that the court's characterization was exaggerated. *One*'s counsel petitioned the Supreme Court for certiorari, urging the Court to read and judge the alleged vulgarity or indecency of the issue for itself. As we shall see, the Supreme Court, in 1957, in a per curiam order, did unanimously reverse the Court of Appeals. The Court wrote no opinion, and we are left in the dark as to the precise grounds for the ruling; presumably, however, the Court simply disagreed with the finding that *One* was obscene. Obviously cases like this presented new and serious difficulty to Postal censorship.

The great mass of material described supplied grist for the mail censorship mill in a decade just past; the cases and categories depicted portray a range of problems which constantly confront censorship. Speaking candidly, Postal lawyers declared that judging it day in and day out was a frustrating business.

4. A DESCRIPTION OF SOME MATERIALS WHICH THE CUSTOMS CENSORS HAVE CENSORED

THE JOB OF CUSTOMS was no less difficult. But in results the two operations reflected important variances in attitude and scope.

Like the Post Office, Customs has kept no meaningful statistics. Perhaps, therefore, the most meaningful approach is to give some examples of representative cases and problems.

The contraband of the period 1946–56 was made up principally (95 per cent would be a conservative estimate) of nudist publications, "art" books featuring photos of nude females, entertainment magazines of the "girlie" variety, paperbound books published primarily in France and Mexico by certain commercial enterprises, small collections of loose photographs, and commercial movies. Infrequent categories of obscene articles are rare and erotic books, paintings, gadgets and statuary, silk prints, and pictures on articles of apparel.

During the period 1946–56 the inflow of nudist and "art" publications, usually magazines or picture booklets, ranged from lots of several thousand (rare) to small shipments of one to ten (common). These importations were usually addressed to private individuals in all parts of the country rather than commercial dealers; most came through some large central port like New York. The materials originated, for the most part, in Scandinavian countries, Holland, Germany, and France. The Bureau has doubted the authenticity of many as genuine publications of genuine nudist groups or sincere efforts at photographic art. No one knows how many of these publications, all told, appeared at our national borders, let alone how many were stopped, in any given year. Customs officials at the port of New York estimated (unofficially) that 3,106 magazines were confiscated in 1955 and 2,874 during the first eight months of 1956. In the port of Seattle, where normally traffic in such things is light, several commercial shipments running into the thousands were stopped in 1955. In general, Bureau officials believed, as of 1956, that importation—or attempted importation—was increasing. It still is.

The obscenity—or alleged obscenity—of these materials derived, of course, from the fact that they consisted of pictures of people, mostly girls, without clothes and usually without any retouching. But at least since the *Parmelee* case in 1940, the Bureau, unlike the Post Office, rejected the view that *all* such photos were obscene. Theoretically, of course, the standard was the "community's" notion of decency; increasingly the Bureau construed that notion to be more liberal, and the decision to confiscate depended on such factors as artistic quality of the pictures, as it appeared to non-professional viewers; the pose—its "suggestiveness"; mixing of the sexes; retouching or concealment of the genital areas; and—perhaps strange to say, if libidinous impact is to be the test—the attractiveness of the figure photographed (the prettier the models, the less likelihood of an obscene creation). It mattered not whether these magazines were imported privately or commercially; in either case they were judged strictly on their merits, and thus in a sense in the abstract, by the criteria noted above—criteria which are hard to articulate, let alone apply.

Bureau officials openly admitted in 1956 that they could not agree among themselves about how to apply the criteria in many cases. Many officials at the ports, given a free hand, would simply have confiscated all nudist magazines, for they believed, probably with good reason, that in most cases the motivation to import these reflected a prurient interest in the pictures. But centralization of decision-making in Washington meant that all cases except those involving materials "unquestionably" obscene (and only rarely would a nudist publication be in such a class), the magazine must be referred to Washington. The result was that a line was drawn and redrawn over the years; it was drawn in Washington, and officials in the field were hard pressed to describe it, as well as irritated by what they thought was indiscriminate discrimination between nudist materials of similar nature. "Censorship here has been loose as a goose," declared one San Francisco official in 1955.

French and Spanish-language entertainment magazines featuring pictures of nude or semi-nude girls seem to have made up another fairly big category of obscene publications seized at the ports in this period, 1946–56. The text of these is foreign, but the pictorial matter which made up the bulk of the format seldom needed textual explanation—girls displaying themselves in strip sequences or disporting themselves in the country, the shower, the seashore, or nightclubs—sometimes in mixed company. Often these pictures were arranged in some sort of story sequence. Frequently, the quality of photography seemed superior to the American counterpart. Almost invariably, when magazines with many pictures of this kind were found, they were confiscated on the theory that they were too much for average Americans to take.

The books which the Bureau seized during this period constituted a significant number of the total number of seizures made in a year. No one in the Bureau knows—or seems willing to estimate—how many volumes were seized yearly. A New York estimate, which is probably far too low (more books are seized in New York than in other ports) indicated that 358 different volumes were confiscated in 1954, 298 in 1955, and 2,911 in the first eight months of 1956, including one seizure of a commercial importation of 2,500. Most of these condemned importations were small shipments of one to five books.

Since Bureau policy permits no divulging of the titles of these books except where the titles have been disclosed through other sources, analysis of the precise nature of this printed obscenity is difficult. Titles range widely; indeed, speculating, the total list of confiscations over a decade would probably include almost all of the world's notorious erotic literature. Included among seized books, for example, have been very rare and often very expensive items such as unusual editions of Ovid and oriental "pillow" books and "marriage manuals." Occasionally, too, volumes of such alleged "classics" as the *Decameron* were seized, not for the text, but because the illustrations were deemed too erotic. Cases like these were not at all run of the mill, and they usually presented very special problems for Mr. Cairns.

The bulk of the books banned by Customs was made up of inexpensive paperbounds. The overwhelming majority came from a few notorious publishers in France and Mexico. The Paris publishers of Henry Miller's works have shipped many, many volumes to this country, and countless copies of these have been destroyed by the government, as have paperbound editions of Nabokov (though *Lolita* was later cleared), Jean Genet, Frank Harris, D. H. Lawrence, Cleland's *Fanny Hill,* and De Sade. But these authors and a few others who appear to have standing in some circles as avant-gardes probably complete the list of writers with any reasonable claim to literary standing whose works have been openly published abroad, shipped here in quantity, and seized.

Other books published by the Paris publishers of Miller, Harris, *et al.,* and their counterparts—that is, publishers who aim at an English-speaking audience—would appear to have little if any literary standing anywhere among any people. Their *raison d'être* would seem to be the depiction of sexual activity for readers who want just that.

Foreign movies presented an unusual problem. Nearly all films designed for exhibition in American theatres have come in via New York. All are reviewed there very carefully, and this may sometimes include news films and technical or documentary matter. Customs officers have been frank to admit that criteria for censorship have been *sui generis:* Figuratively speaking, the reported court cases which deal with books or magazines were thrown to the winds, and rigid mechanical criteria applied.

In the period 1946–56, the theory was that overt nakedness on the screen in almost any situation (except in blurred or very abbreviated sequences or "documentary" or "scientific" films of native tribes) would be offensive to community standards. In the implementation of this, standard films really were judged sequence by sequence, not "as a whole"; and despite the Bureau's tolerance of pictures of unclothed people in other media—e.g., "art" and "nudist" magazines—there was virtually none in the movies. Any episode or scene featuring nudity or partial nudity in any form, despite the consummate artistry of the whole work or its non-erotic impact when viewed in its entirety, has been enough to ban the entire film.

Perhaps the best way to describe what the Bureau did is to give some specific case histories drawn from the records. When the movie *Adorable Creatures* was imported for commercial exhibition here, a Customs film reviewer in New York studied it and wrote this memo:

Picture begins with a wedding; as the couple gets into the car, the bridegroom tells the bride she is the only one he has ever loved. A voice in the background reminds him of his past romantic escapades, and the balance of the picture flashes back to his life before marriage. His first conquest was a married woman with two children. His next love was a young woman with whom he went on a trip to the mountains to ski. He was hurt in an accident, and the girl continued skiing without him. She met a former girl friend and they compared notes as to their present romantic interests. The girl friend is there with the father of a former beau; she says it's more lucrative that way. They each exaggerate about the merits of their respective male companions. They finally exchange partners and each of the girls moves into the hotel suite of the other man. The last of his romantic interludes is with a much older woman. She was enchanted with him immediately and asked a mutual friend to introduce them. Her secretary also falls in love with him, and tells the young man her employer's age; in jealous desperation the older woman has her secretary arrested for theft. The hero finally marries the girl next door.

Objections: Reel 2, bedroom scene, man and woman on bed, man opens buttons on woman's dress. Reel 7, girl in bathtub, breasts exposed. Man enters her room, she asks him to get her robe, she rises in tub (girl seen nude in silhouette). Reel 8, woman in sheer negligee, man embraces her and fondles her breast.

The Deputy Collector (probably after viewing the parts deemed objectionable by the reviewer) recommended seizure; Washington (on the basis of a letter from him) concurred; but the importer, after making the appropriate request, was given permission to bring the film in after the objectionable scenes had been cut.

A more serious fate befell a French film entitled *Touchez bas au Crispi.* After a one-paragraph statement of the plot, the reviewer noted these objections:

Reel 1: Man puts his hand on the breast of a girl. Chorus girls dancing with minimum cover on their breasts. Life sized photo on wall of manager's office showing naked girls. This appears off and on in this reel and in reel 4. Photos of girls without any cover with pubic hair (various scenes, reel 4). Language used in film is often rough: such typical words as "merde" etc., also subtle remarks like the man, taking the girl into his arms, looks down her décolleté and says: "I am happy to see my little friends in good shape." The girl answers: "It has been a long time that you have not visited them."

Here, apparently, some of the objectionable matter (e.g., scenes in the manager's office) could not be cut without chopping the entire film too much. Here, too, the reviewer's objections (accepted by his New York superiors) went beyond the exhibition of nudity; the words spoken, though in French, were deemed objectionable. Informed of these criticisms, the importer himself decided against further efforts to have the film exhibited here, and, with the Bureau's permission, exported it back to France. One might add that the film was of the gangster type; the scenes, while perhaps bold for American audiences, may well have had some basis in reality.

The reviewer's objections to *The Sheep Has Five Legs,* were:

Reel 2: scenes in Beauty Salon—women—naked breasts *see entire reel.* Reel 3: Man draws on a window a picture of a woman's head with large breasts, with witty comments. Reel 6: Native girl, naked, waist up with flowers partly hiding her breasts.

The film was released after total or partial deletions were made of the allegedly objectionable material.

Here are the objections to *Wages of Fear* (which won a "Grand Prix" at Cannes):

Reel 1 (and 2) small ten year old boy walks around naked waist down. Girl scraping floor—her breasts almost exposed. Reel 3: naked colored woman taking shower. Reel 4: man in very scant underwear walks, putting his pants on. First impression is that he is naked. Reel 5: natives practically naked stand watching oil fire.

The objectionable sequences here were abbreviated. Interestingly, in this country, among private groups, the film aroused opposition not on grounds of obsceneness, but because it was allegedly anti-American. In response to this criticism the distributors made very substantial cuts of those parts of the film which depicted the United States oil company in an unfavorable light.

These cases are typical of hundreds. But Customs censorship, which in a real sense is a limited form of national movie censorship, has been confined almost entirely to the depiction of nudity or excessive physical familiarities between the sexes. There are no tabus, as in Hollywood's voluntary censorship code, against making crime pay or against narcotics or even against bawdy bedroom farces, sacrilege, illegitimacy, or the depiction of promiscuity in a light vein, so long as the camera avoids scenes of sexual activity. The "theme" and the "morality" of the plot have seldom if ever provided the basis for censorship. Such celebrated movies as *I Am A Camera* and *The Miracle,* which provoked great controversy and instances of state or local censorship or vigorous condemnation by church groups, have passed Customs with, at most, only temporary delay. The case of the movie called *The Bed* further illustrates this point. Of this film, the reviewer had this to say:

> Film is made of four separate stories called "Le Billet de Logement", "Le Divorce", "Riviera Express", and "Le Lit de la Pompadour". Four men in a car are stranded for two hours at a small railroad station. Each of them tells his most unforgettable experience. The first one is about a captain in the British Army, who just after invasion spends a night at the house of a French woman. She is pregnant, and as soon as he is ready to go to bed, she starts to have pains, so he spends the entire night helping her in childbirth. Everything ends happily, as she gives birth to a boy. (Scenes very realistic).
>
> Second story: A rich man, in order to get a divorce from his famous actress wife, hires, through a special New York agency, a good-looking girl, who is to spend the night with him in a big hotel. They have to pretend being in love so that all the personnel of the hotel could be witnesses to the adultery (very suggestive conversations between the two and others involved in the story). The girl and the man finally fall in love and spend the night together and later get married.
>
> Third story: A truckdriver who meets a young girl on the road, helps her change a tire. She later invites him to her house, where after a dinner he goes to bed. She comes in, gets into bed with him. Giving her space on the bed, the man falls on the floor, and wakes up to see that all this was just a dream.
>
> Fourth story: About the bed of Madame de Pompadour, which is sent by the President of the French Assembly to his mistress,

but which is by mistake delivered next door, to another girl. From then on the story shows how this bed, . . . [brings] "luck" to the girl, she becomes mistress to many men, and becomes the sensation of Paris. Bed scenes play the major role. All four stories are very suggestive (speech and action), although no nudity is shown, the second story in particular, and especially because action takes place in New York City, where according to the story, divorces are made simple, and special agencies lending "good" girls for the night, accepting $1,000 from the man as guarantee that he will not touch the girl. In this particular case, the man loses his deposit. Film is full of subtle and suggestive remarks.

The reviewer recommended that his superiors see this film. They did, and released it.

In the case of the controversial *La Ronde* (barred by many local censorship agencies in this country), the reviewer recommended that it pass:

Film consists of a series of events called The Round (Merry-Go-Round). Each represents a love affair between two individuals at various times in adult life. Several women are involved. While no nudity is shown, each affair results in what is obviously a sexual result. Stars are Simone Simone and Danielle Darrieux.

The film was released without any censorship.

Not very often has the Bureau prevented entry of a film *in toto* when the importer has earnestly sought to bring it in. One such case involved *Clochemerle,* where the reviewer recommended detention after concluding:

This entire film lampoons the Catholic clergy and borders on the blasphemous. Its subject matter, the latrine, is quite obnoxious and the emphasis on promiscuity is dwelt on to the point of vulgarity.

Apparently the eventual decision in New York was to seize this film, but the importer, on learning its nature, decided not to contest the case and, with Bureau permission, re-exported the film before any final decision could be made. But almost uniformly the rulings finding a film "obscene" were based on the idea that specific portions of it were contraband, and if an importer petitioned for permission to bring the film in after these had been excised, the request was almost always granted. In essence, then, the principal impact of this censorship of "obscene" movies is the chopping out of a few moments of a film simply to prevent American audiences from seeing much, if any, nakedness on the screen.

Movies apart, much of the material censored may well have been obscene beyond cavil under existing legal criteria—even assuming these criteria are ill defined. But the fact that Customs may have been right in most of its judgments, hardly answered all problems. The Bureau exercised, in theory and to an unknown extent in practice, plenary power over the right of American citizens to have access to foreign publications. If the Bureau decided that a work was obscene, then, in theory, no ordinary American citizen was to be allowed to read it.

5. A DOUBLE STANDARD: THE SECRETARY'S DISCRETION TO ADMIT SPECIAL BOOKS TO SPECIAL PEOPLE

THERE WAS ONE WAY whereby an American citizen might be able to read a work which Customs had ruled inadmissible: persuade the Secretary of the Treasury to use the discretion granted him by the Tariff Act of 1930 to admit "classics" or "books of recognized and established literary or scientific merit" when imported "non-commercially." But this discretion proved of little practical benefit to the ordinary citizen. For the Bureau's policy, which had been worked out in the earlier decade, was to discreetly discourage all but the most forceful requests. In order that a work might be released under the Secretary's discretion, it was and has always been necessary to show the special standing of: (1) *the work,* i.e., that it is a "classic," or has "recognized and established" "merit" *in this country,* among persons who the Bureau (through its Washington officials—particularly Mr. Cairns) would recognize as experts in the field encompassed by the work; (2) *the importer,* i.e., that there exist very persuasive reasons why the particular petitioning importer should be allowed to receive the item in question.

The Bureau decided, *ex parte,* whether a book in question enjoyed sufficient recognition to warrant the status needed for discretionary release. And note, too, that one, very important, agency-made qualification: without a "substantial and reputable body of *American* critical opinion indicating . . . meritorious quality" [emphasis added], Mr. Cairns had declared in 1938, the discretion would never be exercised in favor of any book. This isolationist construction hardly seems required by the text of the statute, let alone by the apparent legislative intent. But the Bureau nevertheless adopted it.

The difficulties in deciding whether a book had the required standing are reflected in Customs censorship of *Lady Chatterley's Lover* (the book which Senator Smoot had vowed would only come in over his dead body). In 1928 the Bureau had characterized this book as a "gross exposition of obscenity, filth and lewdness"— the antitheses of a work of merit. From the outset, discretionary releases were summarily refused. In 1931 a book collector made a strong plea, submitting considerable evidence of English acclaim. Replied the Bureau: the book had no standing here as a work of merit. The ruling was followed on many occasions (for many Americans now seemed to want to read this book) until 1933. Then a Philadelphia lawyer petitioned; he appeared to plead book-collecting as his warrant for a special dispensation; he also intimated his willingness to litigate if the Bureau ignored his request. The lawyer got what he wanted; there was no explanation for this reversal of policy. In 1934 there were apparently some further denials of petitions; and there was an exchange of memoranda reflecting full review of the problem in Washington and the conclusion of the Bureau that the "literary merit of this book has *not* been established" [emphasis added]. Yet later that same year a copy of the book was released to a petitioning professor. In 1935 the Bureau again reopened the question of the book's literary merit. "I have satisfied myself," wrote Mr. Cairns, that this is a "work of literary standing in the sense that it is constantly discussed in the best literary journals . . . . [It is] a serious work put forward by an eccentric but indubitable genius." When a Maine Senator wrote on behalf of a constituent, the book was very promptly released, and since then the Bureau has apparently continued to release it, providing the importer showed some special standing. We are, perforce, left in the dark as to what happened in 1935 to supply the "recognition" to *Lady Chatterley* which had been wanting the year before.

The treatment of Henry Miller's *Tropic of Cancer* and *Tropic of Capricorn* and other books also affords an interesting example of the problem of judging literary recognition and merit. These books were denied clearance under the Secretary's discretion because, according to the Bureau, the books were obscene and their merit was still to be "recognized" in this country. This conclusion, which meant in theory that no one should be allowed to read these books, was made *ex parte,* without any sort of official notice to the country at large or to particular importers. Apparently no open effort was undertaken by the Bureau to find out, for example, whether outstanding teachers of modern literature in American universities might agree with George Orwell, who wrote an essay praising one of these books as the decade's best novel, but Orwell's praise was not, in theory, persuasive because, though he wrote in English for any English-speaking reader, he remained an Englishman and thus a foreign critic. In like fashion the views of Ezra Pound on Miller ("an unprintable book that is fit to read") or Aldous Huxley ("a bit terrifying but very well done") were probably more or less irrelevant. The views of domestic critics were what counted.

One is prompted to ask how, except via the illegal activity of smuggling, American critics were going to have the chance to render a verdict if, in fact, the books were totally inadmissible. In any event, Miller's works were smuggled, and there were certainly some domestic "experts" who had praised this author—Edmund Wilson, for example, as well as the chairmen and members of the English departments of a variety of universities.[2]

2. The chairmen of the English departments of Pennsylvania, Harvard, Princeton, Columbia, Yale, Brown, and Cornell universities, and Williams, Dartmouth, and Swarthmore colleges were asked by the authors of this study whether "familiarity with the works of Miller is typically part of the general background of the teacher of modern English." The question was perhaps too vague to warrant much reliance on the answers, but, in summary all appeared to agree that familiarity with Miller is "typical." Miller is not taught as assigned reading matter in formal courses of instruction (except possibly *sub rosa*), but most chairmen stated their belief that his works are discussed and at least mentioned in lectures. Opinions differed very widely as to the extent of Miller's literary merit; many younger teachers were enthusiastic about him, but three or four chairmen observed that if this author were not treated as such a *cause célèbre,* so that it was "fashionable" to be all for him, and if his works were allowed to circulate freely, the free market place (rather than the black market place) of ideas might tend to reduce the high standing he enjoys; on the other hand, others were of the opinion that Miller's works should be

Even conceding the "merit" or "classical" status of a book, the importer could seldom secure it simply by saying: "I want it because the critics praise it." He was required to show some special scholarly or professional need for the work. Over the years the Secretary's discretion permitted museums and research libraries to import what they needed; the Bureau leaned over backward for them. Individuals usually fared less well, although there was no uniform treatment.

Importers were given no formal notice of their right to petition for discretionary release of seized material. There were no published regulations reflecting in any detail the criteria established in the 1930's and used by the Bureau to decide: (a) whether a book was a "classic" or had "established and recognized literary or scientific merit," (b) whether a particular importer had demonstrated sufficient status or justification to obtain release of the work.

Bureau file material on the handling of the several books published in Vienna and written by a Dr. Edward Fuchs on the history of sexual morality reflects the difficulty of judging both these questions. On many occasions various persons attempted to import these works, which, although written in turgid German prose, were well larded with all sorts of illustrations, some extremely erotic (a "disgusting", redundant "parade of obscenity," in the words of a former official). The Bureau's file material shows that respectable opinion can be mustered for the conclusion once avowed by a Bureau official that "these books" are "decidedly of a shady (i.e., pseudo-scientific) character" and therefore unfit for discretionary release. Contrariwise, statements in the files by doctors, sociologists, and librarians (including a former Librarian of Congress) hold that the works are scholarly and the pictures highly relevant and useful to the text. At various times the Bureau seems to have barred the book altogether because of its lack of scientific status. The work was confiscated from the household effects of several obviously literate, Viennese refugees entering this country; it was taken away from many other importers who presented no special scholarly credentials to the Bureau. On the other hand, during the same interval, the book was released as a special scientific work to a psychiatrist, a law professor

studied in courses dealing with contemporary literature, and they flatly asserted that the only reason these books are not assigned is that the circulation of his books is legally restricted.

(whose field was domestic relations), a Ph.D. student of art history, and a lawyer whose only avowed interest in the work was biblio-philia and intellectual curiosity—but who threatened showdown litigation if he did not get what he wanted.

The existence of the authority to release books in special cases was not well known, nor was it ever the policy of the Bureau to make the general public aware of its existence. The discretion itself was exercised inconsistently from work to work, and, indeed, from person to person with reference to the same work. At least until the now-famous case involving Dr. Kinsey's importation, in 1957, the average citizen could expect little relief in the statutory dispensation of the Tariff Act of 1930.

6. ANOTHER DOUBLE STANDARD: FEDERAL CRIMINAL ENFORCEMENT CONTRASTED WITH FEDERAL CENSORSHIP

THE FEDERAL STATUTES provide that if obscene materials are in fact "knowingly" mailed or imported, then the mailer or importer shall be liable for criminal prosecution. From 1946 to 1956 there were no prosecutions for importing obscenity; there were only between 150 and 250 arrests per year for violations of the Postal laws, of which over 90 per cent resulted in convictions with pleas of guilty by the defendants in the vast majority of cases.[3]

The biggest category of materials forming the basis of prosecution were private letters relating erotic or shocking ideas or experiences. Where such letters passed between willing communicants, U.S. prosecutors seldom did anything about the "violation" of the law, unless these exchanges reached the dimension of a "sex club" with many participants. In other situations, however, these private letters were not willingly received; the recipient was embarrassed, perhaps subjected to even greater emotional dislocation. These cases may be classified as private "assaults"; typical examples include a first-class mailing of a sordid epistle from a husband to an estranged wife, letters from unrequited lovers, or filthy anonymous letters to people in public life or in the "news," or the attempted

3. The following discussion centers about the period 1946–56; however, with the changes noted in Part IV, it is equally applicable to the present.

dissemination of homemade photos or movies depicting sex acts. Frequently these creations were the product of unbalanced minds, but the Postal Service has assumed that it cannot afford to ignore them; for sometimes the authors of these works might follow with physical violence; frequently they would continue to "assault" by mail until incapacitated. Accordingly, a good deal of time was spent in tracking down these violators; if the case seemed serious, it went to the U.S. Attorney, who then decided whether to go further. When a prosecution was brought, psychiatric examination was frequently ordered by the federal judge.

Two recent Los Angeles cases will illustrate the range of problems confronting prosecutors who attempt to control private exchanges. An Air Force officer engaged in correspondence with the wife of another officer. At the trial the issue of the obscenity of the correspondence was not contested, and although the woman was acquitted (because of a problem of unlawful obtaining of evidence), the officer was convicted by the court sitting without a jury. He was sentenced to probation on condition of psychiatric treatment. Here was a non-commercial, consensual use of the mails by two willing adult participants. One might immediately question whether the coercive power of federal criminal prosecution should be brought to bear on these maladjusted persons—whether the matter is one for federal concern or whether corrective action in this type of case comes, more appropriately, from the local authorities. The federal prosecution was brought because the prosecuting authorities concluded that the actions described in the letters and pictures (cited by the U.S. Attorney as "stomach revolting" in nature) indicated that both defendants were potential menaces to society; the defendant had once engaged in similar correspondence with another woman, and he possessed a vast collection of "hard-core material"; the woman defendant had five children living with her, and she had kept the correspondence, which had lasted over a five-year period, in her own home.

In another non-commercial case, three "sex club" members were given sentences ranging to ten years imprisonment. Their correspondence reflected commission of sexual acts which, themselves, may have been criminal in nature. One picture (which was a subject of the prosecution) showed one defendant performing sexual acts with the ten-year-old daughter of another defendant. The father,

who had been on probation for a prior offense, had his probation revoked and was remanded for observation. Again the gist of the
wrong here was the sexual misconduct of a few persons; their use
of the mails was more or less incidental to the wrong committed.
The justification for federal regulation of moral standards and
obscenity distribution rests primarily on the inability of the states,
through local enforcement, to combat out-of-state commercial distributors who use the mails to circulate. Thus, it may be questionable whether the Comstock Act should, as a matter of policy, be
used to put federal prosecutors in the business of dealing with
maladjusted persons who engage in gross sexual misbehavior, but
whose use of the mails is not at all the gravamen of the wrong
done and bears little relation to the need for corrective action.

"Non-commercial" cases like those described appear to have
constituted at least one-half of all the federal prosecutions brought
over the past years; in the great majority of those cases, the defendants have pleaded guilty; in the great majority the problem was
what to do with apparently irrational and possibly dangerously
maladjusted persons; in many the federal prosecutors were doing
what could be done—and perhaps should be done—by local
authorities.

Thus, the "non-commercial" cases were a problem quite apart
from federal criminal enforcement directed at "commercial" distribution of alleged obscenity. The "non-commercial" cases probably had no real deterrent impact on those who distributed erotica
for profit. It thus is misleading to quote the gross federal statistics
on arrests and prosecutions as indications of the extent to which the
United States government was prosecuting mail-order commercial
exploiters of obscene material.

In the absence of statistical breakdowns and in the absence of
centralized decision-making, generalizations about whom and what
kinds of commercial traffic the prosecutors have attempted to suppress must rest on treacherous ground. Only a few important areas
need to be considered here—the big cities, particularly New York,
Chicago, and Los Angeles, for the major commercial mail-order
operators did their business there; and, until 1958, all offenders
had to be prosecuted in their home communities if they were to
be prosecuted at all. Since 1885 the courts had interpreted the
Comstock Act to require prosecutions only in the place from which

the mailings had come. Very recently this rule of venue was changed by Congress. The nature of this change is discussed later, but the experience up to 1958 indicates that the government confined its attention to a relative handful of serious commercial offenders.

U.S. Attorneys seldom prosecuted unless they themselves were satisfied that the violation was flagrant enough to make conviction by a jury a relative certainty. Thus where the case involved so-called hard-core, pornographic pictorial matter distributed commercially —and these cases are apparently not too prevalent—an indictment would follow. Where the case involved simply a mailing operation in pictures of nude females—nudity, but nothing more—the pattern varied. Dorothy Tager and many others escaped criminal proceedings, and postal inspectors familiar with the Los Angeles area frankly told the Kefauver Committee that it would be hard to win a conviction if the attempt were made. A former U.S. Attorney in another district reported that grand jurors only laughed at some of the items (in the form of nudist materials) presented for indictment.

The celebrated case of Samuel Roth, which started in 1955, typifies the difficulties. Roth mailed: (1) a magazine called *Good Times,* which contained nudes, mail-order advertising for other purportedly obscene matter, and some quite erotic stories; (2) a magazine called *Nus,* which was, indeed, made up of nudes; (3) "Strip Sets," a series of photos portraying complete disrobing and other photos of nudes; (4) a book called *American Aphrodite;* and (5) advertisements for these things which were sent (via mailing lists) to persons all over the country. Indeed, the government had many witnesses—including midwestern housewives and the head of a home for problem children—to show the indiscriminate extensiveness of Roth's solicitation.

Roth was indicted on many counts for these mailings. A trial lasting many days ensued. The defense presented a psychologist who insisted the materials would have no effect on most people. The U.S. Attorney who tried the case felt differently. He was particularly anxious to secure convictions for the pictorial matter, hoping, in his own words, to "set a standard," to "draw a line" indicating and "warning" that materials of this kind would henceforth be treated as criminal contraband by federal prosecutors and courts in the New York area. "There are many people who are

watching . . .," he told the jury: "This stuff will sell. [Other distribu-
tors] are going to be interested to see whether you are going to
make it legal or not."

The jury deliberated for thirteen hours. Their verdict acquitted
Roth on all but four counts: apparently those counts pertaining to
advertising and mailing *Good Times* and *American Aphrodite* were
the basis for the conviction. Quite possibly it was a compromise verdict, but at the same time a puzzling one and in many ways a dis-
appointment to the government. After a long and hard-fought trial
and hours of jury deliberation, the prosecution failed to fix a very
positive standard; there was scant indication that the jury had condemned many of the nude pictures which the prosecutor had condemned.

On the other hand, there have been convictions of vendors of
nude photos in other areas. In Philadelphia, officers of the Burlesque Historical Co. were convicted by a jury for *advertising* the
sale of (in their own terms) "sex-sational . . . all revealing colored"
photos which, they trumpeted, would bring out "every Charm of the
Female Form Devine" [sic]—"the sexiest of poses." In Baltimore,
the operators of a business called the Soloday Co. were jailed (for
three months) for retailing and wholesaling "millions" of pictures
of "nude women," and this conviction, said former Attorney General Brownell, set "an important precedent."

Inasmuch as Los Angeles is frequently referred to as the combined Sodom and Gomorrah of the obscenity field, it is of interest
to examine the course of prosecution and conviction in that district.
In the two-year period from July, 1954, to July, 1956, there were
a total of fourteen criminal prosecutions under the Comstock Act.
Most appear to have involved small mailings of outright pornography or "private assaults." One involved the manager of "Banner
Books"—a mail-order business in pseudo-scientific sex manuals
apparently containing much pornography. One Los Angeles acquittal involved movies of a nude woman in a series of episodes
with a statue of a dog. Most large operators in retouched pictures
of nudes, like Mrs. Tager, were never even arrested or indicted,
apparently because the U.S. Attorneys doubted that juries would
convict them. Two trials of a purveyor of a striptease movie (which
defense counsel, himself, characterized as "pretty rough") produced
no conviction.

This pattern has continued. In an eighteen-month period from 1958 to 1960, the U.S. Attorney in Los Angeles initiated eight prosecutions against commercial disseminators out of a total of thirteen cases. In four of these commercial cases, the defendants pleaded guilty. In the remaining commercial cases, two defendants were convicted, one was acquitted, and one was discharged after trial produced a divided jury which was unable to reach a verdict. The acquittal involved an attempted prosecution for advertising obscene materials. The jury's verdict was apparently based upon its conclusion that the materials advertised were not obscene, and the prosecution failed to persuade the court, as had been successfully done in another circuit, that this was irrelevant if the advertisements represented the ware as obscene. The sentences in the other cases ranged from three years probation to five years in jail. In one of these cases the defendants were husband and wife: a team of photographer and model. They distributed through the mails nude and highly suggestive pictures of the wife. As further bait for customers, a piece of adhesive tape, was strategically affixed, fig leaf style. The husband was given a five-year sentence and the wife a three-year sentence.

In his *Annual Report* for the year ending June 30, 1958, the Attorney General of the United States had this to say:

An alarming increase in the supply of risque material and pictures of nudes has underscored the need for relentless and vigorous enforcement of the federal obscenity statutes (18 U.S.C. 1461–1465). These statutes, however, only cover obscene matter which has been placed in the mails or in interstate commerce. The local sale, distribution, or display of obscene material is primarily a problem for state or local law enforcement authorities. A large scale prosecution was undertaken in the Northern District of Illinois charging various publishers, distributors and corporations with violations of the obscenity statutes. Pleas of guilty and nolo contendere were entered by the corporate defendants and the publishers were forced to clean up their publications resulting in loss of business to such an extent that the magazine suspended publication. In other instances bookstores dealing primarily in material of this type have closed their doors.
A federal grand jury investigation in the Eastern District of Pennsylvania uncovered two separate "pen pal" rings engaging in obscene correspondence. Seventeen persons were indicted for violation of the obscenity and conspiracy statutes. To date, five of the defendants have been convicted.

Despite this vigorous statement, and the protests of the Post Office and other groups about the inundation of obscene literature, the fact remains that criminal enforcement of the Comstock Act was very limited during the period 1946–1956, and thereafter; and one can see this by reading between the lines of the Attorney General's report—by comparing what he has done with what Mr. Summerfield and the Kefauver Committee say needs to be done. Only a very small percentage of the materials against which the Post Office acted civilly were made the subject of criminal prosecutions. Apart from the apparent difference in attitudes of the responsible officials, the fact remains that prosecutors just do not like to lose cases. In the big cities where the mailers resided and the prosecutions were brought, juries seemed to have standards a little more tolerant than those who exercised censorial discretion for the Post Office. Furthermore, when the complaining witnesses (such as the recipients of the material or their parents) lived in distant places, the burden of organizing and pushing a prosecution, including transporting these witnesses from afar, was a deterrent.

Thus enforcement of anti-obscenity law meant one thing to one arm of the government and something else to the other. *De facto,* the Comstock Act's definition of obsceneness was being differently interpreted by different branches of government even if *de jure* the law laid down precisely the same standard (assuming it did in fact permit Post Office censorship). Until there was a major change in the pattern of criminal enforcement, the great bulk of what was to be kept from the mails could be stopped only by administrative censorship, if it was to be stopped at all.

PART IV

The Constitution and

Obscenity Control: Recent

Court Decisions

The year 1957 marked the centennial of Lord Campbell's act. A century of experience had failed to produce a stable solution to the problem of defining and enforcing laws to stop the creation and circulation of undesirable sex expression. The failure was a lesson in itself, a reflection of the fact that standards fluctuated with social change, and conflict between aggressive demands for more freedom from these laws and aggressive demands for more suppression remained irrepressible. At the time, this conflict was one of the more disturbing tensions to plague contemporary American society.

There was ferment in the writing about obscenity law. In England a strong effort was mounted to scrap Lord Campbell's act and the *Hicklin* test and to replace them with more modern legislation proposed by the Society of Authors. And in this country there was also published, under the auspices of the American Law Institute, a model criminal statute which, though unofficial, had an immediate effect on the law. There was also a series of most important court decisions. They resolved some basic constitutional issues and suggested others; they reformulated the definition of obscenity and yet left application of the "tests" as difficult as ever. In short, the law was decidedly in a state of flux, and this is its condition today.

I. THE SUPREME COURT SPEAKS ON THE HICKLIN STANDARD; THE AMERICAN LAW INSTITUTE PROPOSES A NEW TEST

EARLY IN THE SPRING of 1957, a unanimous Supreme Court wrought the demise of *Hicklin*-oriented obscenity standards. The Court struck down a Michigan statute which had used Lord Cockburn's "test" almost in its exact terms. Michiganers, by order of their legislature, were not to have access to any books which would "tend" to "incite" juveniles to "immoral" behavior. Alfred Butler, a bookseller, had allegedly violated this command by selling an admittedly serious, well-received novel, John Griffin's *The Devil Rides Outside;* and he had been punished as a criminal for that sin.

The high Court reversed this conviction. The "incidence" of this Michigan statute, wrote Justice Frankfurter, was to "reduce the adult population of Michigan to reading what was fit for children." Juvenile misbehavior, no doubt, called for strenuous counteraction, but to combat it with this kind of anti-obscenity law was to "burn the barn to roast the pig," and no bookseller should be sent to jail by enforcing such an unreasonable statute. Thus, by the Court's decision, standards for defining obscenity which had been used continuously albeit uncritically, in some states and for seventy years or longer by federal censorship, were now, in 1957, found to be unconstitutional.

Following upon the decision in *Butler v. Michigan,* the American Law Institute (a group of judges, scholars, and lawyers whose purpose, *inter alia,* is to synthesize and reduce principles of law to clear language), published a proposed redefinition of criminal obscenity legislation. The quest of the Institute, in this particular endeavor, was to frame a new, "rational" obscenity statute which would "reflect changes in men's views of the importance of freedom of expression." Perhaps the underlying premise of this Model Penal Code proposal is reflected in these excerpts from the report which proposed it: "Psychiatrists and anthropologists see the ordinary person in our society as caught between normal sex drives and curiosity, on the one hand, and powerful social and legal prohibitions against overt sexual behavior. The principal objective of [the proposed statute] is to *prevent commercial exploitation of this psychosexual tension.*" (Emphasis added.) Again: "Society may legitimately seek to deter the deliberate stimulation and *exploitation of emotional tensions* arising from the conflict between social convention and the individual's sex drive." Thus: "The gist of the offense we envisage, therefore, is a kind of [commercial] 'pandering.'"

Consistent with this end, the Model Penal Code defined "obscenity": "A thing is obscene if, considered as a whole, its predominant appeal is to prurient interest, i.e., a shameful or morbid interest in nudity, sex, or excretion, and if it goes substantially beyond customary limits of candor in description or representation of such matters."

The code then proscribed *all* dissemination except: (1) "dissemination not for gain" among adult "personal associates," (2) dissemination "not for gain" among juveniles, and (3) dissemination to "institutions" and "persons" having "scientific" or other "special justification" for receiving.

By a coincidence of circumstances, the Model Penal Code was destined for an extraordinary reception. It did not languish as a dustcatcher on the bookshelves of law libraries. On the contrary, it found its way to the United States Supreme Court, and particularly onto the desk of Mr. Justice William Brennan, who gave the new work some thoughtful attention, since he was at that very time drafting a decision for the Court on the subject.

2. THE SUPREME COURT SPEAKS ON
THE COMSTOCK ACT: A PYRRHIC
VICTORY FOR THE POST OFFICE

IN THE WAKE of *Butler v. Michigan,* three more cases had come before the Supreme Court. One was a Comstock Act prosecution (the *Roth* case); the second was a California prosecution under a typical, state anti-obscenity criminal statute (the *Alberts* case), and the third was a prosecution under a New York statute authorizing courts to enjoin future sale of certain books adjudged "obscene" (the *Kingsley Books* case). The sole issue to be reviewed in each case was the validity of each particular statute; in no case was the Court required to consider whether the particular petitioners before it were guilty, whether the works before it were in fact obscene, whatever the standard to be used—and, of course, none of these statutes defined any standards. By the terms of its orders granting review, the Court was simply to decide whether state legislatures and Congress could enact these penalties against distribution of things obscene. In a real sense, the Court had confined itself to a determination of the abstract issue of power.

The federal case concerned Sam Roth's conviction for advertising and mailing the book *American Aphrodite* and the magazine *Good Times.* A lengthy trial had produced: (1) evidence that Roth had flooded the country with advertisements of these and other materials; (2) impassioned condemnation of them by the prosecution witnesses; (3) "expert" testimony from a defense psychologist that, though titillating, they were harmless. All this information went to the jury along with the materials. The trial judge told the jury: convict Roth if these things he mailed had "a tendency to excite lustful thoughts ... The test ... is the effect of the book, picture or publication considered as a whole ... upon the average person ... you [must also] judge [each item] ... by present day standards of the community ... Does it offend the common conscience of the community? ..." The verdict was guilty on counts involving the book and magazines.

Over the protest of the late Judge Frank, the Court of Appeals had affirmed Roth's conviction. Judge Frank reiterated views he had first expressed in 1949. He wrote, in essence: We are midpoint in the twentieth century, and it is high time for reappraisal of the anti-obscenity laws in the light of experience, science, and today's legal conception of the right of free speech. I doubt the constitutionality of the Comstock Act; I doubt whether Congress has the power to pass such a law. Obscenity dissemination, a ridiculously vague crime, punishes people for selling books or pictures which may only "evoke thoughts" and nothing more. This is carrying governmental suppression too far.

Reviewing what scientific evidence he could muster, Judge Frank went on to assert that there was no demonstrable nexus between "lustful thoughts" and resultant misbehavior, no proof that obscene books produce overt misconduct. In the absence of this proof, said he, the law should eschew suppression. The First Amendment prohibits punishing people for distributing "speech" which simply offends us. Experience and the underlying philosophy of freedom justify the scope of the broad protection. How else can ideas be given adequate protection? Just as with the soapbox political zealots, so with "publishers" like Roth: let them alone as the price we pay for freedom, unless and until we can show that they have produced some tangible danger to society, a danger more "clear" and more "present" than mere stimulation of "lustful thoughts."

These claims were argued in detail with elaborate analysis of published findings—such as they were—of experts. Roth then petitioned the Supreme Court, and certiorari was granted. We will decide, the Court announced, whether criminal enforcement of the Comstock Act does violate freedom of the press. The contrary assumption, reflected in various dicta spanning seventy-five years and a long history of enforcement in the lower courts, was to be reappraised. Weighty, wordy "briefs," not only from the parties, but from various civil-libertarian oriented *amici curiae,* bombarded the Court. And, of course, the case was vital to the United States government. The future of all federal regulation of obscenity—including Customs and Postal censorship—might hinge on it.

On June 24, 1957 the Supreme Court held that the Comstock Act was constitutional.

Justice Brennan, joined by four of his colleagues—a bare majority—wrote the decision. Obscenity, he noted, could be variously defined. Referring to the new, untried test put forth by the American Law Institute, he declared that this formula (identifying obscenity as that which "predominantly appeals to prurient interest") focused on the essence of the badness of things obscene. But, said Justice Brennan, laying down a proposition patently inconsistent with the expressed philosophy of the model proposal, this new "appeal to prurience" test was only a new verbalization—although apparently a better wording—of the old, traditional tests, of the definitions utilized by the trial court in Roth's trial (i.e., "tendency to excite lustful thoughts" or "offensive to the community's conscience").[1] Thus the Model Penal Code's authors were given the honor of immediate endorsement by the Supreme Court along with the implied slight that nothing in their new "test" was really very novel.

Having thus defined the term obscene, the Court swept aside, summarily, the argument that the standards were too vague by simply contradicting the claim. And having defined obscenity, the Court's five-man majority proceeded to lay down the proposition that all publications meeting these criteria are useless to mankind

1. Wrote the framers of the ALI proposal: "obscenity [in our draft] is defined in terms of material which appeals predominantly to prurient interest in sexual matters and which goes beyond customary freedom of expression in these matters. *We reject the prevailing test of tendency to arouse lustful thoughts or desires* because it is unrealistically broad for a society that plainly tolerates a great deal of erotic interest in literature, advertising, and art, and because regulation of thought or desire, unconnected with overt misbehavior, raises the most acute constitutional as well as practical difficulties . . . On the other hand, 'appeal to prurient interest' refers to qualities of the material itself; the capacity to attract individuals eager for a forbidden look . . ." (emphasis added).

and therefore warrant no protection under the First Amendment. Obscenity, said Justice Brennan, is "utterly without redeeming social importance." So whether its circulation creates a "clear and present danger" or no real danger at all is irrelevant. Like libel, obscenity can be suppressed without proof of its impact on behavior because it is not "speech" as that term is used in the First Amendment.

Just as the Court summarily disposed of the vagueness and clear-and-present-danger arguments, so it disposed of the third, the claim that there is no federal power to regulate the content of speech for the purpose of protecting morality. Again the answer was simple: "obscenity" is "not expression protected by the First Amendment," so there is no bar to the assertion of power, and the argument falls with the premise.

All of this did not sit well with some Justices. "The Court seems to assume that obscenity is a peculiar *genus* of 'speech and press' which is as distinct, recognizable and classifiable as poison ivy," scoffed Justice Harlan. "I cannot agree that any book which tends to stir sexual impulses [etc.] . . . is utterly without redeeming social importance." Justice Harlan went on to argue that the constitutional limitations on federal power to deal with obscenity should be far more stringent than those imposed on the states. A state criminal statute could be judged by a more liberal standard of reasonableness under the Fourteenth Amendment, he argued, but there is no express *federal* power to protect morality, and the First Amendment fixes the strictest kind of a limitation on Congress' power to regulate the content of the post. Except for "hard core pornography"—which, presumably, he agreed was not "speech" in the constitutional sense—the United States government lacked the power to enforce anti-obscenity statutes.

Chief Justice Warren, concurring in the result in the *Roth* case, voiced another view. He insisted that blanket proscriptions which were interpreted or which operated to forbid *all* dissemination of obscenity were invalid. He would uphold suppression by criminal prosecution (and perhaps also by prior restraint, though that is not clear), but only when the disseminator engages in "conduct" amounting to "pandering," to commercial exploitation of the obscenity. The "conduct of the defendant," he declared, should be made "the central issue" in every case. Thus, the Comstock Act was valid, but only for the purpose of prosecuting purveyors like Sam Roth and David Alberts:

> That there is a social problem presented by obscenity is attested by the expression of the legislatures of the forty-eight States as well as the Congress. To recognize the existence of a problem, however, does not require that we sustain any and all measures adopted to meet that problem. . . .
> The line dividing the salacious or pornographic from literature or science is not straight and unwavering. Present laws depend largely upon the effect that the materials may have upon those who receive them. It is manifest that the same object may have a different impact, varying according to the part of the community it reached. But there is more to these cases. It is not the book that is on trial; it is a person. The conduct of the defendant is the central issue, not the obscenity of a book or picture. The nature of the materials is, of course, relevant as an attribute of the defendant's conduct, but the materials are thus placed in context from which they draw color and character. A wholly different result might be reached in a different setting.

Two other dissenters of the Court expressed still another view. Devout in the belief, which they have often urged before, that the words "no law" in the First Amendment mean "no law" which punishes "speech" independently of its demonstrable harmful effect, Justices Black and Douglas argued that a far more stringent test must be met before publishers could be jailed because of objection to the content of their work. Prohibiting circulation of expression simply because it promotes "impure sexual thoughts" or "appeals to prurience" is unconstitutional, said Douglas; enforcement of these laws exalts the "Philistines" in their age-old "battle" with "the literati;" and: "If experience in this field teaches anything, it is that censorship of obscenity has almost always been both irrational and indiscriminate. . . . The First Amendment, in its terms absolute, was designed to preclude [government] from weighing the values of speech against silence. . . . Freedom of expression can be suppressed if, and to the extent that, it is so clearly brigaded with illegal action as to be an inseparable part of it. . . . [We] cannot afford to relax that standard, for the test that suppresses a cheap tract today can suppress a literary gem tomorrow. All it need do is to incite a lascivious thought or arouse a lustful desire. The list of books that judges or juries can place in that category is endless."

The companion case from the New York courts, *Kingsley Books, Inc. v. Brown,* was decided the same day. A Times Square book-dealer had been selling a paperbound called *Nights of Horror*—a concoction of pictures and fiction which might have chilled the blood of De Sade. Acting under a new statute which had been pushed by the New York legislature's zealous "Joint Committee on Obscene and Offensive Books," the City of New York had asked for a court order telling the bookseller to stop selling *Nights of Horror,* immediately and forever. The New York judge to whom this complaint was addressed had read the book, pronounced it "dirt for dirt's sake" and issued the injunction: destroy all copies of this book, he told the seller, do not ever sell it again, under pain of contempt of court.

Obliteration of *Nights of Horror* from the annals of mankind could hardly be called a catastrophe. But, in the opinion of many New York publishers, this kind of statute posed a threat of court censorship which, if abused, would operate to prohibit or inhibit sales of, say, a salty bestseller. Even if the danger of a sweeping court injunction against controversial books put out by reputable publishers was remote, the danger of harassment of less powerful booksellers was great—particularly if the statute were copied over the country and enforced zealously by publicity-minded prosecutors in many communities. The specter of continual harassment—threats of injunctions—by zealous city officials, far more than the danger of bad court decisions when controversial cases were finally litigated, was probably their concern. Hence respectable publishers joined to take up the defense of *Kingsley Books, Inc.,* and they asked the Supreme Court to strike down the New York statute.

The Court, by a different majority this time, sustained the statute. Justice Frankfurter, for the majority, wrote: "If New York chooses to subject persons who disseminate obscene 'literature' to criminal prosecution *and also* [emphasis added] to deal with such books as deodands of old, or both, with due regard, of course, to appropriate opportunities for the trial of the underlying issue, it is not for us to gainsay its selection of remedies."

Justices Black and Douglas again dissented. So, too, did Chief Justice Warren; adhering to the view expressed in *Roth,* he refused to uphold a law permitting a total ban against a publication without taking account of the publisher's "conduct"—his method of distribution and his motives.

Consistent with the philosophy he expressed in dissent in *Roth,* Justice Harlan voted with the majority in *Kingsley Books;* this case concerned state legislation rather than a federal law, and, as noted, in his view that difference is significant.

On the other hand, Justice Brennan, in a somewhat surprising shift, dissented. The vice of New York's "prior restraint" (i.e., its censorship type of statute), as he saw it, was the failure to guarantee a jury trial on the issue of obscenity. Only with this jury-trial "safeguard" could there be assurance of "competent application" of the "obscenity standard." No book should be proscribed unless and until there has been opportunity for a jury determination of its legality.

This cataloguing of the view of the Justices, while confusing, may be basic to analysis and prediction of future development of the law. For among the individual opinions every sort of viewpoint appears. This suggests interesting problems about other cases which might arise.

Two Justices (Black and Douglas) say there can be no suppression of any sex expression, even though we characterize it as "obscene," without evidence of a "clear and present danger" of harm from its publication. One Justice (Harlan) seems to say: no *federal* power; the states can use criminal or civil sanctions, but the United States government cannot, except against "hard-core pornography." One Justice (Brennan) seems to say: jury trials and perhaps criminal prosecutions are a *sine qua non* to assure fair enforcement of the law; there must be a jury trial before a book can be suppressed. A fifth member of the Court, the Chief Justice, says: "It is the manner of use that should determine obscenity. It is the conduct of the individual that should be judged, not [simply] the quality of the art or literature. To do otherwise is to . . . violate the [First Amendment]."

If we take Justice Harlan, Justice Brennan, and the Chief Justice at their words—if these judges abide by their announced views along with Black and Douglas, then it is quite possible that at least five of the Justices would find *civil* enforcement of the Comstock Act, i.e., Postal censorship, unconstitutional. For in the Postal censorship cases there are no jury trials to satisfy Brennan's *Kingsley*

Books qualification; the standard for suppression has not conformed to the standard espoused by the Chief Justice, and three other members of the court (Harlan, Black, and Douglas) have already declared the view that these laws are invalid as an illegal use of federal power. It is thus arguable that the announced views of five members of the Court, divergent as they may be, make for the conclusion that Postal censorship, as practiced, is unconstitutional.

But analysis should not stop there. There are other factors which suggest that the *Roth* decision simply cannot stand as the last word on constitutional limitations without further qualification or explanation.

The prevailing opinion in that case is superficial.

Sweeping assumptions were invoked by Justice Brennan and his four colleagues to support the conclusion that Congress has the power to put people like Sam Roth in jail. Eschewing appraisal of existing experience, the Court in effect said: (1) "obscene" publications can be identified and distinguished from legitimate expression without much risk of much mistake; (2) "obscene" publications (as identified by applying the standards) have no social value whatsoever.

These assumptions may be true in many cases, but there are some where it is very difficult to apply the tests and very difficult to say the accused book is "utterly without redeeming merit," and it is precisely because we encounter these difficulties that the anti-obscenity laws present a threat of excessive inhibition on freedom of expression.

Is obsceneness easy to judge? The Post Office and the Bureau of Customs have not agreed about how much pictorial nudity is too much for the good of the public. They have disagreed frequently enough when it comes to judging fictional works. The Post Office has censored magazines which sell openly in stores in perfectly respectable communities, in communities where the police do not prosecute the distribution. The Bureau of Customs has insisted that depiction of nudity in foreign films be blotted out on the assumption that there is some uniform, nationwide standard condemning nudity, a homogeneous "community conscience," when quite clearly there is none. In short, the standards are not so clear cut that their vagueness is not a problem.

And is it true that all "obscene" works are utterly worthless?

Who is wise enough to say that *Lady Chatterley's Lover*, the forbidden works of Ovid, Miller, De Sade, and Frank Harris, *Memoirs of Hecate County, God's Little Acre, From Here to Eternity, The Woman of Rome,* or even Mark Twain's *1601,* and many of the others which have been proscribed in recent years, are "utterly without redeeming social importance"? Who is confident that he can demonstrate that some or all of these books are or are not worth any man's attention? The Library of Congress carefully preserves copies of almost all books seized by Customs censorship and makes them available either to the general public or at least for restricted use. And if the law operates on the assumption that all "obscene" books are fit only for oblivion, why did Congress, legislating in 1930, speak of "obscene classics" and "obscene" books of "recognized literary merit"?

The portrayal of "sex," admitted Justice Brennan, "has undisputably been a subject of absorbing interest to mankind through the ages"; freedom to discuss or portray it is "guaranteed" as an element of freedom of speech, and the courts must practice "ceaseless vigilance" to assure that freedom. But there the thought was left dangling, and the exhortation died. For we are also told that if you portray sex in a manner which others will evaluate as "predominantly" an "appeal to prurience," an incitement of "impure sexual thoughts" and an offense to the "community's conscience", if you have done this, then, *ipso facto,* the case suddenly changes; you have created something worse than worthless.

3.   THE SUPREME COURT SPEAKS ON

THE OBSCENENESS OF VARIOUS

MAGAZINES AND MOVIES

THE *Roth, Alberts,* and *Kingsley* decisions hardly settled the law. Unresolved were two basic questions: (1) Was federal
censorship, as practiced, constitutional? (2) And how, more precisely, was obsceneness to be measured?

In the fall of 1957 another series of cases came before the Court
which might have produced a more clear-cut statement of these
issues. Alas, they did not.

Three of these were federal censorship cases. The Post Office
had declared "non-mailable" several issues of a nudist magazine put
out by the Sunshine Company. The Post Office had also banned *One*
("the magazine for homosexuals"). Customs officers on the west
coast had seized a quantity of European nudist magazines imported
by one Mounce. In each of these cases the lower courts had upheld
the censorship action, and the Supreme Court was asked to reverse.
The petitioners claimed that (1) the First Amendment forbade
such censorship; (2) even if it did not, the publications were not
obscene and should never have been suppressed.

In each case the court granted the petition, and, without hearing
any argument, summarily reversed the lower court. In no case did
the Court write an opinion. In the Customs (*Mounce*) case, the
lower court was simply told to decide the issues again in light of

the new standards articulated in the *Roth* decision. In the two Postal cases (*Sunshine* and *One*), the Court reversed the judgment and disposed of the cases with absolute finality. However, it wrote no explanation whatsoever for these judgments; it simply cited the prior decision in the *Roth* case. In effect the Court seemed to be saying: these publications cannot be banned; we refer you to what was said in our *Roth* opinion; explain it yourself.

In June of 1959 the Supreme Court handed down another newsworthy, controversial decision. Although the decision did not deal with obscenity law, it did deal with a serious problem of censorship of sex expression, and the Court, again, struck down an attempt to enlarge the area of permissible suppression.

New York's movie censors had banned all exhibition of the film, *Lady Chatterley's Lover,* not because the film was obscene, but because it was "immoral," i.e., it "portrayed adultery as desirable, acceptable and [a] proper pattern of behavior."

All nine Justices joined in the conclusion that this ban was illegal and must be set aside. A majority declared the censorship standard (banning all films portraying immoral conduct as acceptable) unconstitutional. "What New York has done," wrote Justice Stewart, "is to prevent exhibition of a motion picture [simply] because that picture advocates an *idea*—that adultery under certain circumstances may be proper behavior. Yet the First Amendment's basic guarantee is of freedom to advocate *ideas*. The State, quite simply, has thus struck at the very heart of constitutionally protected liberty." (Emphasis added.) Justices Black and Douglas, in a separate opinion, added that they thought all movie censorship should be declared invalid. On the other hand, Justices Frankfurter, Harlan, and Whitaker took a very narrow view of the case: the standard might be constitutional in the abstract, they said, but when used to ban this film the result was unconstitutional censorship because the film itself was neither obscene nor "corruptive" as an "incitement" to commit adultery. "As one whose taste in art and literature hardly qualifies him for the avantgarde," wrote Justice Frankfurter, "I am more than surprised, after viewing the picture, that the New York authorities should have banned Lady Chatterley's Lover. To assume that this motion picture would have offended [even] Victorian moral sensibilities is to rely on the stuffiest of Victorian conventions." And this opinion, that the movie is, in fact, innocuous, seems to have been shared by an overwhelming number of cinema critics who hastened to review *Lady Chatterley* once the Court permitted its broad release.

But critics of the Court still stormed at the decision: if immorality could be so freely advocated, what would happen to the nation in this time of peril? Others scoffed at the Court, at the fact that no less than six opinions, all told, had been written in the case: how was any man to know where the law stood when almost every Justice felt constrained to follow his own independent views on these questions? Actually, it wasn't quite so confusing—if one took the time to distill the gist from each of the opinions. Justice Stewart had written, for five colleagues, that the immorality standard was unconstitutional: that was the point of law settled by the case; Justices Black and Douglas had added their opinion that *all* censorship was bad; Justice Clark had rested his vote for reversal on the proposition that "immorality" was too vague, a point not considered by the majority; Justice Harlan (joined by Frankfurter and Whitaker) had dealt with the film on its merits; Justice Frankfurter had added a thoughtful comment, warning that sex censorship cases should be judged on the narrowest possible ground rather than on broad propositions which indiscriminately struck down state legislation, for, he urged, the field was fraught with controversy and difficulty; Justice Black had written (in a special reply to Frankfurter) that the case-by-case method of ajudication would lead the Court into a quagmire of litigation; the Justices, to do justice to these cases, would have to spend hours viewing films and reviewing censorship agencies, but the minimum duty of the Court, said Hugo Black, was to mark out clear areas where censorship could *not* operate, by striking down all standards which, perforce, depended on the subjective discretion of those who must enforce them. He, himself, believed that all these forms of restraint on mass communication were illegal.

The *Lady Chatterley* movie case demonstrated, at least, that little could be done to enlarge the definition of obscenity laid down in *Roth* without violating the First Amendment; indeed, it suggested that any anti-sex-expression law would pass muster on constitutionality only if it was confined to a serious infraction of the obscenity standard.

Another, recent Supreme Court decision, *Smith v. California,* seems also to have imposed First Amendment limitations on the permissible scope of anti-obscenity laws. Smith was a Los Angeles bookseller. He was arrested for violating an ordinance making it a crime for news vendors, drugstore owners and other merchants to "possess" or "sell" an "obscene" book. Brought to trial, Smith tried to defend on the ground that he knew nothing of the content of the book alleged to be obscene; nor, as a practical matter, could he read all his merchandise; and because he was innocent of the book's content he should be innocent of the crime charged. Smith's lawyer also tried to introduce evidence, via the testimony of a local newspaper's literary editor, that the book's "sex episodes" were within the bounds of the Los Angeles "community standard": what was written here was no more shocking than material to be found in other acceptable novels selling openly in the community. The trial judge rejected both defenses, not because the claims were vague or incredible, but because the anti-obscenity ordinance, according to the trial court, did not permit such defenses.

As the California courts read it, the ordinance said in effect: it doesn't make any difference whether a bookseller is totally innocent of the bad content of a book he keeps on his shelves; if the book is in fact obscene, then a crime is committed simply by possessing it in a store. Thus, booksellers must "act at their peril." Nor, ruled the trial court, does California law require us to hear testimony of any witnesses on community standards in literature. The court (or jury) alone should fix those standards, without even the aid of conceded "experts" on the sexual content and standards of frankness of contemporary fiction.

The Supreme Court (in December, 1959) unanimously reversed Smith's conviction and declared this Los Angeles ordinance unconstitutional. The *absolute* liability—the "sell at your peril"—features of this law imposed an undue inhibition on book vending, declared the Court's majority. Such a law would intimidate vendors, counseling them to stock only the safest books or items for which they (or safe, self-appointed censors) could vouch; and "the bookseller's . . . timidity" in the face of this threat of "absolute criminal liability" would coerce a form of "self-censorship" which could operate to "deplete" stores and "periodical stands" of lawful literature and thus "restrict" the "public's access to forms of the printed word which the state could not constitutionally suppress". And all this impinged too much on press freedom.

Justices Frankfurter and Harlan decided the case on the evidentiary issue. (The majority had not reached the problem of exclusion of the "community standard" testimony, but these Justices thought it was the more serious point). "To exclude evidence" by competent experts on the "community standards or the psychological or physiological consequences of questioned literature, is, in effect, to exclude . . . evidence which goes to the very essence of the defense", wrote Frankfurter. A trial or a law which rules out such testimony violates "due process."

Justices Black and Douglas once again reiterated their views on the absolute nature of the First Amendment. The Constitution should give Americans as much protection in the creation and publishing of sex expression as it does in the dissemination of any sort of political or religious dissent, wrote Justice Douglas; "no law abridging freedom" means *no* law; "freedom of expression can be suppressed [only] . . . to the extent that it is so closely brigaded with illegal action as to be an inseparable part of it."

The ramifications of the *Smith* case are interesting. Justice Frankfurter appears to condemn a practice (i.e., excluding all external testimony about the challenged work) which has flourished (until very recently) in Postal censorship. And arguably, the *practical* effect of the majority's decision (though admittedly it is not the strict legal rule) is to require, in criminal cases, something like the proof which Chief Justice Warren had previously demanded in *Roth's* case: a showing that the defendant had recklessly exploited a questionable book for commercial purposes.

In January 1961, the Supreme Court decided *Times Film Corporation v. City of Chicago.* It was a case deliberately framed to challenge all motion picture censorship. The representatives from the motion picture industry who started it hoped to render the death blow to all such censorship. They failed.

The Chicago ordinance—typical of other cities—requires that all motion pictures be submitted to an administrative board for approval before any public exhibition. It is, indeed, like the licensing which drew Milton's fire several centuries ago.

Times Film Corporation applied for a permit to exhibit *Don*

Juan, but it refused to submit the film for inspection. The very requirement that we seek government approval before "publishing" (i.e., exhibiting) violates the First Amendment, declared the company; it is a classic form of "prior restraint". So Times Film sued for an injunction, claiming, *not* that this film was innocuous (which it admittedly was), *nor* that Chicago's ordinance in particular was continually suspect (which it may be) because of its breadth of standards and procedures, but solely that any and all laws which require any submission of any film before any exhibition on any grounds are unconstitutional; this *method* of controlling exhibition is unconstitutional. The lower courts refused to hear this claim; neither the film, nor any evidence of its contents, nor even Chicago's ordinance in particular are before us, the courts declared; there is no "justiciable controversy"—only a hypothetical claim of the type courts should decline to hear.

Perhaps the Supreme Court, too, might have avoided the rather theoretical issue which Times Film sought to litigate. But the court concluded there was a "justiciable," albeit somewhat abstract, "controversy".

The question, said Justice Clark (for a bare five man majority), is whether, under the Federal Constitution, a state may establish any sort of censorship device to control movies. The answer to that question—at least in the abstract—is "Yes." We limit our answer to movies—impliedly a different sort of medium for mass communicating; we consider only the question whether a state may require some method of examining films for obscenity; we need not stop to declare what this method must be, what must be the limitations in terms of precision of either the standards or procedures for enforcing them, for Times Film claims *all* systems are invalid. But we have said that obscenity—as defined in *Roth*—is unprotected "speech"; in the *Kingsley Books* case we upheld New York's statute permitting injunctions forbidding sale of obscenity by booksellers; and we have heretofore carefully observed, in striking down state movie censorship laws that there *may* be room for some censorship statutes "narrowly drawn". All of these points suggest the answer to the abstract question here: "It is not for this Court to limit the State [as Times Film argues] in its selection of the remedy it deems most effective to cope with [the] problem [of obscene movies], absent, of course, a showing of unreasonable strictures on individual liberty resulting from its application in particular circumstances."

Sustaining a censorship power over obscene films—at least in the abstract—was, perhaps, a conclusion consistent with the prior decisions. But it was a conclusion which four dissenters (Warren, Black, Douglas and Brennan) refused to reach. Chief Justice Warren reviewed the classic arguments against censorship and considerable history of its abuse from Milton's time to Chicago's very recent experience. Perhaps the capstone of this review was this quotation attributed to the policeman in charge of the City's censorship: "Children should be allowed to see any movie that plays in Chicago. If a picture is objectionable for a child, it is objectionable period."

The "censor", wrote Chief Justice Warren, too often "performs free from procedural safeguards" afforded litigants in other disputes. "Beholden" to those who "sponsored creation of his office", and "insulated" from countervailing pressures for tolerance, he finds too readily that which he is commissioned to "suppress". His decision is, too likely, "less contemplated" than it should be. And, in the case of commercial film exhibitors, the burden of disputing that decision, of proceeding to what may be lengthy litigation in the courts, may too often outweigh the advantages of grudging acquiescence in the censor's demand for deletions here and there.

The majority did not really respond to these arguments. Perhaps the reason lies in the abstractness of the only issue which they did decide; their answer might be: admitting a danger of such abuses, we decide only that the Constitution does not forbid any and all systems of censorship simply because danger exists in many.

The narrowness of both the Court's majority and its abstract ruling suggests that many battles are yet to come. The *Times Film* case may well be misconstrued by proponents of censorship. The overgeneralization that the Court has approved censorship may stimulate pressure for creation of censorship boards, and extravagant actions may be condoned.

And if this happens one might venture to predict some possible developments: first, a constant striking down of censorship ordinances in the volume of litigation which is bound to follow, on grounds of deficiencies in the procedures or standards or because erroneous decisions were made on content of the film suppressed.

Second, with cities given their heads, the ensuing surge of censorship may well substantiate the warnings of the dissenters, persuade one or more of the present majority or succeeding members of the Court to curtail the power permitted and ultimately effect either a reversal or a mutilation of the *Times Film* decision.

In any event, it is by no means clear that this movie censorship case carries with it the implication that federal censorship of the mails is constitutional. Without regard to analysis of its present defects of procedure or standards, it is important to note that federal censorship of the content of books, magazines and other published matter in the mails must stand on a different footing because the federal government may not enjoy powers allowed the states in connection with movies. Justice Harlan, for example, who constituted one of the five man majority in the *Times Film* case, took the position in the *Roth* case that the Federal Government enjoys no such power in this field. Other Justices may see other impediments to federal censorial powers. Assuming, as seems proper, that the Chief Justice and Justices Black, Douglas and Brennan will adhere to their views, and that Justice Harlan will adhere to his, the constitutionality of Post Office censorship remains debatable.

4.

SOME SIGNIFICANT LOWER-COURT
DECISIONS RANGING FROM DR.
KINSEY'S COLLECTION TO LADY
CHATTERLEY'S LOVER

IN ADDITION TO THESE Supreme Court decisions, there have been others from the lower courts; they also added significant parts to the new mosaic of law which developed in the period since 1957.

Far-reaching were the possible ramifications of the so-called *Kinsey* case. Dr. Kinsey and his associates at the Institute for Sex Research (an affiliate of the University of Indiana) had attempted to bring into the country all kinds of foreign pornography. Their purpose, of course, was social-science research. But Customs officials at New York pounced on the importation. The Institute applied for a discretionary release under either the Tariff Act's special proviso or some other, implied, exception to the law. A long period of dickering with the government followed.

By no stretch could most of the seized materials be characterized as "classics," works of "scientific merit," or by any other ennobling synonym entitling the Institute to the dispensation expressly allowed by the tariff statute. Here were materials ranging from photographs of scribblings on lavatory walls, to cheap offsets, to expensive, glossy, but decidedly pornographic matter. If these works were to be judged in the abstract under the *Roth* standards, they were patently obscene. But the Institute urged admission on the grounds of its own scientific purpose. In fact, all agreed that the materials were necessary in the furtherance of bona fide research, that they would be kept from the general public, and that if released they would be held "under security conditions . . . for the sole use of the Institute staff or of qualified scholars engaged in bona fide research." What the Institute really sought, therefore, was an exception based, not on the merit of the materials, but on the special qualification of the recipients to receive them—a test difficult indeed to square with the traditional theory of the Tariff Act and with anti-obscenity laws generally.

Conceding that a few exceptions had been made in the past, in similar cases, for medical men, the Acting Secretary of the Treasury now refused the relief. The government went ahead with court forfeiture proceedings, and the Institute for Sex Research and the Trustees of Indiana University appeared in opposition. The government's lawyers argued that release in this case would create impossible problems of enforcement in the future: Customs officials would be confronted with analogous claims, with requests from all sorts of scholars or pseudo-scholars for release of obscene books for special study; and how could the Bureau undertake the task of examining the motivation and credentials of all these potential claimants?

In a careful opinion, the District Judge rejected the government's argument and directed release of the impounded works. Few can quarrel with the result. Yet, the implications of the decision, which the government did not choose to challenge by further appeal, are still to be fully realized. Judge Palmieri had read an implied exception into the law, an exception which could be extended quite far.

As Judge Palmieri noted:

> The Government raises a *concurrus horribilium,* maintaining that there are no workable criteria by which the [Tariff Act's ban on obscene importations] may be administered if it is interpreted [to require release to scholars like Kinsey]. . . . But . . . I fail to see why it should be more difficult to determine the appeal of libelled matter [i.e., the material seized by Customs] to a known group of persons than it is to determine its appeal to a hypothetical average man. The question is not whether the materials are necessary, or merely desirable for a particular research project. The question is not whether the fruits of the research will be valuable to society. The Tariff Act of 1930 provides no warrant for either customs

officials or this Court to sit in review of the decisions of scholars
as to the bypaths of learning upon which they shall tread. The
question is solely whether, as to those persons who will see the
libelled material, there is a reasonable probability that it will appeal
to their prurient interest.

Thus, the professed rationale of the decision was simply this:
that importation in Kinsey's case would cause no harm to the recipients or to the public interest, whereas censorship might curtail
freedom to read in a serious way. Surely, other cases where these
conditions could exist can be easily imagined. Would not the rationale of the decision be broad enough, in theory, to require release of
the works of Henry Miller to any professor whose motives for importing were not prurient but intellectual? Indeed, why should the
private citizen, capable of handling psychic responses evoked by
viewing the obscene, be denied the freedom to read if his motives,
too, were scholarly?

Perhaps anticipating such issues, the Judge wrote:

> . . . [The] theory of this decision, rightly interpreted, affords no
> comfort to those who would import materials such as these for
> public sale or private indulgence. A showing that multiple copies
> of a particular piece of matter are sought to be imported by the
> same person should raise an extremely strong inference against
> any claim that the material is sought for allegedly scientific pur-
> poses. And, while I express no definitive opinion . . . it would
> seem that any individual, not connected with an institution recog-
> nized to be conducting bona fide research . . . will not easily estab-
> lish that he seeks importation for a reason other than gratification
> of his prurient interest.

In short, the court expressed a word of caution. But it did not
rule out the possibility that the freedom of access accorded Kinsey
should be available to others in deserving cases. The thrust of the
decision seemed to cut deeply, if narrowly, into the foundations of
Customs censorship.

Some months after the *Kinsey* case, the Post Office was forced
into newsworthy litigation, having run afoul of the courts over
Lady Chatterley's Lover. A commercial publisher in the United
States had at last dared to print an unexpurgated edition (perhaps
concluding that the market prospects, now, far outweighed the
legal risks). Not only was the book printed in a paperback format

for drugstore sales, but the publisher deliberately courted Postal sanctions by advertising a mail-order distribution as well.

The Post Office ruled that neither the book nor advertising for it could pass via the mails to the public. Litigation followed in the U.S. District Court in New York. Judge Bryan's opinion added no startling, new concept to the law; he purported to apply the Model Penal Code test, the *Ulysses* test, and the community standard. The importance of the decision seemed principally in the result. Americans could now read *Lady Chatterley;* it suddenly sold openly and widely with immunity, and this was, perhaps, the strongest sexual fare which many of the book's readers had ever read with knowledge that their reading was expressly sanctioned by law. Indeed the legality of the book was reinforced when, some months later, the Court of Appeals upheld Judge Bryan's ruling.

These are the propositions that influenced the court: (1) the book had, prior to the Postal censorship, been published and sold through the normal, open channels by responsible, reputable persons; (2) it had been read by a wide adult audience; (3) it had been praised for its quality, its value, by responsible, qualified critics; and (4), in the court's own opinion, the book's total dominant effect on a reader was not dangerous stimulation of lust, nor was its "predominant appeal" to "prurient interest," nor did it violate the community standard. In essence, then, the case carried the law a step further in degree in the direction charted by the *Ulysses* decision: books which have genuine value to some responsible, thinking elements of society simply cannot be totally suppressed, notwithstanding the fact that they contain indisputably detailed erotic or graphic descriptions of sexual behavior.

Of interest, too, were several state court decisions. The highest court in Massachusetts and the highest court in New York both ruled that a film, *The Garden of Eden,* portraying life in a nudist camp, with nudists as nudists, was not obscene; and thereafter "nudist" films began to appear in greater volume in many areas. Several other decisions cleared some entertainment magazines which were standard drugstore fare—items which, only a few years before, would have been grist for the mill of most censors. The Supreme Court of Pennsylvania struck down a state criminal statute aimed at the exhibition of obscene films: again, apparently, the sweep of the law was too broad. The Oregon Supreme Court nearly became the first high court to declare, notwithstanding the *Alberts* decision, that all anti-obscenity laws in that state were invalid; by a narrow vote of four to three the court failed to make the jump. A federal judge enjoined Chicago's censorship of the film *Anatomy of a Murder;* the censors had objected to the very blunt (and lifelike) courtroom treatment of the rape issue, to the use of such words as "contraceptive," "panties," and so on. The judge said: (1) the "common conscience" of the general public would surely tolerate such depiction; (2) this censorship patently "exceeded constitutional bounds."

Thus, standards were relaxing. To some observers this legal trend was socially desirable; to some the effect was deplorable. To others it was confusing: were the courts really running too far ahead of the temper of the times? Or was the populace too worried about hobgoblins?

5.   A SUMMARY

WHERE DOES THE substantive law now stand? These observations may at least sum up some basic propositions.

1. There is constitutional power in both the state and federal governments to punish, criminally, people who distribute obscene creations.

2. Obscene creations are those which "appeal predominately to prurient interest," stimulate "libidinous impulses," and overstep the "community's standard" of what is decent. The Model Penal Code's prurient interest concept seems to have been adopted, not only in federal courts but in many states as well, as a new or cumulative criterion. The effect is to tighten the standard, and restrict the permissible scope of operation of anti-obscenity laws—particularly censorship. And it is doubtful if any broader, more inclusive definition of censorable sex expression would be permitted under the First Amendment.

3. But precisely how these standards are to be applied in particular cases is difficult to say. For example: (a) There is a great mass of "borderline" material, and its obsceneness is a matter of conjecture, depending on circumstances such as who will judge it and against what background of experience. The Supreme Court has indicated that neither a nudist magazine nor one for homosexuals

should automatically be decreed obscene, at least for purposes of postal censorship. (b) Books which enjoy high literary standing may not be obscene, even though they contain much erotic or blunt depiction. Whether true or not, as a scientific proposition, courts may continue to hold that a book of quality can't be "obscene" on the theory that quality itself disintegrates the effect of impure parts no matter how extensive. (c) Ordinarily, the measuring stick to make the judgment "is it obscene" is the "average man" (though little is known about "average" sexual instincts or "average " notions of decency). This is the teaching of the *Butler* case and others. But, where the audience overtly solicited and exposed is a juvenile group, or (as in the case of the Klaw materials on sadism) is an otherwise susceptible class, a serious problem exists which the courts have yet to answer. (d) Conversely, as in *Kinsey's* case and as suggested in the *Smith* case, there is now authority that it is not enough to determine that a work is obscene in the abstract—even where it is judged liberally by the "average-man" measuring stick. In censorship cases, where the circumstances permit it, there must be investigation into the circumstances of the actual case to the end that qualified recipients won't be denied freedom to read materials which will not in fact harm them and may be needed by them in the pursuit of mature interests. In criminal cases it must be shown that the defendant acted in a reckless manner with regard to the book which is questioned.

4. States may authorize use of some sort of censorship system as a means to prevent exhibition of obscene movies. There is every indication that the substantive standards must be strict and narrow, and the adjective guarantees must be liberal—the procedures for notice, hearing and full and prompt review in the courts. It remains to be seen just what kind of censorship can be carried on. The court has yet to speak definitively on the subject.

5. Finally, there is doubt whether federal censorship of the mails as it has been practiced is constitutional. Five Justices have stated positions which are inconsistent with the theory and practice, heretofore, of the Post Office. If the operation is to continue, changes are probably required to restrict it to a far narrower area.

PART V

Changes in Obscenity

Control Since 1957

In 1958, as a result of some of these judicial decisions, representatives of the Post Office, Bureau of Customs, and Justice Department attempted to reformulate standards and procedures and better integrate their operations.

For a number of reasons, including fear of adverse publicity and public misunderstanding, the effort failed. Each agency continued to run its own operation independently; each sought to adjust to the various court decisions as best it could.

I. THE BUREAU OF CUSTOMS CENSORS CHANGE THEIR WAYS

THE RAMIFICATIONS OF THE Supreme Court's rulings in the nudist magazine cases (*Sunshine* and *Mounce*) were baffling to Customs officials.

The volume of these importations was greater than ever. In the typical European version, the pictures were large, bold, and not retouched. The court decisions had suggested no explicit criteria for judging obsceneness here; indeed, the Supreme Court had summarily reversed lower court rulings which had been based on the most painful but explicit articulations of criteria. The Bureau's criteria, according to an unofficial memo, turned on the apparent authenticity of the publication as a vehicle of the nudist movement, whether the pictures were accompanied by genuine textual explanation and advocacy, whether too many pictures—in the mind of the viewer—were too "suggestive," too "prurient." This meant, in practice, that most magazines were released. Foreign "art" and "model" studies were judged by the same criteria, but with something of a presumption against their sincerity and authenticity in the usual case. This meant that the same picture of women unclothed might or might not be treated as obscene depending on whether the ostensible purpose of the publisher was to exhibit nudism as practiced by nudists or simply to exhibit the model. Commercial importers were generally treated no differently than private individuals. The Bureau apparently remained more lenient in its pictorial standards than the Post Office.

In the wake of the *Kinsey* case there came an increasing volume of petitions from importers seeking the release of books detained. Some asserted scholarly interest; others asserted only the right of adult Americans to read what they chose. In March of 1959, the Bureau released books by Henry Miller to an individual scholar in New York, analogizing his case to the *Kinsey* case. The ruling was publicized, and the publicity seems to have spurred more petitions for similar releases. The "concurrus horribilium," the specter raised by government lawyers in the *Kinsey* case, loomed. In response to many inquiries about its release policy, the Bureau replied that libraries could import "obscene" books in "appropriate cases" if the books were to be used for someone's "bona fide scholarly research" and kept out of "general circulation." While "individual scholars" could also "file applications," they must show, e.g., by a "certificate" from a "college" official, their institutional connection and their "need" for the obscene material.

These criteria could hardly answer all the hard cases at hand, nor do they reflect the whole story. Decisions concerning when to release and when to hold were not easy to make, let alone make consistently. Who was qualified to receive the *Kinsey* dispensation? An obviously pornographic French paperback novel was released to a petitioner who simply averred he was a "Ph. D. psychologist" studying the "personality" of certain authors as "projected" in their works. But a teacher of literature at a small midwestern college was denied works by De Sade which he had ordered for research purposes. "Ask your library to order them," was the Bureau's only consolation. The same technique was used to dispose of the petitions of other alleged scholars. But a returning tourist, who was separated from his copy of De Sade by a New York inspector, was able to win it back by aiming loud protests and meaningful threats of litigation at Washington. A New York business executive was denied a copy of Henry Miller's *Tropic of Cancer* for his "personal library," but the "director" of a planned-parenthood group who sought the same work for the same purpose was granted relief.

A number of cases have also arisen over importation of works like *Kama Kala* or other serious studies of "Indian erotology."

For example, there is a scholarly, expensive, impressive volume which discusses the absence of a "concept of sin and secretiveness" in various phases of Indian culture. The point is documented with many stark photographs of bas reliefs and statuary on the walls of certain ancient temples which portray sexual activity in a most graphic, "pornographic" form. These temples and their statuary are in India, for all who can afford to go there to see. But photographs of these scenes were not for Americans to see in America— at least according to some rather recent rulings. Presumably, only very special persons may have the work.

Foreign movies presented their perennial problems. As before, most films entered through New York, and Customs enforcement there is still largely the work of the Deputy Collector. The criteria of earlier years has probably slowly relaxed, although scenes of nudity or excessive familiarity are still cut or deleted regularly. The movie *La Loi* (based on the novel, which has had some acclaim here), contained a scene in which "Briganti kisses the woman at the cleavage in her breast." This, said the Bureau, "is an extensive action" and must be cut so that the kiss is suggested rather than portrayed. A "breast feeding" scene in a Swedish film was largely deleted; so was a scene showing briefly the nudity of performers in a French nightclub. *Les Amants,* a French film which received "rave" reviews in Paris and a total ban in Italy, was a tough problem. The "love scenes are, at best, difficult to describe" wrote the Customs official who screened it. Indeed so. One long, continuing scene of embracing and kissing apparently put Paris on its ear, if we are to believe Art Buchwald's account in the *Herald Tribune.* After some deliberation, including a screening in Washington, the film was cleared. So were others, which perhaps only a few years ago would have been stopped or cut up considerably. A French film shows two lovers enter a room; they disrobe and get in bed. Where should the line be drawn? Another film portrays the downfall to debauchery of its hero—all very candidly. How much candor can the United States government permit?

These film and book cases typify some constant, troubling problems of contemporary customs censorship. Who is entitled (under a *Kinsey* or Secretarial dispensation) to receive an otherwise obscene book? What is to be the basic policy in an era of shifting tastes, techniques and tolerance with movies? There is no certain answer to these questions. That there is need for serious re-appraisal of the operation of federal censorship in these areas seems clear. The American Civil Liberties Union has issued a protest to Secretary Dillon, calling attention to some book seizures reflecting, obviously, bad judgment. Litigation now looms over other episodes: a detention of Miller's *Tropic of Capricorn* may supply the vehicle for a test case apparently desired by a prospective American publisher; a case testing the current movie standard, however it may be verbalized, is also probable.

There are other problems which are, perhaps, even more disturbing to some Customs officials. Beginning in the summer of 1960, and increasingly thereafter, inspectors in New York discovered quite by accident that unprecedented quantities of pornographic materials—mostly pictorial—were being sent into this country via first class mail. These letters were postmarked from many European countries, but particularly from Scandanavia. Advertisements were found: mimeographed, misspelled, and crude in all other respects; for a few American dollars the recipient could buy a picture portraying any sex act he desired to see portrayed, including episodes with animals. And the pictures confiscated suggest that this advertising is seldom fraudulent.

The control of obscenity sent here via first class, sealed mail is a burdensome business. Customs officials cannot open suspect letters. If suspicious, they must ask the post office to ask the addressee for permission to open the letter. If assent is denied, the letter will be returned to the sender. If permission is granted and the suspicion is verified, then forfeiture proceedings are initiated—a notice to the addressee and a request for his "assent to forfeiture." If that is not forthcoming, then the material is libeled in court; periodically this is done.

A lot of man hours have been expended here. In the Port of New York an estimated 121,000 "personal" envelopes, each containing "packets," were detained and ultimately seized in a six-month period during 1960–61. Several employees of the United States were required to spend full-time doing nothing but the clerical work of notifying the addressees of this patent pornography.

2.   THE POST OFFICE CENSORS

CHANGE THEIR WAYS

SIGNIFICANT CHANGES HAVE occurred in the Post Office Department since 1957. They were hastened by a shift in personnel. A new "General Counsel" (the old-fashioned term "Solicitor" was at last abolished) took office in 1958. Shortly thereafter, the Chief of the Mailability Division, a lawyer who had served long and zealously and whose predilections had significantly influenced the enforcement pattern for many, many years, retired. More or less contemporaneously, a special assistant for fraud and obscenity matters was appointed to act as the General Counsel's adviser, technician, and perhaps conscience-keeper.

Yielding to the pressure both of court decisions and of its critics, the Post Office had already begun promulgating new rules to govern the procedure for decision-making in non-mailability cases. The new regime hastened this process. Henceforth, said the new rules, when a work is deemed non-mailable, the General Counsel must serve a "complaint" and a "notice of hearing" on the mailer, and those who wish to contest this decision will be afforded opportunity for a formal hearing patterned after the Administrative Procedure Act. In addition, the rules spelled out procedures to facilitate prompt disposal of cases where prompt delivery—if, in fact, the mail was not obscene—was desirable.

A second major change created the position of "Judicial Officer" within the Department. Subject only to the prerogative of the Postmaster General himself to supersede him, the Judicial Officer was given the job of reviewing the findings and conclusions of the Hearing Examiners, who presided as agency "trial judges" at the hearing of contested cases.

Prior to 1958, the General Counsel, or Solicitor, had exercised the power to review and revise the conclusions of the Hearing Examiners; he thus enjoyed, in theory, the power to set aside decisions adverse to the disposition of his own office. Now, the judging function was totally divorced; that power was taken out of the hands of lawyers who acted as initiators and prosecutors of censorship cases, and it was put into the hands of a lawyer who was not responsible to the "prosecutors" and whose sole function was to judge their cases independently. Creation of the new post of Judicial Officer, coupled with the new procedure for hearing non-mailability cases, meant that two separate officers, each acting independently, would have to agree that material was obscene before any restraint on circulation would be imposed. Finally—certainly an important step—each censorship decision would be based on a written record with a written decision issued to support it. Obviously, these more exacting procedures, along with the dispersal of power, would make for greater safeguards against abuse.

A third reform attempted to narrow the scope of mail blocks to comply with the *Sunshine* and *Tourlanes* cases. In those cases the courts had twice told the Department to confine its mail blocks to mail related to an enterprise found unlawful. Twice the government had sought to have these decisions set aside in the Supreme Court; twice the Solicitor General of the United States had gravely announced that this *Sunshine—Tourlanes* rule would destroy the effectiveness of the mail-block sanction. And even after these rulings were twice rendered, the Post Office could not bring itself to comply. But now, in 1958, the Department adopted the simple expedient of giving persons whose mail was "blocked" the opportunity of coming into their local post office, opening the impounded mail under supervision, and withdrawing all communications unrelated to the business of selling the obscene matter. Indeed, the General Counsel recently told a congressional committee that there is not much difficulty in administering the sanction this way.

A fourth significant change—also a tightening of the mail-block processes—has very recently been imposed upon the Post Office by Congress.

One of the most persistent problems confronting the Department over past years has been the matter of *interim* mail blocks. The problem here may seem technical, but it is quite crucial. Assume postal inspectors find a mail-order business in New York distributing materials thought to be obscene. The General Counsel will initiate proceedings looking towards a mail block—an order directing the local postmaster to impound the distributor's incoming mail. But the courts have required that formal hearings be held *before* the impounding order can be issued. Experience indicates that a considerable period of time is consumed in this process, which requires serving the distributor with a formal complaint; affording him opportunity for a formal answer; then a trial-type hearing before the Hearing Examiner who must, thereafter, issue a recommended order; and, finally, opportunity for appeal to the Judicial Officer who issues the final order, in the Departmental decision in the case. During this period the alleged offender stays in business selling materials which the Post Office has condemned as obscene.

The Department's lawyers have long sought the power to impose, *summarily,* temporary mail blocks—interim impounding orders to last during the administrative proceedings.

Prior to 1956 interim orders were issued without any statutory authority. When the Department went after an alleged offender it would sometimes cut off all his incoming mail without any prior notice or hearing. But by 1955, after a series of legal skirmishes, several Federal judges had plainly indicated that, in the absence of statutory authorization, this kind of summary impounding was illegal. In 1956, thanks in part to the publicity of the Kefauver hearings and to pressure from the Post Office, legislation was pushed in Congress to grant authority for interim impounding. But the bill passed only after Senator Monroney had, by amendments offered both in committee and on the Senate floor, put serious limitations on the power: interim impounding orders could be issued for a twenty-day period only; thereafter, the Post Office was required to petition the local district court for an extension of the order; nor could any interim order be imposed against copyrighted material or against publishers who enjoyed a second-class permit.

The 1956 law left Postal lawyers unsatisfied. The twenty-day temporary impounding period was too short, and for various reasons the Department had an unhappy history with applications for judicial extensions. On some occasions there was apparently a lack of liaison with local U.S. attorneys: the applications were filed too late. On other occasions the federal courts (in California) turned the Department down: the judges simply ruled that the materials in question were not obscene, or not so patently obscene as to warrant imposition of interim impounding.

By 1958 Postmaster General Summerfield personally became an active combatant in the anti-obscenity effort. He began a fight to rid the mail block law of "technicalities" impeding his lawyers. At the same time a House subcommittee, headed by Congresswoman Kathryn Granahan of Philadelphia, began a broadgauged, widely-publicized investigation of "smut peddling" in the mails. Mr. Summerfield and others supplied the committee with lurid descriptions of the "flow of filth"; and many congressmen were ceremoniously shown the Department's "Chamber of Horrors"—an exhibition room in the Department containing some shocking materials which Postal officials had previously found in the mails. (This special tour apparently became quite a talked about experience on Capitol Hill, both officially and unofficially.)

Mrs. Granahan introduced a bill to give Postal officials power to impound, without holding any hearings, for a forty-five-day period; the courts were not to interfere with this summary impounding unless it was found that the Post Office had been "arbitrary and capricious" in its action. Before the House committee Mr. Summerfield and his General Counsel argued cogently for the bill; and it was, as newspaper reports put it, "shouted through the House."

In the Senate, however, matters were a little different. Pressure for passage remained intense: Senator Clark (of the Senate Post Office Committee) received no less than 30,000 letters urging action. Many of these communications were, avowedly, the product of organized church drives, campaigns touched off by the previous publicity. But Senator Clark and Senator Monroney (who made up the majority of the subcommittee to which the bill had been referred) also appreciated the arguments of the opponents of the Granahan bill. These opponents ranged from civil libertarian groups to a number of Justice Department lawyers who became convinced that Mr. Summerfield's Department was asking for too much censorial power.

The authority which Mr. Summerfield sought was certainly susceptible to abuse. Departmental experience had showed just how these interim impounding orders could be used to destroy sedentary booksellers. Some years before, for example, Postal lawyers had imposed a "temporary" mail block on Gershon Legman, publisher-author of *Love and Death*. This book is a serious, vehement condemnation of the emphasis on sex and sadism in postwar American literature and movies. On one or two occasions Legman's polemic uses four-letter words; beyond that it can hardly be reproached, and presumably no court would ever find it obscene. But the Postal lawyers did, and Legman was driven out of business by their "temporary" mail block.

Given overzealous Postal officials, abuses like this could occur if carte-blanche powers to issue mail blocks were allowed. Notwithstanding the pressure put upon them, Senators Monroney and Clark held the Granahan bill in committee while their staffs explored less drastic alternatives. The Department of Justice also remained firm in its opposition. By mid-summer of 1960, Congress was caught up in the haste of a waning session and an impending election year, and the prospects for the Granahan bill receded. Postmaster General Summerfield was finally persuaded to accept and endorse a substitute measure or face the prospect of no legislation at all.

The upshot was that the Granahan bill was rewritten from stem to stern. Instead of permitting Postal lawyers to issue interim blocks, the bill now required the Post Office to apply to the appropriate district court for the issuance of a temporary order. The courts, not Postal lawyers, were to determine whether the case warranted interim action: if, after a full hearing, the court should find that there was "probable cause" to believe that a "violation" was occurring, then, and only then, the court could issue an interim order for a period long enough to cover the formal administrative hearings. All publications enjoying second-class mail privileges were exempted from the statute; they could not be reached by "interim" orders.

The requirement of going into court to secure an impounding

order seems to have been precisely the obstacle which the Post
Office wanted to avoid when it started its campaign for new legislation. But a combination of factors—notably two Senators who
shared grave misgivings with a few of the Attorney General's
lawyers—had blocked Mr. Summerfield. The rewritten bill passed
the Senate and the House in a rush, and the Post Office accepted
the compromise.

Whether the new law, requiring the Post Office to operate
directly through the courts, will prove very effective for Mr.
Summerfield's original purpose—a blitz against "borderline" distributors—is open to question. But the theory of the "Granahan-
Monroney law" (as Senator Clark dubbed it) suggests an interesting question. For the limited purpose of issuing temporary mail
blocks, Congress had shifted the entire decision-making process
in these cases from the Post Office to the courts: Why not do the
same thing with other postal powers—why not require *all* censorship cases to be initiated, directly, in the courts?

3. EXAMPLES OF THE POSTAL PROCESS: A MAIL-BLOCK PROCEEDING AND SOME RECENT CASES

THE TYPICAL POSTAL anti-obscenity case today deals with a distributor of nude pictures, borderline "stag" movies or cheap, erotic books. Inspectors, by tracking down complaints and following up "come-on" advertisements, gather data about the operator's business, samples of his wares, and proof of their distribution. Once on the track of such a case, they must move fast to be effective, for, typically, the operation is a fly-by-night business. If the purveyor can fill a volume of orders, he will often be happy to quit and set up a new enterprise when the government begins impounding his orders (although some of these "businessmen" do try to build up a "trade name" and a group of steady customers).

Having investigated, the inspectors will put their case to the General Counsel, and, infrequently, to the Department of Justice and a U.S. Attorney for possible criminal prosecution. Postal lawyers, having no worries about persuading jurors to convict or the pitfalls of a court trial, have been less restrained about using the sovereign power against these enterprises. If nudity is the prime ingredient of purveyor's mail-order wares, the Department will try to put him out of business.

A mail-block proceeding is initiated by filing a complaint with the Hearing Examiner (the Department's "trial judge"). At the same time, the General Counsel must decide the delicate, but often crucial question: What shall be done pending the hearing and a final decision on the complaint? If left alone for two or three more weeks the operator (he is now called a "respondent") may be able to peddle hundreds, perhaps thousands, more pictures. Under the new law of 1960 (amending section 259(b) of the Postal Code) the Department's lawyers must now refer the case to the local U.S. Attorney's office, who must petition the local district for the interim impounding order, presenting evidence to show "probable cause" of a serious violation of the law.

But assume now, in the absence of an interim impounding order, that a hypothetical case against a purveyor comes on for a hearing before the Post Office Department's own "judges." What happens in practice? The respondent may refuse to do legal battle with the Postal lawyers, and, if he does default, the impounding order will be issued. Or he may sign an "affidavit of discontinuance" —pledging just that in return for a promise by Postal lawyers to drop the case. But many respondents hire lawyers and make a contest of the matter. They will file "answers" and related pleadings which raise all sorts of contentions—e.g., applications to move the site of the administrative trial to the respondent's community, motions to make the complaint more precise (by requiring the General Counsel to spell out the ingredients of obsceneness in each of the condemned pictures). There will also be denials that the matter in question is "obscene" and allegations that the mail-block power is unconstitutional. There may be further requests, sometimes quite plausible on their face, for postponements of the hearing to secure more time to arrange a trip to Washington (after all, Los Angeles, where a good many alleged violators live, is a long way off). These questions must all be decided by the Hearing Examiner or Judicial Officer, who must also hurry the proceedings along in the interest of efficient enforcement.

Trial of a typical case has been, if we are to judge from the cold records, a redundant, often mechanical business. The Postal lawyers present the offending materials and testimony showing that they were in fact mailed. An inspector may tell what he has learned about the *modus operandi* of the respondent's distribution. The rest of the prosecution is argument. The materials are obscene, Postal lawyers say, because their predominant appeal is to prurience, their

dominant effect is libidinous, and they violate the community standard. No evidence to prove the actual existence of a community
standard on these particular pictures is offered, nor is any evidence
to establish, scientifically, the probability of incitement to lust
or similar harm. The respondent may claim that in the absence
of "proof" on these points, the case for censorship falls short of
the mark. Not at all, is the retort: the things speak for themselves;
"proof" of obsceneness is simply derived from inspection of the
pictures. The Postal prosecution rests. The respondent may then
argue and perhaps attempt to "prove" from propositions put forth
by his witnesses, that these pictures are no worse than those to be
found in many other publications freely circulating via newsstands,
or in barbershops, barracks, battleships, and countless other "communities" where men congregate. Sometimes "expert" witnesses,
arguments based on the writing of "experts," or both, will be
offered to sustain the claim that average men would not regard the
offending items as indecent; that they are, in fact, no more "indecent" than many other pictures of more renown; that the libidinous impact of the pictures is ephemeral and trivial, if existent at
all. This sort of evidence often has been urged perfunctorily, but,
however presented, it has more often been rejected than accepted.
It is the mandate of the law (the Department still seems to say)
that the Post Office, not outsiders—even expert outsiders—must
appraise the community's "standard" and the libidinous impact and
"predominant appeal" of such pictures. The Post Office's judge,
alone, must decide whether these standards have been transgressed.
On the other hand, when it is asserted that the offending material
has some social value as an educational, literary, or artistic production, the respondent may be allowed more opportunity to have an
"expert" testify. As to what the expert may say, that is, how far he
may be allowed to talk about the ultimate issues, there is, as yet,
confusion. In the *Lady Chatterley* case, where the publisher put
forth much expert testimony in defense of the literary quality and
value of the book while the government produced none, Postmaster General Summerfield simply said, in effect: I don't believe
these "experts." Understandably, the Department has been chary
about "expert" testimony. Who is qualified to give it? What shall
be its form?—its function?—its weight?

In the typical case described, the decision will be for the government. It is usually held that general circulation of pictures of nude young women will arouse impure sexual reactions in the audience solicited; such displays appeal to prurient interest and are not acceptable to the aggregate morality of the American people.

Judging the obsceneness of this "borderland" pictorial material is by far the most common problem to come before Postal officials today. And, as the United States government told the Supreme Court: "There is an unlimited range of poses . . . and it is impossible . . . to have a clear and sharp line as to what is obscene." Evaluating these things, suggested the Judicial Officer, may indeed be a "non-rational process." Thus, in one "non-mailability" proceeding, the magazine *Rogue* was cleared with no verbalization of the reasons beyond this statement: "While [the magazines] are replete with stories concerning sex and pictures of partially nude females, I do not believe that they transcend current community standards." On the other hand, *Men's Digest,* a similar, albeit less literate and more daring magazine, was barred, and the articulation of reasons was equally cryptic: "It is not necessary to elaborate on the exact content of [the magazines]. They are in evidence. . . . Upon application of [the *Roth* standards] I conclude [they] are obscene." Somewhere between these two publications lies the current line of legality. Perhaps further attempt by the Post Office to describe the location would be a tedious waste of print as well as an undignified exercise.

An interesting variant of a borderline case arose in New York. Promoters of the movie *Naked Maja* tried to send postcards portraying on one side a color photograph reproduction of Goya's painting and on the other a plug for the film ("the most breathtaking canvass that ever came to life"). Some cards also advertised the film *Some Like It Hot.* The General Counsel found all of them non-mailable—the Goya reproduction was too prurient when used for these advertising purposes. A hearing followed, enlivened by the distributor's persistent attempts to have a psychologist swear that the cards, in his opinion, would have no harmful effect "on average persons." The Hearing Examiner refused to hear such claims, and, "applying all the yardsticks," he "found as a fact" that these Goya reproductions were "obscene." The Judicial Officer concurred. When the case was appealed to the courts, the Department of Justice, having taken over the defense of the censorship action, withdrew its defense and, in effect, reversed the Post Office by abandoning any effort to sustain its order in a court contest.

Even more controversial were two attempts by Postal lawyers to suppress mailed publications quite different from the borderline material. The book *Lady Chatterley's Lover* was the first. There the decision was made by Postmaster General Summerfield himself. (The Judicial Officer noted that the book had "for many years been held non-mailable" by both Post Office and Customs, and he suggested that any "reversal" must come from the top.)

Mr. Summerfield's explanation for his decision was indeed cryptic. The book, he declared, was "replete" with "filthy," "smutty," "degrading," "offensive," "disgusting" words and descriptions of sexual acts. These filthy words and passages "outweighed" its merit, notwithstanding the uncontroverted contrary testimony of outstanding critics and notwithstanding the total absence of any "proof" in the record to sustain his own vigorously stated conclusions.

More recently, Postal lawyers pursued a "beatnik" magazine. The first issue of *Big Table* is definitely not for the reader who insists on precision of meaning; nor, perhaps, is it for the squeamish. One story, "Old Angel Midnight" by Jack Kerouac, was described by John Ciardi in the *Saturday Review* as:

> . . . thirty-five pages of free association in several languages (of which Kerouac is no certain master) and in gibberish (of which he recognizably is). Add a random of bilingual puns. Add four-letter words at will. Add even—here and there—a glimpse of orderly perception in the whirling chaos. What one comes out with (minus the four-letter words) runs: "God's asleep dreaming, we've got to wake him up! Then all of a sudden when we're asleep dreaming, he comes and wakes us up—how gentle! How are you Mrs. Jones? Fine Mrs. Smith! Tit within Tat—Eye within Tooth—Bone within Light, Like—Drop some little beads of sweetness into the stew (O Phoney Poetry!)—the heart of the onion—That stew's too good for me to eat, you!—" Or: "Sor god denoder pie your pinging lief bring Ida Graymeadow Wolf babe oo brooding in the is-ness seastand graygog magog bedonigle bedart ooo!"

The "dirty words" printed in the midst of all this free association caught the eye of Postal censors. Likewise with another tale, "The Naked Lunch" (which Mr. Ciardi thought was "powerful— a masterpiece of its own genre").

Big Table was withheld from its handful of subscribers, and the editors were not allowed to mail even a few copies to some lawyers and psychologists for critical appraisal of the book's obsceneness. After some delay, the case was heard; several critics testified (some apparently without much enthusiasm) that all this verbal surrealism was, e.g., a "valid," "serious," "artistic" effort, "a recognized school of writing." Perhaps so. Certainly there was no contrary testimony, expert or otherwise, condemning the stories. But the Postal Judicial Officer, emphasizing the filthiness of the offending "four-letter words," ruled the magazine obscene. The American Civil Liberties Union entered the case, publicized it, and sued Mr. Summerfield. Eventually the Department of Justice persuaded (or coerced) the Post Office to back down.

Of course, *Big Table, Lady Chatterley,* and Goya's *Maja* were not "typical" cases. But they did demonstrate the difficulties which persist even after zealous efforts to reform procedures and restrict censorial discretion.

4. FEDERAL CRIMINAL ENFORCEMENT IS EXPANDED; CONGRESS IS AROUSED

IN 1958, A SEEMINGLY technical amendment to the Comstock Act was pushed through Congress. It abrogated a long-standing court-made rule which required criminal prosecution for mailing obscenity to be brought in the district where the materials were mailed. In practice, the long-standing rule had meant that purveyors operating in Los Angeles and New York could only be indicted and tried in those areas, where prosecutions were hard to win.

For years, with varying degrees of zeal, Postal officials had urged Congress to break the alleged bottleneck created by the venue limitation. Finally, in 1958, with another bill in the hopper, the necessary momentum was generated in a House Judiciary Committee headed by Francis Walter.

A score of witnesses representing "clean-up" civil or religious movements backed the change. In vain a few civil libertarian groups protested to Mr. Walter and his colleagues, pointing out that enactment of this bill would create new risks for reputable publishers and booksellers; it would subject them to community standards which might be quite different from their own, to the disparate standards of every American community into which their books might be sent. A firm in New York, for example, might mail a few copies of *Peyton Place* into some distant rural community where prejudice against books of that sort runs strong. A pliant or zealous prosecutor might be persuaded to press for an indictment. At the worst, the New York seller might be convicted. Even if he were eventually acquitted, the opportunity to harass him would exist, and that possibility would deter bold exercise of freedom to publish, for "persecuted" publishers could be forced to transport lawyers, witnesses, and other ammunition for defense to a distant, hostile place. Such harassment, it was said, would "violate" the "spirit," if not the letter, of the First and Sixth Amendments.

These protests were given short shrift: "Everyone squawks the amendments these days," retorted Congressman Chelf, while Chairman Walter insisted, with much logic, that the place where the "damage was done" should be the place where the wrongdoer was brought to book. But the Senate was more receptive to the book publishers' complaints. While the bill was finally reported out and passed, the Judiciary Committee openly warned that United States prosecutors were not to abuse their new power.

The Department of Justice, *so far,* has been mindful of the warning. There appears to have been no abuse of the kind foreseen. Indeed, despite strong, continuous, pressure on the United States government—pressures felt at every level: on Congressmen, Postal Officials, local prosecutors and the Attorney General—criminal enforcement of the Comstock Act has remained limited. There seems to be an unofficial policy favoring prosecutions only when "hardcore" obscenity is disseminated. Again, unofficial policy restricts venue either to the place of mailing or to an area where a large volume of material is sent—to areas where the dissemination has had an "impact," as one government lawyer put it.

Today, few federal prosecutors would seriously entertain the plan of proceeding against mail distribution of a book like *Lady Chatterley*—or, for that matter, against an off-beat publication like *Big Table.* The Department of Justice would, presumably, exercise close rein over prosecutors who might choose to court such controversy. Indeed, despite the new "venue" law, there have still been relatively few prosecutions of the purveyors whose activities are the basis for so many mail blocks. While it remains difficult to articulate the precise difference in standards, there plainly is one, and the two operations—criminal enforcement and censorship—are still managed quite independently. True, the Postal Inspection Service digs up most of the cases, and in that sense it supplies continuous liaison between those who must prosecute and those who must censor. But, the standards for illegality are worked out quite independently. Postmaster General Summerfield continued to deplore the "multimillion dollar traffic" in obscenity. He bombarded Congress and the country with dire warnings.[1] But, the Attorney General's department obviously concluded that only a fraction of all this traffic is criminal contraband.

In the meantime, public consternation, confusion, and controversy increased. A congressional committee headed by Kathryn Granahan of Philadelphia, in the summer of 1959, heard a barrage of protests from ministers, women's clubs, juvenile-court experts, policemen, district attorneys, judges, and Postal officials. As soon as that investigation ended, Senator Kefauver's subcommittee on juvenile crime took up the refrain. A constitutional amendment on obscenity was proposed.

While newspaper headlines were recounting all this redundant, albeit newsworthy protest, Judge Bryan's *Lady Chatterley* decision was handed down, adding fuel to the flames. The decision was attacked by Mr. Summerfield in a statement which was blown up and tacked on many post office walls. The Postmaster General's refrain was picked up by many members of Congress. The Supreme Court, which had come in for serious attack for decisions in other fields, was now damned indiscriminately for destroying established law and order in this field.

Yet, liberalizing court decisions—ranging from affirmance of

1. In January 1961 a new Postmaster General, J. Edward Day, former lawyer and insurance executive, replaced Postmaster General Summerfield. As one of his first official acts, he closed the "chamber of horrors," the room set aside for exhibition of samples of confiscated pornography to demonstrate to visiting Congressmen, clergymen, Women's Clubs and others the evil nature of the traffic, the need for stern laws. "The pictures will be returned to the files where they belong," an aide of the new Postmaster General stated. "Besides, we need every bit of space we can find around here for offices." Secondly, Mr. Day announced (per the *Washington Post and Times Herald* of February 3, 1961,) that the Post Office would no longer engage in publicizing anti-obscenity campaigns. He promised the "toughest crackdown ever conducted" against "violators of the laws against mailing pornographic materials", but it would go on "without fanfare." A far cry from Mr. Summerfield, whose anti-obscenity publicity had even included a stamp cancellation reminding the public at large, constantly, to "Report Obscene Mail to Your Postmaster."

Lady Chatterley's Lover decision by the federal court of appeals to the clearance of other controversial movies by state courts, for example, *The Lovers*—continued to make headlines. Lawrence's book became a best seller, widely praised, widely denounced. Magazines like *Playboy,* "avant garde" only a few years ago for their boldness, became staple items on the newstands of even conservative neighborhood drugstores. A change in the community standard of tolerance had probably occurred, even over a period of a few short years, and notwithstanding the most vehement protests from the community itself. Senators Scott and Mundt introduced similar bills to establish a "National Commission on Noxious and Obscene Matters and Materials" with the broad, vague mandate to "study" traffic in obscenity—"a matter of grave national concern", and to "formulate" a new legislative program "for the suppression of such traffic." A joint bill, co-sponsored by twenty-seven other senators, creating the Commission, was passed unanimously and loudly by the Senate, in the summer of 1960. A similar House bill, also widely supported, did not reach the floor that session. But future passage seemed likely.

What was happening?—sober, intelligent objective Americans wanted to know. Where were we going? Where should we be going?

PART VI

Proposals for the Future

1. WHY DO WE SUPPRESS OBSCENE PUBLICATIONS?

THE PRECISE FUNCTION of laws, state and federal, aimed at suppressing obscene books has never been identified very clearly. The multitude of sources—case reports, legislative debates, and commentaries which are supposed to explain why we have such laws—speak a babel of ideas.

Diverse explanations have been variously worded, sometimes dogmatically asserted, over the years. Although cataloguing is risky because it oversimplifies, there follows an attempt to restate and evaluate some of the rationales.

1. *Obscenity laws are necessary to prevent people from thinking bad thoughts and thus adopting corrupt attitudes.* This "corruption of the populace" thesis holds that publications which inculcate immoral attitudes toward sex should be characterized as obscene and suppressed. One basis is more purely puritanical: simply that it is "bad" to think bad thoughts. Another is somewhat more sophisticated: If such creations are allowed to circulate, they may gain some acceptance; men will cease to condemn conduct which is bad—evil in the abstract and harmful in fact. Thus free circulation of obscenity will produce a slow but sure enervation of moral standards; society will come to condone immodesty, promiscuity, adultery, and similar conduct; basic institutions—religion and

the family—will crumble. As the Supreme Court once wrote, long ago:

> The foundation of a republic is the virtue of its citizens. They are at once sovereigns and subjects. As the foundation is undermined, the structure is weakened. When it is destroyed, the fabric must fall. Such is the voice of universal history.

Pretermitting the question of the validity of the premises, it is difficult to support the conclusion that all works which are "corrupting" must forthwith be destroyed and put out of mind, through the *force of law,* in order to save our institutions. If all books which taught bad attitudes or evoked bad thoughts were proscribed, then the proscription would be vast indeed—intolerably so. Past experience, notably experience with enforcement of the obscenity laws under the broad, vague *Hicklin* mental sanitation concept, or with the *Esquire* fiasco, and more recently with the movie, "Lady Chatterley," demonstrates the dangers of authorizing the government to act against anything simply because it may induce such corruption in the populace. Moreover, our standards about what is corrupting have certainly never been unchanging, exact constants. Few would argue, today, that many of the books once banned as "corrupt" are, today, corrupting; many would argue that some of these works have precisely an opposite effect. Clearly, the best remedy against noxious speech should simply be more speech—speech, like the teaching of religion, ethics, and aesthetics, that will persuade men to know and reject what is wrong and thus work out their own salvation as self-reliant men. Surely in a free country the ultimate responsibility and the best hope for exercising good judgment in matters of morality, just as in matters of polity, must rest with the people themselves, not with a paternalistic sovereign.

2. *Obscenity laws are necessary to prevent sexual misbehavior among adults.* This second justification is based on the theory that publications or movies which depict sex in the manner we characterize as "obscene" cause bad conduct—not just bad beliefs. In many censorship cases it has been assumed that a particular book will have a strong "libidinous" or "stimulating" impact on adults if they are allowed to read it; this stimulation will cause many readers to engage in some sort of conduct—a physical action, not just a mental reaction—which society may legitimately condemn. The

aim of the law, it is suggested, is to identify that kind of sex expression which does produce this bad conduct and curb its circulation.

The essential difficulties with this theory are that it is vague and that it is unsupported by evidence in any particular case. (And we are speaking here of acceptable scientific evidence, not personal opinion). What kind of sexual misconduct (on the part of adults) is, in fact, caused by exposure to what kind of expression?

Consider, for example, the following: John Doe is an adult, an "average man"; he is, in Judge Woolsey's words "l'homme moyen sensuel." John Doe wants to buy and read *The Memoirs of Fanny Hill*. That book, it seems fair to say, is deliberately and flagrantly erotic; indeed as pornography it is a "classic" (the Harvard Library once insisted that Customs release an imported copy precisely because the book was the "classic" piece of obscene literature of the English-speaking world).

Can we let Doe have the book? Present laws, as officials interpret them, say "No." But, if Doe reads Fanny's *Memoirs,* what harm will befall him? What are the probabilities that he will forthwith become promiscuous or otherwise anti-social in his sexual conduct? Do the facts that the book has endured through the decades and is still very readable and is regarded as a sort of "classic" make it more or less harmful? If Doe reads it, will he respond any more or less than if he reads something duller—albeit perhaps even more pornographic? Does the case change, do we know with any more certainty what the result will be, if the work suppressed is a nudist or a girlie magazine? Or a movie featuring a scene where the heroine disrobes? Or an account of a sex crime splurged pruriently in a tabloid?

As of the moment, there seems to be no generally accepted answer to these questions. One, oft-cited, exhaustive "expert" study of the available, reputable, "scientific" evidence concludes that there are no conclusions: we simply cannot isolate the impact on behavior of one book, one set of pictures, or even one sequence in a movie, as opposed to another, and generalize about the effect this communication will have on "normal" adults. Neither can we generalize about any class of books nor any of the various media to which we are exposed.

There are, it would seem, many variations to gauge the immedi-

ate libidinous impact of a work, let alone its influence on later behavior: the cultural background of the reader, his psychodynamics,
his physical circumstances and condition when he reads it, the character of the obsceneness of the book and its peculiar relationship
to the characteristics of the reader, and so on—all of these may
affect the impact of some item depicting sex activity or nudity. There
is evidence (Kinsey's findings for example) to verify the assumption that viewing erotic material often may stimulate a sexual
arousal in many men. But we are told nothing about the meaning,
the effects of this transitory feeling.

Clinical opinion is divided; we are offered many unproven hypotheses. The draftsmen of American Law Institute's Model Penal
Code recently surveyed the "scientific" literature and reported that
"there is no psychiatric consensus," nor is there consensus in any
other of the "social sciences"; thus "we know little or nothing about
the consequences of reading obscene or shocking literature." Two
other leading legal scholars on obscenity law also surveyed the
literature and found no evidence of "a single effort of genuine research" to test the "effect of sex literature upon sex conduct." Even
the United States Government, arguing in behalf of the validity of
the Comstock Act, tacitly admitted the absence of evidence and
was careful to avoid premises which assumed that there was proof
of specific cause-and-effect relationship. Indeed, one might snidely
suggest that if there is a precise cause-and-effect relationship,
government employees such as policemen, movie censors, and other
officials exposed repeatedly to condemned eroticism should be periodically re-examined for their own and society's safety.

Yet, despite the admitted lack of evidence supporting any particular hypothesis concerning the effect that reading an obscene book
will have on conduct, a great many eminent persons and groups insist—as a matter of opinion—that there may be some sort of a
dangerous relationship in many cases. At least, it is often asserted
that widespread, continuous dissemination of obscene expression
will breed anti-social attitudes and thus may stimulate many adults
to sexual misbehavior—though the precise nature of this misbehavior is seldom defined. The Kefauver Committee's report and the
testimony of some "experts" before the Committee reflects this
confusion, this self-serving confidence coupled with uncertainty. The
Committee's conclusion seems to be that obscenity must be assumed

to exert a bad influence in the mass, especially on juveniles, but apparently on adults, too, though evidence to prove this is admittedly lacking. Congresswoman Granahan's House Post Office Committee recently reached similar conclusions; in fact, that Committee was emphatic, albeit indiscriminate, in its assertions.

Law-enforcement officials, judges who sit daily in criminal or juvenile courts, clergymen who work with people in trouble, social workers, and some psychiatrists (others, of course, strongly disagree) have vigorously claimed that the reading of obscenity has definitely triggered much of the day's sexual criminality. They repeatedly point to actual criminal cases with which they are familiar; but careful analysis may well show that juvenile cases are often used to support conclusions framed in terms of adults and that, in any event, most of these wrongdoers suffered from serious mental disorder or psychological defects to begin with; many case histories cited are simply not cases involving "average adults," even tolerating a lot of leeway in one's concept of the general average. Indeed, there is some psychiatric opinion that the reading of these materials sometimes decreases, rather than increases, anti-social sexual behavior— that there is a sublimation and cathartic effect induced by the reading, a release of otherwise aggressive sexual drives without actual physical aggression. Again, there is respectable opinion that, in the main, those who engage in aggressive conduct are simply non-readers of anything, be it trash or even obscenity.

Yet newspaper editorialists and most of the public certainly share a generalized, imprecise but strong impression that obscenity circulation breeds crime or sexual misbehavior. The American Law Institute, even as it deplored the void of knowledge about any particular cause-and-effect relationship, proceeded to promulgate its new, "rational" legislation on the assumption that widespread commercial circulation of all sorts of obscenity will cause undesirable psychological consequences among adult readers and therefore should be deterred. Again the assertions are based more on suppositions strongly felt than on external evidence scientifically marshalled—for, as most admit, there is little if any persuasive empirical data to be marshalled; there are only opinions and clinical judgments.

Those who do argue a cause-and-effect hypothesis may also insist that the skeptics cannot be allowed to carry the day simply by shifting the entire burden of proof. They point out that scientific certainty is difficult if not impossible in this field, that conclusions must be based on fragmentary data and knowledgeable conjecture, and that the beliefs or intuition of an overwhelming majority are not to be set aside by reason of the doubts of the few or the unavoidable dearth of scientific data. There may be no proof to support any sweeping generalizations, but that hardly compels rejection of all hypotheses justifying anti-obscenity laws.

Suppose there were no laws—no laws at all: Recent experience surely indicates that widespread, continued mass dissemination of strongly erotic works among adults would occur. And if widespread, continuous dissemination of varied forms of obscenity occurs, then there is surely a probability (how strong it is, no one knows) that the behavior of some adults would be affected in a serious way over the long run. For, the psychiatrist cautions, there may well be no certain standard of "normality" among "average adults" in this field. There may, on the contrary, be a host of variables. There is some empirical data suggesting that, varying with the circumstances, some kinds of obscenity may have a stronger appeal and arousal impact on some people than on others. And the very fact that we cannot generalize about the impact of obscenities on viewers may well indicate that repeated exposure of those who do seem to be attracted to this expression could, when this condition of easy availability is coupled with other factors, cause socially harmful conduct among some of these people, even though these "some" may be otherwise "average adults."

This risk may not be proved sufficiently "clear" and "present" to justify, *by itself,* any anti-obscenity legislation. But the question is whether this risk, *when coupled with other justifications,* makes a case for the imposition of limited restraints on the mass dissemination of obscene matter.

3. *Obscenity laws are necessary to prevent sexual misbehavior by youthful and sexually maladjusted persons.* Many proponents of vigorous anti-obscenity laws concede that too little is known about the impact of obscene publications on the conduct of "average" adults to justify the existence of the laws on that ground. Yet they insist that obscene publications influence the conduct of what we might call a class of "susceptible" people—sexually maladjusted adults, adolescents, perhaps, too, very young children.

Again, the evidence to show what kind of material affects what kind of person in what kind of way is lacking. For example, two very eminent students of juvenile delinquency (Dr. and Mrs. Glueck of Harvard), made exhaustive studies of the background of five hundred anti-social delinquents and reported no evidence at all that viewing obscenity caused their delinquent conduct. Other studies suggest similar conclusions. Yet, again, many persons who deal with juveniles in a criminal setting—law enforcement and court personnel—insist that, in case after case, the offender was exposed or was an addicted reader of allegedly obscene matter. All this probably proves little either way; nevertheless, the probability of misconduct occurring as a result of viewing obscenity seems greatest when we limit the cause-and-effect hypothesis to juveniles and maladjusted or mentally disordered adults.

Yet, the whole history of anti-obscenity law demonstrates the danger of setting up a standard which proscribes all publications of books fit for adults simply to prevent "susceptibles" from reading these books. Indeed, precisely such a Hicklin-type standard was condemned as unconstitutional in the *Butler* case. Consequently, to the extent that our laws are to be limited simply to the goal of preventing broad distribution of obscene creations to this specially defined audience, we must make it quite certain that these same laws do not impose unwarranted restraints on the freedom of "normal" adult people. The danger, if any, to youth is too often cited as the justification for new restrictions on the freedom of adults.

4. *Obscenity laws are necessary to protect parental interests.* Somewhat analogous is this argument, often voiced by irate parents: "I don't care if obscenity doesn't affect the behavior of young people, I just don't want commercial vendors or movie exhibitors tempting my kids to buy, read or see this stuff behind my back."

Strictly speaking, the assertion here is not that the material may affect behaviour, but that obscenity has a strong attraction to many teen-age youths; many will read it if they can; and, if there were *no* laws, it would be difficult indeed for parents (in today's hectic, urban world, where parental influence is surely less than it was generations ago) to control or offset frequent exposure to sex expression repugnant to reasonable parents.

Of course, parents have no absolute, overriding, legal right to bring up children as they choose. But our norms do put a high value on the privilege of the parent to teach as he sees fit in matters of morality; and in various ways, law surely has reflected, indeed articulated, that value.

In today's world no parent can expect his child to be insulated from all the erotic stimuli which seem omnipresent in mass communications. But is not the parental interest here strong enough to deserve some recognition and protection?

Even assuming that exposure of an adolescent to erotic stimuli or shocking pornography or sex sadism does nothing to the personality and future behavior of most children, should we permit all children to be fair game for any purveyor? Postal files indicate that often youngsters are recipients of advertisements of cheap mail-order erotica, and these cases frequently produce the strongest kind of outrage and denunciation among parents—a feeling that the purveyor is a malicious intruder. The justification for the purveyor's conduct, for deliberately soliciting youngsters—or even recklessly soliciting names on a list when any reasonable man would know that this list contains many youths—seems hardly sufficient to outweigh the desirability of some minimal controls against such conduct.

5. *Obscenity laws are necessary to prevent unjustified infliction of emotional disturbance.* There is also the argument that obscenity controls are needed to protect the average adult from a psychic hurt produced by exposure to that which outrageously offends his moral code. By virtue of their upbringing, religious beliefs and other factors, many people cannot tolerate obscene things; they regard them with horror or loathing, and exposure causes that kind of psychic sensation. In tort law, courts have increasingly recognized a right to recover for the "emotional disturbance" which, it is assumed, can ensue when one is subjected to "extreme and outrageous" verbal assaults or analogous conduct. Just as filthy insults might well disturb many people, too, in a similar sense, mental disturbance (shame, disgust, outrage, fear) may very well result among people who are unjustifiably forced to view or read things depicting sex or speaking of sex in a way which transgresses precepts universally taught and devoutly believed. A function of anti-obscenity law, it is sometimes implied, is to prevent infliction of such mental disturbance.

Care must be taken to distinguish here between voluntary as

opposed to involuntary exposure. One who reads pornographic matter by choice, or even with some forewarning, is scarcely in a position to complain about any psychic hurt. Most people, today, are exposed to things seriously obscene only by their own volition. On the other hand, exposure is sometimes not by choice, but is more or less unavoidable, as in the case of highly erotic advertising conspicuously put in a public place, or, to relate the matter to postal law, the recurring case of one who receives in the mail, unsolicited, with no warning, a message put in a very obscene form. Such recipients may, under some circumstances, suffer a kind of unsought, psychic harm analogous to that suffered by the victims of other verbal assaults which tort law now condemns.

6. *Obscenity laws are necessary to prevent commercialized stimulation of psycho-sexual tensions.* The American Law Institute has offered a new articulation of the rationale of a modern anti-obscenity law. Says the Institute: "The wall of secrecy with which society has surrounded sexual behavior tends to build up in the individual strong feeling of the shamefulness of sexuality. . . . Literary or graphic material which disregards the social convention evokes 'repression-tensions,' i.e., mixed feelings of desire and pleasure on the one hand, and dirtiness, ugliness and revulsion on the other. . . . Society may legitimately seek to deter the deliberate stimulation and exploitation of [these] emotional tensions . . ." Thus: "the principal objective [of the law should be] . . . to prevent commercial exploitation of this psycho-sexual tension."

The Institute has thus suggested a new, provocative insight: obscenity is bad, not in the abstract, nor because it demonstrably triggers misbehavior, but rather because of its unsettling influence. Our culture—our entire upbringing, in a very formidable way—makes men fear the obscene even while they are drawn to it. If profit-motivated purveyors are allowed to stimulate such tensions, some sort of psychological harm to many individuals may result. But are most men normally drawn to obscene expression? How strong is the attraction? Do they, upon exposure or thereafter, suffer strong feelings of conscious or unconscious guilt? How serious is the resultant anxiety or tension? What effects might it have on behavior? These are questions to which psychiatrists and others have not yet responded to any degree.

Indeed, the Institute's study elsewhere admits that we know

"little or nothing" about the effect of reading "obscene" or "shocking" matter; and surely it is hard to say what kinds of books, pictures, or advertisements evoke serious "psycho-sexual" tensions. Again, if it is only deliberate, commercial stimulation of tension which is to be stopped, then why not limit the law's proscription to precisely that conduct?

Nevertheless, as *one,* if not the sole nor conclusive justification for anti-obscenity legislation, this suggested rationale seems important. The Model Penal Code experts have described—in psychiatric terms—an evil, possibly latent, in obscenity which other writers seem also to have perceived, from D. H. Lawrence to Margaret Mead to thoughtful judges. Because the scientific evidence is not all in, it hardly follows that the hypothesis must be rejected. Indeed, this hypothesis may be more readily open to empirical examination and evaluation than others.

7. *Obscene publications may be banned because they form no useful part in the exposition of ideas or the advancement of the arts.* Here the argument is, strictly, that regardless of whether they work harm on the morals, psyche, or behavior of people, obscene publications may still be suppressed at the will of the majority because they are socially useless; they stimulate glands alone—not the intellect, nor even that more amorphous but also more important element of personality, the human spirit.

No doubt the bulk of what is intercepted as obscene lacks worth by almost any standard—society might lose little by losing most of it. But (Justice Brennan and his four colleagues to the contrary) who is to say that this bold assertion is wholly true?

Experience with enforcement of anti-obscenity laws demonstrates the difficulty of this rationale. We have already recounted these cases in detail. A substantial number of books which have recently been found "obscene" clearly have other important characteristics, at least to a substantial number of responsible persons. Who can say, in such circumstances, that these proscribed works are "utterly without redeeming social importance"? To take one very significant case, the book *Lady Chatterley's Lover:* one might concede, *arguendo,* that this work is "obscene" for some purposes because of the detail and extreme emphasis in so many of its parts on the sexual act. But even if this be conceded, surely only the Philistine can deny that Lawrence's book is, at least in part, but in a real sense, a social tract—a protest against what has happened to culture and man in industrialized, "civilized" England. Nor can it be denied that discriminating readers have appreciated this author's artistic power to use words to communicate. However, until 1959 the book was vigorously denounced as seriously obscene by both federal censors and state courts. These decisions may have been wrong all the time, but the experience and an objective appraisal of the book may show how erotic writing can be combined in a large measure with literary value or social advocacy. The next major court case may well involve new litigation over one of the forbidden novels of Henry Miller, which would present precisely the same phenomena in even bolder form.

The Library of Congress carefully preserves copies of books condemned as obscene by the Bureau of Customs; it makes many available to the general public and eschews attempts to judge the worth of these books in humble recognition of man's frailties to make such judgments. Many great libraries of the world also maintain large collections of erotica. While society vigorously condemns obsceneness as a form in which to couch ideas, it remains a fact that men have used the form to express themselves—to describe human conduct, fictional or true; to express ideas, good or bad, but ideas nevertheless. This use of obsceneness in communication has surely been true of other great cultures, and, because some things which are quite obscene may also be important reflections of man's culture, thinking and ideas, Congress, when enacting the Tariff Act ban, authorized the Secretary of the Treasury to permit entrance of obscene "classics" and obscene works of scientific or "literary merit."

The tests for obsceneness, no matter how we phrase them, are too susceptible to error induced by ignorance or the influence of the times to operate as a sure sift to sort that which has social value from that which has none. Strong judges have resisted popular pressure to suppress works which, at the time, were vigorously condemned. But less tolerant judges and many censors—operating under the same laws—have not. Framers of standards and commentators on the subject have long wrestled with the persisting problem: how to make sure that worthwhile works can escape the law's ban. The "rules" about judging works as "a whole," about evaluating their "dominant effect" or "predominant appeal" reflect the struggle to devise a formula which will provide a loop-hole to save all good books.

Alas, not only is it difficult to know how to judge the worth of many works when we evaluate them "as a whole," but this concept—that the law protects art and condemns only trash—if pushed too far, seems to produce embarrassing paradoxes. Some works having notable qualities of artistry and the power to communicate effectively may also partake of the very qualities which constitute "obsceneness," which make us fear it. A good writer who attempts to appeal to prurience may do a much better job than a dull hacker; the good writer, of course, should have no special license to put out what inferior creators may not. Nevertheless, let us beware of any dogma which insists all works currently deemed obscene can be committed to the bonfire with no loss to mankind.

Instead of the hypothesis advanced by the Court in the *Roth* case, is it not more realistic to say that obsceneness is a characteristic which sex expression may have, that there are infinite degrees and many forms of obsceneness, that the more obscene a work becomes the less likely it is to have much value to most men as useful expression? But we should recognize, too, that some things obscene, indeed some things very obscene, may still have value as expression for at least limited purposes.

The argument justifying the banning of all obscenity for its "utter lack of value" as speech is thus a dangerous generalization. Absence of value can be a criterion to measure obsceneness and a reason for justifying suppression. But it is, at most, only *one* justification, and it should not be regarded as the conclusive justification for suppression.

2.   SHOULD WE CONTINUE TO SUPPRESS OBSCENE PUBLICATIONS?

CONSIDERING THE HISTORY of obscenity suppression, the dangers to expression of ideas, to art, and to literature, the imprecision in ascertaining what is and what is not obscene, and the lack of conclusive arguments for its retention, one may ask: Have the supporters of suppression carried their burden of proof in this area which is so fraught with constitutional implications?

In the past, and today, strong voices have protested restraints imposed in the name of obscenity. They have called attention to the abuses committed in its name. They have challenged its rationality, its validity. They have pointed to the duality of society's standards—suppressing in public, leering in private. What has all this accomplished, they have asked. Where are the benefits which outweigh the damage? Let us abolish controls; they say, let us permit open circulation of all kinds of representations. The harm of suppression, including its own contribution to shame, must be eliminated. Until there is proof—clear and convincing—of the harm which obscenity is alleged to cause, let us remove these restrictions on man's ability to communicate to man, no matter what the content may be.

Challenging arguments. Yet, there remains the unsettling feeling that the harms which have previously been singled out as the law's possible target *may* occur if all controls on the circulation of obscenity were abolished. Absent *all* legal controls, obscenity, in

[203]

many variant forms, could be pandered openly by profit-minded purveyors (and it is naive to think there are not many of these in
our land), pandered to all sorts of recipients—to sexually maladjusted people, to youths, to potentially addictable adults. The risk
of some sort of a reasonably direct influence on the behavior or
personality of some of these people would increase. Absent *all* controls, sensitive people or the children of sensitive parents, against
their consent, could be freely exposed to filthy or erotic expression
without restraint, and some psychic harm would be more likely to
occur. Individuals could be subjected to real affronts to their privacy
and dignity.

Rational evaluation of the two positions and an objective choice
are difficult indeed. What is here involved is a conflict of hypotheses, of deeply held values and assumptions. This, like all important
controversies, cannot be resolved by a neat syllogism or orderly
equation.

And it is this fact which is the point of departure for the remainder of this work, regardless of our own preferences. Given the
imprimatur of the *Roth, Alberts* and *Times Film* cases for support
—for "legality" of suppression—it is, in our view, unrealistic to
expect our present society to abolish obscenity control. Schizophrenic
though our society may be—affirmatively tolerating a great deal
of condemned sexual expression even while we fitfully urge purges
upon ourselves—there does seem to be a very strong, persistent
social urge to control or suppress obscenity. There is a deep popular
intuition here, unrefined as it is, and popular intuitions of such
strength are not to be ignored.

Perhaps if the negative were ultimately proved, if thoughtful,
comprehensive, empirical studies and expert opinion were to agree
and to demonstrate that the assumed harms (whatever they may
be) are phantom fears and that suppression itself is harmful in
subtle psychological ways, then repeal of these laws would be possible. However, the fact is that such a consensus does not exist to
the extent where we can expect lawmakers to act upon it. The
direction of change must be to evaluate particular techniques of
control, to refine the standards, and to assure that freedom to publish cannot be impetuously limited from time to time by the power
of government acting on the prejudices of articulate pressure groups.

Accordingly, this work turns to exploration of these aims.

3. WHAT OBSCENITY IS AND WHAT

IT IS NOT

THE LAW TODAY operates on the premise that once something is "obscene," *nobody* should see it. This would seem to go too far. It puts government (fellow citizens who happen to have official titles) in the role of telling everyone else what he shall never write or read.

The dichotomy which holds that a work is either fit or unfit is a heritage of the past, subtly developed in the minds of men as literacy and mass communication became a condition of life. It is a dichotomy which makes controversial decisions a matter of real controversy. Surely there would be less concern when a particular work is judged obscene if the law stopped acting on the assumption that *all* dissemination must then cease. In view of our uncertain state of knowledge about the existence of evils from exposure, in view of man's dangerous prejudices and his oft-demonstrated fallibility, and in view of the dangers to freedom from too much repression, that assumption should be rejected.

To keep suppression at a minimum, we should forbid circulation of obscenity only when the transaction—the manner of circulation —involves conduct which more justifiably permits governmental interference.[1]

1. In the words of Chief Justice Warren in the *Roth* case: "The line dividing the salacious or pornographic from literature or science is not

Thus, in determining the proper area within which the force of government may suppress dissemination, it is necessary: (1) to define obscenity as a form of sex expression and (2) to determine what kinds of circulation may be prohibited.

We would also stress a concept which is probably self-evident, yet frequently overlooked when courts and legislators begin characterizing obscenity as if it were poison ivy. There can be no line demarking obscenity from non-obscenity; there is only a continuum; obsceneness is a quality of which a work partakes, once we can reasonably describe its predominant appeal or effect; but the fact is that a work may meet these tests and yet hardly be a serious offense against the standards. There are degrees of offense, and the degree of obsceneness (however we define obsceneness) must be an important factor in judging whether, in any particular case, the particular sanction is warranted.

Dealing now with the matter of definition, a number of proposals for broadening or narrowing the standard have recently been offered.

1. There have been persistent efforts to frame a definition which would drag in, as an adjunct of obscenity, depictions of violent crimes, bloodshed, or "horror" which, though perhaps very noxious, are devoid of overt sexual content. Undoubtedly, America's apparent preoccupation with crime and physical violence in its mass media constitutes a social problem; possibly it is a problem which is, psychologically, related to preoccupation with sex. But control of the depiction of crime and cruelty *per se,* under the guise of controlling the depiction of sexual activity or nudity, would be opening a vast new field, one which presents issues of its own and must be treated separately, if at all.

2. Similarly, there persists the idea that all communication portraying and condoning abortifacients, contraception, adultery, or other illicit practices must, *per se,* be incorporated within our concept of the obscene. But the Supreme Court has made it quite clear that the First Amendment forbids such action, and certainly repression of this kind of "speech" goes far beyond the narrow

---

straight and unwavering . . . It is manifest that the same object may have a different impact, varying according to the part of the community it reaches . . . *The conduct of the defendant is the central issue, not the obscenity of a book or picture."*

social objectives set forth for anti-obscenity law. Men may differ
vehemently as to the morality of Lady Chatterley's conduct or the
practice of contraception; that is not the issue. The question is
whether the government is ever to be the arbiter of these matters,
for we are dealing now with ideas and information, with discussion.
As long as the First Amendment is law, it must not be the function
of government to say what is "right" and suppress dissent. Of
course, portrayal of these matters *may* become obscene, not because the subject is automatically obscene, but only because of the
form in which the expression appears. But the ideas—hateful or
not—should stand or fall on their merit.

3. The American Law Institute has included within its definition
of obscenity depictions which are predominantly "filthy" (in a
sexual sense) or "scatological" rather than erotic in the aphrodisiac
sense. There has always been some confusion (reflected in the history of the Comstock Act) as to whether this kind of communication is, technically, obscene. Psychologically the "filthy" category
seems to be related and to shade imperceptibly into the erotic
category; indeed, often the two characterizations overlap to a considerable degree in the thinking of judges and lawmakers. While
there is some basis for believing that the epithet "filthy," as it
appears in the Comstock Act, was intended as a word of art to
encompass a prohibition not included by the term obscene, the
effort to build a distinction and worry over classification seems
pointless. An excess use of four-letter scatological or sexual words
is bad, if it is bad, for substantially the same reason an excess
emphasis on the erotic is bad: the social harms to be avoided are
probably much the same for all practical, present purposes.

4. Some, like Judge Frank and Judge Bok, have suggested that
the test be made far more restrictive than it is now, that the law
concern itself only with that depiction of nudity or sexual conduct which creates a clear and present danger, or a substantial likelihood of criminal (or perhaps simply "undesirable") behavior on
the part of persons exposed to it. But these proposals seem unrealistic because they are so extreme; while proof of the danger—or
lack of danger—created by a distributor's circulation of erotic
material should clearly be relevant, a rule which required proof
of a "clear and present danger" would virtually bar all suppression.
This is going further than society seems yet prepared to go.

5. New definitions have also been proposed by some psychiatrists (theoretically, perhaps, those most qualified to make a scientific definition). One doctor, after a detailed study, has suggested that the "pornographic criterion" should be based on such factors as (1) "asexual sexuality," (2) "emphasis on erogenic zones of the body," (3) "monotony and infantilism in the emotions," (4) "emphasis on parts rather than a whole." Other psychiatric experts have suggested that there are other, similar, definite characteristics inherent in all genuinely obscene writing and that these same characteristics are absent or only incidental and subordinate in literature which should not be censored. The plea is that the courts recognize these suggested criteria and the distinction between genuine obsceneness and expression which is "realistic" and "frank" about sex, but not psychologically structured in the "hard-core," "genuine" pornographic form. These various tests should be helpful as an insight into the ingredients of "obsceneness"; to the extent that they appear to be scientifically valid, they should be developed as bases for expert testimony which will help judges evaluate any challenged material. (Indeed, as will be detailed later, the procedure for judging obsceneness should affirmatively encourage such inquiry, particularly in controversial cases.) But it is risky to suggest that these diverse psychiatric concepts should simply be substituted for the existing legal standards. In the first place, these concepts would be difficult for lay law enforcers to comprehend. In the second place, there is apparently no psychiatric consensus on the concept of "obscenity" which would justify the adoption by courts or legislatures of some particular new formulation of words espoused by only one or a few experts. Psychological criteria such as those which have been suggested can and should be used by government officials, lawyers, and courts as guides to proper evaluation of questioned materials, nor is it necessary to reformulate existing legal criteria to permit their effective use. The existing legal standards laid down in *Roth's* case call for examination of the "appeal" of questioned materials, their potential "effect" on readers, and the apparent "motive" of the creator. Proposed psychological criteria also appear to focus on these issues, and psychological evaluation along the lines suggested by the psychological commentators should be clearly relevant evidence where it is available. Since psychologists are still struggling with the concept of obscenity and

the question of its impact, the law should be on more solid ground if it permits wide latitude in hearing the contentions of experts and yet desists, at this time, from embracing any particular view as a matter of substantive law.

6. Some outstanding critics of existing obscenity law from the American Civil Liberties Union have urged that the only material which should be suppressed is "hard-core pornography," material *solely* devoted to depicting, verbally or pictorially, the sexual act. It is urged that any broader definition (such as that of the American Law Institute Code) trenches upon man's freedom to express ideas. The hard-core pornography test also has the merit of reducing the element of vagueness, so inherent in obscenity proscriptions, to a minimum. But this suggested test, like the proposed "clear and present danger" formulation, is probably unrealistic: it goes too far in permitting open circulation of materials which society simply will not tolerate today. One need not strain his imagination to conceive of material—ranging from writing to motion-picture scenes— that would fall outside of the proposed new definition (if the proponents of the hard-core test mean what they say); yet this material could be extremely erotic and presumably well beyond existing community standards. Indeed, there is probably much material afoot today that is not strictly pornographic but is still patently obscene; much of this material has little if any "redeeming social importance" as the expression of ideas or feelings. Nor is it necessary to go to the extreme of the hard-core definition to develop a tighter screening process in the enforcement of anti-obscenity law, a process which will give better protection to freedom of expression and thought.

7. The suggestion has also been urged that the test for what may be suppressed should focus directly, in terms, on the question: Does the condemned material have any redeeming idea content or other social or artistic value? Yet such a "test" would invite the exercise of much subjective discretion by those who judge and would probably promulgate much dangerous confusion. We would reject such a test as *the* standard. We would accept it as one (of a number) of relevant inquiries. The goal of the law must be to protect the expression of ideas, but the goal must be broader than that: even expression which may seem devoid of value—if it is not affirmatively noxious and if it is not circulated in a noxious way—must be protected in order to guard interests which freedom is designed to pro-

mote. The Supreme Court seems to have told us that the tests laid down in *Roth's* case are to be applied in a way that will protect speech of any redeeming value. The constitutionality of anti-obscenity law seems premised on that assumption. One way to assure that the existing tests will be properly administered is to permit the fullest freedom for those who defend books against obscenity charges to adduce testimony showing wherein the work does have value. Of course "expert" testimony in this field lacks scientific certainty and may sometimes reflect bias. But the "expert," properly characterized, is the witness with special knowledge of his subject based on experience and study. When men who have engaged extensively in the work of evaluating and criticizing literature give us information about a novel—the theme of the book, the techniques of its author, its reputation among critics—there is every reason why this testimony should be heard and given weight to the extent believed. Precisely on this count, there was, for example, something very amiss in the government's case against *Lady Chatterley*. The defenders of the book produced testimony to show that it was widely read by students of our literature and that an important segment of these readers put a high valuation on it as a novel. These assertions, factual in nature, were simply brushed aside, and the government's failure to meet such evidence epitomizes the deficiency of its case for total censorship. Indeed, one might go so far as to suggest an evidentiary "rule of law" for the relatively few cases where an allegedly serious work is prosecuted. If credible testimony is produced to show that a book has circulated through some open channels and if a substantial segment of reputable "experts" (we put to one side the definition of an "expert"; the problem is not insurmountable) believe the book has value in its field, then its prosecutors must come forward—under pain of losing their case—with outside testimony which either refutes the testimony given or shows that in the *particular case at hand,* because of the distribution methods of this particular defendant, his circulation should be suppressed. This rule is put in adjective terms and suggested as a corollary to the existing substantive rule already adopted by the Supreme Court.

In sum, existing legal standards, as re-formulated by the Court in the *Roth* case, have the merit of defining obscenity in terms which, if relatively vague, are more comprehensible than others which one could realistically propose. These standards also direct attention to the existence of characteristics that presumably make obscenity harmful when its dissemination is totally uncontrolled. Thus, existing tests are related to supportable reasons for controlling the thing condemned, and they also have the merit of a gloss of experience and case-by-case interpretation. Courts have worked with them; psychiatrists, literary experts, and others can also—or should be able to do so if the law is properly administered.

Vague these tests may be, but the danger to freedom from this vagueness can be significantly mitigated once it is posited that obsceneness is not, alone, grounds for the absolute prohibition of a book or picture, but only grounds for preventing some kinds of circulation of it.

Accordingly, obscene expression should be concerned with that which is devoted to depicting nudity, sexual behavior, excretion (and bodily functions related thereto) in terms which are erotic, shocking, or both. But, more precisely, a work is only "obscene" if, judged as a whole:[2]

2. The mandate that a work be "judged as a whole" seems necessary where the work to be judged can be treated as an integrated unit. A particularly graphic description or a sequence of vulgar vocabulary may play an important and specific role in accomplishing an author's over-all purpose. The "work as a whole" criterion, as we have seen, prevents the ripping of a passage or scene out of context, and it permits the decision-maker to evaluate the allegedly offensive passage in a desirable perspective.

But in some situations it is not so easy to know how to judge a work as a whole, indeed, in some situations it is arguable whether that criterion should be applied.

Take, for example, the case of an offending story in a collection, an offending poem in an anthology, an unobjectionable book with offending illustrations. Physically, of course, these offending parts are inseparable from the work as a whole, and if the parts are held to be obscene and illegal, then the whole book must be condemned. From the standpoint of the rationale of the "work as a whole," discerning the author's dominant purpose and the basic appeal of the offensive material, it is arguable that the offending parts must be judged apart and the entire work condemned if these parts offend. The Model Penal Code seems to take that position.

There are substantial risks here; once the door is opened to permit the barring of a book because of one independent offensive part, the way is open for censors to bar the book when the offensive part is not so clearly independent, and not so clearly obscene; and experience has shown that censorship is a self-expanding process.

Perhaps the problem can be resolved if the same test is here applied as has been urged throughout this work: the evaluation of the degree of

(1) its basic appeal is solely to prurient interests *and*

(2) its predominant effect is stimulation of sexual desires or morbid sexual impulses, *and*

(3) it offends current minimal standards of candor.

These are cumulative, not alternative, criteria; and, we repeat, it should also be recognized that there are degrees of obsceneness. The degree to which a work is obscene is a significant factor in determining whether its circulation is to be suppressed or punished in any given case.

Most important, *obsceneness of itself should not mean illegality.* It should no longer be enough that an artist, author, publisher, bookseller, or movie exhibitor has created, sold or exhibited something which is, abstractly, "obscene." Rather, criminal liability or

---

obscenity with the disseminator's conduct and apparent purpose as manifested by his advertising and distribution methods. It is not too difficult to imagine a pornographic tale sandwiched in between innocuous stories, where the entire advertising campaign to sell the book is based upon its pornography; again the border-line book where the detailed illustrations are the big selling-point. The advertising and purveying of Boccacio's *Decameron* via the "girlie" magazines, though presumably not illegal, uses such offensive methods, emphasizing the purported salacity of some of the tales. In the rare case, there might be a reason why this kind of huckstering of the work should be the subject of condemnation, if we are to continue to have laws against obscenity. But where the allegedly offensive part is at least reasonably related to the over-all work (be it anthology, collection, or novel with illustrations) and where the work is not advertised or exploited by emphasis upon this part, there should be no condemnation.

What about movies—for example, the present Customs practice of excising a few feet of film from foreign films, where there has allegedly been too much nudity or familiarity? Here, of course, it is physically possible to delete the offending parts without destroying the entire film. But precisely because of that there are dangers in the continuation of this practice.

Most of the foreign films which have suffered this kind of editing have been widely accepted, if not prize-winning productions. There is something demeaning about the spectacle of federal officials scrutinizing every foot of a film so that no American can see a few feet of a scene which has been widely shown abroad. Moreover, it bears repeating that these motion pictures are being imported for open commercial exhibition. Local authorities would seem to be the place where responsibility for action should be imposed. Again, only when particular parts are seriously obscene, where they can be shown to be clearly irrelevant or unnecessary to the theme, plot, and the value of the work as a whole, and only where the work is being used to exploit the offending part itself, should there be any censorship. For once the power is granted more broadly, it is too easy to require excision of the film, and this is what cautious federal administrators have often done.

censorship should also depend on the nature of the use of the obscene expression. The conduct of the disseminator must be as important as the abstract quality of the speech condemned; suppression through the force of law must depend on an analysis of that conduct and on whether the particular circulation—taking account of the degree of obsceneness of the work—is harmful enough to justify suppression.

4. THE REAL TARGET: THE "PUR-VEYORS," NOT THE BOOKS

THE PROBLEM, THEN, is to identify that kind of conduct, that kind of publishing or distribution activity, which substantially increases the likelihood that circulation of the work will produce harms to society and which, therefore, may be prohibited.

1. *"Assaulting" people with obscenity* is one possible area of prohibition. In more precise terms, this conduct is the intentional use of obscene expression to shock people or subject them to emotional distress, against their consent, without justification, and under circumstances transcending community standards and involving a likelihood that mental disturbance—serious affront, shame, fear or disgust—will in fact result. The man who draws obscene pictures in public places where others must see them, the zealot who intentionally mails an obscene epistle or tract to others under circumstances where the recipient is highly likely to read it and be offended, the crank (who may be far from harmless) who intentionally sends a letter that is both epithetical and indecent—these people, while perhaps often mentally disordered, may be restrained. Again, admittedly, the standard of conduct is hardly precise, and again illegality must depend on the degree of obsceneness of the expression, the nature of the audience exposed, the actor's relationship

to it, his intent—using that word in the traditional legal sense—
and the justification, if any, for his actions. Nevertheless a point is
reached where privacy and feelings deserve protection, where the
law can demand forbearance.

2. *Knowing circulation of obscene materials to adolescents, or
to an audience with abnormal interests in obscene matter.* Undoubtedly, it is here more than anywhere else that the public demands effective restraints on bookstores, mailers, movie theaters,
and newsstand vendors. Most vehement community protests have
usually, in fact, been concerned with dissemination aimed at juveniles. While there may be little evidence linking the viewing of
things obscene to juvenile crime or to sex crimes in particular, the
specter of a purveyor standing outside a school building is an extreme example of conduct which American communities simply
will not tolerate. The interests of freedom of speech—promoting
conditions whereby mature men can have the fullest freedom of
thought and expression—are seldom advanced by such conduct.

An analogous category of conduct is the advertent selling to
those who, by reason of mental disorder or abnormality, very likely
will be stimulated to sexual or related misbehavior—behavior condemned by our law in other statutes—by exposure to certain kinds
of obscene material. Some types of material (e.g., Klaw's weird
brand of sex sadism, booklets depicting male nudity, and other material aimed at homosexuals) may produce harmful stimulation on
this special class of people. There has been considerable testimony
to this effect by law-enforcement officials and some psychiatrists.
In any event, this again is a narrow range of conduct where the justification for the dissemination, in terms of protecting the development of art, literature, and entertainment, seems attenuated.

Accordingly, another area of prohibition should be distribution
to adolescents or persons with abnormal interests when the materials are obscene and when the distributor knows or clearly should
know that his audience or a substantial segment of it is made up of
these groups. Clearly, what should be required in both these situations is a course of conduct, not, ordinarily, one sale of borderline
material to one juvenile. The distributor's conduct should constitute
a serious infringement of the standard, its seriousness to be judged
by the volume of his sales to the protected group, the degree and

nature of the obsceneness of the materials, and the motive behind his behavior.

3. *Reckless commercial exploitation of obscenity* is another category warranting discussion, although, in many instances, the conduct underlies the previous two categories. Selling salacity has become big business. Some vendors go just as far as they can to cash in on prurient tastes by emphasizing through advertising and otherwise the erotic or indecent character of the work, by inducing interest in this obsceneness for its own sake. When the commercial exploiter of obscenity uses the mails to sell, he has little or no knowledge of the nature of the audience to which he sells, and his reckless quest for a market may put him in contact not only with adolescents, but with adults who might be affected seriously. Thus this commercial exploitation increases the likelihood that the obscene work will produce harms which society may legitimately seek to prevent. True, there is the frustrating problem of vagueness; it is impossible to be exact in defining either the conduct proscribed (exploitation) or the thing (obscenity) proscribed.

When, for example, does a disseminator of "art" photos or pin-up magazines become a commercial exploiter of obscenity? The answer will never be easy when we are dealing, for example, with the case of a sedentary, street corner magazine vendor. But at least when the case concerns use of the mails, there are realistic criteria which can be applied, and the decision whether to suppress or punish becomes far more rational if we try to apply them. Thus, in each case the cumulative weight of these variables should be examined: (*a*) the degree of obsceneness of the materials—the degree to which they contain the noxious ingredients of obscenity and lack literary or artistic or any other social value; (*b*) the nature of the advertising, the extent to which the disseminator has attempted to induce purchases by developing interest and desire for the materials essentially because they partake of the quality of obsceneness and for no other reason; (*c*) the extent to which the disseminator has put the materials or the advertising in circulation—the volume of his business or his contacts; (*d*) the nature of the audience solicited; (*e*) the nature of the methods used to select this audience; (*f*) the motives of the disseminator in engaging in this distribution: was it his intent to use care in controlling circulation of this obscene work? Or was he indifferent to the consequences of the circulation he induced?[3]

In sum, our proposal is that the law concern itself more with anti-social *conduct* in the circulation of obscene forms of communication and less with the idea that obscene creations, like deodands of old, must be totally expunged from the face of the earth. Of course, such works may be bad, ethically, morally, or aesthetically, and also valueless. History shows that it is vain to think that we can repress them totally from the annals of mankind, just as it shows that men have made bad mistakes in judging books allegedly bad.

Making the conduct and motives of the distributor essential elements of a proscription on speech is not a new technique in the law. Defamatory statements, an extremely vague category of speech, are often actionable only if coupled with behavior or "motives" deemed improper under vague standards. So, too, the privilege of publishers to print articles which "invade the privacy" of "public figures" (and violation of privacy may be an even vaguer category of prohibited speech) can be lost and the speech made actionable if the publisher through "improper motives" goes so far as to engage in "commercial exploitation" of the story—to use words which courts have used. Some courts have developed the notion of commercial exploitation as defeating privilege in these fields; the same can be done with respect to obscenity.

Moreover, as a matter of legal precedent, the propositions advanced here are not really novel to the law of obscenity. To some

3. In the case of Federal action against a publisher of borderline magazines or materials, mailed over a continuing period, the inquiry should also consider past issues of the magazine or other past conduct directly related to the circulation transaction now under inquiry. Such evidence—if it is in fact evidence of a *continuing* publication enterprise—reflects the motives and methods of the enterpriser. Moreover, realistically, Federal coercive action should be aimed at the publisher or distributor who has become a nuisance by his continuing circulation of materials which become progressively more obscene or which are distributed more and more recklessly. It is this kind of course of conduct which should be the law's concern. Another important inquiry should relate to the extent to which the mails, rather than other channels (which can be policed locally), are being used for the alleged business of commercial exploitation—is this case important enough to be made a "federal" case, literally and figuratively? (See, infra, pages 222–223, for discussion of the need for Federal inaction where the local government can act effectively to deal with the publisher.)

extent, the nature of the dissemination has always been a matter of great significance.

Since a very early time, the courts seem to have agreed that it was no violation to sell an obscene work to a doctor if the purpose of the sale was related to the practice of his profession. Long ago Judge Learned Hand, in two criminal postal cases, spoke of "privileged" distributions of otherwise obscene works; the privilege he envisioned seemed to encompass any prudent circulation to mature adults without commercialization; he cautioned that an allegedly obscene book should no longer be judged by "an absolute standard independent of [the] readers" to whom it was addressed. What is this but an argument that the conduct of the defendant-distributor as well as the content of the book must be a decisive issue in each censorship or criminal case? In the *Dennett* and *Popenoe* and *Consumers Union* cases, where the courts dealt with marriage manuals and contraception information, the emphasis, again, was on judging the method of dissemination rather than the materials alone; the courts eschewed a rigid standard which would make a work either fit or unfit; they said in effect: illegality depends on what is circulated, to whom and how. In 1956, a panel of judges of the Court of Appeals, in the *Sunshine* case, reversed a Postal ban on a magazine which purported to be an established organ for the nudist movement; the court admonished the Post Office to make more of an investigation before it issued a blanket order withholding the publication from all subscribers. The Department, said the court, must find whether the publishers were "profitably pandering" the work, or attempting to send it only to subscribers in connection with a "sincere" espousal of the cause of nudism—in short, what was the course of conduct of the publishers? In 1957, the American Law Institute expressly recommended that:

> The following shall *not* be criminal offenses . . . :
> (a) dissemination, not for gain, to personal associates other than children under sixteen;
> (b) dissemination, not for gain, by an actor below the age of 21 to a child not more than 5 years younger than the actor;
> (c) dissemination to institutions or individuals having scientific or other special justification for possessing such material.

In essence, then, the Institute, while apparently rejecting our classification (which appears to have been suggested by one of its ad-

visers) would still make conduct—the nature of the distribution—
an important element in determining whether the law should operate to suppress a publisher. Again, in 1957, Chief Justice Warren
urged this kind of approach. His opinion in *Roth's* case was somewhat cryptic, but his point was that the obscenity statute would be
unconstitutional unless a more restrictive standard, which took account of the defendant's conduct, was read into it. And, of course,
the district court in *Kinsey's* case relied on analogous principles
when it permitted the importation of admitted obscenity because
importation would work no social harm on the receiving group or
anyone else.

In any event, the standard proposed herein is not suggested just
as something theoretically desirable. The standard here proposed is
a minimum reform, vital to the continued implementation of federal anti-obscenity enforcement.

SHOULD FEDERAL CONTROLS BE
ABANDONED?

ASSUME THEN THAT legal controls over the circulation of obscene publications are to be limited to the types of dissemination described above, what should be the role of the federal government? Do we need any federal policing at all?

Arguments about the extent to which federal power should be used to suppress reading or viewing of obscenity have truly ranged far and wide. One zealous congressman recently introduced a bill which would go the whole way in using the ostensible bases of federal power, the commerce and postal clauses of the Constitution. The proposal was that anyone who sells or possesses an obscene book would be guilty of a federal crime if the book or any materials used to create it (e.g., the ink) had passed through interstate commerce or the mails. At the opposite end of the spectrum is the contention forcefully urged by such well-known lawyers as Morris Ernst and O. John Rogge in *Roth's* case that the First, Ninth, and Tenth Amendments, read together and in historical context, impose an absolute legal prohibition against creation of any federal laws or law-enforcement programs aimed at policing the morality of literature.

The *Roth* decision summarily rejected these arguments. It seems clear that Congress has limited power to proscribe some distribution of obscenity through the mails and, presumably, in the channels of commerce, foreign or domestic. Whether *censorship* by Postal officials, as it has been practiced, is constitutional, may be doubtful, as we have already indicated in the analysis of the opinions in the *Roth* case. But assume for the moment that both criminal enforcement and censorship practiced pursuant to more limited standards would be constitutional. There remains the question whether, as a matter of policy, the federal government should engage in any of this business. Why not leave the whole job of policing publications and movies up to the states?

Much can be said for abolishing all federal law enforcement. Admitting the need for controls, there are dangers inherent in using the vast powers of our national government to suppress reading. Under our Constitution, which delegates only some tasks to the federal government, there is no authorization, in terms, for any national law of any sort on this subject; the job of protecting morality, like the job of enforcing most other traditional criminal laws, is left to the states; and certainly the local level seems the appropriate place for imposing this particular responsibility. Of course the power to police the mails and the channels of commerce has been "implied" by the courts, but the more Congress legislates, in the exercise of the "implied" powers, to put federal officials—Postal and Customs inspectors, FBI agents, U.S. attorneys, federal judges—in business to protect citizen morality, the more likely our central government can usurp the whole field by subordinating local authorities and local courts to the policies of Washington.

Justice Harlan's dissent in *Roth's* case warns against the possibilities of abuse and of "deadening uniformity" resulting from excessive enforcement of existing federal laws. It is one thing, he notes, for the police and courts of one community to raid stores and fine booksellers and suppress *Lady Chatterley's Lover* or *Memoirs of Hecate County* in a particular community; it is quite another for a relatively few federal officials in Washington to decide that no one, anywhere in the country, should have access to certain books and then attempt a nationwide suppression by acting against all importation, all domestic distribution in the mails, all interstate shipment. Suppression of controversial books on this broad scale is theoretically possible today; indeed, such would seem the mandate of federal legislation.[4]

Accordingly there seems little justification for invoking the constitutional power to regulate domestic commerce to give the Department of Justice power to police all interstate shipment of books. The states themselves should be competent to police the outlets; the federal government should be denied the power—which, in theory, it now enjoys—to say in effect that it may stop all domestic interstate distribution of publications disapproved by Washington.

On the other hand, there is a very real question whether the states—even if they so desired—could, as a practical matter, deal with mail distribution.

The cold fact is that mail order dissemination is a major avenue for traffic in obscene materials today and a difficult business to control. Collectively these enterprises constitute big business, reputedly growing bigger every year. Similarly, foreign disseminators, sitting safely beyond the reach of our police, can, in the absence of federal policing, carry on the same type of mail operation; indeed, they are in a better position to sell materials which are far more erotic than our domestic products.

The machinery of state and local law enforcement is not capable of combating these mail-order operations. Local police cannot and certainly should not spend their time investigating the content of the domestic mails, let alone foreign matter. Again, local police, especially in more sparsely settled states, may be impotent to extradite out-of-state persons who use the mails to distribute locally.

If, then, there are to be controls over the mail distribution of obscenity, the federal government must do the policing.

But the federal operation can be restricted. As a matter of policy, the sovereignty of the United States government should be concerned only with cases involving substantial use of the mails (to

4. Federal enforcement does produce anomalies. Take for example, the *Kinsey* case. Dr. Kinsey's Institute for Sex Research, is a branch of the University of Indiana, itself an arm of the Indiana state government. Yet, in effect, the federal government attempted to prevent the State of Indiana from importing materials which a state institution deemed useful in its own research and for its own purposes. So, too, Postal censorship has prevented materials from passing through the mails and into communities where the local courts have acquitted the same materials, allowing local dissemination. One need not be a dogmatic advocate of states' rights to find something amiss in this situation.

the exclusion of other means) and operations otherwise beyond the convenient reach of local authorities. The government should also be barred, as a matter of constitutional policy, from banning *all* circulation of works which a few officials in Washington conclude are obscene; enforcement should be limited to curbing the kinds of dissemination activity which we have already singled out.

If those standards are postulated and followed, then the argument about abuse and "deadening uniformity" posited by Justice Harlan loses much of its force. Adult Americans will have a broader, better protected right to read than they have heretofore enjoyed.

6. SHOULD WE ABOLISH FEDERAL CENSORSHIP AS A TECHNIQUE OF SUPPRESSION? ONE ALTERNATIVE: RELIANCE ON THE CRIMINAL LAW ALONE

ASSUMING A FEDERAL operation, must we continue to have Post Office censorship? Why not limit federal power over obscenity in the mails to the enforcement of criminal penalties?

Censorship, far more than criminal law enforcement, poses the dangers envisioned by Justice Harlan. If we simply contrast experience with Postal censorship against experience with criminal enforcement of the Comstock Act, it is apparent there have long been differences in the scope of proscriptions and the exercise of discretion. Despite the very recent introduction of new procedural safeguards in the decision-making process, Postal censorship is still enforced by a handful of officials operating in Washington, removed from the variances of local community tolerances and attitudes, removed from any direct accountability to judges and jurors. The same observation applies to the Bureau of Customs and the informality of its administrative procedures makes for possibilities of abuse, even though there has, in fact, been little in recent decades.

Criminal law administration is less streamlined and more inefficient than censorship, hedged in as it is by all the traditional protections accorded the accused and all the practical obstacles which frustrate prosecutors. Precisely because it is inefficient, criminal law enforcement (in the federal courts) is less likely to result in the suppression of good books or essentially innocuous publications or in the suppression of harmless circulations. To secure a conviction in a criminal case, the prosecutor must decide that the effort of prosecution is worth his time and the taxpayers' money. Grand jurors must indict. Judge and jurors both must be persuaded of the obsceneness of the work. And remember, too, the context in which that issue is decided: the question is really whether the work is so obscene that the defendant should go to jail for distributing it, a sobering possibility which often seems to mitigate juror hostility to the publication itself when the case falls near the borderline.

These practical facts of law administration can and do make a great difference in net results. Within the past decade, federal criminal enforcement has operated selectively against only some of the more noxious disseminators, whereas censorship has operated against many publications of dubious danger. For years *Lady Chatterley's Lover* has been suppressed; the public has been given to understand the book was contraband. But it is doubtful if the Department of Justice, at least during the recent years of suppression, would ever have acted against any reputable bookseller who sold the work without exploiting it. Yet the popular notion that the book was too obscene to be safely read was spawned in large part by the sheer psychological force of a decision by Postal and Customs censors, a decision backed, metaphysically, by the majesty of our federal government. This is a good example to support the argument that federal anti-obscenity enforcement should be limited to criminal prosecution of the disseminator whose materials are seriously obscene, whose conduct as a distributor is seriously antisocial, and who can not be curbed except by conviction in a federal court.

Until recently there was a practical answer to the argument that obscenity control should be limited to criminal sanctions and that censorship should be abolished. Disseminators, it was said (and with much accuracy), operated in big cities where the local authorities did not seem to be interested in prosecuting, perhaps because juries were generally somewhat lenient. Moreover, under the federal statutes, the disseminator could only be prosecuted in the place from which he had mailed the item, not where it had been received. Not only was it difficult to persuade the prosecutors at the point of mailing to begin the prosecution, there was also the prob-

lem of the time and effort and expense of bringing the witnesses to
the big city for the prosecution. All of this added up to few prosecutions.

This alleged deficiency of the criminal remedy no longer exists.
We now have the recent amendment to the Comstock Act in 1958,
permitting the prosecution to be brought at the place to which the
materials have been sent. The dangers inherent in this amendment
have been discussed previously. But one consequence is that a very
strong argument for the retention of censorship simply no longer
exists. If the Los Angeles operator sends a flood of advertising circulars into Nebraska and recklessly engages in the business of selling
"stag" material there, he can be prosecuted in Nebraska.

Why then should there be any retention of federal censorship?

Arguably, a non-criminal means of suppressing obscenity should
be retained because it is the fairest as well as the most efficient way
to police the "borderland" disseminators. It has been urged that
some who sell "borderline" publications have no design to violate
the law, and it has been suggested by a leading authority in book
publishing that criminal penalties are often harshly inflicted on
essentially innocent booksellers; a civil remedy would thus impose
less of a hardship on these "violators." It has also been urged that
Postal censorship is the only effective way to control that considerable number of less "innocent" distributors who constantly skirt
the line between hard-core pornography and less salacious material.

These arguments can hardly be answered dogmatically. No doubt
abolition of Post Office censorship would entail a risk. But probably
not so much of a risk as we were led to believe by Mr. Summerfield,
despite his impressive publicity campaign. Quite probably Post
Office censorship does *not* deter, today, the very purveyors who are
its principal target. While censorial sanctions can visit destructive
consequences on more responsible, sedentary publishers, they do not
seem to stop, nor even impede in a very serious way the fly-by-night
operators. The criminal remedy seems to be the only effective check.
Moreover, since censorship periodically oversteps its legal limits,
and since court reversals are often the result, it is probable that censorship has indirectly played into the hands of the commercial exploiters by producing court cases (e.g., *Lady Chatterley* and *Sun-*

shine Magazine) which only embolden them to convert freedom into license.

The criminal remedy is far better designed for what we have suggested is the only job which the law should undertake: control of those who, with knowledge of what they are doing, exploit obscenity commercially or otherwise direct it at some particular audience. If standards such as have been suggested are imposed, if the courts exercise vigilant control over prosecutors and jurors, then the risks of excess should be minimized.

Even if Post Office censorship of domestic mail were to be abolished, there would still remain a difficult problem with respect to censorship of materials mailed into the United States from abroad.

The difficulty is that foreign sources of distribution are for all practical purposes beyond the jurisdiction of our laws. A seller of obscene books who sets up shop just over the border in Mexico or even in Europe can exploit not only the tourist market there, but also the domestic market here with mail advertisements.

This use of the United States mails by foreign purveyors can be just as reckless and potentially harmful as that of any U.S. counterpart, yet absent Customs controls, the foreign distributor cannot be controlled effectively. It is virtually impossible to use the criminal law against him.[5] Nor are the existing criminal penalties (which are aimed at Americans who import) an effective or even desirable method of controlling most shipments: most importers probably do not act culpably enough to warrant prosecution under laws which require "knowing" importation; most importation is for limited private use; and it is doubtful that prosecutors or jurors would want to convict a private individual for ordering an erotic book for his personal use. Whether these recipients should be punished is debatable, to say the least.

However, unless there is some regulation at the border, the

5. The various international extradition treaties and international covenants outlawing obscenity would hardly be effective devices to make foreign booksellers subject to U.S. laws when they have never been physically present here. Even if the foreign nations (which may, after all, permit publication to take place because there has been no violation of their obscenity standard) are willing to extradite, the processes here are so cumbersome and time consuming that they would be impracticable to deter foreign publishers.

public must face the distinct possibility that foreign dealers will use our postal system to send mail-order advertisments here and then sell, in increasing volume, materials to an unseen audience, recklessly selected. They will do precisely what will be forbidden to domestic publishers; indeed, there is evidence to indicate that this foreign exploitation goes on today in sufficient volume so that if controls were abolished today the mischief would increase considerably tomorrow.

Assuming that mail-order distribution of obscenity should be controlled, the necessity for some Customs censorship seems clear. But, in line with the philosophy previously discussed, this censorship should be limited to controlling importation of patently serious matter sold in volume via the mails, material which emanates from foreign sources of commercial exploitation. Except in extreme cases, there should, as a matter of policy if not law, be no interference with commercial importations by persons whose activities can be policed locally (e.g., importations by commercial movie distributors or neighborhood bookstores which use open commercial channels to reach the public); nor (except in extreme cases) should there be interference with casual, private importation where the book has any value—either intellectually or because it is a rare or unique item (as opposed, e.g., to mass-produced material) and where the importer is a responsible adult and where there is no prospect of further resale or wide distribution of the material received. These controls should be exercised in accordance with stricter and more formal procedures, which may also serve to narrow the area within which official discretion can operate. At most, Customs enforcement can only be a holding operation, a deterrent to foreign exploitation. When the government tries to do more, when it tries to meddle with the reading habits of private citizens and save souls through a broader, total censorship, it is entering upon dangerous ground.[6]

6. Proposals for standards and procedure for Customs censorship are more fully detailed on pages 235–237 and in Appendix VI-6.

7.

ANOTHER ALTERNATIVE: PRESERVE A CIVIL REMEDY BUT SUBSTITUTE COURTS AND JURORS FOR POST OFFICE ADJUDICATIONS

WE HAVE DISCUSSED one alternative to Post Office censorship—total reliance upon the criminal law as the sole means for controlling dissemination of obscenity. There is another alternative which would still permit civil as well as criminal controls and yet cut down on the discretionary powers of the Postmaster General and his subordinates, that is, turning the decision-making power over to the courts: Let the Post Office perform only an initial investigative and screening function; require all decisions and confiscation orders to be made by the courts; forbid any stoppage of mail or any mail block until and unless a court orders such action; make it obligatory that the Post Office, like other anti-obscenity enforcement agencies, prove its case in court before any sanctions are imposed.

This proposal finds precedent in the *theory* of the Tariff law as expressed by the Senate in 1930. Why, indeed, should Post Office officials act as the nation's arbiters of obscenity problems? Even assuming, for the moment, that non-criminal controls are to be used by the United States government to suppress undesirable domestic mail circulations, why should the power to decide where lines shall be drawn be reposed in the Postmaster General or his personal delegates?

Adjudicatory powers involving the exercise of discretion and the authority to take action which affects the freedom or property of particular individuals are usually turned over to some executive official or agency when, for one reason or another, Congress assumes that the enforcement agency will possess some particular expertise not possessed by the courts and when there are complex questions of details of policy which can best be resolved by these experts and when, in other respects as well, the courts do not seem to be apt instruments for the development and enforcement of regulatory action. Thus, the Interstate Commerce Commission—to cite one example—is assumed to be expert in problems of rates, divisions of rates, the need for particular kinds of transportation service and the development of transportation policy; to it Congress delegated powers to enter orders directly affecting the interests of common carriers, and court review of the agency's action is limited. The Commission's officials live with these regulatory problems; the problems are the agency's *raison d'être*, and the commissioners are supposed to become increasingly familiar with the mass of data upon which, presumably, a wise choice of policy alternatives and wise adjudicatory decisions must be based.

Post Office control of obscenity is hardly analogous to the controls exercised by the typical regulatory agency. The special "expertise" which may be relevant in deciding obscenity cases is hardly an expertise which can best be developed by officials who act directly under a political appointee such as the Postmaster General. The expertise of his Department lies in the development of methods for the efficient carriage of mail, not in screening it for acceptability. There is no particular reason why a Postal official—be he lawyer or experienced politician or mail handler—should be deemed, simply by virtue of his official title, peculiarly competent to say what other citizens may see or read.

The determination of such issues seems the very kind of judgment that, to the extent it is to be entrusted to anyone, is best entrusted to courts *and juries* under our system of government. If experience shows anything, it shows that the judicial branch of government will operate best to safeguard freedom—although this is not to assume that the courts have always operated well. Just as the courts decide what is obscene for purposes of enforcing criminal anti-obscenity laws, so they should decide what is obscene for purposes of enforcing other anti-obscenity laws.

It is true that there has been, at various times, a large volume of potential censorship cases under the Postal laws. Some may fear that if the courts are required to do the decision-making in the first instance, they will be flooded with suits by the government asking for mail blocks, interim orders, and non-mailability rulings. But this fear no longer seems valid. If the substantive standards urged here are employed, fewer and fewer of these proceedings should take place. Surely the added burden of several hundred court proceedings (at the very most) is not too great a load for the federal courts, bearing in mind that the cases will, to some extent, be spread throughout the country.

Some may argue, cogently, that preserving the administrative adjudicatory process will serve as an added check to protect publishers worth protecting; it will keep ill-advised cases out of the courts; it will provide a prompter, less expensive forum for these publishers to secure an initial determination of the issues. Against these must be weighed the fact that Postal censorship would probably be more confined and discreet if the law said that no censorship sanction could be imposed except by order of the courts. Ill-advised cases should arise less often if the Post Office knows that the initiation of such cases will be a waste of its time and funds.

When it comes to use of the non-mailability sanction—the power to stop a publication from reaching its subscribers—it seems desirable, at the very least, to change the law so that the Post Office will be required to go to court and there, with the burden of proof against it, persuade the court that the non-mailability order should issue.

The original Comstock Act, the very law under which the Department now operates, did *not* in terms give to the Post Office the non-mailability power which it has actually exercised for many years. Rather, the statute seemed to be directed toward the use of the criminal law, which meant judicial action. The present administrative operations have crept into our law by practice and by congressional condonation, but never with full review of their implications.

Experience over the past years with Post Office administration has hardly shown that the benefits of administrative enforcement outweigh the difficulties of censorship. It is quite true that in the past several years a new generation of Postal lawyers has seriously attempted to improve that administration. But the extent of administrative censorship may still depend upon *who* is in charge. Another change in leadership might produce more restrictive attitudes. New procedural safeguards probably would not stop overzealous political appointees from attempts at harassment such as have occurred from time to time in the past decade. The courts are a safer repository of our freedom.

8. REFORMS TO BE MADE IF THE EXISTING CENSORSHIP SYSTEM IS RETAINED

IF NEITHER OF the preceding two alternatives is adopted, and to the extent that federal censorship of the mails is to be retained, there are still some desirable changes to be made in the existing Postal and Customs systems. These suggested changes are discussed and explained in detail in the Appendix. The principal points may be summarized.

Post Office:

1. The substantive standards of censorship should be brought into line with the criminal standards. Post Office officials should not initiate censorship unless they are convinced that the activities of the disseminator, if continued, would be the subject of criminal proceedings.

2. The Postal power to revoke or deny second-class mailing privileges on the grounds of obscenity should be abolished. The second-class mailing privilege is an economic subsidy which should have no relation to the question of whether the publication is obscene. The power to withhold second-class mailing privileges is easily susceptible to abuse, e.g., by merely threatening to use it, by delaying action on applications; since there are other sanctions, both criminal and civil, the need for this particular sanction would seem doubtful at best.

3. The mail-block sanction should be revised. Mail-blocks should be imposed only when the Post Office reasonably concludes that criminal prosecutions should or will follow. Temporary or interim mail blocks should be imposed only by the Courts. Their duration should be the least possible time required for the Post Office Hearing Examiners to determine that the offense appears to be serious enough to warrant this extreme sanction.

4. The non-mailability sanction should be employed only *after* hearings have been held to determine the illegality of the mailings. Interim stoppage of mail should be authorized only by courts and confined to cases serious enough to warrant contemporaneous criminal proceedings or cases where the alleged violator has committed prior adjudicated violations of a similar nature.

5. The Post Office should seek and retain the use of qualified "experts"—intelligent, objective outsiders with special knowledge that may be helpful from time to time in Postal deliberations. These experts may be able to aid the Department in charting general lines of enforcement policy and in helping officials in Washington to appraise existing "community standards," to evaluate publications under investigation, and to formulate objective findings on the nature and volume of commercial mail-order circulations (as opposed to repetition of the loose "facts" put out in the Department's press releases).

Moreover, the Post Office should permit the use of experts by both sides in its administrative hearings. The Department should not attempt to impose broad controls on publications which have obtained standing among a substantial segment of responsible critics; even if others violently disagree with this favorable expert judgment, the Department should eschew the role of the arbiter. Where credible expert testimony is produced to show that a book has acceptance and has been circulating openly in parts of the country, the Post Office should stay its hand unless confronted with a particular case where the circulation efforts are peculiarly offensive.

6. All Postal decisions should be reviewed *de novo* by the courts with a right of trial by jury. There has, at least until the *Lady Chatterley* case, been some confusion whether a Post Office decision, when challenged in court, is presumptively correct—whether it should be set aside only if there has been "an abuse of discretion."

The difference between Postal proceedings and those of other "regulatory" agencies has already been discussed, and there seems to be no policy reason to differentiate the Post Office from the Bureau of Customs on this score. The Customs decision is, legally, entitled to no weight in the libel (court) proceeding; the burden of proof is always on the government to show that the publication should not be admitted into this country. So it should be with the Post Office.

7. While the Post Office should advise the American people what it is doing, it should scrupulously refrain from attempting to mold public opinion. In the interest of improving public understanding, the Post Office should make information reflecting the extent of its operations freely available, with objective publicity on the nature of the publications which it is suppressing. The rather recent practice of reprinting decisions of the Judicial Officer for public use is a substantial improvement. But information must be put forward with cold objectivity. The comprehensive and unprecedented effort of the former Postmaster General to make people afraid of obscenity and to mobilize public opinion for stricter enforcement should be halted. Of course the head of a department may request Congress for new legislation when he thinks it is in the public interest to do so. But that is a far cry from developing grass-roots lobbying efforts through speeches, the appointment of special "consultants" whose role seems to be to stir up public fear of court decisions, the continuous outpouring of press releases. The Post Office is both a law enforcing and an adjudicating agency. The field of adjudication is indeed a delicate one. If the Postmaster General is to be given adjudicatory powers, he should act under the discipline which judges must accept as part of their role. Courts cannot and should not attempt to manipulate opinion in this way; and in like fashion it is unseemly for the Postmaster General to issue public statements criticizing judicial decisions which have enjoined his censorship. The job of criticism can be left to private citizens.

Bureau of Customs:

Because of the impracticability of the criminal law as an enforcement device, censorship will probably be retained for materials coming from abroad so long as there is to be any federal anti-obscenity enforcement. One must conclude that within recent years the Customs censorship operation has worked pretty well insofar as public complaints or court reversals are concerned. But that, we believe, is because of the personal restraint of those who have made the decision to insure broader protection in the future. There are several changes which may be in order.

1. The objective of Customs censorship should be limited to controlling the flow through the mails of seriously obscene materials from recognized foreign sources of commercial exploitation. Censorship should be limited to the commercial exploitation of flagrantly obscene materials which have little or no value as "speech" in the First Amendment sense; other importations usually present no real threat since the volume is slight and subsequent distribution can be policed locally.

2. Release should be allowed to importers who put forward circumstances showing plausible justification for their importation and absence of harm resulting from release. This may well be what the *Kinsey* case (and probably other Constitutional decisions) require. Thus, even though a particular importation may come from a source of "commercial exploitation," the importation should not be intercepted if the importer shows any special circumstances for the importation.

3. Release should normally be allowed in the case of commercial importations where it can be shown that the domestic activities of the importer can be policed locally. Movie cases would seem to be an important example of this category.

4. The Customs administrative procedures should be formalized. The present corps of administrators are human and will not retain their jobs forever. Over the years, our judicial system has attempted to erect safeguards through procedural protections against the whims and caprices of judges and executive officials. Similar safeguards should be adopted by Customs, so that a change of personnel will not create the problems which the Post Office has so long endured. There should be fuller notification to importers of their right to challenge the administrative decision to impound; there should be a formal opportunity for the importer to appear and defend his claim; separation of the function of seizing from that of judging should be effected.

5. The Bureau's decisions should be a matter of public record. The present policy of withholding titles of seized matter is unduly paternalistic; it is inconsistent with Postal policy, where decisions

are now published; it is an unnecessary abridgment of freedom of information.

It should be emphasized that all of these suggestions are based on the assumption that censorship will be retained as a method of attacking the obscenity problem. It may be that if all are adopted, censorship will operate only within the most narrow limits. But we think that prior experience coupled with the lack of significant data as to the effects of obscene publications puts a heavy burden of justification on those who advocate the retention of any censorship at all. It is a power which is simply antithetical to the best American traditions.

PART VII

Concluding Comments
on Censorship

This work has attempted to trace the development of federal censorship and to discuss many hard problems which have appeared over the years and which still exist today.

Federal anti-obscenity enforcement is of course only one example, one part, of a system of laws and law enforcement in this country directed towards controlling this kind of expression. But the history and recent experience of federal enforcement, both criminal and censorial, reflect dramatically the basic conflicts which these laws present—the conflicts between interests of freedom and the interests of preserving order, morality, and virtue, in the high sense of those words. Thus, analysis of the federal system of censorship should afford opportunity for understanding the problems of censorship generally.

Justification for obscenity regulation seems to have been the product of intuitive impulses and imprecise assumptions. From the nineteenth-century beginnings of modern law-making in this field, the lawmakers have rarely spent much time diagnosing with dispassion the evils which the laws were supposed to remedy, although they have felt very strongly the need for proscriptive prescriptions. The notion that distribution of this kind of human expression results in tangible harm to those exposed is probably supported by less "verifiable" information than are most legislative assumptions.

Since the concept of obscenity seems destined to survive in our culture, since the urge to suppress will remain persistent, since there may be some real dangers to be faced, continuous efforts should be undertaken to restate the assumptions underlying repressive laws and to check their validity by the best techniques available. Until we know more than we do, enforcement of obscenity measures—and the measures themselves—may continue to suffer, from time to time, from irrational influences which trench upon men's liberty.

In any event, censorship as a device to enforce broad-gauged anti-obscenity laws is dangerous. It is dangerous because in many ways it operates to permit the delegation of anti-obscenity law-making power to a few persons who, so experience reflects, often are peculiarly affected by those irrational influences. Unless the most stringent controls are put upon them, those who censor are given, in effect, the power to say what the law means; the appointed censors thus become legislators or courts, but without the restraints which our system puts upon those traditional forums of law-making.

While no one can very well document the degree of harm, if any, which censorship may have done to our culture by inhibiting expression, the assumption herein is that the very process of censorship can, if legally sanctioned, undermine the concept and the institutions of freedom; the philosophy which justifies censorship is the antithesis of the philosophy which ought to underlie our First Amendment. Policing all reading of all citizens is hardly a worthy goal of government, and the law should eschew such a goal in theory as well as practice.

Government should not engage in a quest for "obscenity" wherever it may be found with the purpose of expunging it whenever found. Rather, the hand of the censor or the policeman should be stayed unless the function of anti-obscenity enforcement would in some way be served by invoking repressive means: *i.e.,* the protection of youth from purveyors who seek them out, the deterrence of unsolicited "assaults" of obscenity, and the prevention of reckless commercial exploitation which creates similar risks. These goals have been defined, and we have stressed the point that the conduct of disseminators and the degree of obsceneness of the material should be important ingredients of the test for determining when government may suppress.

Substantive and procedural changes are important, but in the final analysis, the impact of any censorship system may depend as much on the *who* as on the *how*. Strict standards help to depersonalize; but absolute protection from personal predilections is impossible, as is constantly indicated by the different results reached by different officials in applying the same theoretical standard to the same material.

Vigilance by the articulate segment of the public which appreciates the values of freedom can also correct or deter abuses. History may well show that this is the best of all safeguards. Fortunately for America, no one likes to be called a censor, let alone a censor in error.

Regrettably, government—the officials who speak for it—sometimes make it difficult to learn all the objective facts of a censorship operation. Law enforcement officials in this field have usually been more strident than dispassionate about discussing the problems before them. Yet, violent condemnations may only whet prurient appetites and abet the interests of publisher panderers. If rational laws are to be framed and if informed decisions are to be made by legislators, censors, policemen, prosecutors, courts, and the American public, then the problems we face must constantly be put forth objectively and mature debate encouraged. The very process of mature debate, rather than fear and frenzy born of dogmatic condemnation of all things immoral, may teach us to meet the conditions we must, perforce, face as free men should.

APPENDIXES

NOTES TO THE TEXT

NOTE: Appendix II lists books, articles, and other secondary materials that deal generally with the subject of censorship, obscenity law, and freedom of the press. Most of these are cited here simply by author and title; the complete citation can be found in Appendix II.

Appendix III contains an alphabetical listing and full citation of all reported court cases mentioned in the notes below. Unreported cases and Post Office administrative decisions mentioned are cited in full, where possible, in this Appendix.

Appendix IV gives the text of some principal statutes and regulations pertaining to federal censorship of obscenity.

Reference is made throughout this Appendix to various rulings in the General Counsel's "non-mailability" files. These files contain correspondence, memoranda, and instructions to local postmasters and inspectors issued over the Solicitor's signature. They are broken down into categories of violations, "obscenity" being one. The obscenity cases, in turn, are broken down into categories of materials ("books," "magazines") and listed alphabetically within each category. Each separate file represents a separate case. All the files dealing with published matter were examined by this study. Memoranda reflecting most rulings were made, and these are located in the files of the Institute of Legal Research of the University of Pennsylvania Law School.

Reference is also made throughout this Appendix to various Customs rulings reflected in the Bureau's files. The Bureau in Washington (its Penalty Division) maintains both an informal card file of publications that have been referred from Customs offices around the country to Washington, and more complete files of correspondence and instructions issued from Washington relative to each publication that has been reviewed. The entire card file and selected correspondence files were examined for purposes of this study. Similar files, maintained by the Deputy Collector in charge of the Restricted Merchandise Division of the Port of New York, were examined. Memos of pertinent rulings are on file in the Institute of Legal Research of the University of Pennsylvania Law School.

PART I

I-I

For general historical material on the First Amendment relevant to the discussion in the text, see, e.g., Chafee, *Free Speech;* Cooley, *Constitutional Limitations;* Emerson, "Doctrine of Prior Restraint"; Duniway, *Freedom of the Press in Massachusetts;* Rogge, "Congress Shall Make No Law"; Schofield, *Constitutional Law;* Rutland, *Birth of the Bill of Rights;* Schroeder, *"Obscene" Literature;* J. M. Smith, *Freedom's Fetters* (a careful and scholarly account of the Alien and Sedition Acts); Grant and Angoff, "Massachusetts and Censorship." And see, for a broader bibliography, Swindler, *Bibliography;* and Emerson and Haber, *Political and Civil Rights,* II, 270–90. For two strong, oft-quoted statements on the rationale of press freedom generally, in the *Areopagitica* tradition, see Meiklejohn, *Free Speech,* and John Stuart Mill's essay, *On Liberty.*

Blackstone's famous statement about prior restraints may be found in his *Commentaries,* IV, 151. An 1803 American edition by the (then) renowned Virginia law scholar and judge, St. George Tucker, contains an interesting comment to the effect that our First Amendment is a total bar to all federal regulation of the press (see I, 198; IV, 151 *et seq.*). The quotation from Jefferson is taken from Padover's (ed.) *Jefferson,* pp. 384–85. For a further interesting statement by Jefferson, see *Writings of Jefferson,* ed. Ford, VIII, 464. For Madison's comments, see I *Annals of Congress* 704, 737, and his *Writings,* ed. Hunt, p. 341.

For debates on the establishment of the postal system and postal rates, see *Annals of Congress,* 1st Cong. (Vol. II, ed. Gale and Seaton, 1834), pp. 1580–82, 2236, 2357, 2409; 2d Cong. (1849 ed.), pp. 214, 229, 237, 241, 254, 282–85, 298. See, generally, Rich, *History of the Post Office*, pp. 68–91, 111–27.

George Washington's view that newspapers and periodicals should be circulated via the government mails at either no charge or at nominal cost is reflected in *Writings of Washington,* ed. Fitzpatrick (1940), XIII, 161 ("Memorandum of Matters To Be Communicated to Congress," November, 1793, which says: "Might it not be expedient to take off the tax upon transportation of Newspapers, etc."); *ibid.,* p. 169 (Fifth Annual Message, December, 1793; recommends "repeal" of charges on "transportation of public prints"); *ibid.,* XII, 210 (Fourth Annual Message, 1792; recommends that Congress investigate postal rates; stresses "the importance of facilitating the circulation of political intelligence and information"). See also Washington's *Writings,* ed. Ford (1891), XI, 290–91 (letter to John Jay, July 18, 1788). That Washington believed, at the same time, that newspapers were irresponsibly defamatory seems clear from contemporaneous expression. See, e.g., *ibid.,* XII, 179 (letter to Randolph, August 26, 1792); XII, 310 (letter to Henry Lee, July 21, 1793; some newspapers are "diabolical," "outrages on common decency"); XII, 204 (letter to Gouverneur Morris, October 20, 1792). See also Rich, *History,* pp. 68–69, 111–15.

For the debates on President Jackson's proposal to ban abolitionist literature from the mails, see *Register of Congressional Debates,* 24th Cong. 1st sess., pp. 26–33, 1103–71, 1721–37. See also Deutsch, "Freedom of the Mails"; Rogge, "Congress Shall Make No Law"; L. Rogers, *Postal Power,* pp. 105–15.

I-2

For accounts of the extent of writing and circulation of obscene literature in sixteenth, seventeenth, eighteenth, and nineteenth century England, see, e.g., Ginzburg, *Erotica;* St. John-Stevas, "Obscenity"; Scott, *"Into Whose Hands";* Alpert, "Judicial Censorship"; Kronhausen, *Pornography And The Law;* St. John-Stevas, *Obscenity And The Law.*

For early English cases and other source material reflecting the status (and lack of it) of "obscenity law" at various periods prior to the passage of the Obscene Publications Act and the case of *Queen v. Hicklin,* see, e.g., *Queen v. Read* (1708); *Rex v. Curl* (1727); *Rex v. Wilkes* (1770); Hawkins, *Pleas of the Crown,* ed. Leach (1788), pp. 130, 355; Vagrancy Act (1824), 5 Geo. 4 c. 83 § 4; Stephen,

Digest of Criminal Law (4th ed., 1887), p. 117. See also, for citations, the scholarly footnote 1 in the opinion of Justice Frankfurter in *Smith v. California* and Justice Brennan's opinion in *Roth v. United States.*

For the earliest meaningful American cases reflecting the evolution of legal restraints on publications deemed obscene, see: *Knowles v. State* (Conn., 1808); *Commonwealth v. Holmes* (Mass., 1821); *State v. Appling* (Mo., 1857); *Commonwealth v. Sharpless* (Pa., 1815). See also *Revised Statutes of Massachusetts,* c. 130, sec. 10 (1836), and 7 *New York Statutes at Large* 309 (1867) (early statutes punishing publication of obscene materials). See Wharton, *Criminal Law* (2d ed., 1852), p. 739.

Anti-vice societies were very much a product of the nineteenth century. Notable examples include the English Society for the Suppression of Vice, the New York Society for the Suppression of Vice, and the New England Watch and Ward Society. For an interesting protest against early efforts at anti-vice society book censorship in England, see 13 *Edinburgh Review* 333 (1809). The first International Congress of anti-vice groups to propose means to control obscene literature was held in Switzerland in 1893. See the *Nation,* LVII, 323 (1893), for an account. Thereafter, such gatherings became regular occurrences. For history of the development, during the nineteenth century, of the copyright doctrine prohibiting court recognition of property rights in "immoral" or "obscene" works, and for examples of extreme and rather "strait-laced" judicial pronouncements applying this doctrine, see Rogers, *Copyright and Morals.* For the views of Robert Ingersoll, see, *The Works of Robert Ingersoll* (12 vols., 1900), especially XII, 215.

The first Tariff Statute is set out in 5 *Statutes at Large* 566 (1842). The statute provided for an *in rem* libeling procedure in the district court whereby contested seizures would be adjudicated by a judge and jury. See *United States v. Three Cases of Toys* for the first reported contested case illustrating this procedure. During the entire history of this statute, there have been very few reported instances of contested litigation.

In an effort to track down the origins of the statute of 1842 and to gain more familiarity with contemporary understanding of its meaning and function, the usual sources of legislative history were examined. Research into the origins of this statute included a search in the National Archives for possible earlier bills going back over a six-year period: there were none. Correspondence, reports, and papers of the select committee headed by Millard Fillmore to study changes needed in the Tariff Act as well as papers of other congressional committees were examined. The Buffalo Historical Society, which has the papers of Millard Fillmore in its library, reported, on the basis of a brief survey, that there was nothing in these papers for the years 1841 and 1842 bearing on the origins of this part of the tariff law. Treasury Department reports and letters bearing on tariff matters, including letters to and from collectors of Ports of Entry yielded nothing. Neither did official and unofficial Customs manuals. Secondary sources on the history of the Customs Service are also silent. Thus we conclude that there is virtually no recorded legislative history of this law—important though it was, when judged by hindsight. Perhaps, as a helpful assistant in the National Archives put it, after acknowledging defeat: "People just didn't talk about those things in those days."

For the account of the debates and passage of Lord Campbell's "Obscene Publications Act" (20 & 21 Victoria C. 83 [1875]), see Vols. CXLV-CXLIX of Hanshard's *Parliamentary Debates.* For another contemporary appraisal see Lord Broughham's unsigned and hostile article in 3 *Law Magazine and Law Review* 283 (1857). Lord Campbell's *Life of Lord Lyndhurst,* published in 1869 as a supplement to his earlier *Lives of the Lord Chancellors,* contains (p. 201) this comment on Lyndhurst and the Obscene Publication Act: "Having observed from several trials before me the frightful extent to which the circulation of obscene books and prints was carried, and the insufficiency of the remedy by indictment against the publishers, I had introduced a bill giving a power to search for, carry away, and destroy such abominations, under a warrant to be obtained from a magistrate. For some unaccountable reason, Lyndhurst violently opposed this measure, and on the second reading he delivered a most elaborate, witty, unfair, and, I must add, profligate speech against the bill, and moved that it be read a second time that day three months. His motion was rejected, and on the third reading we had such a rough passage of arms that the *entente cordiale* which had subsisted between us for nearly ten years was for a while suspended, and diplomatic relations were not restored between my noble and learned friend and myself till the beginning of the following year." For biographical material on Campbell (by his daughter) see Hardcastel, *Life of Lord Campbell,* reflecting Campbell's restless energy as judge, politician, law reformer, and writer. For an interesting earlier report to Parliament on the problem of commercial distribution of obscene publications, see Gordon and Cocks, *A People's Conscience.* This work recounts several parliamentary investigations into crime and related matters; in the course of these investigations, some of the committees unearthed considerable evidence of commercial traffic.

For the 1857 amendments to the Tariff Act of 1842 see 11 *Statutes at Large* 168. For legislative debates (which did not deal with the anti-obscenity provision) see *Congressional Globe,* 34th Cong., 1st session, pp. 137, 953, 957, 965. For a bibliography of Nineteenth Century state statutes on obscenity, see Justice Brennan's opinion in *Roth v. United States.*

In 1863 the Postmaster General wrote that he had "at different times, excluded from the mails obscene . . . matter on exhibition of its criminal immorality," despite the fact that no statute authorized such action (see H. R. Misc. Document No. 16, 37th Cong., 3d sess.). In 1861 the Postmaster General reported that he was excluding "incendiary" and "treasonable" material (see L. Rogers, *Postal Power,* p. 51). In 1868 the Attorney General advised the Postmaster General that, even in the absence of statute, the Post Office possessed inherent authority to stop mail service to persons suspected of using the mails to defraud (see 12 *Opinions of Attorney General* 399 [1868]). Such assertions of "inherent" power to stop mail deemed noxious have occurred throughout the history of the Post Office, see Paul and Schwartz, "Communist Propaganda in the Mails: A Report On Some Problems of Federal Censorship," 107 *University of Pennsylvania Law Review* 621 (1959).

The first Postal statute on obscenity is set out in 13 *Statutes at Large* 50 (1865). For the short Senate debates attending its passage, see *Congressional Globe,* 38th Cong., 2d sess., pp. 450, 654, 660–62, 965–66 (1865). For further discussion of the legislative history of this statute, see this Appendix, I-3. The Statute of 1865 was re-enacted as part of a general codification of the Postal laws in 1872 (see 17 *Statutes at Large* 322).

For accounts of Comstock's activity in securing passage of the Act of 1873 (17 *Statutes at Large* 598), see particularly Broun and Leech, *Anthony Comstock,* which contains the quotations from Comstock's diary. See also *Congressional Globe,* 42d Cong., 3d sess., Appendix, p. 168 (1873). For further material on Anthony Comstock's activities in general, see e.g., Trumbull, *Comstock;* Cushing, *Post Office.* See also writings by Comstock himself cited in the Bibliography. For further material on George Francis Train (and his account of his encounter with Comstock), see Train's *My Life,* from which the quotation in the text is taken. See also Kilpatrick, *The Smut Peddlers.*

Contemporary newspapers, particularly those of New York, also reflect the scope of Anthony Comstock's operations. For the periods discussed in the text, see, e.g., New York *Times,* February 6 and 9, March 8, 12, 15, 18, 29, April 16, 20, June 4, 17, July 3, 11, 29, August 2, September 30, and October 11 and 31 of the year 1873 for accounts of Comstock's arrests and trials, for violation of the anti-obscenity laws. In July, 1873, Comstock attempted to open and read certain letters addressed to the New York Herald because he suspected that the paper was carrying ads for illegal material. Comstock's rather flagrant attempt to break the seals on private correspondence addressed to the newspaper was resisted by the New York Postmaster. See New York *Times,* July 3, 1873. See *ibid,* February 6, 1878, for a long complaint by Comstock against the courts in which the judges and legal "technicalities" are blamed for his failure to obtain convictions in certain obscenity cases. For hostile press coverage of Comstock's lobbying for the Comstock Act, see New York *Herald,* February 18, 24, 1873. The *Herald* rather gleefully and cruelly noted that a Senate Committee struck out of a Post Office appropriation bill a special provision for Comstock's salary as a "Special Agent" of the Post Office Department (February 24, 1873). But it would appear that Comstock was, in fact, delighted to serve as a "Special Agent" without pay. See Broun and Leech, *Comstock.*

For the legislative sources on the Act of 1873 see *Congressional Globe,* 42d Cong., 3d sess., pp. 1240, 1307, 1358, 1371, 1436, 2004 (1873). For a more detailed analysis of whether the Act of 1873 was intended as a censorship statute, see this Appendix, 1–3, and Paul, "The Post Office."

I-3

The Bennett case is *United States v. Bennett.* See also, Broun and Leech, *Comstock;* New York *Times,* March 19, 20, 21, 22, May 16, June 1, 4, 6, August 9, 1879; New York *Herald,* March 19, 20, 21, 22 (containing a very full account of testimony and proceedings). For other early federal cases see this Appendix, I-4. For the influence of the Bennett case, see Balter, *Federal Obscenity Statutes,* and Kilpatrick, *The Smut Peddlers.*

In 1878, as a result of the arrest of Bennett and the "persecution" of other "free thinkers" an abortive attempt was made by the "National Liberal League" to have the Comstock Act repealed. See 45 *Congressional Record* 1340, 3960, 3473 and *Works of Robert Ingersoll,* Volume 7, pp. 345–347, 215–230.

The debates on the Postal Statute of 1876 (19 *Statutes at Large* 90) may be found in 4 *Congressional Record* 475, 3655, 3687, 4005, 4261 *et seq.,* 4403, 4517. Enactment of this statute was the last time in which Congress amended the basic structure of the Comstock Act; new categories of prohibited matter, e.g., "filthy," have been added (see 25 *Statutes at Large* 496 [1908]), and coverage has been broadened so as to include, e.g., phonograph records (see 69 *Statutes at Large* 184 [1955]). The statute was also significantly amended in 1958, (see 72 *Statutes at Large* 962); but this amendment was directed to its criminal provisions; the purpose was to permit prosecutions against mailers of obscenity to be brought in districts where the material is received as well as in districts where it was first deposited in the mails. This 1958 change created no other new substantive powers. For purposes of determining whether the Comstock Act was intended to authorize "censorship," we must go back to the Statute of 1865 as broadened in 1873 and revised again in 1876—it is the language enacted on those occasions which is critical. A more detailed analysis of this legislative history appears in the Appendix below. See also Paul "The Post Office."

The *Kreutzer Sonata* incident is reflected in 19 *Opinions of Attorney General* 667 (1890). The opinion advised that those issues of the newspaper (which was printing the book in serial form) which carried non-obscene chapters of the book should not be stopped, but that all issues carrying any obscene portions of the book should be stopped. The opinion is important because it is the first statement to the Post Office plainly declaring the power of the Post Office to use the Comstock Act as a civil censorship statute. See also 26 *Opinions of Attorney General* 555 (1908), where, in an extraordinary opinion, Attorney General Charles J. Bonaparte advised President Theodore Roosevelt that the Postmaster General had power to exclude an allegedly seditious tract (called *La question sociale*) from the mails, even in the absence of any censorship statute, indeed, even in the absence of any statute making advocacy of seditious actions a federal crime; the power of the Post Office to exclude "obscene" matter on the basis of the Comstock Act was assumed and spelled out in the course of this opinion. For further indications of the exercise of Postal power to stop circulation of all publications deemed obscene by the beginning of the century, and for a statement showing the sweep of its censorship powers as of 1917, see the statement of the Postmaster General reported in 55 *Congressional Record* 6257–62 (1917). See *Anderson v. Patten* for the first clear reported case reflecting Postal censorship of a magazine (*The Little Review;* ban upheld; opinion by Judge A. N. Hand).

An Additional Note on the Legislative History of the Postal Anti-Obscenity Acts of 1865, 1873, and 1876. The following is a more detailed analysis of whether, in light of the legislative history and other guides, the Post Office was ever really given, by Congress, the power to stop mail deemed obscene, not as an incident of the power to prosecute the mailer, but irrespective of whether a criminal prosecution of the mails is to follow. (For an even more extended discussion, see Paul, "The Post Office").

A conclusion that no such censorship power is authorized might be based, essentially, on the argument that the Acts of 1865, 1873, and 1876 were all *criminal* statutes, that they created no authorization for

Postal officials to censor—at least when no criminal prosecution followed and when the censorship was not accompanied by arrest and indictment.

It has been argued, recently, by lawyers contesting the Post Office in censorship cases, that this was Congress' "intent" when it legislated. It is urged by these lawyers, who have looked into the history of the passage of these laws, that in none of the recorded debates on any of the enactments did anyone in Congress ever suggest that the Post Office Department would, by virtue of the law to be enacted, exercise the broad censorship power which it later assumed. For a full presentation of these arguments see, e.g., the Brief for the Plaintiff in *Big Table, Inc. v. Schroeder,* Civil Action No. 59Cl382, U.S. District Court, Northern District of Illinois (1960); Brief for Petitioner in *Sunshine Co. v. Summerfield,* U.S. Supreme Court (1958), cited in Appendix III.

A review of the legislative history of the statutes shows that there were some expressions on the floor during debates on these Acts to the effect that no independent Postal censorship power was contemplated, that the power to stop mail in transit only arises after the statute has been invoked as a criminal statute, e.g., after the mailer has been indicted or arrested or perhaps convicted for violating the prohibition. But there were, also, a few expressions which may suggest a contrary intent.

There is, first, the legislative history of the Act of 1865, which may be quite significant because all subsequent enactments built on it. The 1865 bill, as reported, provided that "no obscene book shall be admitted into the mails," and further that "all such obscene publications deposited in or received at any Post Office or discovered in the mails, shall be seized and destroyed or otherwise disposed of, as the Postmaster General shall direct." In the Senate, Jacob Collamer of Vermont, a proponent of the bill, admitted that he was "not entirely satisfied with it" because, in the bill as written: "the first part of it provides that if such publications are in the mails, the Postmaster may take them out; and the latter part provides a penalty and punishment for those who put them into the mails. The Senate may adopt the whole of this section or the latter part of it without the first part." Senator Johnson then raised questions about whether the bill as reported would "let the Postmaster break seals?" Collamer observed: "there is not a word said about seals in the section." He went on to observe that the bill might be objectionable because "it might be made a precedent for undertaking to give [the Postmaster] a sort of censorship over the mails . . . like throwing out the abolition papers that used to be talked about." Senator Johnson moved to "strike out the First part, so as to leave it merely an offense [to mail the publications] . . . ; it would be establishing a very bad precedent to give authority to postmasters to take anything out of the mails" and to permit them to "break seals." Senator Sherman then said: "I would much prefer if the Senator would be satisfied, with simply striking out the second clause of the first paragraph. *I think the prohibition against publications of this character going into the mails ought to stand* [emphasis added]. We are well aware that many of these publications are sent all over the country from the City of New York with the names of the parties sending them on the backs, so that the postmasters without opening the mail matter may know that it is offensive matter and improper to be carried in the mails. I think there-fore *the legislative prohibition against carrying such matter when it is known to the postmasters should be left* [emphasis added]. Probably the second clause allowing him to open mail matter should be struck out; and I suggest to the Senator to modify this amendment by merely moving to strike out the words 'but all such obscene publications de-posited in or received at any post office, or discovered in any mail, shall be seized and destroyed or otherwise disposed of as the Postmaster General shall direct'." Senator Johnson agreed to this modification of his amendment. It is arguable that Senator Sherman was arguing for a censorship authorization. But his remarks were ambiguous, and it may be doubtful that he was so understood. In any event the Senate deleted the words "all . . . obscene publications . . . discovered in the mails shall be seized and destroyed . . . as the Postmaster General shall direct." But the bill did, still, say: "No obscene [publication] shall be admitted into the mails," and it went right on to impose criminal penalties for "knowingly" mailing obscenity (*Congressional Globe,* 38th Cong., 2d sess. pp. 660–62 [1865]).

Congress enacted a general codification of Postal laws in 1872. There was no discussion of any relevant section under study here. The codi-fication added language to the anti-obscenity law to the effect that, in addition to obscenity, no "letter upon the envelope of which, or postal card upon which scurrilous epithets have been written 'should' be carried in the mail" and went on to impose the same criminal penalty in the same language as before. There was also another section in the code providing that all material "which may be seized or detained for violation of law shall be returned to the . . . sender or otherwise dis-posed as the Postmaster may direct" (see 17 *Statutes At Large* 320, 323). This might reflect an intention to enforce the anti-obscenity provision by censorship methods. But again there was no indication whether this provision authorizing "disposal" of matter which "violated the laws" was applicable to enforcement of the prohibitions against mailing obscene and scurrilous matter (see *Congressional Globe,* 42d Cong. 2d sess., pp. 5, 15, 71, 783–800, 4092 [1871–72]).

In 1873, the bill (which became the Comstock Act) provided, in essence, that "no obscene . . . publication [and various other items, e.g., contraceptive and abortifacient matter, and "things intended . . . for immoral use"] shall be carried in the mail"; and any person who shall "knowingly" mail any of the "hereinbefore mentioned articles or things" was to be criminally punished. It seems probable that the basic purpose of this bill, which was to be a new act supplanting the Act of 1865, was to broaden the coverage of the latter to include advertising circulars and to include, within the prohibition, contraceptive and abortifacient matter, things "designed" for "immoral use" ("immoral" in a sexual sense) and postcards and envelopes containing "scurrilous" or "indecent" "epithets." Comstock wrote to Representative Merriam listing the kinds of "abominations" which were being sold via the mails, and describing his own activity to suppress the trade. He then wrote:

> There are various ways by which this vile stuff has been disseminated. First, by advertising in the above-mentioned papers. Some weeks there is not a single advertisement in some of these papers that is not designed either to cheat or defraud, or intended to be a medium of sending out these accursed books and articles. . . .
> Secondly. These abominations are disseminated by these men first obtaining the addresses of scholars and students in our schools and colleges and then forwarding these circulars. . . .
> You will please observe that this business is carried on principally by the agency of the United States mails, and there is no law to-day by which we can interfere with the sending out of these catalogues and circulars through the mail, except they are obscene on their face; and there are scores of men that are supporting themselves and families to-day by sending out these rubber goods, etc., through the mails, that I cannot touch for want of law. . . .

Another purpose of Congress at this time, apparently, was to pass additional anti-obscenity legislation prohibiting importation from abroad and prohibiting circulation within the District of Columbia. There was no real discussion at all of the proposed legislation relating to importation, though it clearly appears to have broadened the coverage of the Act of 1842 by including printed as well as pictorial obscenity. No doubt Senator Casserly had this proposal in mind when he made his objection against authorizing Customs interference with the importation of books—an objection aimed, perhaps, at quite a different anti-obscenity operation than policing the domestic mail, but still an objection against "censorship." No one responded to Casserly. Later he said: "I wish to withdraw the remarks I made, because I understand [this part of] the bill relates to the mails altogether, and not to the customhouse." It is possible, in view of Casserly's concern, to argue that no censorship could have been intended in the Postal law, but it may be doubtful whether Casserly or anyone else really gave any attention to the question whether censorship of the domestic mails was authorized. See *Congressional Globe*, 43d Cong., 3d sess., pp. 1371, 1436 (1873); see also other sources cited in the *Globe*, and noted in this Appendix, I-2.

The Act of 1876 made what would appear, at first blush, to be a most significant change in wording. The Comstock Act was rewritten to provide that "Every obscene [publication, etc.] . . . is declared to be *non-mailable matter and shall not be conveyed in the mails or delivered* from any Post Office or by any letter carrier" (emphasis added). But, as noted *supra* in the text (p. 28), there was no definitive explanation of the import of this specific change, although there was some discussion of the scope of the obscenity provisions when the bill was introduced in the House. The original purpose of the Act of 1876 appears to have been twofold: (1) to amend Revised Statutes, Section 3894, the prohibition against mailing lottery materials: the Act of 1876 purported to ban *all* lottery matter, not just all *illegal* lottery matter as had originally been provided; thus, the Postal prohibition was to apply even in states where lotteries, under certain circumstances, had been made legal; (2) to amend the penalty clause of the Comstock Act: the Act of 1873, as seen, listed all sorts of prohibited matter—e.g., obscene publications, abortifacient and contraceptive "things," and "information" and advertisements; however, its penal clause provided only that anyone who knowingly mailed the "hereinbefore mentioned *articles* or *things*" would be criminally liable; the draftsmen of Comstock's Act had failed to include express reference to mailing the "hereinbefore mentioned" *publications;* and the Act of 1873 also failed to provide expressly for punishment of those who mailed advertisements. To cure this omission, the 1876 bill rewrote the 1873 act by listing all the items previously banned (obscene books, prints, pictures, things designed for immoral use, scurrilous "epithets" on wrappers or postcards, and advertisements for any of these items) and by declaring all this matter to be "non-mailable"; the bill then went on to say that "any person who shall knowingly . . . [mail] *any matter declared by this section to be non-mailable matter* . . . shall be guilty of a misdemeanor." It is thus arguable that the language classifying various sorts of material as "non-mailable matter" was the draftsman's device for accomplishing the result he wanted to accomplish in the penalty clause. When the bill was first brought up on the House floor, Representative Conger objected to language in the penalty clause apparently making those who received obscenity criminally liable. He added: "The power given by this law to every one of the thousands of postmasters throughout the country to interfere for the purposes named with the correspondence of the people or their newspapers is a great power, apparently in violation of the assured rights of the citizens. . . ." Chairman Cannon of the Postal Committee assured Congress that the "proposed bill *in no wise changes the law except to provide a penalty for the circulation of obscene literature*" (emphasis added); and he went on to explain the "oversight" in the Comstock Act. "I will state to the gentleman," said Cannon, "that he has misconceived the provisions of the proposed amendment." Cannon then went on to argue that the bill would not punish innocent receivers. Representative Hoar of Massachusetts asked questions about the meaning of the prohibition against things adapted for any "immoral purpose." Was it not too broad? "There was a time when throughout a large section of this country every newspaper which thought slavery was wrong was considered immoral and was taken from the mails by the postmaster." To which Cannon replied again that the bill makes "nothing non-mailable that is not now non-mailable; it merely provides a penalty." Further, the prohibition on "immoral things," he suggested, had to do with things immoral in the sense that they were "obscene." He went on to say: "*Nor, sir, does this bill give any right to any postmaster to open or interfere with anybody's mail. It is like anything else, before you can convict, you must offer and make proof*" (emphasis added). Presumably this was said in reply to Hoar's objection to authorizing Postmasters to take newspapers deemed "immoral" from the mails.

James Garfield then called attention to the fact that a newspaper editor had recently been indicted for printing "a crazy contribution from George Francis Train, wholly theological in its character [an attack on the Trinity doctrine]. . . . It has occurred to me [that] the act we passed last year [in 1873?] is liable to constructions of this character. . . . We ought to be exceedingly careful in all our legislation touching this subject. . . . Where freedom of opinion and of the press lie on the border of obscenity is a difficult question, and I would be glad if the Committee . . . would consent to reference of this bill to the Committee on the Judiciary . . . in order that they may go over the whole subject and inquire whether we have not used terms too broad and too general in the original bill. . . ." At this point Chittenden promised, if the bill were recommitted, to reveal a case of "oppression against an honorable and an innocent man" in Brooklyn. Mr. Bland asked whether a newspaper report of the "Beecher Trial" would be prohibited. Hoar raised an objection that a newspaper publisher might be "exposed" to the standards of juries all over the country; apparently, he wanted the venue of prosecutions limited to the place of publication. Thereupon, Chairman Cannon agreed to recommittal of the bill for further study (4 *Congressional Record* 695–96). Thus, it appears that there were some members of Congress who had genuine reservations about the scope and meaning of the Comstock Act. Regrettably, however, this discussion was all too short, and on the question of whether the bill was intended to authorize an independent Postal censorship operation, it was all too vague. Chairman Cannon reported the bill back to the floor later in the session. No changes significant for purposes of the present discussion were made. The bill was thereupon passed by the House. In the Senate the discussion was confined almost entirely to the lottery provisions, though Senator Morrill did make fleeting allusion to the broad scope of the prohibition against publishing things deemed immoral (see 4 *Congressional Record* 4261 *et seq.*).

The "Comstock Act" was codified in the Post Office Code (but with other plainly criminal sections) until 1909, when it was codified, along with many other criminal statutes, in what has become Title 18 of the U.S. Code, the criminal part of the Code (see 35 *Statutes at Large* 1129, 1153 [1909]).

A statute enacted in 1888 (25 *Statutes At Large* 496, now codified as 18 U.S.C. 1463) prohibited mailing of envelopes or wrappers containing defamatory, "scurrilous" or "obscene" expression; this, Congress declared, was "non-mailable, and shall not be conveyed . . . nor delivered . . . *and shall be withdrawn from the mails under such regulations as the Postmaster General shall prescribe.*" (Emphasis added.) This seems like the language of censorship; although the law contained criminal penalties, it seemed to authorize independent civil enforcement, and the debates on the bill indicate that some in Congress opposed the bill for fear of censorship, although some proponents apparently asserted that no such censorial power would exist. But the debates were very brief; it is simply not clear whether Congress recognized the difference in language between the law of 1888 and the Comstock Act. See 19 *Congressional Record* 2206, 4230, 4934, 4941, 6104, 7660, 8189, 8555. See also Paul, "The Post Office."

An interesting analogy to the problem of Post Office censorship of obscene publications existed by virtue of the first lottery laws (15 *Statutes at Large* 196, [1868]). This statute, as first enacted, provided that "No [lottery material] shall be carried in the mail; any person who shall knowingly [mail such material] shall be [punished criminally]." Its structure was thus quite identical with the anti-obscenity law. The Attorney General, in 1878, advised the Postmaster General, in a formal opinion, that apparently there was no power to seize or detain suspected lottery matter in the mail under this Statute (as codified in Re-

APPENDIXES

vised Statutes §3894) unless the seizure was incident to enforcement of
the criminal law. The thrust of the opinion was apparently that the
anti-lottery law was a criminal statute, not one which provided for an
independent civil sanction (see 16 *Opinions of Attorney General* 5
[1878]; see also 12 *Opinions of Attorney General* 538 [1868]). This
early reading of the lottery law might require, by analogy, a similar interpretation of the similarly constructed obscenity law.

In behalf of the proposition that there is no statutory power to censor
obscene publications by barring them from the mail, one can make the
further argument that, regardless of the ambiguity and paucity of legislative history, any statute which purports to grant law enforcement
powers of such a delicate and controversial nature must speak clearly
and be read strictly; thus, the grant of censorship power should not be
inferred in the absence of a clear-cut purpose; moreover, the Comstock
Act as amended and codified in 18 U.S.C. 1461 is basically a *criminal
law,* codified in the chapter on criminal laws, and criminal laws traditionally are rigidly rather than liberally construed. Thus, it can be
argued, there is no censorship power, and the Post Office has been acting illegally for the past eighty-eight years.

Nevertheless, as suggested in the text, and notwithstanding the two
lottery law opinions of the Attorney General cited *supra,* the Comstock
Act, especially as amended in 1876, *seems* to grant a censorship power
even if the procedure for enforcing this power and the limits on it are
left undescribed. Moreover, as explained in the text, the Post Office did
in fact begin to exercise the power to stop any mail it deemed obscene
—irrespective of criminal enforcement of the statute—and this administrative practice became firmly established and Congress has never repudiated it, and, at least until recently, the courts have never cast doubts
upon it.

Indeed, in 1920 Justice Brandeis wrote (in the *Milwaukee Journal*
case, 255 U.S. 407, 421, in an opinion where Brandeis, himself, was protesting against enlargement of Postal censorship to include the power
to revoke second-class permits): "Power to exclude from the mails has
never been conferred in terms upon the Postmaster General. Beginning
with the Act of March 3, 1865, c. 89, §16, 13 Stat. 507, relating to obscene matter and the Act of July 27, 1868, c. 246, §13, 15 Stat. 196,
concerning lotteries, Congress has from time to time forbidden the de-
posit in the mails of certain matter. In each instance, in addition to pre-
scribing fine and imprisonment as a punishment for sending or attempting to send the prohibited matter through the mail, it declared that
such matter should not be conveyed in the mail, nor delivered from any
post office nor by any letter carrier. By §6 of the Act of June 8, 1872, c.
335, 17 Stat. 285, (Rev. Stats., §396), the Postmaster General was em-

powered to 'superintend the business of the department, and execute all laws relative to the postal service.' As a matter of administration the Postmaster General, through his subordinates, rejects matter offered for mailing, or removes matter already in the mail, which in his judgment is unmailable. The existence in the Postmaster General of the power to do this cannot be doubted. The only question which can arise is whether in the individual case the power has been illegally exercised."

In light of our own investigation of the legislative history, we cannot be as certain as Brandeis that the censorship "power" of the Post Office to "remove [allegedly obscene] matter" from the mails "cannot be doubted." We think, on the contrary, that there is a basis for doubting that there was a clear Congressional purpose to authorize the power. But we cannot conclude, ourselves, that the Post Office *must* be said to be acting illegally, today.

Of importance as evidence that the statute means what the Post Office has long said it means are: the long period of congressional silence plus manifestations of affirmative acquiescence in the use of the civil censorship sanction by many congressional committees concerned with legislation in the area; congressional augmentation of the Post Office's civil sanctions (e.g., by enactment of 39 U.S.C. 259(a), the mail-block law); earlier court decisions, not questioned until recently which have certainly assumed, but without discussing the issue, that the independent Postal censorship power is granted by the statute (see, e.g., *Anderson v. Patten; American Mercury v. Kiely*). In the more recent (1957) case of *Sunshine Book Co. v. Summerfield* a divided full bench of the Court of Appeals for the District of Columbia upheld the statutory power of the Post Office to stop "obscene" mail in transit, though three dissenters doubted whether the Comstock Act really does authorize this power and, if so, whether it is constitutional. The Supreme Court reversed *per curiam* without suggesting that there was no statutory censorship power. In the more recent *Lady Chatterley* case, *Grove Press v. Christenberry*, the Court of Appeals for the Second Circuit avoided the question; assuming, without deciding, that the Post Office could exclude obscene books, it went on to hold that this book was not obscene.

After reviewing all the arguments and history, the only conclusion we can stress is: when Congress enacted and later amended the Comstock Act, no real thought was given to the question whether the statute should authorize an independent "censorship" program as well as criminal enforcement of the proscription. Nor has Congress ever really reviewed the issue since then. Nor has any court decision carefully explored the issue. It is, therefore, a matter well worth the review of the courts should the occasion for careful review ever be presented. See, for amplification, Paul, "The Post Office."

I-4

For interesting contemporary account of the *Jackson* case, see New York *Times* March 19, May 1, 19, June 1, 1878.

For an excellent history of the general expansion of the Post Office's power to exclude objectionable matter from the mail, see Lindsey Rogers, *Postal Power*, pp. 48–60, 97–126. Some of the leading cases, mentioned in the text and reflecting this evolution of power are: *Ex parte Jackson* (1876) (constitutional power to exclude lottery material sustained; broad dictum that Congress may fix conditions to the content of the mails); *Ex parte Rapier* (same) (1879); *United States v. Bennett* (1878) (first definitive, reported federal case on Comstock Act; Hicklin test followed and adopted); *Swearingen v. United States* (1896) and *Rosen v. the United States* (1896) (Hicklin test approved by the U.S. Supreme Court); *Dunlop v. United States* (same) (1897); *American School of Magnetic Healing v. McAnnulty* (1902) (Postmaster General has broad discretion in fraud causes; judicial review limited); *Public Clearing House v. Coyne* (1909) (mail blocks in fraud cases sustained; constitutionality of Comstock law assumed); *Milwaukee Publishing Co. v. Burleson* (1920) (the *Milwaukee Leader* case; power to revoke second-class permits sustained).

For statutes reflecting the expansion of Postal *censorship* power after 1876, see, e.g., 25 *Statutes at Large* 187 (1888) (indecent, libelous matter appearing on wrappers or envelopes); 25 *Statutes at Large* 496 (1888) (adding obscene private letters to the Comstock Act); 35 *Statutes at Large* 1129, 1138 (1909) ("filthy" matter also added as a new category); 37 *Statutes at Large* 240 (1912) (prize-fight pictures declared non-mailable excluded); 41 *Statutes at Large* 1060 (1919) (motion-picture films added). See also the cases cited in this Appendix I-4; Rogers, *Postal Power*, pp. 158–80. Justice Brandeis' dissenting opinion in *Milwaukee Publishing Co. v. Burleson* contains an account (255 U.S., p. 424, n. 1) of the proposal to ban mail service for publishers of [religiously] "immoral" works. He wrote: "In the Sixty-third Congress, Third Session (1915) a bill, H.R. 20644, was introduced to deny absolutely the use of the mail to any person who, in the opinion of the Postmaster General, 'is engaged or represents himself as engaged in the business of publishing any books or pamphlets of an indecent, immoral, scurrilous or libellous character.' It was objected: The 'bill would invest one man . . . with the power to destroy the business of a publisher without affording any opportunity for trial by jury, according to regular court practice. The punishment which may be inflicted upon a publisher by the Postmaster General under the provisions of this bill is most severe, absolutely depriving him of the privilege of using the United States mails, even for legitimate purposes. . . . Furthermore, this bill makes it possible for the Postmaster General to inflict what is practically a confiscatory penalty for an offense not clearly defined. . . . Under such circumstances as these it is not safe to leave to the decision of one man, after an *ex parte* investigation, a decision which will involve the freedom of the press. Trial by jury and a penalty inflicted for each specified act is the only safeguard against an arbitrary and tyrannical power.' The bill failed of passage. Hearings before Committee on Post Office and Post Roads, February 1, 1915, On Exclusion of Certain Publications from the Mails, pp. 38, 39, 63rd Cong. 3d sess."

The first fraud statute is 17 *Statutes at Large* 322 (1872). See also 25 *Statutes at Large* 874 (1889). The "Fictitious Name Statute," originally designed to permit mail blocks in fraud situations and later used as a legal basis for mail blocks in obscenity cases, is 25 *Statutes at Large* 873 (1889). The modern "mail block" statute was enacted in 1950, 64 *Statutes at Large* 451, and codified as 39 U.S.C. 259(a) and recently re-codified as 39 U.S.C. 4006.

I-5

Rulings of the Customs Court are to be found in a series of reports called Treasury Decisions under the Customs Laws (cited hereafter as TD), published since 1857. For illustrative rulings discussed in the text, see, e.g., 52 TD 37 (titles of works condemned not listed); 54 TD 42907 (a shipment of books including *Ulysses* and *Aphrodite*); 56 TD 47 (*Decameron*); 56 TD 10 (Balzac's *Droll Stories*); 51 TD 2 (*Well of Loneliness*); 56 TD 17 (*Enduring Passion*); 56 TD 20 (*The Wild Party*); 56 TD 14 (pictures); 57 TD 26 (*Well of Loneliness*); 59 TD 20 (*Temptation of Saint Anthony*); 61 TD 42 (*Story Teller's Holiday*).

Other rulings made during this period are reflected in the files of the Penalty Division of the Bureau of Customs. For contemporary secondary source material reflecting the extent of Customs and Postal censorship and controversy over it prior to 1930, see, e.g., Schroeder, *Obscene Literature;* Haight, *Banned Books;* Dennett, *Who's Obscene?* Ernst and

Seagle, *To the Pure;* Gilfond, *Arbiters of Obscenity* and *Customs Men;* Weeks, *The Practice of Censorship* (contains episode on A. Edward Newton); remarks of Senator Cutting in 9 *Congressional Digest* 3 (1930) (reprinting excerpts from his Senate speeches attacking a Custom enforcement of the tariff ban); Rogers, *Extension of Federal Control.*

The account of the Dennett case is taken from Dennett, *Who's Obscene?* and *United States v. Dennett.*

The *History of Prostitution* incident is discussed in Schroeder, *Obscene Literature,* p. 68. See also secondary sources cited in this Appendix I-6.

Other Post Office incidents discussed in this section are based on rulings found in the files of the General Counsel of the Post Office which reflect the Department's "non-mailability" rulings issued during this period. Most of the earlier rulings, i.e., prior to about 1940, are no longer available, but, as of 1956, enough had been retained in the files to give a fair sampling of the scope of censorship, as practiced during the period 1920–30. Memoranda of each of these rulings are on file in the Institute of Legal Research of the University of Pennsylvania Law School. The case involving the banning of the magazine, *The Little Review,* was litigated: see *Anderson v. Patten;* and the Postal decision was upheld by Judge Augustus Hand (who was then a district judge). His opinion suggests considerable personal doubt as to the obsceneness of the story, but he felt constrained: (1) to follow the *Hicklin* formula, and (2) to defer, in cases of doubt, to the discretion of the Postmaster General. The opinion is worth contrasting with the later views of Judge Hand enunciated in the famous *Ulysses* case discussed in the text on p. 65. The case involving the banning of *American Mercury* was appealed to the Court of Appeals, where Judge Mack's injunction against the Post Office was set aside on the ground that there were no grounds for granting such relief because, apparently, the magazine had already been delivered to all its subscribers before the Postal ruling had been implemented. The opinion of the court (per Judge Manton) contained broad dicta to the effect that postal discretion in non-mailability cases should not be reversed unless the censorship decision was clearly wrong (see, *American Mercury Inc. v. Kiley*).

PART II

II-1

The Tariff Act of 1930 is printed in 46 *Statutes at Large* 688 and codified as 19 U.S.C. 1305 (a).

The debates over its enactment covered the period October, 1929, to February, 1930, and are scattered through Volume LXXI of the *Congressional Record,* Parts 3, 4, 5, 6 (1929–30). See, particularly, pp. 1068–69, 3695–96, 4118, 4432–39, 4445–46, 4451, 4455–60, 5416–20. See also the *New York Times* for October 10, 12, 13, 19, November 7, and December 24, 1929; March 7, 1930.

II-2

For discussion of the "ground-breaking" work of the New York state courts during the late twenties and early thirties, see Cairns, "Freedom of Expression."

The federal cases discussed in the text are: *United States v. Dennett; United States v. Ulysses; United States v. Parmelee.* For two other noteworthy cases involving interpretation of the term "obscene" for purposes of applying the Comstock Act in criminal cases, see *United States v. Levine* and *United States v. Rebhuhn.* Both decisions were rendered by Judge Learned Hand. Other significant cases occurring during the period 1930–45 were *United States v. Consumers Union, Inc.,* dealing with the Comstock Act's ban on mailing information on contraception and creating an exception when this material is mailed to married persons seeking such help on the advice of a physician, and *Walker v. Popenoe,* which set aside a Postal ban on Dr. Popenoe's booklet, *Preparing for Marriage.* This case is discussed at length in the text, p. 95.

II-3

For an account of Huntington Cairns's background and work with the Bureau, see Chafee, *Government and Mass Communications,* Chapter 13, and the monographs by the Attorney General's Committee on Administrative Procedure, entitled *The Post Office Department* (1940), pp. 32–33, 95, and *Administration of the Customs Laws* (1940) pp. 116–22. For a discussion by Mr. Cairns of obscenity problems, see his article, "Freedom of Expression," from which the quotation in the text is taken.

The account of Customs enforcement during the period 1930–45 is based on an examination of Bureau files reflecting rulings made during this period and on interviews with Mr. Cairns and Mr. Irving Fishman, Deputy Collector of the Port of New York.

II-4

The Post Office rulings described here are reflected in rulings in the "Non-mailability Files" of the General Counsel. In addition, some of these rulings were publicized in the press; data on rulings involving the periodicals *Studio, PM,* and *View* were drawn from the files of the American Civil Liberties Union in Princeton University Library. For an oft-cited state court decision, upholding a ban on *Strange Fruit,* see *Commonwealth v. Isenstadt.*

Material reflecting widespread use of the revocation sanction by the Post Office during the period 1940–44 is to be found in files of the American Civil Liberties Union at Princeton University; see, e.g., Vol. 2349, pp. 63, 77, 235; Vol. 2435, p. 139; Vol. 2436, p. 74. These materials contain correspondence between publishers, Postal officials, and ACLU staff members as well as press releases. See also the critical speeches of Senator Langer, 89 *Congressional Record* 3820–24, 4328–34 (1943), discussing this phase of Postal censorship, listing titles of banned magazines and reprinting news articles.

Postmaster General Frank Walker's observations on the second-class privilege are to be found on p. 12 of the *Annual Report of the Postmaster General for 1942.* The official reports of the *Esquire (Hannegan v. Esquire)* case are cited in Appendix II. Quoted excerpts from the trial are taken from the opinion of the Court of Appeals.

For significant Supreme Court decisions during the period 1946–56 see, e.g., *Winters v. New York* (the "crime magazine" case; New York statute declared invalid because its description and standards of prohibited publications was too broad and too vague.); *Burstyn v. Wilson; Gelling v. Texas; Holmby v. Vaughn; Superior Films, Inc. v. Department of Education* (movie cases; censorship prohibitions declared unconstitutional because they were too broad and vague; the *Burstyn* case is the leading case; the others are *per curiam* decisions simply citing *Burstyn*). See also *Hallmark Productions v. Carrol* for a similar Pennsylvania movie censorship case where the court applied those decisions and declared the Commonwealth's censorship statute unconstitutional. Other cases dealing with limitations imposed by the courts on federal censorship are cited in this chapter note.

The *Hecate County* case is *Doubleday Doran v. New York*. The case was litigated through the New York state courts and all the way through the U.S. Supreme Court, but none of the judges ever wrote an opinion explaining why the book was "obscene." An account of the argument of the case appears in 17 *U.S. Law Week* 3117, October 26, 1948; during the course of the argument Justice Jackson opined that perhaps the book should be treated as obscene when sold in "the vicinity of St. Patrick's Church" but not when sold to the denizens of "Greenwich Village."

For the Court's major dictum that "obscene" speech is not speech protected by the First Amendment, see Justice Murphy's opinion, speaking for a unanimous court, in *Chaplinsky v. New Hampshire*. Actually the dictum, when read in the context of the *Chaplinsky* case, may not have been intended (at least by its author) to state so broad a proposition as it was later assumed to state. Chaplinsky had been jailed for disorderly conduct; he had argued with a policeman, cursed and loudly called the officer "a God damned Fascist." In part Chaplinsky argued he had a First Amendment right to curse policemen to their face. The Court unanimously rejected the argument—with the dictum noted in the text. Justice Murphy might well have had obscene epithets rather than publications with any pretense of seriousness in mind. See also the 1952 case of *Beauharnais v. Illinois,* which repeated the dictum and gave it a much broader connotation in the course of a decision upholding an Illinois law outlawing defamation of races or religious groups.

The long and interesting opinions of Judge Curtis Bok (then of the Philadelphia Court of Common Pleas, now of the Supreme Court of Pennsylvania) and the late Judge Jerome Frank (of the U.S. Court of Appeals) on the meaning of the term "obscene," which voice skepticism of the validity of anti-obscenity restraints (as then defined), are to be found in *Commonwealth v. Gordon* and *Roth v. Goldman.* Both judges dealt particularly with the question of the harmful impact of allegedly obscene expression on persons exposed to it; both doubted, in light of available evidence, that there was any. Other cases reflecting new judicial concern about the scope of obscenity law when enforced in the federal context are: *Walker v. Popenoe; Door v. Donaldson; Sunshine Co. v. Summerfield; Tourlanes Co. v. Summerfield.*

For a leading study published by a behavioral scientist in 1954, surveying existing studies and expressing doubt as to the validity of the claim that "bad books" have a "bad psychological impact," see Jahoda, *Impact of Literature.*

For a leading, critical treatment of the law of obscenity and its validity under the First Amendment, published in 1951, before constitutional issues had been litigated, see Lockhart and McClure, *Literature, the Law of Obscenity and the Constitution.*

No attempt is made here to list all the scholarly studies and comments dealing with trends in postwar literature and reading and the relation of these trends to changes in moral values. On this general subject, however, see e.g., Wagner, *Parade of Pleasure;* Ellis, *Folklore of Sex;* and Sorokin, *Sex Revolution,* for detailed comment and description of this aspect of contemporary American life, each author presenting a somewhat different reaction to the danger presented by the present emphasis on sex in mass communications, and on the growth of distribution of salacious materials. See also Lerner, *America as a Civilization.* For an interesting history of the business aspects of the development of the so-called "sophisticated" (and more expensive "girlie" magazines like *Playboy, Tiger, Gent, Gem, Dude, Nuggett,* and others, see the long article captioned "Racy Reading," in *Wall Street Journal,* April 19, 1957, p. 1, col. 1. This discussion traces the phenomenally rapid growth in circulation—almost entirely via newsstand sales—of these magazines, notably *Playboy* and *Nuggett.*

Discussion in the text, pp. 83–86 (on the increasing volume of sales of allegedly obscene materials, via the mails), is based on, *inter alia:* interviews with Solicitor Abe M. Goff of the Post Office; Mr. David Stephens, Chief of the Postal Inspection Service; and various Postal inspectors and other Postal officials formally interviewed in the course of field studies; examination of the "non-mailability files" of the Post Office; a survey of the various reported hearings of Senator Kefauver's Subcommittee of the Judiciary Committee Investigating Juvenile Crime and the reported hearings of the Gathings (House Select) Committee to "investigate Current Pornographic Materials." The published *Hearings* and *Reports* of these committees (see Appendix II for full citations) contain estimates of the volume of the trade; the estimates, of course, are highly speculative. See, particularly, the Kefauver Committee's *Hearings,* subtitled *Obscene and Pornographic Materials,* which contain the most revealing data. See also the *Annual Reports* of the Postmaster General for the years 1950–56. For an indication of Samuel Roth's commercial success, see, e.g., 169 *Publishers Weekly* 241, 1035 (1956). See also *Report of the New York State Joint Legislative Committee, Studying Publications and Dissemination of Offensive and Obscene Material* (1957); also 1956, 1955, 1954, and 1949. Other material in the possession of this committee, which we examined, was also revealing.

We have profited from the research and help afforded by two seminar papers by University of Pennsylvania Law School students, written in 1958; Yampell, *A Study of the New York State Joint Legislative Committee Studying Publication of Offensive and Obscene Material;* Pfannebecker, *The Kefauver Committee: Obscenity and Related Matter and Its Causal Relationship to Juvenile Delinquency.* These papers summarized much of the testimony presented to these committees and their "findings."

III-2

Discussion of Customs procedures for screening and intercepting suspected obscenity are based on our field-study interviews with Customs personnel in Washington and in the ports of New York, Los

Angeles, Chicago, Philadelphia, Baltimore, and St. Paul-Minneapolis
(see the Preface). A brief official description of Customs operating
procedure is set out in 19 *Code of Federal Regulations* 1305 (1957)
and in the *Customs Manual.*

In New York, the biggest port of entry in terms of volume, the
various functions of detection, opening, and inspection are performed
by three different categories of employees: "inspectors," "segregators,"
and "V.O.P.'s" (standing for "Verifier, Opener, and Packer"). In the
smaller ports, where the volume of business is less, the entire operation
of detection, opening, and inspecting may be performed by one official.
According to the terms of the Universal Postal Convention of 1952
(Article 77) and the various conventions between the United States
and other countries, sealed parcels may be opened for inspection by
Customs officials. The Universal Postal Convention states that matter
exported in sealed parcels shall bear an endorsement on the outside of
the package authorizing Customs examination. Where no such endorsement appears, the Bureau of Customs, via the Post Office Department,
sends a form to the addressee authorizing inspection. Unless the form is
returned, the package will not be admittted. The citizen is forced to
waive his rights to the privacy of the seal even though the purpose of
compelling disclosure of the nature of his property may have nothing
to do with revenue enforcement and may be solely for the purpose of
detecting contraband.

As noted, Customs officials do not inspect all published matter entering the country. In 1956, one of the notorious Paris publishers, who
puts out a great many of the books regularly seized, reported in response to an inquiry by a college bookstore in Massachusetts (which
had experienced loss, via U.S. Customs censorship, of Lengel's *School
for Sin* and *Helen and Desire*) that "the U.S. Customs find about 30%
of our shipments."

Decision-making at each port of entry is exercised in theory by the
Collector, in fact (in large ports) by a subordinate. In New York, during the period in which our surveys were conducted, this official was
Mr. Irving Fishman, Deputy Collector in charge of the Restricted Merchandise Division, who gave so much assistance to this study; in smaller
ports the comparable official may simply be called a "deputy collector"
or an "assistant collector," or he may have some other title. In all ports
the cases are funneled through one or two key officials who exercise the
Collector's decision-making power.

Seizure without referral to Washington was authorized by a
Bureau directive promulgated in 1955. The directive told collectors, in
effect: You can seize any matter which is *"unquestionably* obscene"
(emphasis added). It went on to say that any "book or other publica-

tion identical with an edition" already ruled obscene by the Bureau in a "ruling made since 1940" may be treated as unquestionably obscene. This directive was promulgated to save time, man hours, and other costs, and to relieve Washington of the burden of deciding routine cases. This directive, amending the *Customs Manual* (in June 15, 1955), was preceded by an earlier directive (July 6, 1954) which limited the "unquestionably obscene" discretion to pictorial matter. Before 1954 (and since 1937) *all* suspect matter was referred to Washington.

Discussion of Customs censorship of movies is based on interviews with Irving Fishman and Huntington Cairns and on an examination of a sampling of 150 movie files in Mr. Fishman's office. These files (one for each film) are made up of the reviewer's report and correspondence between Mr. Fishman and the importer and Mr. Fishman and Mr. Cairns and the Bureau's ruling in each case.

During the period 1953 to 1956, no more than three or four films per year were censored by Customs officials in Los Angeles. One film was stopped in San Francisco—the first ever to be stopped there—and was sent to New York on instructions from Washington, where it was censored. Recently, more films have been imported through west coast ports.

With respect to discussion in the text concerning Customs procedures following detention of suspect obscenity, the following is typical of notices sent to the importers:

Sir or Madam:
You are advised that a mail package addressed to you from abroad, found to contain printed material, has been temporarily detained pending a determination as to its admissibility under the provisions of Section 305 of the Tariff Act of 1930 (as obscene). As soon as a final decision is made, you will be further notified.

After there has been a "final" administrative decision to seize, a seizure "notice," with an "assent to forfeiture," will be mailed to the importer instead of his book. The form for the letter used in New York is as follows:

You are advised that a mail package addressed to you from France, containing a copy of the book entitled . . . has been seized as in violation of the provisions of Section 305 of the Tariff Act of 1930.
Section 305, above referred to, deals with the prohibition from importation into the United States of obscene or immoral articles. There is enclosed herewith an Assent to Forfeiture for the above described merchandise. If you desire, you may sign this form and

return it marked for the attention of the undersigned, in which event the prohibited merchandise will be disposed of in accordance with existing law and regulations.

In some ports, allusion to referral to the courts for libeling is conveyed even more cryptically; in at least one, in 1956, the Collector's form letter really appeared to "apply the screws"—albeit unintentionally —to get the importer's signature on the assent, *viz.,* "If the [assent] form is not returned to us, it will be necessary to refer the matter to the United States Attorney for appropriate action." There was no explanation of what the United States Attorney will do, and a person unschooled in the provisions of Section 305 (a) (19 U.S.C. 1305(a) might well speculate that the "appropriate action" would involve grand juries and worse rather than the initiation of a law suit to libel the material. In the port where this somewhat ominous reference about referral for "appropriate action" to the U.S. Attorney concluded the letter, officials estimated that the Bureau received about an 80 per cent return on its requests for assents to forfeiture. Estimates, in 1956, seemed to run about the same in other ports; it is probable that over 75 per cent of the Bureau's seizures never go to court.

Material which is seized is either destroyed or sent to the Library of Congress. The Library does not collect obscene or pornographic materials as such; it receives such materials because it is a repository for publications produced the world over. Wherever any materials might have some relevance or use in the fields of literature, the social sciences, psychology, psychiatry, or anthropology, they are retained. Selection criteria are broad, for the Library is not worried about protecting the public; it is worried about retaining all materials—anything which may reflect some facet of the world's culture or may be useful for research.

Once selected by the Library, the material may or may not be catalogued: outright pictorial pornography is usually not; most books formally published are. The Library has no formal criteria to make this decision on the eventual disposition of a book; but the primary considerations have to do with the potential use or demand for the book by serious readers or scholars. If the material is catalogued, it may even go straight to the regular shelves for reader use, or more likely, to the so-called Delta collection—Delta being a symbol which simply indicates that due to the nature of the book, there is a greater risk of pilfering or mutilation, and therefore all reading must be done in a special room under special surveillance. But any adult whose motives are not patently prurient can probably have access to books in the Delta collection. There is no censorship here; Americans are allowed to read the very works which other arms of the government are energetically attempting to suppress.

The description of the court proceedings resulting in forfeiture of materials seized by the Bureau is based on interviews with U.S. Attorneys in New York and Chicago.

The procedures outlined in the text and described above deal mostly with mail censorship. The same basic procedures are followed in the case of freight, though of course, the methods of interception differ. In the case of freight shipments, a spot-check system is used for purposes of securing compliance with the Customs laws. The technique is dependent on the valuation of the merchandise. That valued under $250 comes in via "informal entry papers" (a general statement of content and value prepared by the importer and filed in the customhouse). Whether or not the Bureau will go behind these papers depends on the incidence of spot checks or on other circumstances, i.e., on the grounds for suspicion towards this particular package on the part of the inspector who checks the entry papers and the external appearance of the goods while they are on the dock. Freight valued at over $250 comes in via "formal entry"; there is a regular sampling of some percentage of all these shipments—and a complete examination whenever suspicions are aroused. Items selected for examination are referred to expert appraisers who examine the merchandise with great care. In passing, it might be noted that many of these experts really know their job; in New York, the Bureau's art expert has sometimes detected fraudulent imitations, to the consequent chagrin and expense of an "expert" importer. The procedure on the piers with respect to the handling of passenger baggage is familiar to all Americans who have been tourists abroad. Spot checks are made, and "key" questions asked. An untold number of tourists seem to bumble into an admission that they are carrying postcards, "stag" movies, or obscene books, but no one really knows how many of these and other items may slip by.

It is interesting to note that Customs procedures, because they lack the ingredients of procedural due process, are subject to the same criticisms which were long leveled at the Postal operation. But Customs procedures have never, in fact, been subjected to the same public criticism as were the Postal procedures prior to 1958. Moreover, the court decisions which required the Post Office to comply with the Administrative Procedure Act are probably inapplicable to the Bureau's censorship operation because there exists for the importer, under the Tariff Act, a right to a complete "trial *de novo*" in the courts, and the Administrative Procedure Act (5 U.S.C. 1005) does not apply to administrative adjudications which the courts can review in a trial *de novo*. Thus, under the letter of existing law there is probably no need for the

Bureau to comply with the formal procedures which the courts have ruled govern Postal action; but the question whether this result is desirable remains debatable (see text, pages 90–91).

Discussion of Post Office procedures for censorship is largely based on our field-study interviews with Postal officials. A description of these field studies is set forth in the Introduction to this work. Discussion of specific "non-mailability" cases is based on rulings reflected in the General Counsel's case files on "non-mailable" matter. See this Appendix, III-3, for a description of these files.

For other published material describing procedure in the Post Office on non-mailability rulings, see De Grazia, "Obscenity and the Mail;" a "Note" entitled "Postal Sanctions: A Study of the Summary Use of Administrative Power," in 31 *Indiana Law Journal* 257 (1956); Cutler, *The Post Office Department.* The "Acheson Committee" (Attorney General's Committee on Administrative Procedure) published a monograph on Post Office administrative procedures generally, entitled *The Post Office Department;* see pp. 29-33 for the criticism of non-mailability "censorship" procedures and p. 95 for the Post Office's reply. See also the testimony of various Postal officials in the *Hearings* of the Gathings Committee.

The "Popenoe case" is *Walker v. Popenoe.* See also the 1941 case of *Pike v. Walker,* which implied disapproval of Post Office procedures.

For court decisions on the development of the Administrative Procedure Act and applying it to Postal censorship, see *Wong Yang Sung v. McGrath; Gates v. Hederlein; Door v. Donaldson.* The quote of Solicitor Roy Frank about the alleged inapplicability of the act is from the *Hearings* of the "Gathings Committee," p. 277.

A most interesting insight into the Post Office Department's early hostility to the Administrative Procedure Act can be perceived from the complaint of Daniel J. Kelly to members of the House and Senate Judiciary Committees in 1952. This was about sixteen months after the Supreme Court had, by virtue of its decision in *Gates v. Hederlein,* required the Department to enforce the fraud laws (and, by implication, the obscenity laws) in conformity with the Procedure Act.

Kelly was the Department's First Chief Hearing Examiner. He reported that the Chief Inspector of the Post Office was hostile to the Procedure Act and was attempting to "intimidate the hearing examiners . . . who were . . . merely endeavoring to perform their function 'in an impartial manner' as required by this Act."

In a more detailed statement Kelly spelled out his complaint with charges that Postal inspectors, acting under policy formulated by their Chief, were refusing to initiate fraud cases because of their distaste for the formality, strictness of proof, and the delay required by adherence to the act. It was also charged that the inspectors were lobbying to secure an exemption from the act, notwithstanding the apparent implication of the Supreme Court decisions that the Constitution required adherence to the basic rules of the act.

Mr. Kelly's charges were vigorously denied by the Postmaster General. In a communication to the committee members, he admitted the Department's desire to be exempted but denied attempts at intimidation and declared that Kelly was simply "fearful" lest he "lose his independent status as a hearing examiner."

No matter who was right in this controversy, the inability of the Department to live happily with the act is readily apparent. Copies of the Postmaster General's reply to Mr. Kelly and other memoranda on this dispute are in the files of the Institute of Legal Research.

For further discussion of the problem of supplying formal hearings in Postal cases, hearings *first,* prior to any stoppage of mail, see text, Part V, pp. 175–178. Our discussion of the unreported *Playboy, Confidential,* and *Rogue* cases is based on discussions with Postal officials and counsel for the magazines. In addition we have examined the records of these cases furnished by counsel.

Justice Douglas' opinion (written in connection with stay-order proceedings) expressing doubts about the validity of summary mail blocks appears in *Stanard v. Oleson.*

The legislation authorizing such blocks (Pub. L. No. 821, 84th Cong., 2d sess.) was codified as 39 U.S.C. 259 (b) (see Appendix V-2 for more recent changes).

The legislative history of Section 259(b) is interesting. As originally drafted the bill provided that: "Whenever the Postmaster General shall determine," during section 259(a) [mail block] proceedings, that interim mail stoppage is "necessary to the effective enforcement of" the law, "he may enter an interim order directing that mail addressed to [the respondent] be held . . . for a period of twenty days. . . ." Notice of the interim mail block, which could thus be summarily imposed, must be sent to the respondent. The interim mail block would expire after twenty days unless the Post Office petitioned the local District Court for an extension to last until the end of the administrative hearings. Issuance of the interim mail block was exempted from Administrative Procedure Act.

On the Senate floor, Senator Monroney offered an amendment:

I realize that a serious problem exists in trying to prevent the fraudulent use of the mails for raising money in phony deals, or for the transmission of salacious or pornographic material. It is to meet this problem, and this problem alone, that the proposed legislation was brought before the distinguished Committee on Post Office and Civil Service. In reporting the bill the committee states:

"The Committee recognizes that even in its present form the bill gives the Postmaster General extraordinary and summary powers to impose a substantial penalty by impounding a person's mail for up to 20 days in advance of any hearing or any review by the courts. Such power is directly contrary to the letter and spirit of normal due process, as exemplified by the Administrative Procedure Act, which requires a hearing before any penalty may be imposed. The Post Office Department has made its case for this legislation on the grounds that a temporary and summary procedure is required to deal with fly-by-night operators using the mails to defraud or to peddle pornography, who may go out of business— or change the name of their business or their business address— before normal legal procedures can be brought into operation." I am in sympathy with the bill if the purpose is to be confined to the seizure of a person's mail pending a legal hearing within 20 days; but I cannot fail to recognize the grave danger if the act should be misused, and 20 editions, we will say, of a newspaper or magazine which some Government official might dislike, should be impounded. During those 20 days bankruptcy could be brought about through the process of 1-man rule and 1-man censorship. My amendment would exempt regular publications, such as newspapers and magazines, which are entered as second-class matter; and also books and other publications which are registered under the Copyright Act. Thus no single individual in the Government would be given the power of censorship or the power to freeze the receipt of mail by reason of an order of the Postmaster General or any of his officials. [See 102 *Congressional Record* 12289 (1956).]

Senator Monroney's exemption was accepted by the handful of senators on the floor, and the bill passed. Later the protection afforded to publishers of copyrighted materials was eliminated (see 72 *Statutes at Large* 940 [1958]), apparently in recognition of the fact that a copyright is no guarantee against obsceneness. See *Senate Report* No. 2386, 85th Cong., 2d sess. (1958).

The *Sunshine* and *Tourlanes* mail-block cases are *Sunshine Publishing Co. v. Summerfield* and *Summerfield v. Tourlanes Publishing Co.*

It must be emphasized that the Postal procedures which obtained in 1956 were considerably revised in 1958 and 1959. For the new, reformed rules on non-mailability cases, see 22 *Federal Register* 8999-9000 (1957), amended by 24 *Federal Register* 4026 (1959) and published in 39 *Code of Federal Regulations,* Part 203. For discussion of these changes see *supra,* p. 173, and this Appendix, pp. 287–288. For current rules governing mail-block cases, see 39 *Code of Federal Regulations* Part 201 (1961).

III-3

Discussion of the Postal non-mailability rulings in this chapter is based on our study of General Counsel's files on non-mailable matter; these files contain correspondence, memoranda, and, sometimes, exhibits pertaining to each ruling. Each of the rulings discussed herein has been verified by the file material; in a number of cases we have obtained additional information from the mailer, publisher or from the files of the American Civil Liberties Union in New York and at Princeton University.

Figures on the number of "non-mailability" rulings per year are not regularly reported; sometimes the Postmaster General's *Annual Report* has contained an estimate.

The "non-mailability" files are broken down into several classifications: books, magazines, newspapers, calendars, etc. The individual case files are arranged alphabetically by title.

In attempting to determine the extent of and impact of Postal censorship on various publishers, we addressed letter inquiries, in 1956, to the membership of Magazine Publishers Association and the Book Publishers Council, and this list of book and periodical publishers was later supplemented by additions selected from various directories of publishers. We received about a 50 per cent return to our questionnaire to the book publishers; no established book publisher reported any serious interference from Postal censorship, and, save for a few cases (most of them are reported in the text), none reported any direct interference with their own circulation efforts. A much smaller number (about 35 per cent) of the membership of the Magazine Publishers Association (which totaled, as of 1956, about 375) replied. None reported any recent experience (within the past five years). This Association is, however, made up of publishers which are unlikely to experience censorship difficulty. See a Resolution of the Association, dated September 30, 1954, condemning "salacious repulsive and otherwise objectionable matter in magazines" and calling on members to advocate "vigilant and vigorous, but fair enforcement of legislative bans against such objectionable material." Our efforts to secure answers to a questionnaire addressed to publishers which were not members of the Magazine Publishers' Association resulted in a low return. All publishers of "girlie" or the "men's" type of magazine who did respond indicated that they had few, if any, mail subscribers at the time and, thus, no occasion for difficulty.

A substantial majority of publishers, both book and magazine, writing as individuals, indicated concern about the mere existence of Postal censorship; only two publishers, a small one in New Mexico and a large one in New York, advised us that they emphatically favored increased exercise of the power. The Book Publishers' Council has been a vigorous opponent of Postal censorship and, during the recent past, of every legislative attempt to extend its powers. The Magazine Publishers' Association has, apparently, not been as vigorous an opponent (indeed, note the resolution just quoted). The president of the Magazine Publishers' Association wrote to us: "some of our people have felt that the Association [in its official capacity] should not become involved in a study that might develop criticism of the Post Office." This comment seemed true of only a few magazine publishers asked, personally, to give information.

We also circularized the membership of the American Booksellers Association—this time by a mimeographed letter-questionnaire. The replies were too few to be meaningful, but of approximately seventy reporting stores, only two or three, apparently, had encountered any censorship, and these cases had to do with importations.

With respect to the book rulings on *From Here to Eternity* and *The Woman of Rome,* we are indebted to counsel for the publisher for furnishing us with additional information about these incidents.

With respect to the *Lysistrata* case, see De Grazia, "Obscenity and the Mail"; Mr. De Grazia was counsel for the book's owner in this case; his encounter with the Post Office led him to conduct a fuller, personal study of Postal censorship, which in turn led to the publication of his article; and we are indebted to him for considerable initial help in our study.

The *Art International* case is based, not only on examination of Postal files, but also on examination of correspondence and material in possession of the bookseller and interviews with him. The *Natural History* case is also based on correspondence with the publisher as well as on material in the Post Office files. There are, in the files of the Institute of Legal Research, reports of a number of other magazine cases similar to the above incidents. For example, the president of Camera Craft Publishing Company reports (by letter dated January 26, 1956) that the Post Office objected to a nude in a photographic magazine although it "was probably the most innocuous nude we have ever published. . . . This occurred after the issue had been mailed . . . [but] the upshot of the matter was that *we were required to show a dummy of the magazine* to the local postmaster prior to printing *for the next three or four issues* until we had once again established a clean bill of health" (emphasis added). A typical ruling from the Chief Hearing Examiner's office on the "mailability" of photographic magazines which featured female nudes is the case of the publication, *Classic Photography*, in 1956, which was denied a permit for second-class rates after the Hearing Examiner found that the pictures, all admittedly by leading photographers, "inspired lust" and "were offensive to the community standard."

For Eastman Kodak's "private" censorship see Chernoff and Sarbin, *Photography and the Law*, p. 59, which reprints a statement (the gist of which was confirmed to us by the Eastman Kodak Co.) reflecting the company's policy. There is in the files of the Institute of Legal Research an interesting case where a customer of Eastman sent an undeveloped color picture of a copy of Goya's "Duchess of Malba." The company refused to return the developed picture until a vigorous protest was filed. The company then wrote: "In our judgment, confirmed by rulings we have had from the Post Office Department in similar cases, we cannot legally return such pictures without a satisfactory explanation of the circumstances surrounding the taking of the pictures and their intended use." For a case illustrating the legal problems in enforcing Eastman's policy, see *Hendricks v. Eastman Kodak Co.*

Discussion of the *Playboy* and *Confidential* cases is also based on additional information furnished by counsel for the magazines, including copies of the pleadings and orders of the District Court. The cases are not reported.

Discussion of the Dorothy Tager case is based on a long typewritten, autobiographical statement furnished by Mrs. Tager to the Kefauver Committee. This statement was furnished us by James Bobo, Esq., counsel for the Committee. Her sworn testimony before the Committee supports this statement in substantial detail. It appears in the Kefauver *Hearings* subtitled *Obscene Materials,* cited in Appendix II.

Discussion of mail-order businesses similar to Mrs. Tager's operation is based on our inspection of material in the case files of the Hearing Examiner's Office, material in the possession of the Kefauver Committee and the New York State Joint Legislative Committee Studying Publication and Dissemination of Offensive and Obscene Material, and advertising material collected through our own investigation. Anyone who doubts the availability of this material need only scan the advertisements in any "girlie" magazine and many of the magazines "for men" and put himself on the mailing list of some of these purveyors. See also Kilpatrick, *The Smut Peddlers.*

The first mail-block act was the "Fictitious Name" Statute, 25 *Statutes at Large* 873 (1888), as amended; 39 U.S.C., 255. As a legal device to stop businesses using the mails to sell obscene matter, it has now been supplanted by 64 *Statutes at Large* 451, as amended; 39 U.S.C., 259(a) *et seq.* For legislative history of Section 259(a) and Postmaster General Donaldson's request for its enactment, see *Senate Report* No. 2179, 82d Cong., 2d sess. (1950). 39 U.S.C. 259(a) has, very recently, been re-codified as 39 U.S.C. 4006.

The quote describing Klaw's publications is from Geoffrey Wagner's *Parade of Pleasure.* For discussion of this material see also *Report of the New York Joint Legislative Committee To Study Publication of Comics for 1956.*

The pictures in Klaw's publication (he also sold movies, e.g., of "girl wrestlers," "sorority initiations") did not feature nudity or sexual activity between females and males. Their appeal to and impact on "average" adults may be debatable. When the Post Office went after Klaw via a mail-block proceeding, Postal lawyers adopted—perhaps they felt they were forced to do so—the unusual strategy of introducing detailed psychiatric testimony to show that Klaw's "sado-masochistic," "fetishist" pictures had special attraction to a limited class of people who might very well be stimulated into undesirable behavior or "fantasy" from exposure to them. Ordinarily of course, the Department took the position that no expert testimony should ever be admitted in these hearings because of its alleged lack of value. What the Department seems to have promulgated in the *Klaw* case was a special standard to apply to this special category of communication. The Hearing Examiner also decided simply that Klaw's publications were offensive to the "community standard of decency." He rejected attempts by Klaw's lawyers to introduce pictures from other sources portraying similar sadism, e.g., in art, literature, newspapers, and movies. The mail-block order was upheld in the courts with little consideration of the issues, in *Klaw v. Schaeffer.* While few may quarrel with the *result* in Klaw's case, the Post Office's theory does suggest troublesome questions, and the case should be compared with the more recent Court of Appeals decision in *Volanski v. United States,* holding that the government cannot prove obscenity by simply attempting to show that certain photos of nude women would have an adverse effect on a limited class of abnormal people. See also discussion of the problem of setting special standards for "Klaw-type" material in Part VI of the text, p. 215, and this Appendix, pp. 301–303.

The *One* magazine case is *One, Inc. v. Oleson.* Our discussion has been helped through correspondence with counsel to the publisher, who furnished us with a history of the magazine and a number of copies for illustrative purposes.

III-4

Discussion of Customs rulings noted herein is based on examination of card files and correspondence files, reflecting detentions and seizures under Section 305 of the Tariff Act, in the Bureau of Customs in Washington. We are particularly indebted to Mr. Reuben Klaben, an attorney with the Penalty Division of the Bureau, for assistance on this aspect of our project. Our survey is also based on an examination of file material (rulings on books and movies) in the office of the Deputy Collector in charge of Restricted Merchandise in the Port of New York; an examination of seized materials sent to the Library of Congress by the Bureau after seizure proceedings were consummated; examination of seized and detained materials in the Port of New York and interviews with the Customs officials during the various Customs field studies, described in the Preface to this book. The ruling and memoranda on the movie censorship cases are all drawn from the files of the Deputy Collector of Restricted Merchandise for the Port of New York.

Two significant District Court decisions dealing with nudist magazines were *Sunshine Book Co. v. Summerfield* and *United States v. 4200 Copies International Journal;* both cases were later reversed by the U.S. Supreme Court, the latter under the title *Mounce v. United States.* See discussion in the text, pp. 152–153.

III-5

Discussion of the Bureau's policy on administering the Secretary of the Treasury's discretion (the proviso in 19 U.S.C. 1305[a]) to admit "classics" and works of "literary" or "scientific merit" is based on interviews with Huntington Cairns, Esq., and examination of file material in the Bureau. See also, Cairns, "Freedom of Expression," Chafee, *Law and Mass Communications.*

On Henry Miller, see Perles, *My Friend Henry Miller,* which contains a good deal of biographical material and a bibliography of critical writing about his works. George Orwell's essay on Miller, entitled "Inside the Whale" (published in *A Collection of Essays*), is also of considerable interest. We are indebted to Mr. Miller for the use of his unpublished essay entitled "Obscenity in Literature." It sets forth an explanation of how he came to write his "obscene" books, as well as his philosophy on legal controls on sex expression. Of his works, Miller writes that his purpose is: ". . . to reveal myself as openly, nakedly and unashamedly as possible. If I be asked why I should want to do this I can only answer—because my nature or my temperament compels me to do so. I am interested in life, all life, and every aspect of it. The one life I know best of all is my own. Examining my own life, describing it in detail, exposing it ruthlessly, I believe that I am rendering back life, enhanced and exalted, to those who read me. This seems to me a worthy task for a writer and one for which I have had illustrious predecessors. . . ."

III-6

Discussion in this section is based primarily on our interviews with U.S. Attorneys, attorneys with the Department of Justice, and members of the Postal Inspection service (see Preface describing the scope of these field studies). A follow-up field study of the situation in Los Angeles was made in March, 1960.

We are indebted to Mr. George S. Leisure, former assistant to the U.S. Attorney of the Southern District of New York, for supplying detailed information and insight in connection with the *Roth* case.

Some statistics on the numbers of arrests (and sometimes for convictions) may be obtained from the Postmaster General's *Annual Reports*. The figures for arrests for violation of the Comstock Act for the period 1946 through 1956 are: 1946—175; 1947—248; 1948—194; 1949—170; 1950—171; 1951—134; 1952—187; 1953—172; 1954—136; 1955—200; 1956—224 (source: Postmaster General's *Report* for 1956, p. 113). The published *Hearings* of the Kefauver Committee (particularly the publication subtitled *Obscene and Pornographic Matter*) also contain a good deal of useful material reflecting the difficulties of prosecuting the so-called borderline dealers.

For an interesting case where the mail order operators of the "Burlesque Historical Co." were convicted for sending out advertisements of purportedly obscene material (which actually was not) see *United States v. Hornick*.

On the question of whether and when federal prosecutors should seek indictments in the "non-commercial" cases of the character described in the text, see Schwartz, "Federal Criminal Jurisdiction and Prosecutor's Discretion," in 13 *Law and Contemporary Problems* 64 (1948). For a general, non-critical study of the Postal Inspection Service, see Makris, *The Silent Investigators*. The quote from the Attorney General's *Report* for 1958 is found on pp. 220–221.

PART IV
IV-1

The *Butler* case is *Butler v. Michigan.* We are indebted to Emanuel Robbins, Esq., attorney for Mr. Butler and the publisher of *The Devil Rides Outside* for supplying useful background information on the development of this case.

The American Law Institute's *Model Penal Code, Tentative Draft No. 6* (see Bibliography for full citation) was published on May 6, 1957, several weeks *after* the *Roth* case had been argued before the Supreme Court. It is interesting to note that, despite the Supreme Court's later, extensive reliance on the Model Penal Code, none of the parties who argued the case made any reference to it, presumably because they were, at the time of argument, unfamiliar with it.

IV-2

The *Roth* case is *United States v. Roth.* The companion cases from the state courts were *Alberts v. California* and *Kingsley Books, Inc. v. Brown.*

See text, Part I, pp. 31–33, for more on the argument that the federal government lacks power to enact anti-obscenity laws because the Constitution grants no express power to the national government to legislate in the field of morals and because the First Amendment's flat prohibition ("no law") was meant to re-emphasize and nail down the prohibition against any exercise of an implied congressional power to regulate the content of the press in the interest of protecting morality. This argument was strongly urged by O. John Rogge, Esq. (counsel for Roth), and Morris Ernst, Esq. (who appeared in his own personal capacity as in *amicus curiae*). Mr. Rogge later spelled out his contention in his scholarly series of articles, "Congress Shall Make No Law." Mr. Ernst appears to have raised the same contention as long ago as 1935 in testimony during a congressional hearing; see *Offenses Against the Post Office, Hearings before Subcommittee No. 8 of the Committees on Post Office, House of Representatives, 74th cong., 1st sess.* (1935), pp. 83 *et seq.*

For comment by the draftsman of the ALI Model Penal Code on the Supreme Court's assimilation of the Code's test for obsceneness with the traditional tests, see Professor Schwartz's article, "Criminal Obscenity Law." For two recent comments on the *Roth* case, see Lockhart and McClure, "Censorship of Obscenity" and Kalven, "The Metaphysics of Obscenity."

IV-3

The Supreme Court cases decided in the fall of 1957 and discussed in the text are *Sunshine Book Co. v. Summerfield, Mounce v. United States,* and *One, Inc. v. Olesen.* In addition see the 1957 case of *Times Film Corp. v. Chicago,* wherein the Court set aside a blanket ban on the film *Game of Love* imposed by Chicago's Chief of Police pursuant to a municipal ordinance. Of further interest is the case of *Adams Theatres, Inc. v. Newark,* where the Court, again without writing any opinion, upheld a city ordinance banning exhibition of nude people in live stage productions.

The *Lady Chatterley* movie case is *Kingsley Pictures Corp. v. Regents.* The *Smith* case is *Smith v. California.* For a sequel to the doctrine laid down in the *Smith* case, suggesting the problems of drawing the line on the rule requiring *mens rea,* see *People v. Schenkman.* Sources reflecting violent congressional reaction to these and other federal court decisions in obscenity cases are cited in Appendix V-4.

The 1961 *Times Film* case is *Times Film Inc.* v. *City of Chicago.*

IV-4

The *Kinsey* case is reported under the title, *United States v. Thirty One Photographs Etc.* We are indebted to Morris Ernst and Harriet

Pilpel, counsel for Dr. Kinsey, for furnishing background information on the development of this case.

The *Lady Chatterley* book case is *Grove Press v. Christenberry*.

We are indebted to Yashuhiro Okudaira, of Japan, for a seminar paper containing a full discussion of a decision of the Supreme Court of Japan holding that this book is "obscene" in that country. A jury in England acquitted a seller of the book in 1960, thus, apparently legalizing its public sale in that country.

The state court cases discussed in the text are *Excelsior Pictures Corp. v. Regents* and *Commonwealth v. Monix* (involving the film *Garden of Eden*).

The *Anatomy of a Murder* decision is *Columbia Pictures Co. v. Chicago*.

The Oregon case is *State v. Jackson*.

PART V
V-1

Information on recent Bureau rulings and procedures was supplied by the Deputy Collector of Customs, Restricted Merchandise Division, New York, and descriptions of Bureau rulings are drawn from case files in this office. The file on the movie *Les Amants* (*The Lovers*) reflects the fact that this film was apparently banned in its entirety in several European countries. Additional information has been drawn from the files of the American Civil Liberties Union. See letter of Patrick M. Malin to Douglas Dillon, January 23, 1961, and reply, March 25, 1961, in these files for ACLU's broad attack on Customs procedures.

V-2

The changes made in Postal procedures for initiating and hearing contested cases are reflected in the procedural rules adopted by the Department over this period. See 24 *Federal Register* 4026 (1959) ("Rules of Practice in Proceedings Relative to Mailability"), which amended 22 *Federal Register* 8999 (rules of practice first promulgated November, 1957). These rules now appear in 39 *Code Federal Regulations* 203 (1959). See also 23 *Federal Register* 3775 (1958), 39 *Code Federal Regulations* 201 (1959), for "Rules of Practice in Proceedings Pursuant to the Administrative Procedure Act under 39 U.S.C.

259, 259(a) and 732"; 24 *Federal Register* 3592 (1959), 39 *Code Federal Regulations* 204 (1959), for "Rules of Practice in Proceedings Relevant to the Denial, Suspension or Annulment of Second-Class Mail Privileges," as amended by 39 *ibid* Part 201 (1961 Supplement).

The illegality of the procedures which obtained up to 1958 was strongly suggested by the decision in *Pinkus v. Reilly* (holding that there is no proper separation of functions when general counsel's subordinate initiates complaints and general counsel makes the decisions.) See also *Borg Johnson v. Christenberry.*

The Judicial Officer was created by order of the Postmaster General (see 23 *Federal Register* 2817 [1958]). Legislation has been introduced to confirm his independent status as the Post Office judge on mailability matters (see H. R. 7506, 86th Cong., 1st sess. [1959]). The First Judicial Officer, Charles Ablard, served until March, 1960, when he resigned—with newspaper rumors of disagreement over enforcement policies of the Department. See the *Washington Post and Times Herald,* March 9, 1960.

The records of all cases initiated under the new procedures are contained in the Judicial Officer's office and are available for public inspection. For some illustrative cases reflecting the procedures and problems described in the text, see, e.g., *Pigalle Imports,* P.O.D. 1/138 (1959); *Holly Watkins,* P.O.D. 1/32 (1958); *Regal Arts,* P.O.D. 5/180 (1958); *Milco Specialties,* P.O.D. 1/96 (1958).

For discussion of the persisting problem of "interim" mail blocks see also text, pp. 97–99, and Appendix III-2, *supra.*

The practice of the Post Office Department prior to 1956 is illustrated by cases such as *Stanard v. Oleson* and *Williams v. Petty.* See also the Judicial Officer's opinion in *In re Tigron,* P.O.D. 1/153 (1959).

The legislative history of the 1956 statute (Pub. L. No. 821, 84th Cong., 2d sess., which, until August, 1960, was 39 U.S.C. 259[b]) is discussed is Appendix III-2. See 102 *Congressional Record* 12289.

For background of the interim impounding legislation of 1960 and the hearings before Mrs. Granahan's House Post Office Subcommittee, see its *Hearings* subtitled *Detention of Mail.* See also the Kefauver Committee *Hearings before Subcommittee of the Judiciary Committee on Constitutional Amendments* (86th Cong., 1st and 2d sess.) subtitled *Control of Obscene Matter.* The Post Office's General Counsel, in his testimony before these committees, listed and discussed several unreported cases as illustrative of the difficulties encountered by the Post Office in attempting to use the interim impounding power authorized by 39 U.S.C. 259 (b). See also *Toberoff v. Summerfield.*

As noted in the text, there are considerable dicta in the decisions of some federal judges to the effect that interim impounding orders, imposed summarily without any hearing, are unconstitutional (see, e.g., *Walker v. Popenoe,* the opinion of Justice Douglas in *Stanard v. Oleson,* and *Greene v. Kern*). On the other hand, the use of summary sanctions has been sustained in several district court cases see, e.g., *Williams v. Petty; Schillaci v. Oleson*). A full and careful discussion of the problem appears in the Judicial Officer's opinion in the case of *In Re Tigron Distributors,* P.O.D. 1/153 (1959). And note *Monart v. Christenberry* and the Court of Appeals' opinion in *Sunshine v. Summerfield,* sustaining interim non-mailability orders.

The Gershon Legman case, cited by way of example in the text as an illustration of the way in which the mail-block power can be abused, is based on file material in the Post Office General Counsel's non-mailability files and on information supplied by Mr. Legman. Other cases might also be cited; see, e.g., *Cadillac Publishing Co. v. Summerfield.* Reference should also be made to the rather unique case of "Cowboy Pink" Williams. In 1953, Williams, an Oklahoma politician (and former lieutenant governor) attempted to sell (via mail orders) postcards with this message inscribed on them: "Cattlemen's Convention and Public Ass-Kicking—All Day Picnic at the Head of Salt Creek the day after you are foreclosed. All cattlemen who voted for Ike will have their ass kicked free, and all the crow they can eat." Williams' enterprise was promptly suppressed when the Post Office declared the cards "obscene" and imposed, summarily, a mail block (before holding any formal hearings) against "Cowboy Pink." See *In re Pink,* P.O.D. 2/207 (1953), and *Williams v. Petty.* While the taste of these cards is certainly open to question, one might still ask: if they were "obscene," was it a crime to mail them? If not, was summary impounding justified?

For further legislative history of the Granahan bill (H.R. 7379, 86th Cong., 1st and 2d sess.), see *H.R. Report No. 945,* 86th Cong., 1st sess. For the Senate discussion, see 106 *Congressional Record* 11310 (June 9, 1960), where Mr. Summerfield's willingness to compromise was announced by Senator Kefauver (who had previously sponsored Mrs. Granahan's bill in the Senate, S. 2562, 86th Cong., 1st sess.). Senator Kefauver introduced a new bill (S. 3654) which was similar to the legislation finally enacted. Senator Monroney then reported out his revised version of the Granahan bill; see *S. Rept. No. 1818,* 86th Cong., 2d sess. For further Senate discussion and enactment of the revised bill, and for an account of the legislative history on the Senate side, see 106 *Congressional Record* 14420–23 (1960). The text of the new interim impounding law (Pub. L. No. 673, 86th Cong., 2d. sess., amending 39 U.S.C. 259[b]) is set forth in Appendix IV.

V-3

The *Rogue Magazine* case is *In re Greenleaf Publishing Co.*, P.O.D. 4/202 (1958). The *Men's Digest* case is *In re Camerarts Publishing Co.*, P.O.D. 1/66 (1959). The *Naked Maja* case is *In re United Artists Co.*, P.O.D. M-15 (1959); *Big Table* is *In re Big Table, Inc.*, P.O.D. 1/150 (1959). Following the Post Office decision finding *Big Table* non-mailable, the publisher sued and won an injunction in the District Court (see *Big Table v. Schroeder*). For John Ciardi's discussion see the *Saturday Review*, June 27, 1959, p. 22.

The *Lady Chatterley* case (in the Post Office) is *In re Grove Press and Readers Subscription, Inc.*, M-16, M-18 (1959). For an interesting series of news articles (by Helen Dudar) on the history of the *Lady Chatterley* case, see the *New York Post*, February 8–12, 1960. See also the American Book Publishers Council's *Censorship Bulletin*, June, 1960, issue, which reviews considerable newspaper comment about the case.

V-4

For the 1958 amendment to the Comstock Act (Pub. L. 796, 85th Cong., August 28, 1958, 72 *Statutes At Large* 962, amending 18 U.S.C. 1461) permitting "venue" of criminal prosecutions to be brought in the district into which the allegedly offending material is mailed, see *Hearings before Subcommittee No. 1, Committee on the Judiciary, House of Representatives, on HR 2542, HR 3033, HR 3498, HR 3663, HR 6239, HR 7829, and HR 10353, January 27 and 30, 1958*, 85th Cong., 2d sess. See also *House Report* No. 1614, 85th Cong., 2nd sess.; *Senate Report* No. 1839, *ibid*; and *Conference Report* No. 2624, *ibid*. This legislation overruled the prior court-made rule that prosecutions can *only* be brought in the district where the material is deposited into the mails. See *United States v. Ross* for the leading decision to this effect, although the rule was laid down many years earlier in *United States v. Commerford*. Compare 18 U.S.C. 3237, which makes other offenses against use of the mails "continuing offenses."

For indication that the venue power bestowed by the 1958 amendment can be abused, see *Steiner v. Hocke*, which was a suit by California distributors to enjoin a federal prosecution initiated against them in Michigan; the plaintiffs alleged that a California district judge, in a previous proceeding reviewing a Postal "mail block" order, had ruled that the material was not obscene. Information on other removal cases has been furnished to us by the U.S. Attorney for the Southern District of California in interviews and correspondence during March, 1960. For another case indicating the possibilities of wide variance in federal jury standards, see *Flying Eagle Publications, Inc. v. United States*—prosecution of publishers of *Manhunt*, a "detective" magazine which sells widely in drugstores.

In the fiscal year which ended June 30, 1959, the Post Office Department made 315 arrests after about "4,000 separate investigations" of alleged violators of the Comstock Act. This was a marked increase over earlier years. See *Control of Obscene Matter, Hearings before Subcommittee on Constitutional Amendments and Subcommittee to Investigate Juvenile Delinquency*, 86th Cong., 1st and 2d sess. (1960), p. 9. It is probable that well over half of the actual prosecutions concerned private mailings, homemade pornography, and instigators of correspondence clubs.

For examples of the very dire predictions of Mr. Summerfield against "the flow of filth," see his testimony in the above hearings. See also his testimony before the "Granahan Committee" (*Obscene Matter Sent Through the Mail, Hearings before the Subcommittee on Postal Operations*, pp. 3–9). Perusal of the reports of these published committee hearings furnishes some reflection of the extent of the public concern over the obscenity problem. For a more sober estimate of the volume of mail-order obscenity, see Lacy, "Obscenity and Censorship."

An indication of the extent of congressional and public concern over the problem of obscenity in the mails may also be gleaned from a sampling of the Congressional Record for the 86th Cong., 1st sess. The months of June, July, and August, 1959, when *Lady Chatterley* made headlines, reflect over fifty different speeches or insertions in the Record on this one topic by at least twenty-five different legislators (see 105 *Congressional Record* 8110–17855 *passim;* Appendix, 4400–8647 *passim*).

For the "Mundt-Scott Bill" to establish the "Commission on Noxious and Obscene Matter and Materials" (S. 3736, 86th Cong. 2d. sess.), see 106 *Congressional Record* 14078–82 (1960), which reprints the favorable *Report of the Senate Committee on Government Operations* and the text of the bill. See also the companion House bill, H. 11454, introduced by Representative Oliver, a member of the Granahan Committee. See 106 *Congressional Record* 6409 (1960).

PART VI
V-1 and 2

The various rationales for anti-obscenity legislation which are discussed herein constitute our own synthesis derived from all we have read about the law of obscenity in legal and other materials. A somewhat similar cataloguing of some of the objectives we list appears in Professor Louis B. Schwartz's unpublished, preliminary draft and comments for the American Law Institute's Model Penal Code provisions on obscenity, entitled *Article 207, Sexual Offenses and Offenses against the Family* (mimeographed, 1956).

A great deal has been written about the need for and the rationale of, obscenity prohibitions, particularly about the social harms allegedly caused by mass circulation of obscene matter, the relation between mass circulation of obscene material and moral or social standards of conduct, and the extent to which exposure to obscene material directly causes undesirable, physical behavior on the part of the persons exposed.

We do not attempt to catalogue, here, all that we have read on these questions; but we believe the works mentioned below are important examples. The materials cited demonstrate (1) the divisions of opinion and the variety of assertions and hypotheses offered in justification of obscenity regulation or in opposition to it, (2) the fact that there are few if any conclusive propositions to be laid down about the effect which exposure to obscenity may have on either adult or juvenile conduct.

Our listing below is broken into several broad categories of works, each category composed of writings approaching the subject from the standpoint of some different insight, professional expertise, or background of experience. The groupings we have made, with some general observations about each, are as follows.

(1) *Comment by Psychiatrists.* Meaningful material written for laymen is remarkably meager. Nor does there seem to be any precise consensus—a fact which may be understandable but, which is nevertheless frustrating to those laymen in search of positive answers. Undoubtedly, too, the non-psychiatrist with no orientation toward dynamic psychiatry experiences difficulty in appreciating the psychiatrist's observations and insights. The psychiatric sources do seem to teach that one effect of reading or viewing erotic or shocking material may be the stimulation of fantasies—fantasies which are, at least in part, the product of unconscious, perhaps repressed, sexual or aggressive urges. The feelings thus evoked obviously may have more impact on the behavior of a sexually "maladjusted" adult or juvenile—the individual who already has difficulty in handling sexual or aggressive impulses. Some psychiatric authorities seem to believe that the fantasies and feelings evoked by exposure to erotic stimuli will often trigger a release of the maladjusted person's suppressed feelings; the release may simply take the form of a sort of psychic masturbation or perhaps, also, physical masturbation and nothing more; indeed, some authorities have even asserted that this kind of "release" is beneficial for persons with strong, suppressed impulses because the experience operates as a "safety valve" for "deviates" or "potential offenders." But other authorities seem to believe that the fantasies and ensuing stimulation may, in some cases, produce aggressive conduct; thus the experience of exposure to "obscene" stimuli is asserted by some to be a factor causing harmful misbehavior *among already maladjusted persons;* but precisely how this stimulation works, and the extent to which obscenity, apart from the many other influences and stimuli, can trigger harmful external conduct, seems most unclear. Indeed, there is apparently some question whether, if "obscenity" were unavailable, a less erotic stimulus would not be used to achieve the same effect. A few authorities seem to suggest that materials depicting extreme violence and sadism may suggest—teach, in an intellectual sense—ideas and methods for misconduct to deviate persons; and, in this sense, it has also been asserted that obscenity is a "cause" of dangerous behavior. Again, of course, the thesis, even if true, is limited to the impact of some forms of obscenity on a small class of readers who are admittedly already prone to misconduct. Whether obscene writing and pictorial matter can be singled out as a *sine qua non* scapegoat remains controversial. None

of the psychiatric assertions is based on statistical evidence; all are simply clinical judgments.

For the view that the effects are probably not harmful and may even supply, to some people, a useful release, see Abse, "Psychodynamic Aspects"; Kronhausen, *Pornography and the Law;* Watson, *Psychiatry for Lawyers.* See also Karpman, *The Sexual Offender;* Ginzburg, *An Unhurried View;* Eliasburg, "Art: Immoral or Immortal"; Scott, *Into Whose Hands;* Havelock Ellis, "The Revaluation of Obscenity" (in *More Essays of Love and Virtue*), and *Studies in the Psychology of Sex.* For statements from psychiatrists suggesting the dangers of exposure of maladjusted adults or juveniles to some kinds of erotic or sadistic stimuli in the various forms of communication, see the testimony of Drs. Benjamin Karpman and George Henry before the Kefauver Committee, reported in its *Hearings.* See also, for an extreme assertion that viewing obscene matter causes adolescent crime, the testimony of Dr. Nicholas Frignito (a psychiatrist of the Philadelphia Municipal Court) before the Granahan Committee, reported in its *Hearings.* Reference should also be made here to Frederick Wertham's controversial book, *Seduction of the Innocent,* which argues, on the basis of the author's clinical experience, that "crime comics" (those depicting excessive violence and sadism) were a significant influence in producing juvenile behavior in many cases studied by the author. Interestingly, Dr. Wertham apparently makes no assertions about obscene or erotic matter which is devoid of physical violence.

(2) *Comment by Psychologists and Other Behavioral Scientists Discussing the Cause-and-Effect Problem on the Basis of Empirical Evidence.* As noted, the psychiatric views cited above are clinical judgments, and there simply are no scientific, empirical studies which attempt a direct answer to the questions of the effect of exposure to obscene stimuli on external conduct. The consensus of a number of psychologists is that there is no statistical evidence which gives any real support to any cause-and-effect thesis. Perhaps the most complete review of the sources of "evidence" is to be found in Jahoda, *Impact of Literature.* Dr. Jahoda wrote a summary of her conclusions (namely, that there are no conclusions to be drawn) which is set forth by Judge Jerome Frank in his opinion in *United States v. Roth.* A similar, widely publicized, briefer survey of the "evidence" was published by a group of Brown University psychologists (Drs. Nissim Levy, Lewis Lippsitt, and Judy Rosenblith) in the *Brown Daily Herald* of May 13, 1958, and reprinted in the American Book Publisher Council's *Censorship Bulletin* of August, 1958. These authorities state that "there is no reliable evidence that reading or other fantasy activities lead to anti-social behavior." This negative conclusion is largely drawn from an analysis of

existing empirical studies of factors causing Juvenile crime; and the authors conclude that none of the existing studies attributes any importance to exposure of youth to obscene matter. For a further survey of the absence of evidence, see McKeon et al., *Freedom To Read.*

The "negative" statements listed above are now frequently cited by other commentators to support generalizations to the effect that there is no relevant empirical evidence at all. But several reports on empirical research, which have *not* been cited (as far as we can see) in the legal and general literature on sex censorship, do seem of some relevance because they give us further insights into the nature of response to erotic stimuli. These studies may also point the way to further hypothesizing and experimentation. (For assistance in finding and evaluating this material we are indebted to Dr. Julius Wishner and Dr. Robert Cairns of the Department of Psychology of the University of Pennsylvania.)

Thus, several studies report experiments wherein male subjects were exposed, e.g., to pictures of nude females and thereafter given a "Thematic Apperception Test." The results indicate that, at least where exposure to the stimuli takes place in some "permissive" situations, fantasies about sexual activity were quite likely to be aroused in the subjects, and such fantasies are more likely to be stimulated in men who report more sexual activity. Further experimentation has indicated that sexual fantasies (as a response to erotic stimuli) are less likely where persons are exposed to the stimuli in a "non-permissive" setting (e.g., in a gathering where a formal atmosphere prevails); in this setting the subjects tended to avoid sexual fantasy. See Clark, "The Projective Measurement of Experimentally Induced Levels of Sexual Motivation," *Journal of Experimental Psychology,* XLIV, 391 (1952); Mussen and Scodel, "The Effects of Sexual Stimulation under Varying Conditions on TAT Sexual Responsiveness," *Journal of Consulting Psychology,* XIX, 90 (1955); Epstein and Smith, "Thematic Apperception, Rorschach Content and Ratings of Sexual Attractiveness of Women as Measures of Sex Drive," *Journal of Consulting Psychology,* XXI, 473 (1957).

Studies of the physical response of males to the viewing of sexually oriented "love scenes" in movies and books report, generally, a significantly increased respiratory rate and galvanic skin response in the viewer—particularly in adolescents. Drisesens and Woods, "Psychophysiological Behavior under Various Types of Literature," *Journal of Abnormal and Social Psychology,* XXX, 484 (1936); see also Clark and Treichler, "Psychic Stimulation of Prostatic Secretion," *Psychosomatic Medicine,* XII, 261 (1950), reporting an increase in acid phosphatase (a secretion of the prostate gland) in a small sample of

males who reported feelings of arousal after exposure to a pornographic film and no increase in one male who said he was repelled by
the film.

Other investigators have used the self-reports of subjects as a method
of obtaining information about their response to exposure to obscene
stimuli. Kinsey, in *Sexual Behavior in the Human Male* and *Sexual Behavior in the Human Female,* indicates that 54% of his male subjects
(contrasted with only 12% of his female subjects) experienced definite sexual "arousal" when viewing pictures of nude persons of the
opposite sex; and the data seems to suggest that direct, unambiguous
erotic depictions are more likely to have a more immediate stimulating
effect on males than more subtle material; this is probably not true of
females.

While none of these findings about arousal may take us very far
when it comes to making verified assumptions necessary for the formulation of a rationale for anti-obscenity legislation, some of the studies
do suggest that the amount of sexual feeling which is caused by erotic
stimuli may be a function of such variables as the subject's guilt in-
hibitions, the conditions under which exposure to the stimuli takes
place, the subject's "sex drive" (as measured by physical indices), his
environment, his aggressiveness and other patterns of behavior. Thus,
there is empirical evidence that the same erotic material may have a
quite different effect on different persons and a quite different effect
on any particular person, depending on where, when, and how he is
exposed to the material. See also a study attempting to correlate preferences of males for various types of nude females with "an allegedly
important aspect of orality, namely dependency" (Scodel, "Hetero-
sexual Somatic Preference and Fantasy Dependency," *Journal of Consulting Psychology,* XXI, 371 [1957]).

Some studies of delinquent juvenile males suggest that they are more
aroused by sexually suggestive stimuli in terms of fantasy projection
than are non-delinquent males. See, e.g., Chapter 4 of Bandura and
Walters, *Adolescent Aggression* (1959); Haines, "Juvenile Delinquency and Television," *Journal of Social Therapy,* I, 192 (1955). See
also studies investigating the correlation between reading sexually suggestive or erotic materials and delinquency: Lorang, *The Effect of
Reading on Moral Conduct and Emotional Experience* (1946); Haines,
op. cit.; Blumer and Hauser, *Movies, Delinquency and Crime* (1936).
The controls imposed upon these investigations may well be open to
question. For a devastating criticism of research in this area, see Adler,
Art and Prudence.

Going further afield, there is for the layman a great deal of confusing
literature on the influence of comic books and movies on juvenile be-

havior; much of it seems inconclusive and much of it does not seem to be based on empirical research having much validity. For studies which may be of some relevance to the obscenity problem, see, e.g., Hoult, "Comic Books and Juvenile Delinquency," *Sociological Research*, XXXIII, 279 (1949); Lorang, *op. cit.;* Pfuhl, *Relationship of Crime and Horror Comics to Delinquency;* Charters, *Motion Pictures and Youth* (1933); Blumer and Hausen, *op. cit.,* (asserting a number of findings, e.g., about sexual arousal, which were reviewed and roundly criticized in Adler, *Art and Prudence*).

For a rebuttal to the conclusions which Dr. Jahoda, Judge Frank, and others draw from the absence of statistical, scientific evidence relating the reading of obscenity to misbehavior, see the statement by Rev. Terrence Murphy, *Evidence as to the Social Harm Caused by Potentially Objectionable Publications,* printed in the *Hearings* of the Granahan Committee (subtitled *Obscene Matter Sent through the Mail*). The extreme difficulty of adducing empirical "evidence" on the effects of stimuli in mass communications and the unfairness of drawing negative conclusions are suggested in Father Murphy's article. For further criticism of Judge Frank's "no evidence" conclusions, see Schmidt, "Justification of Statutes Barring Pornography." For a more general survey of the effects of reading on attitudes, see Waples et al., *What Reading Does to People,* a work which suggests that books do influence development of character and the personality of youth; but this study makes no particular observations on obscenity, nor does it make conclusions on the direct relationships between reading and behavior.

(3) *Anthropological Insights: The Concept of Obsceneness in Other Cultures.* Several studies consulted in this field indicate that there is a fair consensus that "obscenity" is a relative concept depending upon the sources of one's culture. While sex has, apparently, been a universal source of "tabus," depictions of sex and sexual behavior held to be "obscene" and "illegal" in our culture may be acceptable in others, and vice versa. Men do seem to develop, along with the development of a higher social order and more refined norms of behavior, very strong conceptions of what is right and what is wrong in sexual behavior and in portraying it or talking about it; they thus develop strong hostilities, fears and proscriptions; but the standards defining what is made obscene are variable. See La Barre, "Obscenity: An Anthropological Appraisal"; May, *Social Control of Sex Expression;* Mead, "Sex and Censorship"; Ford and Beach, *Patterns of Sexual Behavior;* Bourke, *Scatologic Rites of All Nations.*

(4) *Historical and Contemporary Descriptive Studies of the Extent and Nature of Sex Expression in Our Western Culture and in the United States.* For sources showing the fluctuations of "community

standards" at various times within our own Western civilization, the persistence of expression which we now tend to characterize as erotic or obscene in art, literature, the theatre, and social behavior, and for a history of the various attitudes which various groups in our culture have taken toward the problem of controlling sex expression, see, e.g., Taylor, *Sex In History;* May, *op. cit.;* Honigman, "A Cultural Theory of Obscenity," *Journal of Criminal Psychopathology,* V, 715 (1944); Fuchs, *Illustrierte Sittengeschichte;* Adler, *Art and Prudence.*

Several interesting descriptive studies have been made of the extent of erotic and "obscene" stimuli in the contemporary material of the mass media. Dr. Sorokin, in his *The American Sex Revolution,* compares the conditions of today with other times or other places and asserts that discussion of sexual behavior, illicit behavior, and erotic emphases in books, magazines, movies, and other materials have vastly increased, that such stimuli have, historically, produced harmful attitudes leading to degenerate conduct and social disintegration in other places and eras (the decline of Rome is said to be an example); it is further argued that unless the use of erotic stimuli is controlled, today's increasing volume of obscene matter will produce various harms to our own culture. See also Wagner, *Parade of Pleasure.* On the other hand, Albert Ellis in *The Folklore of Sex,* takes note of the same phenomenon but insists that the ensuing danger, if any, lies in trying to impose fear of obscenity by teaching puritanical and unrealistic attitudes toward sex; for a rigid attitude causes immature curiosities and emotional tensions in the persons exposed. See also Mead, "Sex and Censorship."

(5) *A Limited Sampling of Comment on Assumptions Underlying Censorship by Other Sources.* The religious point of view—that mass-volume circulation of obscene materials is undermining attitudes toward morality in sex—is well argued in Cannon, *A Sickness in Society,* and in Gardiner, *The Catholic Viewpoint on Censorship;* see also Wagner, *Parade of Pleasure.* An attack on this type of justification for more censorial controls appears in Larabee, *Cultural Context of Sex Censorship;* Blanshard, *The Right to Read;* and McKeon et al., *Freedom to Read.*

(6) *Comment by Legal Scholars.* For a small sampling of some of the discussion by legal scholars evaluating evidence of social harms caused by obscenity, see, e.g., Schroeder, *Obscene Literature and the Constitution;* Ernst and Seagle, *To the Pure;* Alpert, *Judicial Censorship;* Lockhart and McClure, "Literature, The Law of Obscenity and the Constitution"; American Law Institute, *Model Penal Code, Tentative Draft No. 6;* St. John-Stevas, *Obscenity, Literature and The Law.* The opinions of the late Judge Jerome Frank in *Roth v. Goldman* and *United States v. Roth,* and of Justice Bok in *Commonwealth v. Gordon,*

also contain a very full review. See also Lockhart and McClure, "Censorship of Obscenity." The above, of course, is only a small sampling of the writing by lawyers about the rationale of anti-obscenity law.

(7) *Comments by Law-Enforcement Personnel and Legislative Bodies.* For a few examples of the emphatic cause-effect claims of law-enforcement officers, see, e.g., the article by J. Edgar Hoover, "Let's Wipe Out the Schoolyard Sex Racket"; the testimony of David Stephens, Chief of the Postal Inspection Service, in the Granahan *Hearings* subtitled *Obscene and Pornographic Literature.* See also the statements of various law-enforcement officials in the Kefauver Committee *Hearings,* both those of 1959 and those subtitled *Obscene and Pornographic Materials* (1954). Considerable law-enforcement testimony is presented in the *Report of the New York State Joint Legislative Committee on Obscene and Offensive Literature for 1949;* also for 1955, 1956, and 1957. The conclusions of the Kefauver Committee on whether obscenity is a cause of juvenile crime (discussed in the text) are set out in *Senate Reports* Nos. 62, 1466, 2055, and 2381, 84th Cong., 1st sess. (1956), and *Senate Report* No. 130 (*Juvenile Delinquency*), 85th Cong., 1st sess. (1957). *Senate Report* No. 2381 is entitled *Obscene and Pornographic Literature.* The conclusions of the Granahan Committee are contained in *Obscene Matter Sent Through the Mail, Report to the Committee on Post Office,* 86th Cong., 2d sess. See also the *Reports* cited *supra* of New York's joint legislative committee. See also, for an effective presentation of the law-enforcement point of view, an address by Lois L. Higgins, director of the Illinois Crime Prevention Bureau, before the American Association for the Advancement of Science, December 28, 1959, entitled *Obscenity and Delinquency.* And see, finally, *Hearings before the Subcommittee on Special Education of the House Committee on Education and Labor on HR 11454* (A bill to establish a "Commission on Noxious Printed and Pictured Material) 86th Congress, 2d session (1960).

VI-3

The "test" or "definition" of obscenity projected in the text is, of course, a combination of the American Law Institute's "prurient interest community standard" formulation and the *Ulysses* test. Apparently, the Supreme Court in the *Roth* case meant to approve both these tests as the federal standard, although the Court's assumption seems to have been that the ALI formulation was, essentially, simply a rewording of the *Ulysses* test. We believe, along with the ALI draftsmen (see

Schwartz, "Criminal Obscenity Law"), that there is a difference in emphasis between the two, but unlike the ALI draftsmen we see no reason why all the tests should not be combined. Other possible, alternative tests are suggested in the American Law Institute's unpublished monograph prepared in 1956 in connection with the Model Penal Code and entitled *Sexual Offenses and Offenses against the Family*, and in the Institute's *Model Penal Code, Tentative Draft No. 6.* Psychiatric criteria are stated in Kronhausen, *Pornography and the Law,* and in Eliasburg, *Art: Immoral or Immortal.* See also an excellent unpublished monograph of the American Civil Liberties Union, entitled *Obscenity, Censorship and Free Speech,* which argues for a test limited to "hard core" pornography.

We reject any attempt to proscribe contraceptive or abortifacient information. *Kingsley International Film Co. v. Regents,* extending constitutional protection to abstract advocacy of the idea of adultery, should be broad enough to protect discussion of contraception. The decisions in *U.S. v. One Book Entitled "Married Love," U.S. v. One Book Entitled "Contraception,"* and *Consumers Union v. Walker* all drew a clear distinction between informational books dealing with sex education, birth control, etc., and obscene books; in each case a manual which dealt in detail with the physiology of conception was absolved of any taint of obscenity. The *Consumers Union* case suggested serious doubts about the limits of Congress' power to proscribe works on birth control except when circulated indiscriminately, doubts which seem implicit in the Supreme Court's dismissal in June 1961 (*Poe v. Ullman*) of an attack on Connecticut's prohibition on the "use" of contraceptive devices, based on the state's failure to enforce the law for some 75 years.

We include "scatological" and similar "filthy" expression in the proposed concept and standard for obscenity on the grounds that the law has traditionally done so and that, psychologically, the concepts are associated. See discussion of this in ALI, *Model Penal Code,* p. 33; see also the Court of Appeals discussion of the obsceneness of Henry Miller's *Tropic of Capricorn,* in *Besig v. United States.* But compare, with these cases, *Verner v. United States* and *Limehouse v. United States,* which purport to recognize a distinction between "filthy" and "obscene" matter. In the *Big Table* case (Post Office non-mailability order entered against the magazine *Big Table* on the ground that stories contained an excess of "four-letter words" and excessive "discussion" of "defecation, the genitals, sexual relations, perversions and aberrations in the lowest type of language") the Judicial Officer stated his personal opinion that the term "filthy" and "obscene" should be assimilated; but he expressed doubt whether the Comstock Act, properly construed, provided for such assimilation. We think the question is probably academic, and, in any event, *Big Table* affords an excellent example of why—if there is to be a law against circulation of "obscene" material at all—the proscriptive standard should include matter which is, in essence, "filthy" in the sense previously described.

VI-4

With respect to the "conduct test" proposed in the text—namely, "knowing circulation of obscenity to . . . an audience with an abnormal interest in obscene matter"—we believe this is one of the more difficult and yet important areas of concern. The difficulties were described before the Granahan Committee (see its *Hearings* subtitled *Obscene Matter Sent through the Mail,* p. 196) by Harold K. Wood, then a U.S. Attorney, now a federal district judge. Said Judge Wood:

> This approach to the transmission of filth for profit utilizes two effective theories of influence. This first is based on easily recognized forms of obscenity. This material in printed and photographic form depicts the obscenity and lewdness commonly associated with nudity, immoral acts, suggestiveness, specific references to obscene language, and descriptions of commonly understood antisocial activity along sexually abnormal lines.
>
> The second theory of influence, and *no doubt the worst* (emphasis added) appears to be something not commonly associated with the known moral standards of obscenity. This theory takes the form of carefully prepared photographs, writings, and drawings, which use as their spearhead of influence, symbols and other visual stimulus psychologically proven to induce thoughts and conduct along sadistic and masochistic lines to satisfy compelling sexual needs. The subject matter conveyed in these materials is not necessarily the portrayal and glorification of direct abnormal sexual conduct. These materials do not have as their object the most common types of immodest display ordinarily identified with obscenity and lewdness. Rather, they portray individuals in many cases fully clothed, performing and submitting to acts of violence on members of the same sex. Some of these materials show fully dressed women physically restrained and being subjected, to acts and threats of violence by other women, which at first glance appear to be unconnected in any way with commonly recognized concepts of obscenity. They are designed to appeal to persons inclined to perversion and the minds of the adolescent.
>
> Medical testimony has indicated that such influences, can and do accomplish an actual distortion of human values in the minds of

those reached. This permanent plan of moral distortion is eventually converted into notions of sexual dominance accomplished by terrorism, violence, force, and brutality.

While it may be that this particular kind of material, so deplored by Judge Wood (and see also, for a strident indictment of it, the *Report of the New York Joint State Legislative Committee on Obscene and Offensive Publications for 1955* (also 1956), is often not obscene according to the established standard, we think, at least until more reliable and precise scientific information is at hand, that there are obvious dangers in trying to broaden the law to proscribe material which does not offend the obscenity standard. However, where material is of a borderline, obscene variety, then it would seem appropriate to take special account of its special character and special appeal. Thus, where there is competent expert testimony to the effect that the material has a particular and harmful psychological appeal to a group with abnormal interests in such material, *and* where the distributor has good reason to know that an important segment of his audience is purchasing the material because of this special, abnormal appeal, then we believe curbs are in order. An illustrative case, where the government produced such testimony in part, is *Klaw v. Schaeffer.* For a recent Postal case where the Department suppressed mail distribution of two alleged "homosexual" publications which depicted men virtually nude and which allegedly, contained advertising from sources which pandered to homosexual tastes, *Manual Enterprises,* P.O.D. 1/246 (1960). In the hearing on this case the Postal lawyers admitted that "average persons" would simply have "no interest" in the offending materials. But two psychiatric witnesses testified, for the Post Office, to the effect that the publications would have special "appeal" to "homosexuals" or persons with "latent homosexual tendencies" and that the pictures might "arouse" such readers. (The testimony did not elaborate on the effects of such stimulation.) A Postal inspector testified to the effect that materials advertised in the publications had been sold to homosexuals. The Judicial Officer sustained findings that the average reader of *this* publication would be homosexually inclined and that, as regards such readers, it was "obscene." Also approved, apparently more on the basis of intuition than evidence in the record, was a finding that the publication would attract and influence "adolescent" readers.

With respect to the conduct standard, "reckless commercial exploitation of obscenity," it should be noted that we have *not* advocated that the Post Office be empowered to enter mail blocks or non-mailability orders where material is purportedly *advertised* as obscene but in fact is not. At various times the Post Office has proceeded against publishers and booksellers on the theory, not that the books sold were obscene, but simply that the advertising sent through the mails represented the books as obscene. See *Farley v. Simons* for an earlier case. See e.g., *Monart Co.*, P.O.D. 1/246 (1958), for a typical recent Departmental case dealing with a commercial purveyor. For another classic case see *Cadillac Publishing Co. v. Summerfield*—a case which, on reflection, suggests all the difficulties with this kind of censorship (mail block issued against publishers of *Encyclopedia of Sex;* the encyclopedia was innocuous; the advertising, it was said, purported to "promise" the reader that the work was "obscene"). On occasion, the Post Office has used its "fraud" powers against advertisers of purported obscenity. See, e.g., *A.P.R. Industries, Inc. v. Summerfield* (Civil Action No. 5009-55, U.S. District Court, D. C.) for an unreported case challenging a departmental decision of 1955 which held that advertising of certain comic books was fraudulent because, by a stretch of the imagination, the representation that these were "old tyme comics" and "action" comics about "Pop Eye," and "Draggin Lady," and others implied that such materials are "pornographic." (Perhaps one has to be an experienced censor to know the subtlety of these terms.) For a criminal conviction of advertisers of purported obscenity see *United States v. Hornick*. This decision, too, suggests uncomfortable problems in defining its limits. We believe that advertising should never be suppressed unless (1) the advertising is obscene itself (which may often be true of some of the more serious purveyors), or unless (2) the materials are in fact obscene and clearly indicated as such. A U.S. District Court decision, *Poss v. Christenberry*, appears to take an analogous position. See also *United States v. Schillaci* for a criticism of the *Hornick* decision by another federal judge.

With respect to the conduct standard, "assaulting people with obscenity," the underlying premise in justification of this control is that it is possible to inflict severe emotional distress by exposing some persons to seriously obscene matter directed particularly at such recipients. Postal inspectors have told us that the victims of private mailing assaults do in fact suffer such upset in many of the "private mailing" cases which are the basis for so many prosecutions today. In the law of torts, civil liability is increasingly recognized for the "intentional infliction of emotional disturbance"—a tort which includes very similar conduct. See the American Law Institute's *Restatement of the Law of Torts*, Section 46 (1948 Supplement). The theory is that intentionally engaging in extreme and outrageous conduct which causes emotional upset may result in a harm sufficiently serious to warrant compensation. A very recent New York case, *Mitran v. Williamson*, holds that civil damages can be recovered by the female recipient of an obscene letter from its author.

For earlier cases mentioned in the text which suggest that the "conduct of the defendant" is to be considered in a criminal prosecution under the Comstock Act, see Judge Hand's opinions in *Rebhuhn v. United States,* and *Levine v. United States.* In the development of the civil action for "invasion" of one's "right of privacy" by publication of the facts of one's private life, it would appear that "commercial exploitation" of the details of the private life of a person who is, for some purposes, a public figure is an element which, if present, may defeat the defense of privilege. See for example, the recent discussion, *Jenkins v. Dell Publishing Co.*

VI-5

For a case reflecting the difficulties which face the states and local prosecutors in combating mail order distributors in distant states, see, e.g., *Cooper v. McDermott.* In this case Philadelphia authorities sought to extradite California booksellers who had, apparently, sent (it is not clear by what means) publications into Pennsylvania but had never physically entered that state themselves. The majority and dissenting opinions elaborate some of the problems inherent in construing the extradition laws in such situations, and the case itself reflects the cumbersomeness of the extradition procedure.

VI-6

For discussion of the criminal "Venue" legislation of 1958, 72 *Statutes at Large* 962, see text, pp. 185–186, and this Appendix, V-4. At this writing, U.S. Attorneys and lawyers in the Department of Justice were unprepared to venture an opinion on the effect of this legislation.

VI-7

The proposal that the Post Office's adjudicatory powers in the field of censorship be shifted to the courts is not new. See, for example, Chafee, *Law and Mass Communications* I, 231. Senator William Langer made a similar proposal in his attack on Post Office censorship in 1942 (see 89 *Congressional Record* 3820, 4328); and at various times in the past, bills have been proposed in Congress to accomplish the result. The previous General Counsel of the Post Office Department has also discussed the idea seriously with various critics of Post Office censorship. And, of course, the "Granahan-Monroney law," providing for interim impounding (Pub. L. 673, 86th Cong. 2d sess., amending 39 U.S.C. 259 (b)); see text pp. 176–178 affords a concrete example of shifting decision-making power from the Post Office to the courts.

VI-8

This appendix is devoted to a more detailed discussion of recommendations for substantive and adjective changes in federal anti-obscenity censorship.

Assuming that civil enforcement of federal anti-obscenity laws will be continued—that Congress will demand the use of censorship, in addition to the threat of criminal penalties, as a device to suppress circulation of obscene materials—there remains a need to make changes in today's system.

At the outset the question might be asked: why not merge the mail-policing functions of the Post Office Department, the Bureau of Customs, and the Department of Justice? Instances of variance in policy, procedures, and criteria have been cited throughout this work. What is obscene to one agency has not always been obscene to another; in a sense the United States government has uttered conflicting judgments in passing on the legality of many publications; clearly, a personal element is involved in decision-making, and why, then, should there not be a more centralized exercise of discretion to achieve more uniformity?

There is something of an administrative precedent for merger of Postal and Customs censorship activity into a unified command; the precedent is the system used (until 1961) to censor foreign political propaganda. Communist propaganda sent here unsolicited from Iron Curtain countries has been treated as non-mailable by our government on the basis of a complicated (and doubtful) opinion of the Attorney General; to enforce this interpretation of the law, Customs officials screened Iron Curtain mailings and referred cases where the materials were deemed appropriate for seizure to the Post Office (the General Counsel's office), which, in theory, made the decisions (see Paul and Schwartz, "Communist Propaganda in the Mails"). The same technique might, arguably, be used to screen suspect obscene matter.

There has long been a lack of co-ordination between the Post Office and the Department of Justice. Attorneys from both departments have suggested that there have been clear disagreements over Postal decisions in various recent cases. The Department of Justice simply refused to represent the Post Office in the litigation challenging the non-mailability order in the "Naked Maja" (*United Artists*) case (see text, pp. 182–183). The Department of Justice was, at all times, reluctant to defend the Post Office's action in the *Lady Chatterley* case; and after two defeats, the Solicitor General refused Mr. Summerfield's request to petition the Supreme Court for certiorari (to review the case). A similar experience occurred in the *Big Table* case. It would also appear that the Justice Department has not regularly consulted with the Post Office about cases which are to be prosecuted criminally; nor do Postal lawyers consult over potential mail-block and non-mailability cases. The mail block and criminal remedy are not always used together in cases where, logically, it would seem that combined action would be warranted.

While greater consultation between the three agencies would seem in order—with the Department of Justice taking a greater part, particularly in reviewing Postal decisions—a merger of all law enforcement functions would seem to us undesirable. Despite the Communist propaganda precedent, there are practical problems in the way of a merger of the Customs and Postal operation, as a study of the enforcement of the anti-propaganda program has revealed (see Paul and Schwartz, "Communist Propaganda in the Mails"). More important, however, is the question whether it is desirable to set up one agency—which in the last analysis means one individual—in government as the enforcer of censorship standards. Unless one believes in symmetry for the sake of symmetry, there are values to be achieved in diffusion of decision-making responsibility and power and, indeed, in having differences of opinion within government. Uniformity and monolithic censorship augment the hazards of excessive federal censorship.

Assuming that it is desirable to separate responsibility for policing foreign mail and domestic mail and for enforcing criminal sanctions, we would suggest certain changes in the Postal and Customs operations which might supply more protection in the interests of freedom.

I. *Reformulation of the Substantive Standards of Postal Censorship and Co-ordination of Civil Standards with Criminal Standards.* If what has been already stated in this work has validity, Postal censorship should confine itself to the activities of three kinds of distribution operations:

  (1) unsolicited "assaults";
  (2) willful distribution to adolescents or particularly "susceptible" persons;

(3) "reckless commercial exploitation," where the harms embraced in the first two categories are created.

That these classifications may not be precisely definable should not be fatal. A fuller meaning can be imparted as particular questions are answered on a case-by-case basis.

Censorship should operate only when Postal officials can fairly conclude (on the basis of interdepartmental consultation) that criminal prosecutions would be brought against the disseminator of the work if he did not desist from his offending methods of distribution.

II. *Abolition of Postal Power to Deny or Revoke Second-Class Mailing Privileges.*

The lower rates accorded to second-class mail, as was forcefully brought home in the *Esquire* case, may mean life and death to a magazine publisher. Although the Post Office has not applied its asserted power to revoke established second-class mailing permits since the *Esquire* case, and although the Judicial Officer has expressed some doubt whether the power exists (see *In re Greenleaf Publishing Co.,* P.O.D. 4/202 [1958]), a General Counsel has taken the position recently that it does; see his testimony in the Granahan Committee *Hearings.*

To revoke a second-class mailing permit because *past* issues of a publication *retroactively* are thought to justify such a censorship sanction is clearly a dangerous form of censorship, as the experience of the early 1940's would indicate.

While the Post Office has not attempted to revoke permits *previously granted* (on the ground that past issues of the publication were obscene), it has denied initial *applications* for second-class rates to publications which apply for them, where the current issue is believed to be obscene. In defense of this type of censorship Postal lawyers argue that denial of mailing privileges is the most effective way to police many borderline magazines. By refusing cheap rates the Department is able to exert more leverage to force the publication to "clean up" before it develops a subscription market; if second-class rates are to be allowed as a matter of course as soon as the other physical requirements for the permit are met, then (it is argued) the Post Office's only remedy is to try to stop the mailing of each issue of the magazine deemed obscene. Reliance on the non-mailability power, it is said, may be difficult because of the manpower and time pressures imposed on the Post Office. Once quantities of a magazine are deposited for mailing to subscribers, the Department's lawyers must be pretty sure of their case before they can undertake to hold up its delivery. Since interim stoppage of magazines destined for subscribers is a serious matter, and since the Department is not anxious to become involved in such cases if they can be avoided, Postal lawyers prefer to use the power to withhold cheap rates to control borderline publications.

The answer to all this lies, we believe, in use of the criminal sanction or in use of the non-mailability sanction (but with interim stoppage only after there has been a pattern of previously adjudicated offenses). While these remedies may be less efficient, they are also, very definitely, subject to less abuse by overzealous enforcers.

Very recent litigation (*Sunshine Co. v. Summerfield*, Civil Action No. 1125–59, U.S. District Court, D. C.) between the Post Office and its long-standing opponent, the publisher of two nudist magazines (*Sunshine and Health* and *Sun*) reflects the difficulties of permitting use of the mailing-privilege power for "censorship purposes." *Sunshine* applied in 1958 for a second-class privilege. The applications were denied, apparently for two reasons: (1) they were "incomplete" for failure to furnish certain technical information; (2) the Post Office concluded that the magazines were "non-mailable." A number of conferences between Postal and *Sunshine* lawyers ensued. Thereafter, in view of the Supreme Court's decisions (in the separate litigation) holding that other, similar nudist magazines were *not* obscene (*Sunshine Book Co. v. Summerfield* and *Mounce v. United States*), the Post Office abandoned, under pressure from the Justice Department, its claim that the magazines were "non-mailable." But it still denied the application because of technical insufficiencies (e.g., incomplete information on subscribers) and on the ground that the magazines: (1) did not provide information of a "public character," nor were they devoted to arts or science as required by the mail classification statute (see 39 U.S.C. 226, set out in Appendix IV), and (2) they were designed to promote advertising and business for the publisher—a professional nudist organization—in violation of §226. After more than two years of negotiating, with lengthy delays caused in part by the unexplained failure of the Post Office Department to answer letters, the publisher brought suit in the District Court in Washington to compel issuance of the permits. Judge Youngdahl granted this relief. He found that the "Post Office Department [had] handled plaintiff's applications with a gingerly restraint amounting to outright reluctance." Since the magazines were not obscene, had a legitimate list of subscribers (approximately 6,000), and contained bona fide textual discussion of the "precepts of nudism," and since the advertising was general (and not simply for activities promoted by the publisher), the magazines met the requirements of the statute. "Nudism," the court noted, may "not have the public acceptance given the ideas and way of life presented by 'Ladies Home Journal' and 'House and Garden,' but . . . [*Sunshine* and *Sun*] are not for that reason undeserving of equal treatment by the Postal Service." See *Sunshine Publishing Co. v. Summerfield*, Civil Action No. 1/25–59, U.S. District Court, D. C. (1960).

III. *Limitation of the Mail-Block Sanction.*

(1) *Permanent mail blocks.* Mail blocks—stoppage of *incoming* mail addressed to a mail-order purveyor of obscenity—can be a most effective sanction. The mail block cuts off his very *raison d'être;* the orders from potential consumers of his obscenity. A past Solicitor of the Post Office Department once admitted, for example, that he could stop incoming mail directed to General Motors, Inc., if the company was using the mails to circulate an obscene calendar to some of its customers (see De Grazia, "Obscenity and the Mail"). Since that particular Solicitor also found the celebrated Marilyn Monroe calendar obscene (when sold by a small businessman), a test case of his asserted power would indeed have been an interesting matter. But standards for judging illegality can be narrowed, and if mail blocks are, in the future, imposed only when the Post Office reasonably concludes that criminal prosecutions should or will follow, the exercise of the power can be justified to keep the putative criminal from achieving his basic objective and from persisting in seriously undesirable activity. On the balance, therefore, mail blocks should be retained if we are to have censorship at all, provided they are imposed against purveyors warranting criminal prosecution, judged by standards already suggested.

The Post Office should also continue its present practice—a reform recently instituted—of stopping only that part of the offender's incoming mail which is related to the illegal dissemination of obscenity; it should not bar incoming mail which has nothing to do with circulation of obscenity. See *Tourlanes v. Summerfield;* compare 39 U.S.C. 259 (b) as amended by Pub. L. 673, 86th Cong., 2d sess. (1960), which imposes this limitation on interim impounding orders.

In practice, of course, the Post Office has seldom instituted a mail block against a publisher of a variety of publications where only one publication transgresses. The block is and should be imposed upon only those whose principal line is obscene matter. Such a limitation would go a long way to confine the mail-block sanction to the limited objective of serving only as a sanction against obvious purveyors. In these cases the Post Office should be permitted to hold up all mail unless, on the face of the envelope or upon inspection of its contents, it is clearly unrelated to the offending dissemination.

(2) *Interim mail blocks.* The Post Office has cogently argued that if, as the law now requires, it must hold full-blown administrative hear-

ings before a "permanent" mail block can be imposed against a publisher, it should be allowed to hold up his incoming mail pending the completion of this formal hearing. Otherwise, it is said, a final order allowing the block will be meaningless, for the purveyor will have already reaped his gain during the course of the hearings. The hearing process takes about 45 days, it is said, and that is long enough for a distributor, left unmolested, to advertise and to fill a huge volume of orders.

The Post Office has thus demanded authority to move against the suspected violator before its case is proven. It is obviously a serious thing to hold up the incoming mail of a businessman or publisher before he has been judged guilty of any offense. The summary sanction can cripple some small publishers, and society may be the ultimate loser.

As noted, previously, the Post Office nearly won authority in 1960, via the "Granahan bill," to impose, summarily, interim mail blocks for 45 days on alleged offenders. The Senate Office Subcommittee, however, refused to endorse such legislation and rewrote the bill to require the Post Office to petition the appropriate local district courts for an interim order (see text, pp. 176–178, and this Appendix, V-3, for discussion of this legislative history).

This new statute, which became 39 U.S.C. 259 (b) as amended, authorizes the court to issue the interim order for a period subject to the court's discretion, if after hearing, the court finds that there is "probable cause to believe" that the respondent is selling obscenity.

The standard "probable cause" is, unfortunately, somewhat broad and vague. The statute might well have spelled out more precise criteria.

In his testimony in support of the original Granahan bill, the General Counsel of the Post Office Department stated that interim impounding should be used only in "unusual cases." More specifically—though put in informal terms—he suggested that the following criteria should be met before his lawyers seek an interim order: "Is the mailer an old hand, well known as a purveyor of obscenity? . . . Is his operation the type through which he can make a financial killing within a few days or a few weeks so that subsequent action by the Post Office Department would be superfluous? Is he . . . filling the homes of Americans with tons of obscenity which young people would read before the Post Office Department completed its procedure? Or is his material, though perhaps small in quantity, particularly outrageous in lasciviousness?" (see Granahan Committee *Hearings*).

The House Committee on Post Office and Civil Service, in its report (H. R. *Report No. 945,* 86th Cong., 1st sess.) recommending the Granahan bill as originally drafted, also recognized that temporary impounding orders should only be issued in cases of serious violation of the postal laws:

> Consideration would be given to the nature or character of the enterprise conducted through the mails. . . . In the case of enterprises selling obscene material through the mails, the character of the merchandise would be considered in determining whether an interim impounding order should be applied. The nature of the merchandise which is being offered for sale—such as promotion for hard-core pornography—should be considered, as well as the flagrancy of the advertising.
> A second factor which would be considered is the method of operation of the enterprise. Consideration should be made of the likelihood or possibility that most of the profits from the mail-order enterprise will be realized before the Department's case is completed. The hit-and-run operators gauge their mailing operations in such a manner that they are able to reap their huge profits within a very limited period of time.

IV. *Limitation of Non-mailability Sanction.*

The non-mailability sanction is the device by which the Post Office physically prevents offending material from passing through the mails. Until very recently the power was used extensively against many suspect books and magazines; today it is used much more infrequently. Administrative procedures by which these censorship decisions are made have recently been formalized, and a full and fair hearing has been insured. But the fact remains that the non-mailability sanction remains a clear example of a virulent prior restraint: this kind of censorship prevents a publisher from reaching a large audience—if the Postmaster General or his subordinates so desire.

The difficulty with abolishing the non-mailability power altogether is that some publishers seem to push as close to the line, wherever it is, as they can, going over it deliberately but sporadically in the belief that no serious sanction will follow, that the risk of occasional infringement is worth the gain. In policing this zone of borderland violations, it is, of course, easy for the Department to do too much. Yet the risks of overzeal could be curbed if the Post Office, while retaining its power to stop publications in transit, ordinarily only used that power *after* hearings had been held to determine the illegality of the mailings.

It is a serious business to both publisher and subscriber to have mail delayed before any court or administrative tribunal has determined whether there should be any stoppage at all. Indeed, there are court decisions, notably *Walker v. Popenoe,* which declare that this summary use of the mail-stoppage power is illegal. The ruling in this case has always been ignored by the Post Office on the theory that the court couldn't have meant what it said and that some other court decisions are clearly *contra* (see, e.g., *Monart v. Christenberry;* compare the Court of Appeals decision in *Sunshine v. Summerfield*).

It is time for the Post Office to reappraise the law here. The fact is that there is *not,* usually, enough potential harm in delivering one issue of one magazine—whatever one's thoughts about the harm caused by reading or viewing obscene things—to warrant summary censorship (interim mail stoppage) against every publication thought to offend. Thus, *Big Table, Playboy, Confidential,* and *Sunshine* magazines all presented some grounds, according to Postal standards of the moment, for believing the issues might be obscene. Yet, all of these magazines, even if one concedes the Post Office was correct, fell in a decidedly gray area. Their obsceneness was open to serious question, and the possible harm resulting from circulation was conjectural precisely because their illegality was conjectural.

It would be far better, in these cases, to hold a non-mailability hearing without resorting to interim stoppage. True, the magazine would have to be delivered before the hearing could be concluded, and it may well turn out that the Post Office would deliver some publications which offend the standards. But this does not mean that the hearing be useless. For it would still serve as a guide for the future, as a warning to the publisher which, if it went unheeded, would supply grounds for criminal action or summary stoppage in the future.

Interim stoppage of mail—the sanction which makes non-mailability such a dubious sanction—should take place only when there is a large volume of mail involved and, in that event, only in two kinds of cases: (1) when the Post Office and the Justice Department find that the circulation is so serious as to warrant criminal proceedings, or (2) when the alleged violator has committed prior *adjudicated* (albeit administratively adjudicated) violations of a similar nature, and therefore has engaged in a course of conduct which warrants summary suppression of his mail at this time in order to enforce the standards previously fixed and now openly flouted.

Moreover, an interim order directing a local postmaster to hold up delivery of a suspected publication should only be issued by the Department's Judicial Officer upon the petition of the General Counsel. The petition should allege enough to show one of the above two classes of cases beyond doubt; the petition should be filed within two days after the General Counsel has been notified that mail is being detained by the local postmaster, and, of course, the hearing on the final non-mailability order should be held at the earliest practicable time at the publisher's option.

V. *Use of Experts and External Evidence in Formulating and Implementing Censorship Policy.*

Experts can shed light upon the administration of the statute and the formulation of Postal policy, as well as in adjudication proceedings.

In the rare cases which involve serious, controversial materials and also in selected cases considered typical of current enforcement problems, Postal lawyers might at least attempt to use competent, nonlegal experts to give information or advice on the following topics:

(1) *The relation of the material to existing community standards.* Obviously, in one sense, it is impossible to locate a national standard of acceptability with respect to many publications. It is, however, important that the Department keep constantly cognizant of the extent of changes in various particular communities, that it keep itself informed of the extent to which open circulation of particular motion pictures, books, and magazines reflect changes in standards of tolerance.

An examination of censorship experience up to 1956 shows repeated efforts to suppress fiction, magazines, and other materials which, however useless, were selling openly through normal, local channels. The lawyers chiefly responsible for initiating enforcement action in those days seem to have had strong predilections against tasteless, prurient-oriented publishers. They were also insulated from the facts of life: they did not pay much attention to what kinds of books and magazines were being tolerated by metropolitan American communities; nor were they greatly familiar with books which were selling widely; nor were such considerations deemed relevant to judgment.

The Post Office is not charged with uplifting national standards, nor even resisting change; nor is the personal experience of Postal lawyers the criterion; nothing should be censored unless it clearly seems to exceed the current limits of candor, as those limitations may be perceived. The best possible comparisons should be made with other similar material currently on normal, open markets in communities representative of the areas in which suspect materials circulate. The relevant information here can be obtained from a number of possible sources: persons who are engaged in the general study of this aspect of mass communications, persons familiar with the publishing business and trends in it, literary and other critics, and experienced Postal investigators. Again, this kind of appraisal need *not* occur in every case; but it should be undertaken from time to time in typical "borderline" instances—so that the Post Office's borderline will keep in touch with reality.

(2) *Psychological appeal and effect of the material.* There is no certainty here; we have psychological hypotheses rather than demonstrable facts. We know that many psychiatrists may be intellectually opposed to obscenity laws, and we often find conflict in the stated views of these experts. To the layman, this uncertainty and occasional bias may seem to negate the value of their insights. But, since he, too, is biased and suspicious, it is entirely too easy for the layman to discount the value of scientific aid. The fact that psychiatrists cannot conclusively answer all the (perhaps impossible) questions put to them by laymen hardly means that psychiatrists have nothing to contribute.

As previously noted, a number of experts have suggested that there are reasonably precise psychological criteria by which obsceneness (or pornographic purpose) may be judged. At the moment, these theories may not have broad acceptance, but, in all probability, there will be new articulations, further refinements, and more commonly accepted propositions within the profession. Federal censorship, in formulating enforcement policies, can ill afford to ignore, or worse, be hostile to these developments. Rather, our government should be committed, in good conscience, to the furtherance of objective inquiry on all fronts; it should seek all available assistance and promote new interest in scientific inquiry; it should do this even though enforcement officials may have their doubts, and even though many reject some of the opinions now offered. In the long run, history will surely vindicate a liberal policy in this regard; and, just as probably, history's judgment will condemn a policy of hostility or even of indifference to the acquisition of knowledge urgently needed to make the law as rational as possible.

(3) *The value or absence of value of the material as art, literature, scientific, or educational matter.* Evidence that a condemned book has such value should never be rejected when the book is put on trial. It seems shortsighted for enforcement officials to ignore the possibility that such evidence exists when they are making up their minds whether to initiate censorship.

These experts should, of course, be men with special knowledge; their opinions and their assertions of fact about books have value precisely because they have spent a great deal of time analyzing and criticizing books, because their opinions on similar questions have been accorded respect in the community, and because they have knowledge of many subsidiary facts upon which the opinions and general assertions of fact may be based. For example, when an experienced teacher of modern literature states that critics or teachers of modern literature today are usually familiar, as a matter of professional interest, with the "obscene" works of Henry Miller, the statement—even if a broad generalization—is worth evaluating before one decides how far the government should go in suppressing the book. When a professional critic offers the opinion that *Lady Chatterley's Lover* has artistic value because Lawrence has a peculiar power to use words effectively, the opinion, if based on developed skills of analysis and judgment in evaluating such an art, is important evidence in deciding when to suppress circulation of the book; when the critic makes the generalization that this opinion is shared by other, similar "experts," this generalization (even if, in part, a matter of opinion) is again worth our attention; to the extent that the expert has professional knowledge and skill in judgment, the assertion is obviously worth our credence; and if believed, it is a very important piece of evidence to be put upon the scales.

Of course, experts will disagree. But disagreement here, if probed carefully, may be narrowed; well-trained lawyers are certainly used to this task of clarifying and analyzing competing claims; the reasons for disagreement can be exposed, and this very process of analyzing the disagreement may be of value to those who must make the ultimate decision.

This is not a suggestion that the government create, formally, a panel of experts to give public advice on these matters. Rather, it might experiment with consultants without necessarily formalizing the arrangement. The human resources of the government are surely adequate to provide such help; the nation's finest library, mental hospitals, and other institutions are located within easy distance of Washington. The way is open to resourceful lawyers to develop a *modus operandi* which will surely help to improve the hazardous responsibility which, by law, is theirs.

(4) *Use of experts and external evidence in formal adjudicatory proceedings.* In the *Lady Chatterley* case, the publisher of the book produced several experts who testified about the book's plot, structure, and themes, about the relationship of its erotic parts to its central theses, about its literary value, and about its value as a commentary on modern man and his social environment. Evidence in the form of book reviews and similar writings was offered to show community acceptance, indeed, praise for the book by a substantial body of reputable critics.

The government offered no evidence to discredit any of this testimony; in fact, Postal lawyers tried to block much of it—needlessly emphasizing the legalistic (for purposes of an administrative trial) objection that experts are not supposed to give opinions going to "the ultimate issues" of a case. The government relied, in effect, on the impression the book would create in the mind of the man who was to judge it—only this and nothing more—to refute undisputed, external evidence showing that the condemned work, however erotic, contained ideas, i.e., was "speech," in the sense of the First Amendment.

Without giving any explanation, Mr. Summerfield, who made the final decision, did what his "prosecutors" hoped he would do; he simply rejected all the expert testimony and declared the book too "erotic," too "disgusting," and so forth for the Americans to read.

The absence of an articulated judgment and the obvious presence of a gestalt judgment in this decision is disturbing. Surely, more can be done to make decision-making less subjective, less emotional; surely, more can be done to require—in cases like this one where, very obviously, there are competing interests to be weighed—the articulation of reasons for rejecting reputable testimony that socially useful ideas will be suppressed if censorship is imposed.

Indeed, in cases like this one, those who "judge" for the Post Office should *require* those who attack the book to meet the evidence adduced in its defense. More particularly, when evidence has been produced to show (1) that the publication has been circulating through established, open channels of distribution in this country, and (2) that a substantial number of reputable critics believe that the book has social, literary, educational, or other value (for reasons which are set forth), *then* the government should produce evidence beyond the book itself which either (a) tends to undermine the veracity or competence of the witnesses who testify to points (1) and (2) above, or undermines the truth of their assertions, or (b) tends to show that, notwithstanding points (1) and (2) above, the book's erotic content outweighs its merit (that it meets the standard of obscenity, and showing the degree of its obsceneness), and that its distribution *in the particular case at hand* should be stopped because of the conduct of the publisher.

The burden here put on the Postal lawyers—the "prosecution"—is a burden of producing credible testimony, not a burden proving anything beyond reasonable doubt. The purpose of this proposed rule is simply to formalize what should be a basic policy: that the government will not suppress books simply because those in power, having read them, choose, for reasons never articulated, to disbelieve all the external testimony in the book's behalf.

For further discussion of the use of experts in the determination of the obscenity issue, see the discussion in the A.L.I. *Model Penal Code,* pp. 43–49; see also the opinion of Justice Frankfurter and Harlan in *Smith v. California.* On the general problems of admissibility and qualification of expert testimony which are to be encountered in this area, see McCormick, *Law of Evidence,* Sections 12 and 13 (1954 ed.). Our proposal for using the adjective-law technique of shifting—or, perhaps more accurately, creating a *new* burden of producing evidence

when testimony tending to prove certain conditions has been established—has precedent in the law (see Morgan, Maguire, and Wein-
stein, *Cases and Materials on Evidence,* p. 443 [1957 ed.]).

VI. *De Novo Judicial Review of Censorship Decisions in the District
Courts, with the Right to Trial by Jury.*

Although they are probably not authoritative, there are a few court
decisions (e.g., *Roth v. Goldman* and earlier cases such as *Anderson v.
Patten*) which declare that the courts ought only to set aside Postal
censorship orders where there has been a clear "abuse of discretion" by
the administrative officials.

The premise here is that federal judges should not automatically substitute their judgment for that of the Postal administrators; the standard
to be applied when a censorship case is brought into court for review
must be more limited. The argument for this limitation seems based on
the assumption that officials, who are constantly confronted with these
questions, develop an "expert feel"; their "experience" makes them more
competent to make judgments; moreover, Congress, it is sometimes said,
has reposed discretion in these officials, and the courts accept that fact
and defer; it is also argued that it is wasteful for courts to ignore the
Postal decision in reasonably close cases—in the interest of efficiency,
the Department must have the benefit of any doubt.

Except for the *Lady Chatterley* book case (*Grove Press v. Christenberry*), few federal judges have presented (on paper) a careful analysis
of this premise. But the issue is important, for most Postal censorship
cases brought into the courts are likely to be "borderline" cases rather
than clear violations. The question is whether federal judges, in considering these cases, should adopt a frame of reference—i.e., put themselves in a frame of mind—whereby the judge says to himself, in
effect: my job is not to decide this case all over again, but only to decide
whether the Post Office is so clearly wrong that I can safely say that no
reasonable man, properly applying the legal standards, could agree with
the Department's results.

The answer should be no: the courts should not abdicate any discretion when it comes to application of the standard. In these cases, we are
dealing with issues which are peculiarly within the province of courts,
with law which is peculiarly court-made law. Furthermore, constitutional
issues are interwoven in every obscenity case; the First Amendment is
an issue at least latent in every case, for whatever is added to the
domain of censorial discretion is withdrawn from the domain of permissible expression. Experience shows that Postal officials have no
better expertise than other well-briefed mortals when it comes to making ultimate judgments; Postal officials may, indeed, be experts on the

business aspects of managing the distribution of mail, but they are not experts on evaluating the content of mail for purposes of determining its fitness for Americans to read. Nor is the Post Office comparable to a regulatory agency like the FCC, where Congress necessarily must lay down broad standards in a statute and authorize a quasi-legislative agency to fill in the details of policy and regulation. Congress has never expressly reposed any special discretion of this sort in the Post Office; censorship has evolved as a result of departmental assertions of power confirmed far more by congressional silence than by any express consent, let alone mature legislative deliberation; indeed, the ironic fact is that, aside from the Cutting-Smoot debate, Congress, speaking as a body, has never objectively reviewed and declared itself on the censorship problem—and perhaps, until today's excitement dies down, it cannot.

The former General Counsel for the Post Office has admitted that Postal lawyers, aside from their initial familiarity with the applicable legal decisions, have no special "expertise about obscenity determinations because anybody [who studies the court decisions] can decide...." (see his testimony in the Granahan Committee *Hearings*). He goes on to make the point, perhaps valid, that the Post Office does have a special knowledge of "the methods and modes of operations of ... purveyors." Perhaps this is a sound point; perhaps the Department's findings and inferences on purely factual matters—e.g., the size and nature of the audience circularized—should stand where the record adduced at the administrative hearing can support such conclusions. But not so with the Department's conclusions on whether continued circulation of the challenged work is to be suppressed. As Justice Brennan's majority opinion in the *Roth* case makes clear, the validity of anti-obscenity laws is in part dependent on the fact that the courts can practice "ceaseless vigilance" to make sure that the standards are not abused. Lawyers may make the nice technical point that, if review is to be *de novo*, why should the administrative process be required to adhere to the administrative Procedure Act? The answer: there are always subsidiary facts to be found, as indicated above; and, secondly, we are dealing with a subject which is *sui generis*.

Indeed, in view of the precarious validity of censorship under the First Amendment, it seems desirable, not only that court review be *de novo*, but that publishers be entitled to a jury trial on the issue of obsceneness if they so wish. The jury's judgment should simply be available as an additional check upon the courts and the agencies. In 1930, when the Senate rewrote the tariff law, it seemed quite certain to Congress that jury determination of the issues was desirable to prevent abuses. Experience renders some support for that proposition, though it is hardly clear that jurors are always more prone than judges to safeguard the interests of freedom. And, of course, from a pure statistical viewpoint, it is nonsense to say that a jury's verdict reflects the sense of a community, but at least it is true that adding the jury trial ingredient—without in any way diminishing the judge's power—increases the potential braking power of the law to stop excesses. If the objective is to permit censorship but to keep its operations confined to the more serious cases (those which warrant criminal action in the event of continued dissemination), then civil enforcement should be virtually as accountable to the courts as in criminal enforcement.

The Post Office has also urged that the forum for review of its decisions be shifted from the federal District Courts to the Courts of Appeals. One provision in the original Granahan bill (H.R. 7379, 86th Cong.), which passed in the House, embodied this recommendation. The arguments for stripping district judges of their power to enjoin Postal orders have never been spelled out very effectively, but there appears to be a belief that the Department would be better insulated if its decisions could only be attacked in a higher tier of courts. It is also argued that only a more "authoritative" court than a District court should interfere with the Department's actions.

The philosophy behind this proposed change would appear to be the antithesis of a philosophy which favors *de novo* court review of Postal determinations. *De novo* review should include jurisdiction to receive evidence going to the merits of the case. It should also include (as we urge above) the right to a jury decision on the issue of obsceneness. And, finally, the forum for review should be easily accessible and the relief readily available. All of these considerations militate against any change in the site of the review.

VIII. *The Post Office Department Should Make Information Easily Available to the Public; But It Should Scrupulously Refrain from Efforts to Mold Public Opinion.*

Postal censorship is a power which touches basic freedoms, and the issue of how much censorship Americans can properly permit is no doubt destined to excite controversy and study for years to come. The details of the Postal operation—what decisions have been made and why and by whom—have suffered from a lack of healthy, rational discussion. Traditionally, most of the information has simply not been revealed. Since 1958, thanks to reforms of the General Counsel, the records of Postal hearings and decisions are now open to inspection; the Judicial Officer's opinions are available for some general distribution. More could be done to compile and synthesize this information via, perhaps, the Postmaster General's Annual Report. The public should be told the names of any copyrighted publications which the Department has found obscene and suppressed. The public should be told, in clear, objective terms, about the mail-order enterprises which the Post Office is suppressing. Details of the more important censorship cases should be explained—but only in the most objective terms

While the Post Office should strive to make facts available, it should eschew attempts to influence public judgment.

Mr. Summerfield, as Postmaster General, engaged in what was pretty clearly a concerted effort to mobilize public opinion for stricter enforcement of the anti-obscenity laws. The volume of speeches, press releases, and communications to members of Congress was unprecedented.

Of course, no one can quarrel with Mr. Summerfield's motives, nor is it wrong, as a matter of policy, for one in his position to express concern about the degree of purveying going on in the country.

But surely there should be limits to this public-relations activity. The Postmaster General is overseer of a censorship operation. Censorship is not the norm in a democracy. The Post Office should certainly refrain from activities which, in effect, will create a degree of public hysteria that will persuade Congress to augment its censorship powers. It is one thing for the Department to lay its problems before Congress dispassionately. It is another thing to court, openly, the backing of sympathetic religious and civic groups and to question—through press releases and large notices tacked up on Post Office walls—the wisdom of court decisions which overturn Postal decisions: the Postmaster General's pronouncements on *Lady Chatterley*—after the District Court had so emphatically reversed him—were quite questionable.

For similar reasons, one can only view with some alarm the hiring of the wives of two Republican congressmen as "consultants" or the announced (but unimplemented) decision to create some sort of citizen advisory board on obscenity matters—particularly when the indications were that its membership would be weighted with men who, by background or special religious identification, were likely to favor broader controls rather than the risks that broad freedom always entails (see the *New York Times,* November 26, 1959, and the American Book Publishers Council's *Censorship Bulletin* of June, 1960). There are many private pressure groups in the country on both sides of the issue; Congress is hardly insulated from the arguments; the public is hardly apathetic. The creation of another group designed mainly to speak to the public or to Congress—a group which would be no more expert than any other but which would be given the prestige of a quasi-official title—seems ill advised. Indeed, one may question whether this step, in the long run, would not produce a hostile reaction which would work to discredit the entire Postal program. The Post Office, like the Supreme Court, is a decision-making agency even if it is also, like the FBI, an investigative and prosecuting agency. No court worth respect has ever hired hucksters or in any other way contrived to manipulate public opinion to bring about mass assent to its controversial judgments. The Postmaster General must be subject to the same limitations.

SELECT BIBLIOGRAPHY OF SEC-
ONDARY MATERIALS CITED

Books, Articles, and Pamphlets

Abse, D. W. "Psychodynamic Aspects of the Problem of the Definition of Obscenity," 20 *Law and Contemporary Problems* 572
(1955).

Adler, Mortimer Jerome. *Art and Prudence; A Study in Practical Philosophy.* New York and Toronto: Longmans, Green & Co., 1937.

Alpert, Leo M. "Judicial Censorship of Obscene Literature," 52 *Harvard
Law Review* 40 (1938).

American Civil Liberties Union. *Censorship of Comic Books,* 1955.

———— "Obscenity, Censorship and Free Speech" [mimeographed state-
ment], 1960.

American Law Institute. *Model Penal Code, Tentative Draft No. 6,*
1957.

"Lord Campbell's Bill," 3 *Law Magazine and Law Review* 2d Series 283
(1857).

Balter, Harry G. "Some Observations concerning the Federal Obscenity
Statutes," 8 *Southern California Law Review* 267 (1935).

Blackstone, Sir William. *Commentaries on the Laws of England* (ed.
St. George Tucker). Philadelphia: William Young Birch and
Abraham Small, 1803.

Blanshard, Paul. *The Right to Read.* Boston: Beacon Press, 1953.

Broun, Heywood, and Leech, Margaret. *Anthony Comstock, Roundsman of the Lord.* New York: A. & C. Boni, 1927.

Cairns, Huntington. "Freedom of Expression in Literature," 200 *Annals of the American Academy of Political and Social Science* 76 (1938).

Cannon, Ralph A. *A Sickness in Society.* Methodist Board of Temperance, 1958.

Chafee, Zechariah, Jr. *Free Speech in the United States.* Cambridge: Harvard University Press, 1941.

——. *Government and Mass Communications.* Chicago: University of Chicago Press, 1947.

Chenery, William Ludlow. *Freedom of the Press* (1st ed.). New York: Harcourt, Brace & Co., 1955.

Clemens, Samuel Langhorn (Mark Twain). "*1601; or, Conversation at the Social Fireside as It Was in the Time of the Tudors.*" New York: The Golden Hind Press, Inc., 1930.

Comstock, Anthony. *Frauds Exposed.* New York: J. H. Brown, 1880.

——. *Morals versus Art.* New York and Chicago: J. S. Ogilvie and Co., 1888.

——. *Obscene Publications and Immoral Articles of Mail.* New York and Chicago: J. S. Ogilvie and Co., 1888.

Cooley, Thomas M. *Constitutional Limitations Which Rest upon Legislative Power of the States of the American Union* (5th ed.). Boston, 1883.

Craig, Alec. *The Banned Books of England.* London: G. Allen & Unwin, Ltd., 1937.

Cushing, Marshall. *Story of Our Post Office: The Greatest Government Department in All Its Phases.* Boston: A. J. Thayer & Co., 1893.

Cushman, Robert Eugene. "National Police Power under the Postal Clause of the Constitution," 4 *Minnesota Law Review* 402 (1920).

Cutler, Charles R. "The Post Office Department and the Administrative Procedure Act," 47 *Northwestern University Law Review* 72 (1952).

De Grazia, Edward. "Obscenity and the Mail: a Study of Administrative Restraint," 20 *Law and Contemporary Problems* 608 (1955).

Dennett, (Mrs.) Mary Ware. *Who's Obscene?* New York: The Vanguard Press, 1930.

Deutsch, Eberhard P. "Freedom of the Press and of the Mails," 36 *Michigan Law Review* 703 (1938).

Duniway, Clyde A. *The Development of Freedom of the Press in*

Massachusetts. New York, London, etc.: Longmans, Green & Co., 1906.

Eddy, J. P. "Obscene Publications: Society of Authors' Draft Bill," *Criminal Law Review* 218 (April 1955).

Eliasberg, W. G. "Art: Immoral or Immortal?" 45 *Journal of Criminal Law, Criminology and Political Science* 274 (1954).

Ellis, Albert. *The Folklore of Sex.* New York: Charles Boni, 1951.

Ellis, Havelock. *Little Essays of Love and Virtue.* New York: George H. Doran Co., 1922.

———. "The Revaluation of Obscenity," in *More Essays of Love and Virtue.* New York: Doubleday, Doran & Co., Inc., 1931.

Emerson, Thomas I. "The Doctrine of Prior Restraint," 20 *Law and Contemporary Problems* 648 (1955).

——— and Haber, David. *Political and Civil Rights in the United States: A Collection of Legal and Related Materials.* 2 vols. Buffalo: Dennis, 1952.

Ernst, Morris L., and Seagle, William. *To the Pure . . . A Study of Obscenity and the Censor.* New York: The Viking Press, 1928.

Feder, Edward L. *Comic Book Regulation.* Berkeley: Bureau of Public Administration, University of California, 1955.

Fitzgerald, Msgr. Thomas J. "NODL States Its Case," 97 *America* 280 (1957).

Ford, Clellan Stearns, and Beach, Frank A. *Patterns of Sexual Behavior.* New York: Harper & Bros., 1951.

Ford, John. *Criminal Obscenity: A Plea for Its Suppression.* New York, Chicago, etc.: Fleming H. Revell Co., 1926.

Ford, Paul Leicester (Ed.), *The Writings of Thomas Jefferson* (1892–99). New York: G. P. Putnam's Sons, 1904.

The Fortune Survey. "Uncle Sam As Censor," *Fortune Magazine* Vol. 19, No. 6 (June, 1939) 109.

Foster, Henry H. " 'Comstock Load' Obscenity and the Law," 48 *Journal of Criminal Law* 245 (1957).

Freund, Paul A. "The Supreme Court and Civil Liberties," 4 *Vanderbilt Law Review* 533 (1951).

Fuchs, Edward. *Illustrierte Sittengeschichte.* 4 Vols. Munich: Langen (1912).

Gardiner, Harold Charles, S. J. *The Catholic Viewpoint on Censorship.* New York: Hanover House, 1958.

Gardiner, Harold C., S.J. "Moral Principles towards a Definition of the Obscene," 20 *Law and Contemporary Problems* 560 (1955).

Ginzburg, Ralph. *An Unhurried View of Erotica.* New York: Helmsman Press, 1958.

Gordon, Strathearn, and Cocks, T.G.B. *A People's Conscience*. London: Constable & Co., Ltd., 1952.

Grant, Sidney S., and Angoff, S. E. "Massachusetts and Censorship," 10 *Boston University Law Review* 36 (1930).

Haight, Mrs. Anne (Lyon). *Banned Books*. New York: R. R. Bowker, 1955.

Harpster, James E. "Jurisprudence, Obscene Literature," 34 *Marquette Law Review* 301 (1951).

Harris, Albert W., Jr. "Movie Censorship and the Supreme Court: What Next?" 42 *California Law Review* 122 (1954).

Hawkins, Sir William. *A Treatise of the Pleas of the Crown* (Leach ed.). Dublin: Eliz. Lynch, 1788.

Hoffman, Frederick J., and Moore, Harry T. (eds.). *The Achievement of D. H. Lawrence*. Norman: University of Oklahoma Press, 1953.

Holdsworth, W. S. "Press Control and Copyright in the 16th and 17th Centuries," 29 *Yale Law Journal* 841 (1920).

Hoover, J. Edgar. "Let's Wipe Out the Schoolyard Sex Racket," *This Week Magazine* (August 26, 1957).

Huxley, Aldous Leonard. *Vulgarity in Literature; Digressions from a Theme*. London: Chatto and Windus, 1930.

Jahoda, Marie. *The Impact of Literature: A Psychological Discussion of Some Assumptions in the Censorship Debate*. Research Center for Human Relations, New York University, 1954.

Jones, James. *From Here to Eternity*. New York: Chas. Scribner's Sons, 1951.

Kadin, Theodore. "Administrative Censorship: A Study of the Mails, Motion Pictures and Radio Broadcasting," 19 *Boston University Law Review* 533 (1939).

Kalven, Harry, Jr., "The Metaphysics of The Law of Obscenity," *The Supreme Court Review, 1960,* University of Chicago Press, 1961.

Kaplan, Abraham. "Obscenity As an Esthetic Category," 20 *Law and Contemporary Problems* 544 (1955).

Karpman, Benjamin. *The Sexual Offender and His Offenses: Etiology, Pathology, Psychodynamics and Treatment*. New York: Julian Press, 1954.

Kilpatrick, James Jackson, *The Smut Peddlers,* New York: Doubleday and Company, 1960.

Kinsey, Alfred, *et. al., Sexual Behavior in the Human Female*. Philadelphia: W. B. Saunders Co., 1953.

Kinsey, Alfred C., Pomeroy, Wardell B., and Martin, Clyde E. *Sexual Behavior in the Human Male*. Philadelphia: W. B. Saunders Co., 1948.

LaBarre, Weston. "Obscenity: An Anthropological Appraisal" 20 *Law and Contemporary Problems* 533 (1955).

L'Affaire Lolita, Defense de l'ecrivain. Paris: The Olympia Press, 1957.

Larrabee, Eric. "The Cultural Context of Sex Censorship," 20 *Law and Contemporary Problems* 672 (1955).

Lawrence, D. H. "Pornography and Obscenity" in *The Portable D. H. Lawrence.* New York: The Viking Press, 1955).

———. *Sex Literature and Censorship,* (ed. Harry T. Moore). New York: Twayne Publishers, 1953.

Legman, Gershorn. *Love and Death: A Study in Censorship.* New York: Breaking Point, 1949.

Lehmann-Haupt, Hellmut. *The Book in America.* New York: R. R. Bowker Co., 1951.

Lockhart, William B., and McClure, Robert C. "Literature, the Law of Obscenity, and the Constitution," 38 *Minnesota Law Review* 295 (1954).

——— "Censorship of Obscenity: The Developing Constitutional Standards," 45 *Minnesota Law Review* 5 (1961).

———. "Obscenity in the Courts," 20 *Law and Contemporary Problems* 587 (1955).

Makris, John N. *The Silent Investigators: The Great Untold Story of the United States Postal Inspection Service.* New York: Dutton & Co., 1959.

Malin, Patrick Murphy. "The ACLU Replies to NODL," *Civil Liberties,* (September, 1957).

May, Geoffrey. *Social Control of Sex Expression.* New York: W. Morrow and Co., 1931; London: G. Allen & Unwin, Ltd., 1930.

McKeon, Richard, Merton, Robert K., and Gellhorn, Walter. *Freedom to Read: Perspective and Program.* New York: R. R. Bowker Co., 1957.

McPartland, John. *Sex in Our Changing World.* New York and Toronto: Rinehart & Co., Inc., 1947.

Mead, Margaret. "Sex and Censorship in Contemporary Society," in *New World Writing* (Third Mentor Selection). 7 New York: The New American Library, 1953.

Mencken, Henry L. "Puritanism as a Literary Force," in *A Book of Prefaces.* New York: A. A. Knopf, 1917.

Noll, John F. *Manual of the NODL* (n. d.).

Okudaira, Yashuhiro. *"A Comment on the Japanese Supreme Court Decision on 'Lady Chatterley's Lover.'"* Unpublished Seminar paper, University of Pennsylvania Law School, 1959.

Orwell, George. "Inside the Whale," in a *Collection of Essays.* New York: Doubleday and Co., 1954.

————. "Raffles and Miss Blandish," in *Critical Essays*. London; Secker and Warburg, 1946.

Paterson, James. *The Liberty of the Press, Speech, and Public Worship*. London; Macmillan and Co., 1880.

Patterson, Giles J. *Free Speech and a Free Press*. Boston; Little, Brown & Co., 1939.

Paul, James C. N., "The Post Office and Non-Mailability of Obscenity: An Historical Note," 8 *U.C.L.A. Law Review* 44 (1961).

Paul, James C. N., and Schwartz, Murray L. "Obscenity in the Mail: A Comment on Some Problems of Federal Censorship," 106 *University of Pennsylvania Law Review* 215 (1957).

Perles, Alfred. *My Friend, Henry Miller: An Intimate Biography*. New York: J. Day Co., 1956; London: N. Spearman, 1955.

Pincherle, Alberto. *The Woman of Rome*. Translated by Lydia Holland. New York: Farrar Straus, 1949.

Pollack, Jack Harrison. "Newsstand Filth: A National Disgrace!" *Better Homes and Gardens*, Vol. 35 (September, 1957), p. 10.

Pritchett, Charles Herman. *Civil Liberties and the Vinson Court*. Chicago: University of Chicago Press, 1954.

Rich, Wesley Everett. *The History of the United States Post Office to the Year 1829*. Cambridge, Harvard University Press, 1924.

Rogers, Edward S. "Copyright and Morals," 18 *Michigan Law Review* 390 (1920).

Rogers, Lindsay. "The Extension of Federal Control through the Regulation of the Mails," 27 *Harvard Law Review* 27 (1913).

————. *The Postal Power of Congress; A Study in Constitutional Expansion*. Baltimore: The Johns Hopkins Press, 1916.

Rogge, O. John. "Congress Shall Make No Law . . .," 56 *Michigan Law Review* 331, 579 (1958).

Rutland, Robert Allen. *The Birth of the Bill of Rights* (1776–1791). Chapel Hill: Published for the Institute of Early American History and Culture by the University of North Carolina Press, 1955.

St. John-Stevas, Norman. "Obscenity and Law Reform," *The Spectator*, Vol. 194 (February 4, 1955), p. 119.

————. *Obscenity and The Law*. London: Secker & Warburg, 1956.

Schmidt, Godfrey P. "A Justification of Statutes Barring Pornography from the Mail," 26 *Fordham Law Review* 70 (1957).

Schroeder, Theodore Albert. *Constitutional Free Speech Defined and Defended in an Unfinished Argument in a Case of Blasphemy*. New York: Free Speech League, 1919.

————. *Freedom of the Press and "Obscene" Literature*. New York: Free Speech League, 1906.

———. *"Obscene" Literature and Constitutional Law; A Forensic Defense of Freedom of the Press*. New York: Private print for forensic uses, 1911.

Schwartz, Louis B. "Criminal Obscenity Law; Portents from Recent Supreme Court Decisions and Proposals of the American Law Institute in the Model Penal Code," 29 *Pennsylvania Bar Association Quarterly* 8 (1957).

Scott, George Ryley. *"Into Whose Hands," An Examination of Obscene Libel in Its Legal, Sociological and Literary Aspects*. London: G. G. Swan, 1945.

Scott, Ronald C. "Proof of Obscenity." Unpublished seminar paper, University of Pennsylvania Law School, November, 1959.

Smith, James Morton. *Freedom's Fetters*. Ithaca: Cornell University Press, 1956.

Smith, Lillian Eugenia. *Strange Fruit*. New York: Reynal & Hitchcock, 1944.

Sorokin, Ptirim Aleksandrovich. *The American Sex Revolution*. Boston: P. Sargent, 1956.

Stephen, Sir James Fitzjames. *A Digest of the Criminal Law* (4th ed.). London and New York: Macmillan and Co., 1887.

Taylor, G. Rattray. *Sex in History*. New York: Ballantine Books (1960).

Thomas, John L. *Lotteries, Frauds and Obscenity in the Mails*. Columbia, Mo.: E. W. Stephens, 1900.

Thrasher, Frederic M. "The Comics and Delinquency: Cause or Scapegoat?" 23 *Journal of Educational Sociology* 195 (1949).

Train, George Francis. *My Life in Many States and in Foreign Lands, Dictated in My Seventy-fourth Year*. New York: D. Appleton and Co., 1902.

Trumbull, Charles Gallandet. *Anthony Comstock, Fighter*. New York and Chicago, etc., Fleming H. Revell Co., 1913.

Twomey, John E. "The Citizens' Committee and Comic-Book Control: A Study of Extragovernmental Restraint," 20 *Law and Contemporary Problems* 621 (1955).

Wagner, Geoffrey Atheling. *Parade of Pleasure: A Study of Popular Iconography in the USA*. London: D. D. Verschoyle, 1954; New York: Library Publishers, 1955.

Waples, Douglas, Berelson, Bernard, and Bradshaw, Franklyn R. *What Reading Does to People*. Chicago: University of Chicago Press, 1940.

Warburg, Fredric J. "Onward and Upward with the Arts. A Slight Case of Obscenity," *The New Yorker*, Vol. 33 (April 20, 1957), p. 98.

Weeks, Edward. "The Practice of Censorship," *Atlantic Monthly,* Vol. 145 (January, 1930), p. 17.

Wertham, Frederic. *Seduction of the Innocent.* New York: Rinehart, 1954.

Wharton, Francis. *A Treatise on the Criminal Law of the United States* (2d ed.). Philadelphia: J. Kay, jun. and brother, 1852.

Whelan, Charles M., S.J. "Censorship and the Constitutional Concept of Morality," 43 *Georgetown Law Review* 547 (1955).

Williams, J. E. Hall. "Obscenity in Modern English Law," 20 *Law and Contemporary Problems* 630 (1955).

Wolf, William, Jr. "Control of Movies In Pennsylvania." Unpublished seminar paper, University of Pennsylvania Law School, April, 1958.

Zuckman, Harvey L. "Obscenity in the Mails," 33 *Southern California Law Review* 171 (1960).

Selected Anonymous "Comments" and "Notes" in the Law Reviews

(*Note:* A great many fine pieces, written by law students in various American law schools, have been published in the various law reviews of the country. Pursuant to tradition, the authorship of these contributions is undisclosed. We list below only a few of many such commentaries consulted over a long period of time.)

"Censorship of Obscene Literature by Informal Governmental Action," 22 *University of Chicago Law Review* 216 (1954).

"Entertainment: Public Pressures and the Law," 71 *Harvard Law Review* 326 (1957).

"Extralegal Censorship of Literature," 33 *New York University Law Review* 989 (1958).

"The Law of Obscenity: The New Significance of the Receiving Group," 34 *Indiana Law Journal* 426 (1959).

"Obscenity and the Post Office: Removal From the Mail under Section 1461," 27 *University of Chicago Law Review* 354 (1960).

"Postal Sanctions: A Study of the Summary Use of Administrative Power," 31 *Indiana Law Journal* 257 (1956).

"The Supreme Court and Obscenity," 11 *Vanderbilt Law Review* 585 (1958).

Select Bibliography of Legislative Materials Cited in This Work

"Gathings Committee" (1952):
Hearings before the Select Committee of the House of Representatives on Current Pornographic Materials, 83d Congress, 2d session (1952).
Report of Select Committee of House of Representatives on Current Materials, H.R. Rep. No. 2510, 83d Congress, 2d session (1952).

"Kefauver Committee" (1954–56):
Hearings before Subcommittee to Investigate Juvenile Delinquency of the Senate Committee on the Judiciary, 83d Congress, 2d session (1954); 84th Congress, 1st session (1955) (Subtitled: *Obscene and Pornographic Materials*); 84th Congress, 2d session (1956).
Hearings before Subcommittee on Constitutional Amendments and Subcommittee to Investigate Juvenile Delinquency of the Committee on the Judiciary, 86th Congress, 1st and 2d sessions, on S.J. Res. 116, S.J. Res. 133, S. 2562 (1959–1960) (Subtitled: *Control of Obscene Matter*).
Report of the Subcommittee to Investigate Juvenile Delinquency of the Senate Judiciary Committee, S. Rep. No. 1064, 83rd Congress, 2d session (1954); S.Rep. No. 61, 84th Congress, 1st session (1955). S.Rep. No. 1466, 84th Congress, 2d session (1956). S.Rep. No. 2055, 84th Congress, 2d session (1957). S.Rep. No. 2381, 84th Congress, 2d session (1957) (Subtitled: *Obscene and Pornographic Literature*); S.Rep. No. 130, 85th Congress, 1st session (1957).

"Granahan Committee" (1959–60):
Hearings before the Subcommittee on Postal Operations of the Committee on Post Office and Civil Service of the House of Representatives, 86th Congress, 1st session (1960) (Subtitled: *Obscene Matter Sent Through the Mail*); 86th Congress, 2d session (1960) (Subtitled: *Self-Policing of the Movie and Publishing Industry*).
Hearings before the Committee on Post Office and Civil Service, House of Representatives, 86th Congress, 1st session (1959) (Subtitled: *Detention of Mail for Temporary Periods*).
Report to the Committee on Post Office and Civil Service by the Subcommittee on Postal Operations, House of Representatives, 86th Congress, 1st session (1959) (Subtitled: *Obscene Matter Sent through the Mail.*)

"New York Committee":
Report of the New York State Joint Legislative Committee Studying Publication and Dissemination of Offensive and Obscene Material. [Separate "Reports" for the years 1949, 1953, 1954, 1955, 1956, 1957, and 1958 were consulted.]

TABLE OF SELECTED CASES

(This does not purport to be a listing of all federal cases on the subject, and it contains only a few state cases. The selection is intended to list all important federal cases bearing on federal censorship; it includes all reported court cases cited in Appendix I.)

Adams Theatres Inc. v. Newark, 354 U.S. 931 (1957). Lower court opinion: 22 N.J. 472; 126 A.2d 340 (1956). (*Per curiam* decision upheld city ordinance forbidding nudity on the stage).

Alberts v. California, 354 U.S. 476 (1957). (Supreme Court upheld state criminal statute against selling obscene materials).

American Mercury v. Kiely, 19 F2d 295 (2d Cir.) (1927). (Famous "Hatrack" case; magazine sued to enjoin postal non-mailability order; suit dismissed as moot by court of appeals).

American School of Magnetic Healing v. McAnnulty, 187 U.S. 94 (1902). (Court overruled demurrer to complaint seeking injunction to prevent postmaster from impounding mail of plaintiff's healing business).

Anderson v. Patten, 247 Fed. 382 (S.D.N.Y.) (1917). (Early federal district court case sustaining Postal non-mailability order).

Andrews v. United States, 162 U.S. 420 (1896). (Early Criminal case under Comstock law).

Attorney General v. Book Named "God's Little Acre", 326 Mass. 281; 93 N.E.2d 819 (1950). (Holding the book is not obscene).

Bates & Guild Co. v. Payne, 194 U.S. 106 (1904). (Early case on revocation of second-class permits; reflects summary and informal
character of Post Office procedures).

Beauharnais v. Illinois, 343 U.S. 250 (1952). (Illinois "group libel"
statute upheld as constitutional; broad dictum that "obscene"
speech enjoys no constitutional protection).

Besig v. United States, 208 F.2d 142 (9th Cir) (1953). (Henry
Miller's *Tropic of Cancer* and *Tropic of Capricorn* ruled obscene
under the Tariff Act; Bureau of Customs seizure upheld; decision
reads, in part, as if *Hicklin* test was the standard).

Big Table, Inc. v. Schroeder, 186 F.Supp. 254. (N.D. Ill.) (1960).
(Court enjoined postal order declaring magazine non-mailable).

Borg-Johnson v. Christenberry, 169 F.Supp. 746 (S.D.N.Y.) (1959).
(Court enjoined enforcement of fraud order for failure to comply
with Administrative Procedure Act).

Bonica v. Oleson, 126 F.Supp. 398 (S.D. Calif.) (1956). (Post Office
mail block set aside; movies of girls in bikinis may be "dull," but
not "obscene").

Burke v. Kingsley Books, Inc., 167 N.Y. Supp. 2d 615 (1957). (Judicial order, under New York statute, forbidding sale of certain
publications).

Burstyn v. Wilson, 343 U.S. 495 (1952). (Leading Supreme Court
case on motion picture censorship; state cannot ban a film alleged
to be "sacrilegious"; movies are protected under First Amendment).

Butler v. Michigan, 352 U.S. 380 (1957). (Michigan statute codifying
the *Hicklin* rule declared invalid as violation of First Amendment).

Cadillac Publishing Co. v. Summerfield, 227 F2d 29 (D.C. Cir.)
(1955). (Post office administrative procedures challenged; suit
dismissed because publisher failed to "exhaust" administrative
remedy).

Cantwell v. Connecticut, 310 U.S. 296 (1940). (Important background
First Amendment case holding that state cannot forbid activities of
Jehovah's Witnesses by licensing controls, *inter alia*).

Cates v. Haderlein, 342 U.S. 804 (1951). Lower court opinion: 189
F.2d 369 (7th Cir.) (1951). (Postal fraud proceedings governed
by Administrative Procedure Act).

Chaplinsky v. New Hampshire, 315 U.S. 568 (1942). (Conviction for
cursing a policeman upheld; dictum that "obscene" speech is not
protected by First Amendment).

Collier v. United States, 283 F.2d 280 (4th Cir.) (1960). (Criminal
conviction for selling photos of nude males; such pictures do "ap-

peal to prurient interest" of some; "One" magazine case distinguished.)

Columbia Pictures Co. v. Chicago, 184 F.Supp. 817 (1960). (Film *Anatomy of a Murder* not obscene).

Commonwealth v. Gordon, 66 Pa. D. & C. 101 (1949). (Local prosecution for various books, including *Studs Lonigan;* interesting opinion by Judge Curtis Bok holding books are not obscene and suggesting that test for obscenity must be something like clear and present danger).

Commonwealth v. Holmes, 17 Mass. 336 (1821). (Early prosecution for selling an obscene book).

Commonwealth v. Isenstadt, 318 Mass. 543, 62 N.E. 2d 840 (1945). (Prosecution for selling *Strange Fruit;* represents strict approach).

Commonwealth v. Moniz, 336 Mass. 178, 143 N.E.2d 196 (1957). (Conviction for exhibiting motion picture *Garden of Eden* reversed).

Commonwealth v. Sharpless, 2 S. & R. (Pa.) 91 (1815). (Early prosecution for an obscene exhibition).

Consumers Union v. Walker, 145 F.2d 33 (D.C. Cir.) (1944). (Leading case creating exception to Comstock Act's prohibition against circulation of information about birth control).

Donaldson v. Read Magazine, 333 U.S. 178 (1948). (Postal fraud, mail-block power).

Door v. Donaldson, 195 F.2d 764 (D.C. Cir.) (1952). (Mail-block proceedings; applicability of Administrative Procedure Act).

Doubleday v. New York 335 U.S. 848 (1948). Lower court opinions: *People v. Doubleday & Co.,* 297 N.Y. 687; 77 N.E. 2d 6 (1947). (The *Hecate County* case; all decisions are brief *per curiam* orders).

Dunlop v. United States, 165 U.S. 486 (1897). (Early criminal prosecution under Comstock Act).

Excelsior Pictures Corp. v. Regents, 3 N.Y. 2d 237 (1957). (Movie censorship; film *Garden of Eden* ruled not obscene).

Ex parte Jackson, 96 U.S. 727 (1877). (First Supreme Court dictum on constitutionality of laws excluding obscene and other objectionable matter from mails; Court sustained congressional power to exclude lottery matter from mail; further dictum that sealed mail cannot be opened except with search warrant, enjoys protection under 4th Amendment).

Farley v. Simons, 99 F2d 343 (D.C. Cir.) (1938). (Fraud order for advertising of purported obscenity).

Flying Eagle Publications, Inc. v. United States, 273 F.2d 799 (1st Cir.) (1960). (Conviction for mailing alleged obscene magazine,

Manhunt, reversal for errors by trial court; court holds that while publication is not obscene in its entirety, one story and picture may be found to be obscene).

Gelling v. Texas, 343 U.S. 960 (1952). Lower court opinions: 157 Tex. Cr. R. 516; 247 SW 2d 95 (1952). (Movie censorship held unconstitutional; vague standards).

Glanzman v. Finkle, 150 F.Supp. 823 (E.D. N.Y.) (1957). (Mail-block case; scope of the impounding order).

Greene v. Kern, 174 F.Supp. 480 (D.N.J.) (1959), affirmed, *per curiam* 269 F2d 344 (3rd Cir.) (1959). (Postmaster General has no authority to impound mail pending administrative proceedings on alleged fraud).

Grimm v. United States, 156 U.S. 604 (1895). (Comstock Act prosecution; postal inspectors not guilty of entrapment when they order "fancy photographs" etc. and ask for information about how to obtain them).

Grove Press, Inc. v. Christenberry, 276 F2d 433 (2d Cir. 1960). Lower court opinion: 175 F.Supp. 488 (S.D.N.Y.) (1959). (*Lady Chatterley's Lover* held not to be obscene).

Hallmark Productions v. Carrol, 384 Pa. 348, 121 A2d 584 (1954). (Pennsylvania Motion Picture Censorship Act declared unconstitutional).

Hannegan v. Esquire, 327 U.S. 146 (1946). Lower court opinion: *Esquire, Inc. v. Walker* 151; F.2d 49 (D.C. Cir.) (1945). (The famous *Esquire* case).

Hendricks v. Eastman Kodak Co., 262 F.2d 392 (9th Cir.) (1958). (Owner of film has burden to prove it would not be used for exhibition purposes in replevin action to gain possession from processor).

Hochman v. United States, 277 F.2d 631 (7th Cir.) (1960). (Criminal prosecution; defendant who looked at obviously obscene books cannot defend on ground he did not believe they were obscene.)

Holmby Productions v. Vaughn, 350 U.S. 870 (1955). Lower court opinions: 177 Kans. 728; 282 P.2d 412 (1955). (Movie censorship; standard "immoral" is too vague).

In re Rapier, 143 U.S. 110 (1892). (Leading early decision on the scope of the postal power; sustained validity of lottery statute).

Jeffries v. Olesen, 121 F. Supp. 463 (S.D. Cal.) (1954). (Mail-block proceedings; the right to a change in venue).

Jenkins v. Dell Publishing Co., 251 F.2d 447 (3rd Cir.) (1958). (Right of privacy; commercial exploitation of plaintiff's private life).

Kingsley Books, Inc. v. Brown, 354 U.S. 436 (1957). Lower court opinion: 1 N.Y. 2d 177; 134 N.E. 2d 461 (1956). (New York statute authorizing court to issue order stopping the sale of obscene books upheld as constitutional under First Amendment.)

Kingsley Pictures Corp. v. Regents, 360 U.S. 684 (1959). Lower court opinion: reversing 4 N.Y. 2d 349 (1958). (*Lady Chatterley* movie case; state cannot ban film which may portray adultery as acceptable conduct).

Klaw v. Schaffer, 151 F. Supp. 534 (S.D. N.Y.) (1957). Lower court opinion: 251 F.2d 615 (2d Cir.) (1958), vacated as abated by U.S. Supreme Court, 357 U.S. 346 (1958). (Mail block upheld; materials found to be obscene).

Knowles v. State, 3 Day (Conn.) 103 (1808). (Early U.S. prosecution for distributing obscenity).

Lewis Publishing Co. v. Morgan, 229 U.S. 288 (1913). (Second-class rates; classification statute upheld as constitutional).

Limehouse v. United States, 285 U.S. 425 (1932). (Construing the term "filthy" in the Comstock Act).

Mapp. v. Ohio, 29 Law Week 4799 (1961), reversing 11 Ohio Op. 2d 169. Ohio court had sustained statute making mere "knowing" possession of obscenity criminal; reversed on other grounds.)

Milwaukee Publishing Co. v. Burleson, 255 U.S. 407 (1921). (*Milwaukee Leader* case; revocation of second-class mailing permits sustained).

Mitran v. Williamson, 197 N.Y.S. 2d 689 (N.Y. Sup. Ct., 1960). (Woman may sue for civil damages for emotional distress resulting from obscene letter sent by defendant).

Monart v. Christenberry, 168 F.Supp. 659 (S.D. N.Y. 1958). (Non-mailability order and interim impounding sustained).

Mounce v. United States, 355 U.S. 180 (1957). Lower court opinion: 247 F.2d 148 (9th Cir.) (1957). (Customs seizure of nudist magazines; case returned for further consideration by district judge in light of the *Roth* decision).

Mutual Film Corp. v. Industrial Commission of Ohio, 236 U.S. 230 (1915). (Early decision on film censorship; now largely over-ruled).

New America Library of World Literature v. Allen, 114 F. Supp. 823 (N.D. Ohio) (1953). (Enjoining threats by local authorities against bookseller; police must prosecute or leave distributor alone).

Near v. Minnesota, 283 U.S. 697 (1931). (Leading case on the un-constitutionality of "prior restraints" which proscribe future publication).

Oakley v. Summerfield, 231 F.2d 775 (D.C. Cir.) (1956). (Scope of mail blocks imposed against photographer who sold both alleged obscene pictures and "innocuous" pictures).

One, Inc. v. Olesen, 355 U.S. 371 (1958). Lower court opinion: 241 F.2d 772 (1957) (9th Cir.). (Involving *One,* the magazine "for homosexuals").

Parker v. Summerfield, 265 F.2d 359 (D.C. Cir.) (1959). (Mail fraud order sustained against challenge that statute did not authorize Deputy Postmaster General to issue such orders).

Parmelee v. United States, 113 F.2d 729 (D.C. Cir.) (1940). (Customs seizure of book on nudism containing photographs reversed; court applies a "community standard" case).

People v. Schenkman (Court of Special Sessions, N.Y. City), 28 *U.S. Law Week* 3112 (1960). (Criminal prosecution for selling obscene books, including high-priced paperbound with statements suggesting that stories are "sizzling," "wilder than a Roman orgy." Defendant's plea that he did *not* know contents were "obscene" can be discredited; *Smith v. California* distinguished).

Pike v. Walker, 121 F.2d 37 (D.C. Cir. 1941). (Legality of administrative procedures of Post Office Department).

Pinkus v. Reilly, 178 F.Supp. 399 (D. N.J., 1959). (Evidence sustained administrative finding of mail fraud, discussion of Postal procedures).

Police Commissioner v. Siegel, 223 Md. 110 (1960). (Maryland's "Crime Comics Act" held unconstitutional; too vague.)

Poss v. Christenberry, 179 F. Supp. 411 (S.D. N.Y., 1959). (Unless circular advertising obscene matter is itself obscene or matter to be purchased in response to it is obscene, or both, distribution of circular does not violate statute prohibiting mailing of obscene matter, even though circular may suggest that materials for sale are obscene).

Price v. United States, 165 U.S. 311 (1897). (Early criminal case under the Comstock Act).

Prince v. Massachusetts, 321 U.S. 158 (1944). (Power of a state to enact special protections for children; statutes which forbid colporteur activities in the evening upheld on attack by Jehovah's Witnesses).

Public Clearing House v. Coyne, 194 U.S. 497 (1904). (Mail-block power upheld; leading statement of theory that Congress has plenary power over the mails).

Queen v. Hicklin, L.R. 3 Q.B. 360 (1868). (The famous "English Case" which produced the so-called common law test or *Hicklin* formula for determining whether a work was obscene).

Queen v. Read, 11 Mod. 142, 88 Eng. Rep. 953 (1708). (Early prosecution at common law; court holds writing an obscene book is not an indictable offense).

Rex v. Curl, 2 Str. 788, 93 Eng. Rep. 849 (1727). (Early English Case holding that distribution of an obscene book is punishable as a common law crime).

Rex. v. Wilkes, 4 Burr. 2527 (1770). (Early prosecution for uttering "seditious and scandalous libel" and for "obscene and impious libel").

Riss & Co. v. United States, 341 U.S. 907 (1951) Lower court opinion: 96 F. Supp. 452 (W.D. Mo.) (1950). Administrative Procedure Act and its applicability to federal agency).

Rose v. Quigley, 264 F.2d 608 (2d Cir.) (1959). (Suit for injunction to modify scope of postal fraud order).

Rosen v. United States, 161 U.S. 29 (1896). (Criminal prosecution under Comstock Act; dicta stating that *Hicklin* test is the standard, repeating holding in *Bennett v. U.S.*).

Roth v. Goldman, 172 F.2d 788 (2d Cir.) (1949). (Postal ruling against book, *Waggish Tales of the Czechs,* challenged; long, interesting (if discursive) concurring opinion by Judge Frank questioning the rationale for anti-obscenity laws).

Roth v. United States, 354 U.S. 476 (1957). Lower court opinion: 237 Fd 796 (2d Cir., 1956). (Constitutionality of criminal provisions of Comstock Act upheld by Supreme Court; lower court opinion contains Judge Frank's "concurring" opinion questioning validity of Act in light of history and modern "scientific" knowledge).

Saunders v. Oleson, 163 F.Supp. 939 (S.D. Calif.) (1958). (Mail block upheld).

Schere v. Christenberry, 169 F.Supp. 900 (S.D. N.Y.) (1959). (Enforcement of fraud order enjoined because of evidentiary error in hearing).

Schillaci v. Oleson, 161 F. Supp. 227 (S.D. Calif.) (1958). (Interim mail block sustained).

Sinclair v. United States, 338 U.S. 908 (1950). Lower court opinion: *U.S. V. Sinclair* 174 F.2d 933 (3d Cir.) (1949) (*per curiam*). (Criminal prosecution against husband for writing allegedly obscene letter to wife).

Sir Charles Sydlyes Case, 1 Keble 620, 83 Eng. Rep. 1146 (1663). (Early prosecution for obscene behavior; case later cited as precedent to establish common law crime prohibiting circulation of obscene books).

Smith v. California, 361 U.S. 147 (1959). (Ordinance making bookstore proprietor absolutely liable, criminally, for mere possession in his store of book later judged obscene held unconstitutional; must prove some sort of *mens rea*).

Stanard v. Oleson, 74 Sup. Ct. 768 (1954). (Legality of summary, interim mail stoppage pending formal hearings; opinion by Justice Douglas in stay proceedings).

State v. Appling, 25 Mo. 315 (1857). (Early prosecution for distributing obscenity).

State v. Jackson, 385 P.2d 465 (Oregon Supreme Court) (1961). (Oregon court sustains state's criminal anti-obscenity statute by 4 to 3 vote; interesting discussion.)

Steiner v. Hocke, 272 F.2d 384 (9th Cir., 1959). (Suit to enjoin prosecution of California mail-order distributor in Michigan under the 1958 "Venue Act" permitting Comstock Act prosecution to be brought in community where mail is received).

Summerfield v. Sunshine Book Company, 221 F.2d 42 (D.C. Cir. 1954); Certiorari denied 349 U.S. 921 (1955). (Scope of mail-block orders; stoppage of incoming mail must be limited to mail related to the illegal enterprise).

Sunshine Book Company v. Summerfield, 355 U.S. 372 (1958). Lower court opinions: 128 F.Supp. 564 (D.C.) (1955); 249 F.2d 114 (D.C. Cir.) (1959). (Mailability of nudist magazines; Supreme Court summarily reversed non-mailability order sustained by lower courts).

Superior Films, Inc. v. Department of Education, 346 U.S. 587 (1954). (Movie censorship; vague standards).

Swearingen v. United States, 161 U.S. 446 (1896). (Early criminal prosecution under Comstock Act; dicta repeating the *Hicklin* test).

Thomas v. United States, 262 F.2d 844 (6th Cir.) (1959). (Conviction for mailing obscene private letter).

Thornhill v. Alabama, 310 U.S. 88 (1940), (Picketing as "free speech" protected by First Amendment; important discussion of "prior restraints").

Times Film Corp. v. City of Chicago, 355 U.S. 35 (1957). Lower Court opinion: 244 F.2d 432 (7th Cir.) (1957). (Movie censorship; *The Game of Love* ruled not obscene).

Times Film Corp. v. City of Chicago, 81 S.Ct. 391 (1961). Lower court opinion: 272 F2d 90 (7th Cir.) (1959). (Motion picture censorship sustained).

Toberoff v. Summerfield, 256 F.2d 91 (9th Cir.) (1958). (Interim impounding orders; limitations on court power to extend time periods; Post Office must prove within 20 days that extension is "necessary").

Toberoff v. Summerfield, 245 F2d 360 (9th Cir.) (1957). (Interim impounding orders must be based on a finding that such action is "necessary" to the enforcement of 39 U.S.C. § 259 (a)).

Tourlanes Publishing Co. v. Summerfield, 231 F.2d 773 (D.C. Cir.) (1956). Certiorari denied 352 U.S. 912 (1956). (Scope of mail-block orders; impounding must be limited to mail connected with sale of obscene matter).

Tyomies Publishing Co. v. United States, 211 Fed. 385 (6th Cir.) (1914). (Criminal prosecution of Finnish language newspaper; constitutionality of Comstock Act upheld).

United States v. Bennet, 24 Fed. Cas. 1093 (2d Cir.) (1879). (Prosecution for mailing an obscene book; court applied the *Hicklin* test; leading early case construing Comstock Act).

United States v. Chesman, 19 Fed. 497 (E.D. Mo.) (1881). (Book on physiology of sex held obscene for purposes of general circulation; dicta that mail circulation to doctors would be permissible).

United States v. Comerford, 25 Fed. 902 (D.C. Kans.) (1885). (Venue in postal obscenity case must be in district where mailed, not where received).

United States v. Dennett, 39 F.2d 564 (2d Cir.) (1930). (Prosecution for mailing pamphlet, *The Sex Side of Life: An Explanation for Young People*).

United States v. 4200 Copies International Journal, 355 U.S. 180 (1958). Lower court opinion: 134 F.Supp. 490 (E.D. Wash.) (1955). (Customs seizure of nudist magazines; seizure reversed and remanded by Supreme Court).

United States v. Gundelfinger, 314 U.S. 617 (1941). Lower court opinion: 119 F.2d 1023 (3d Cir.) (1941). (Comstock Act prosecution for circulation of pamphlet).

United States v. Harmon, 34 Fed. 872 (Kansas D.C.) (1888). (Prosecution under Comstock Act; long discussion of the standard; *Hicklin* test followed).

United States v. Hornick, 229 F.2d. 120 (3d Cir.) (1956). (Prosecution for advertising material which represented, by defendants, to be obscene).

United States v. Keller, 259 F.2d 54 (3d Cir.) (1958). (Prosecution for mailing allegedly indecent post cards).

United States v. Kennerley, 209 Fed. 119 (S.D. N.Y.) (1913). (Judge Hand on the *Hicklin* standard).

United States v. Levine, 83 F.2d 156 (2d Cir.) (1936). (Criminal prosecution under Comstock Act; opinion by Judge Hand).

United States v. Limehouse, 285 U.S. 424 (1932). (Comstock Act prosecution; "filthy" matter as a category apart from "obscene matter).

United States v. One Book Called "Ulysses", 72 F.2d 705 (2d Cir. 1934). Lower court opinion: 5 F. Supp. 182 (S.D.N.Y., 1933). (The famous *Ulysses* case).

United States v. One Book Entitled "Contraception", 51 F.2d 525 (S.D.N.Y.) (1931). (Holding the above book by Dr. Marie Stopes is admissible under the Tariff Act; Section 305's proscription against importation of "articles" for the "prevention of conception" does *not* apply to books; nor was the book "obscene" simply because it dealt in detail with the subject of contraception, giving information on methods; decision by Judge Woolsey).

United States v. One Obscene Book Entitled "Married Love", 48 F.2d 821 (S.D.N.Y.) (1931). (Decision by Judge Woolsey holding above book by Dr. Marie Stopes admissible and not obscene— primarily on the authority of the *Dennett* case).

United States v. One Unbound Volume, etc. 128 F.Supp. 280 (D.C. Maryland) (1955). (Customs seizure of folio containing pictures of ancient vases, etc. alleged to be obscene).

United States v. Rebhuhn, 310 U.S. 629 (1940). Lower court opinion: 109 F.2d 512 (2d Cir.) (1940). (Criminal prosecution under Comstock Act; significant opinion by Judge Hand).

United States v. Ross, 205 F.2d 619 (10th Cir.) (1953). (Criminal prosecution under Comstock Act; leading case holding that trial must be held in district where the matter was mailed and could not be held in district where it was received).

United States v. Schillaci, 166 F.Supp. 303 (S.D., N.Y.) (1958). (Criminal prosecution; dicta that in prosecution for advertisements the material advertised must be obscene).

United States v. Thirty One Photographs Etc., 156 F.Supp. 350 (S.D. N.Y.) (1957). (The *Kinsey* case; materials collected for scientific research must be released).

United States v. 3963 Bottles Enerjol, 265 F.2d 332 (7th Cir., 1959). (Default decree entered upon failure of drug manufacturer to answer government's interrogatories in action for condemnation and seizure of drugs; prior agreement in mail fraud proceeding did not bar subsequent action under federal Food, Drug and Cosmetic Act).

United States v. Three Cases of Toys, 28 Fed. Cas. 112, No. 16499 S.D.N.Y.,) (1843). (First reported case on Customs seizure of obscene matter).

U.S. Bio-Genics Corp. v. Christenberry, 173 F.Supp. 645 (S.D. N.Y., 1959). (Person who enters agreement of discontinuance with

Post Office Department and who subsequently deviates from his
agreed pattern of conduct cannot, in absence of coercion, have
waiver disregarded).

Verner v. United States, 183 F.2d 184 (9th Cir.) (1950). (Conviction
for mailing "filthy" private letter affirmed; defense that letter
would have no harmful impact on addressee rejected).

Volanski v. United States, 246 F.2d 842 (6th Cir.) (1957). (Criminal
prosecution under Comstock Act; legality of material which may
adversely effect juveniles or some special class of persons, but not
public generally).

Walker v. Popenoe, 149 F.2d 511 (D.C. Cir.) (1945). (Clearing
pamphlet *Preparing For Marriage* and declaring summary stoppage
of mail to be illegal).

Williams v. Petty, 136 F.Supp. 283 (E.D., Okla., 1953). (Interim mail
blocks pending formal hearings).

Winters v. New York, 333 U.S. 507 (1948). (New York statute
aimed at "crime" magazines declared unconstitutional because too
broad and vague).

Wong Yang Sung v. McGrath, 339 U.S. 33 (1950). (Leading case on
Administrative Procedure Act; procedures must be followed where
there is a "right" to a hearing).

Supreme Court Cases of June 1961

Marcus v. Search Warrants, 29 U.S. Law Week 4747 (U.S. Supreme
Ct.), reversing 334 S.W. 2d 119. (Missouri statutory procedure
permitting issuance of search warrants for seizure of allegedly
obscene materials unconstitutional because of breadth, and failure
to protect non-obscene materials.)

Poe v. Ullman, 29 U.S. Law Week 4820 (U.S. Supreme Ct.) (Dismissal of appeal attacking Connecticut Supreme Court of Errors'
sustaining of state statue prohibiting use of contraceptive materials; dismissal based on no "immediate controversy" due to
state's failure to prosecute more than once in 75 years.)

SELECTED EXCERPTS FROM GOVERNMENT STATUTES AND REGULATIONS PERTAINING TO MAIL CENSORSHIP

The "Comstock Act":

18 U.S. Code, Section 1461

§1461. *Mailing obscene or crime-inciting matter.* Every obscene, lewd, lascivious, indecent, filthy or vile article, matter, thing, device, or substance; and—

Every article or thing designed, adapted, or intended for preventing conception or producing abortion, or for any indecent or immoral use; and

Every article, instrument, substance, drug, medicine, or thing which is advertised or described in a manner calculated to lead another to use or apply it for preventing conception or producing abortion, or for any indecent or immoral purpose; and

Every written or printed card, letter, circular, book, pamphlet, advertisement, or notice of any kind giving information, directly or indirectly, where, or how, or from whom, or by what means any of such mentioned matters, articles, or things may be obtained or made, or where or by whom any act or operation of any kind for the procuring or producing of abortion will be done or performed, or how or by what means conception may be prevented or abortion produced, whether sealed or unsealed; and

Every paper, writing, advertisement, or representation that any article, instrument, substance, drug, medicine, or thing may, or can, be used or applied for preventing conception or producing abortion, or for any indecent or immoral purpose; and

Every description calculated to induce or incite a person to so use or apply any such article, instrument, substance, drug, medicine, or thing—

Is declared to be nonmailable matter and shall not be conveyed in the mails or delivered from any post office or by any letter carrier.

Whoever knowingly uses the mails for the mailing, carriage in the mails, or delivery of anything declared by this section to be nonmailable, or knowingly causes to be delivered by mail according to the direction thereon, or at the place at which it is directed to be delivered by the person to whom it is addressed, or knowingly takes any such thing from the mails for the purpose of circulating or disposing thereof, or of aiding in the circulation or disposition thereof, shall be fined not more than $5,000 or imprisoned not more than five years, or both, for the first such offense, and shall be fined not more than $10,000 or imprisoned not more than ten years, or both, for each such offense thereafter.

The term "indecent," as used in this section includes matter of a character tending to incite arson, murder, or assassination.

The "Mail Block" Statutes:
39 U.S. Code, Sections 259(a), 259(b), and 259(c)

(The statutes quoted below are presented in the form in which they appeared during the period covered by this work. Congress has recently re-codified the Postal laws and sections 259(a), 259(b) and 259(c) now appear (with editorial changes only) as 49 U.S.C. 4006 and 4007.)

§259a. *Exclusion from mails of matter relating to the sale and advertisement of obscene, lewd, etc., articles, matters, devices, things, or substances.* Upon evidence satisfactory to the Postmaster General that any person, firm, corporation, company, partnership, or association is obtaining, or attempting to obtain, remittances of money or property of any kind through the mails for any obscene, lewd, lascivious, indecent, filthy, or vile article, matter, thing, device, or substance, or is depositing or is causing to be deposited in the United States mails information as to where, how, or from whom the same may be obtained, the Postmaster General may—

(a) instruct postmasters at any post office at which registered letters or any other letters or mail matter arrive directed to any such person, firm, corporation, company, partnership, or association, or to the agent or representative of such person, firm, corporation, company, partnership, or association, to return all such mail matter to the postmaster at the office at which it was originally mailed, with the word "Unlawful" plainly written or stamped upon the outside thereof, and all such mail matter so returned to such postmasters shall be by them returned to the senders thereof, under such regulations as the Postmaster General may prescribe; and

(b) forbid the payment by any postmaster to any such person, firm, corporation, company, partnership, or association, or to the agent or representative of such person, firm, corporation, company, partnership, or association, of any money order or postal note drawn to the order of such person, firm, corporation, company, partnership, or association, or to the agent or representative of such person, firm, corporation, company, partnership, or association, and the Postmaster General may provide by regulation for the return to the remitters of the sums named in such money orders or postal notes.

§259b. *Detention of mail containing obscene matters—Interim order; jurisdiction of court; appeal; right to examine mail.* Whenever the Postmaster General shall determine during proceedings before him that in the administration of section 259a of this title, such action may enter an interim order directing that mail addressed to any person be held and detained by the postmaster at the post office of delivery for a period of twenty days from the effective date of such order. Notice of such order, advising such person of the holding and detention and setting forth in specific detail the reasons therefor, together with a copy of sections 259a–259c of this title, shall be sent forthwith by registered or certified mail to such person at the post office at which such mail is to be held and detained. Any such order for the holding and detention of mail addressed to any person shall expire at the end of the twenty days after the issuance thereof unless the Postmaster General shall file, prior to the expiration of such twenty-day period, a petition in the United States district court for the district in which the post office in which such mail is held or detained is situated, and obtain an order directing that mail addressed to such person be held and detained for such further period as the court shall determine. Notice of the filing of any such petition shall be given forthwith by the clerk of the court in which such petition is filed to such person, at the post office at which the mail is being detained (or otherwise as the clerk of the court shall determine to be appropriate), and such person shall have five days in which to appear and show cause why such order should not issue. If, upon all the evidence before it, the court shall determine that the continued withholding and detention of mail addressed to such person is reasonable and necessary to the effective enforcement of section 259a of this title, it shall forthwith issue an order directing that mail addressed to such person be held and detained by the postmaster at the office of delivery until conclusion of the proceeding by the Postmaster General or until further order of the court. If the court shall determine, upon all the evidence before it, that the continued withholding and detention of mail addressed to such person is not reasonable or necessary in the administration of section 259a of this title, it shall dismiss the petition and order all mail addressed to such person held or detained in any post office to be released forthwith for delivery. An appeal from the order of the court shall be allowed as in civil causes. Any order of the Postmaster General or of the district court, under sections 259b and 259c of this title, may be dissolved by such court at any time for cause, including failure to conduct expeditiously the proceedings instituted against such person before the Postmaster General with respect to section 259a of this title. When, under any order herein authorized to be issued by the Postmaster General or the district court, a person's mail is detained and held by the postmaster at the office of delivery, such person shall have the right to examine said mail and receive such mail as clearly is not connected with the alleged unlawful activity.

(b) As used in sections 259b and 259c of this title the term "person" means any individual, firm, corporation, company, partnership, or association.

(c) Action by the Postmaster General in issuing the interim order provided for herein and petitioning for a continuance of such order under sections 259b and 259c of this title, shall not be subject to the requirements of the Administrative Procedure Act.

§259c. *Same; application to mail addressed to publishers or agents.* The provisions of sections 259b and 259c of this title shall not apply to mail addressed to publishers of publications which have entry as second-class matter under the Act of March 3, 1879, as amended, or to mail addressed to the agents of such publishers.

[*Authors' Note: Sections 259 (b) and (c), supra which were in force until August, 1960 were superseded by the statute which immediately follows.*]

The Interim Impounding Mail Block Statute.

[The "Monroney-Granahan" Statute (PL 673, 86th Congress, 2d Session, 1960) amending 39 U.S.C. 259 (b) and (c); now codified as 39 U.S.C. 4007.]

(a) In preparation for or during the pendency of proceedings under section 3929 of the Revised Statutes (17 Stat. 322; 39 U.S.C. 259), as

amended and extended by the Act of March 2, 1895 (28 Stat. 964; 39
U.S.C. 259), section 4041 of the Revised Statutes (17 Stat. 323; 39
U.S.C. 732), as amended, and the Act of August 16, 1950 (64 Stat.
451; 39 U.S.C. 259a), the United States district court in the district in
which the defendant receives his mail shall, upon application therefor
by the Postmaster General and upon a showing of probable cause to
believe the statute is being violated, enter a temporary restraining order
and preliminary injunction pursuant to rule 65 of the Federal Rules of
Civil Procedure directing the detention of the defendant's incoming
mail by the postmaster pending the conclusion of the statutory proceedings and any appeal therefrom. Any such order, in the discretion of the
district court, may provide that the detained mail be open to examination by the defendant and such mail delivered as is clearly not
connected with the alleged unlawful activity. Any action taken by a
court hereunder shall not be deemed to affect or determine any fact at
issue in the statutory proceedings.

(b) The provisions of subsection (a) of this section shall not apply
to mail addressed to publishers of publications which have entry as
second-class matter under the Act of March 3, 1879, as amended (20
Stat. 358; 39 U.S.C. 221, and the following), or to mail addressed to
the agents of such publishers.

The "Tariff Act": 19 U.S. Code, Section 1305 (a)

(a) *Prohibition of importation.* All persons are prohibited from
importing into the United States from any foreign country any book,
pamphlet, paper, writing, advertisement, circular, print, picture, or
drawing containing any matter advocating or urging treason or insurrection against the United States, or forcible resistance to any law of
the United States, or containing any threat to take the life of or inflict
bodily harm upon any person in the United States, or any obscene book,
pamphlet, paper, writing, advertisement, circular, print, picture, drawing, or other representation, figure, or image on or of paper or other
material, or any cast, instrument, or other article which is obscene or
immoral, or any drug or medicine or any article whatever for the
prevention of conception or for causing unlawful abortion, or any
lottery ticket, or any printed paper that may be used as a lottery ticket,
or any advertisement of any lottery. No such articles, whether imported
separately or contained in packages with other goods entitled to entry,
shall be admitted to entry; and all such articles and, unless it appears
to the satisfaction of the collector that the obscene or other prohibited

articles contained in the package were inclosed therein without the
knowledge or consent of the importer, owner, agent, or consignee, the
entire contents of the package in which such articles are contained,
shall be subject to seizure and forfeiture as hereinafter provided:
Provided, That the drugs hereinbefore mentioned, when imported in
bulk and not put up for any of the purposes hereinbefore specified, are
excepted from the operation of this subdivision: *Provided further,* That
the Secretary of the Treasury may, in his discretion, admit the so-called
classics or books of recognized and established literary or scientific
merit, but may, in his discretion, admit such classics or books only
when imported for noncommercial purposes.

Upon the appearance of any such book or matter at any customs
office, the same shall be seized and held by the collector to await the
judgment of the district court as hereinafter provided; and no protest
shall be taken to the United States Customs Court from the decision of
the collector. Upon the seizure of such book or matter the collector
shall transmit information thereof to the district attorney of the district in which is situated the office at which such seizure has taken
place, who shall institute proceedings in the district court for the forfeiture, confiscation, and destruction of the book or matter seized. Upon
the adjudication that such book or matter thus seized is of the character
the entry of which is by this section prohibited, it shall be ordered destroyed and shall be destroyed. Upon adjudication that such book or
matter thus seized is not of the character the entry of which is by this
section prohibited, it shall not be excluded from entry under the provisions of this section.

In any such proceeding any party in interest may upon demand have
the facts at issue determined by a jury and any party may have an appeal
or the right of review as in the case of ordinary actions or suits.

The Statute Defining Conditions for the Issuance of Second-Class Mail Rates: 39 U.S. Code, Section 226

This statute was recently re-codified and now appears as 39 U.S.C. 4354.

§226. (*Second Class Matter*); *conditions admitting publications to.*
Except as otherwise provided by law, the conditions upon which a publication shall be admitted to the second class are as follows: First. It
must regularly be issued at stated intervals, as frequently as four times
a year, and bear a date of issue, and be numbered consecutively. Second.
It must be issued from a known office of publication. Third. It must be

formed of printed paper sheets, without board, cloth, leather, or other substantial binding, such as distinguish printed books for preservation from periodical publications. Fourth. It must be originated and published for the dissemination of information of a public character, or devoted to literature, the sciences, arts, or some special industry, and having a legitimate list of subscribers. Nothing herein contained shall be so construed as to admit to the second class rate regular publications designed primarily for advertising purposes, or for free circulation, or for circulation at nominal rates.

Post Office Rules of Procedure for "Mail Block" Proceedings: Selected Excerpts from 39 Code of Federal Regulations, Part 201 *et seq.,* 1959 Supplement.

[The rules set forth below were in effect during the period covered by this book. These rules were slightly revised in 1960 and, as revised appear in 39 *Code of Federal Regulations,* Part 201 (1961 Supp.).]

§201.1 *Scope of Rules.* The rules of practice in this subpart shall be applicable in all proceedings before the Post Office Department wherein the adjudication is required by the Administrative Procedure Act (5 U.S.C. 1001 et seq.) to be determined on the record after opportunity for an agency hearing. The rules in this subpart shall apply to cases instituted under prior Rules of Practice.

§201.3 *Informal Dispositions.* The provisions of this subpart hereinafter appearing shall not preclude the informal disposition of any matter within the scope of this subpart (§201.1), either before or after the filing of a complaint (§201.4), where time, the nature of the proceeding, and the public interest permit.

§201.4 *Formal Proceedings—Complaints.* Whenever the General Counsel of the Post Office Department or his designated representative shall have to believe that any person or concern is using the mails in any manner requiring administrative action under 39 U.S.C. 259, 259a or 732, he shall prepare and file with the Docket Clerk a complaint which shall name the person or concern involved; state the legal authority and jurisdiction under which the proceeding is initiated; state the facts in a manner sufficient to enable the person or concern named therein to make answer thereto; and recommend the issuance of an appropriate order. The person or concern so named in the complaint shall be known as the respondent.

§201.5 *Notice of Hearing and Answer Date.* Upon filing the complaint the Docket Clerk shall issue a notice of hearing. Said notice of hearing shall contain the date and place of the hearing and the time for filing an answer which shall not exceed 15 days from the date of service of the complaint, and a reference to the effect of failure to file an answer or appear at the hearing. The hearing date shall be no more than 30 days from the date of issuance of the notice.

§201.6 *Service of Complaint and Notice of Hearing.* (a) The Docket Clerk shall cause a duplicate original of the notice of hearing and a copy of the complaint to be transmitted to the postmaster at any office of address of the respondent or to the Inspector in Charge of any Division in which the respondent is doing business which shall be delivered to the respondent or his agent by said postmaster or a supervisory employee of his post office or a postal inspector. A receipt acknowledging delivery of the notice shall be secured from the respondent or his agent, which receipt shall be forwarded to the Docket Clerk, Division of Hearing Examiners, Room 5115, New Post Office Department Building, Washington 25, D.C., and shall become a part of the record in the case.

(b) In the event that no person can be found upon whom service of the notice of hearing and the complaint can be effected pursuant to paragraph (a) of this section, or in the event of the refusal of the respondent or his agent to execute the receipt provided for by paragraph (a) of this section, the notice of hearing may be delivered in the usual manner with other mail addressed to the respondent, and a statement to that effect showing the time and place of such delivery shall be made and signed by the postal employee who so delivered the notice of hearing, which statement shall be forwarded to the Docket Clerk and shall constitute prima facie evidence of service of the complaint and notice of hearing.

§201.7 *Filing Documents for the Record.* (a) All pleadings, motions, orders and other documents filed for the record shall be delivered to the Docket Clerk who shall cause the same to be recorded and filed, and copies thereof delivered to the assigned hearing examiner and to all parties to the proceeding. . . .

§201.17 *Judicial Officer.* The Judicial Officer is the officer duly authorized to render a final departmental decision for the Postmaster General. The Judicial Officer, acting for the Postmaster General, may also preside at the reception of evidence and make the final departmental decision. Either party at the time of the filing of the complaint or answer or not less than 10 days prior to the date scheduled for the hearing may petition the Judicial Officer requesting that he preside at the reception of evidence and make the final departmental decision based upon his hearing of the evidence. The reasons for such a request shall be stated in the petition. This matter shall be within the discretion of the Judicial Officer and, if he grants the request of the petitioner, the parties shall be notified of the fact. In all other cases a hearing examiner shall preside at the reception of evidence. In any case before final agency decision has been rendered the Judicial Officer may order the hearing reopened for the purpose of taking additional evidence by the examiner who presided or the Judicial Officer.

§201.18 *Hearing Examiners.* Hearing examiners shall be appointed and qualified pursuant to Section 11 of the Administrative Procedure Act, 5 U.S.C. 101. Proceedings shall be assigned to a hearing examiner by the Docket Clerk on rotation and notice of the assignment given to the parties.

§201.20 *Powers.* With respect to any proceeding assigned to him, the presiding officer shall have the following authority, to:

(1) Administer oaths and affirmations.

(2) Examine witnesses where necessary for clarity of the record.

(3) Rule upon offers of evidence subject to the limitations thereon provided by the rules in this subpart.

(4) Rule upon offers of proof.

(5) Receive oral and documentary evidence for the record.

(6) Grant or deny applications for the taking of depositions in accordance with the rules in this subpart.

(7) Regulate the course of the hearing, maintain discipline and decorum and exclude from the hearing any person acting in an indecorous manner.

(8) Require the filing of memoranda of law and presentation of oral argument with respect to any question of law upon which a presiding officer is required to rule during the course of the hearing.

(9) Hold conferences for the settlement or simplification of issues by consent of the parties.

(10) Dispose of procedural requests and similar matters.

(11) Make initial or final departmental decisions in conformity with the Administrative Procedure Act as hereinafter set forth in this subpart.

§201.21 *Evidence.* (a) Except as otherwise provided in the rules of practice in this subpart, the rules of evidence governing civil proceedings in matters not involving trial by jury in the courts of the United States shall govern: Provided, however, That such rules may be relaxed to such extent as the presiding officer may deem proper to insure an adequate and fair hearing. Irrelevant, immaterial or repetitious evidence shall be excluded by the presiding officer.

(b) The testimony of witnesses shall be under oath or affirmation and witnesses shall be subject to cross-examination.

(c) Agreed statements of fact may be received in evidence.

(d) Official notice or knowledge may be taken of all matters of which judicial notice or knowledge may be taken by the Federal Courts.

(e) Medical or other scientific books or essays will not be admitted in evidence in lieu of oral expert testimony.

(f) Affidavits containing opinions or statements of an affiant will not be received in evidence, except as provided by paragraph (h) of this section.

(g) Testimonials will not be received in evidence of the efficacy or quality of any product or thing sold through the mails.

(h) The written statement of a competent witness may be received in evidence provided that such statement is relevant to the issues, and provided further that the witness whose statement is offered shall testify under oath at the hearing that the statement is in all respects true, and, in the case of expert witnesses, that the statement correctly states his opinion or knowledge concerning the matters in issue.

(i) Objections to the admission of evidence shall include a brief statement of the grounds thereof. Formal exceptions to the rulings of the presiding officer are unnecessary.

(j) At any time prior to the filing of his decision, the presiding officer may, for good cause shown, reopen the case for the reception of further evidence.

§201.25 *Transcript.* (a) Hearings shall be stenographically reported by a contract reporter of the Post Office Department under the supervision of the assigned presiding officer. No oral argument upon any matter shall be included in the transcript unless ordered by the presiding officer. A copy of the transcript shall be a part of the record and the sole official transcript of the proceeding. Copies of the transcript shall be supplied to the parties to the proceeding by the reporter at rates not to exceed the maximum rates fixed by contract between the Post Office Department and the reporter. Copies of parts of the official record other than the transcript may be obtained by the respondent from the reporter upon the payment to him of a reasonable price therefor.

§201.27 *Proposed Findings and Conclusions.* (a) Each party to a proceeding, except those who fail to answer the complaint or having answered fail to appear at the hearing, may, unless at the discretion of the presiding officer such is not appropriate, submit proposed findings of fact, conclusions of law either in oral or written form in the discretion of the presiding officer....

(b) Except when presented orally before the close of the hearing, proposed findings of fact shall be set forth in serially numbered paragraphs and shall state with particularity all evidentiary facts in the record (with appropriate citations to the transcript or exhibit relied upon) supporting the conclusions proposed by the party filing same. Each proposed conclusion shall be separately stated.

§201.28 *Initial Decision.* (a) The hearing examiner shall render an oral initial decision at the close of the hearing when the nature of the case and the public interest warrant. Any party who desires an oral initial decision shall notify the hearing examiner and the opposing party at least 5 days prior to the date set for hearing. Proposed findings may then be submitted either orally or in writing by both parties at the conclusion of the hearing.

(b) If an oral initial decision is not rendered, a written initial decision shall be rendered at the earliest possible date. The initial decision shall become the final departmental decision unless an appeal is perfected to the provisions of §201.29.

(c) The initial decision of the hearing examiner shall include findings and conclusions with the reasons therefor upon all the material issues of fact, law or discretion presented on the record, and the appropriate order or denial thereof.

(d) The Docket Clerk shall cause a copy of the hearing examiner's initial decision to be served upon each party who participated in the hearing.

§201.29 *Appeal from Initial Decision.* (a) Any party of record in a proceeding, except those who failed to answer the complaint or having answered fail to appear at the hearing, may appeal to the Judicial Officer for the Post Office Department by filing exceptions in a brief on appeal within 15 days from the receipt of the examiner's decision.

(g) Upon the perfection of any appeal the Judicial Officer shall make and sign the final departmental decision and deliver the same to the Docket Clerk for transmittal to the parties.

§201.31 *Final Orders.* (a) Copies of the final departmental decision and order shall be incorporated in the record of the proceeding. The Docket Clerk shall cause the order to be published in the Postal Bulletin and transmitted to such postmasters and other officers and employees of the postal service as may be required to put the provisions of said order into effect.

(b) Copies of the decision and order shall be promptly served upon each party to the proceeding.

§201.32 *Public Information.* Copies of all final opinions or orders, except those required for good cause to be held confidential, shall be available for public inspection in the Library of the Post Office Department during regular office hours.

§201.34 *Supplementary Orders.* Whenever the General Counsel or his designated representative shall have reason to believe that any person or concern is evading or attempting to evade the provisions of any order issued pursuant to the rules in this subpart or any prior rules by conducting a similiar enterprise under a different name or at a different address he shall prepare and file with the Docket Clerk a petition with accompanying evidence setting forth the alleged evasion or attempted evasion of the order and requesting the issuance of a supplementary order against the name or names allegedly used. This shall be forwarded to the Judicial Officer. Notice shall then be given by the Docket Clerk to the person or concern that such an order has been requested and of their opportunity to file answer within 10 days of the notice. The Judicial Officer shall, within 10 days from the answer date, make and file a decision granting or denying the supplemental order.

Post Office Rules of Practice in Cases Involving Denial or Revocation of Second-Class Mailing Privileges: Selected Excerpts from 39 Code of Federal Regulations, Part 204 *et seq.*, 1959 Supplement, as amended May, 1959

4. *Application.* A publisher may file an application for entry of a publication as second-class mail (39 CFR Part 22). The Director, Postal Services Division, Bureau of Operations, Post Office Department, rules upon all applications. If he denies the application he shall notify the publisher specifying the reasons for his denial and attaching a copy of these rules. Before taking action on an application, the Director may call upon the publisher for additional information or evidence to support or clarify the application. Failure of the publisher to furnish such information or evidence may be cause for the Director to deny the application as incomplete or, on its face, not fulfilling the requirements for entry.

5. *Revocation.* When the Director determines that a publication is no longer entitled to the permit, he may issue a ruling of suspension or revocation to the publisher at the last known address of the office of publication stating the reasons and attach

6. *Failure to Appeal Proposed Action.* A ruling of the Director shall become final upon failure of the publisher to file a petition in accordance with the requirements of Rule 7.

7. . . . . (b) *Petition.* A publisher may appeal from a ruling of the

Director by filing a petition within 15 days of the receipt of the ruling unless extended by the Director. The petition shall state the reasons the publisher believes the ruling of the Director is erroneous and shall affirmatively show compliance with each provision of law or regulation on which the ruling was based.

(c) *Notice of Hearing.* Upon receipt of the petition the Docket Clerk shall set a date for the hearing and issue a notice of hearing to the parties stating the time and place of the hearing, the date for filing an answer, and the name of the presiding officer assigned pursuant to Rule 13.

(d) *Answer.* The Director shall answer the petition within 15 days after filing and admit or deny each allegation of the petition.

[Sections dealing with hearings, initial decisions, appeal to the Judicial Officer, and his decision are substantially similar to the "mail block" rules quoted above.]

Post Office Rules of Procedure for "Non-mailability" Orders: Selected Excerpts from 39 Code of Federal Regulations, Part 203, 1959 Supplement, as amended May, 1959.

1. *Limitation.* The rules shall be applicable only to cases where the matter offered for mailing shall be of substantial value or quantity. The initial determination of this question by the General Counsel may be appealed to the Judicial Officer.

2. *Initiation.* Upon receipt of mail matter of doubtful mailability under the provisions of 18 U.S.C. 1302, 1461, 1463, 1717 or 1718 submitted by a postmaster pursuant to Sec. 331.6 of the Postal Manual, the General Counsel shall: (a) file a complaint with the Docket Clerk of the Post Office Department or (b) instruct the postmaster to accept such matter for mailing.

3. *Complaint.* The complaint shall: (a) state statutory and/or regulatory authority for withholding the matter from the mails; (b) specify the character or content of the matter which the complainant believes to be nonmailable; and (c) request the issuance of a notice of hearing by the Docket Clerk.

4. *Notice of hearing; Service.* Upon receipt of the complaint the Docket Clerk shall issue a notice of hearing. The notice shall set the time and place for the hearing and assign on rotation as far as prac-

ticable, a Hearing Examiner qualified pursuant to Section 11 of the Administrative Procedure Act. The date set for the hearing shall be within ten days of the date of the filing of the complaint. The notice, together with copies of the complaint and these rules, shall be sent promptly to the Postmaster at the place of mailing to be served upon the mailer or his agent. A receipt therefor shall be obtained and forwarded immediately to the Docket Clerk. If personal service cannot be made, the notice of hearing shall be deposited in the mails for delivery in the regular course which shall constitute valid service. A report of such delivery shall be promptly forwarded to the Docket Clerk.

5. *Compromise and informal dispositions.* The mailer may request a conference with the complainant to consider informal disposition of any question of mailability or apply to the complainant for the withdrawal of the matter from the mails. When such a request is received, the scheduled hearing date will be postponed for such period of time as may be necessary but in no event longer than five days unless specifically requested by the mailer. If no agreement is reached, the proceeding shall promptly be re-scheduled for hearing.

6. *Answer.* The mailer may file an answer to the complaint and appear in person or by counsel at the hearing. The answer shall contain a reply to each allegation in the complaint and shall be filed in triplicate with the Docket Clerk in Room 5115, Post Office Department, Washington 25, D.C., at least three days prior to the date set for the hearing. Each allegation not answered shall be deemed admitted.

8. *Hearing.* Unless otherwise ordered by the Hearing Examiner, the hearing shall be held in Room 5241, Post Office Department, 12th and Pennsylvania Avenue, N.W., Washington 25, D.C., on the date set in the notice.

10. *Initial Decision.* Unless given orally at the conclusion of the hearing, the Hearing Examiner shall render an initial decision within five days of the conclusion of the hearing or of the receipt of the proposed findings if not submitted at the hearing. The initial decision shall become the departmental decision if an appeal is not perfected.

11. *Appeal.* Either party may file exceptions in a brief on appeal to the Judicial Officer within five days after the initial decision unless additional time is requested by the mailer. A reply brief may be filed within five days after the receipt of the appeal brief by the Docket Clerk.

12. *Departmental Decision.* The Judicial Officer shall render a departmental decision or refer the matter to the Postmaster General for decision. The decision shall be served upon the parties and the postmaster.

13. *Expedition.* For the purposes of expedition the parties may, with the concurrence of the Judicial Officer, agree to waive any of these procedures."

Customs Regulations for Enforcement of the Tariff Act: Selected Excerpts from 19 Code of Federal Regulations, Chapter 1, Sections 12.40 and 12.41, as amended by 1959 Supplement.

§ 12.40 *Seizure; disposition of seized articles; reports to United States attorney.* (a) Any book, pamphlet, paper, writing, advertisement, circular, print, picture, or drawing containing any matter advocating or urging treason or insurrection against the United States or forcible resistance to any law of the United States, or containing any threat to take the life of or inflict bodily harm upon any person in the United States, seized under section 305, Tariff Act of 1930, shall be transmitted to the United States attorney for his consideration and action.

(b) Upon the seizure of articles or matter prohibited entry by section 305, Tariff Act of 1930 (with the exception of the matter described in paragraph (a) of this section), a notice of the seizure of such articles or matter shall be sent to the consignee or addressee.

(c) When articles of the class covered by paragraph (b) of this section are of small value and no criminal intent is apparent, a blank assent to forfeiture and destruction of the articles seized, customs Form 4609, shall be sent with the notice of seizure. Upon receipt of the assent to forfeiture and destruction duly executed, the articles shall be destroyed and the case closed.

(d) In the case of a repeated offender or when the facts indicate that the importation was made deliberately with intent to evade the law, the facts and evidence shall be submitted to the United States attorney for consideration of prosecution of the offender as well as an action in rem under section 305 for condemnation of the articles.

(e) If the importer declines to execute an assent to forfeiture of the articles other than those mentioned in paragraph (a) of this section and fails to submit, within 30 days after being notified of his privilege so to do, a petition under section 618, Tariff Act of 1930, for the remission of the forfeiture and permission to export the seized merchandise, information concerning the seizure shall be submitted to the

United States attorney in accordance with the provisions of the second paragraph of section 305 (a), Tariff Act of 1930, for the institution of condemnation proceedings.

(f) If seizure is made of books or other articles which do not contain obscene matter but contain information or advertisements relative to the prevention of conception or to means of causing abortion, the procedure outlined in paragraphs (b), (c), (d), and (e) of this section shall be followed.

(g) In any case when a book is seized as being obscene and the importer declines to execute an assent to forfeiture on the ground that the book is a classic, or of recognized and established literary or scientific merit, a petition addressed to the Secretary of the Treasury with evidence to support the claim may be filed by the importer for release of the book. Mere unsupported statements or allegations will not be considered. If the ruling is favorable, release of such book shall be made only to the ultimate consignee.

§ 12.41 *Prohibited films.* (a) Importers of films shall certify on customs Form 3291 that the imported films contain no obscene or immoral matter, nor any matter advocating or urging treason or insurrection against the United States or forcible resistance to any law of the United States, nor any threat to take the life or inflict bodily harm upon any person in the United States. When imported films are claimed to be free of duty as American goods returned, this certification may be made on customs Form 3311 in the space designed 'Remarks' in lieu of on Form 3291.

(c) Any objectionable film shall be detained pending instructions from the bureau or a decision of the court as to its final disposition.

INDEX